English Lessons

English Lessons

THE PEDAGOGY OF IMPERIALISM

IN NINETEENTH-CENTURY CHINA

James L. Hevia . . . .

. . . .

. . . .

. . . .

. . . .

. . . .

. . . .

. . . .

. . . .

. . . .

DUKE UNIVERSITY PRESS

Durham and London 2003

HONG KONG UNIVERSITY PRESS

Hong Kong 2003

© 2003 DUKE UNIVERSITY PRESS

All rights reserved. Printed in the
United States of America on acid-free
paper ♾ Designed by Amy Ruth
Buchanan. Typeset in Quadraat by
Tseng Information Systems, Inc.
Library of Congress Cataloging-in-
Publication Data appear on the last
printed page of this book.

.   .   .   .

This book is among a series of titles
copublished by Duke University Press and
Hong Kong University Press, a collaboration
designed to make possible new circuits of
circulation for scholarship. This title is
available in Asia, Australia, and New Zealand
from Hong Kong University Press; in the
Americas and Europe from Duke University
Press; and from either publisher in the rest
of the world.

DUKE UNIVERSITY PRESS
Box 90660 Durham, NC 27708-0660
www.dukepress.edu

HONG KONG UNIVERSITY PRESS
14/F Hing Wai Centre, 7 Tin Wan Praya Rd
Aberdeen, Hong Kong www.hkupress.org

Dedication — For Barney

CONTENTS

. . . .

LIST OF ILLUSTRATIONS AND TABLES

Maps

Figures

Tables

ACKNOWLEDGMENTS

This book was a long time in the making and, as a result, has accumulated a host of debts. The first of these began innocently enough when, in 1986, Bernard Cohn suggested that I check out the India Office archives in London for "prize rolls" related to British army looting in China. This is fitting, as Barney had long provided a model for how to study colonialism and imperialism. Most of the topics found here were inspired by his scholarship and intellectual commitments.

In London, Craig Clunas and Verity Wilson at the Victoria and Albert Museum, and Frances Wood at the Oriental and India Office Collections of the British Museum, have provided invaluable assistance and continued friendship over a number of years. Without their guidance and helpful suggestions, research on museum collections, the art market, and the circulation of objects plundered from the Summer Palace of the Emperor of China would have been impossible. Robert Bickers and Aubrey Singer helped me track down some of the looted objects now in other museum collections.

Over the course of researching this book, I benefited greatly from the expertise of a number of research archivists, museum curators, and librarians. These include DeAnne Blanton and David Wallace at the National Archives and Records Administration; Roland Bauman at Oberlin College; Zdenek V. David at the Woodrow Wilson International Center for Scholars; and the staffs of Davis Library at UNC-Chapel Hill, the Library of Congress, the United States Army Military History Institute, the West Point Museum, and the Freer art library. In London the staffs of the National Army Museum, the School for Oriental and African Studies, the Royal Engineers Museum, and the Imperial War Museum; and in Beijing the staff at the Number One Historical Archive all deserve thanks.

I was extremely fortunate to receive a fellowship from the Woodrow Wilson International Center for Scholars in Washington in 1997–1998. Warren Cohen, director of the Asia Studies program, deserves a very special thanks for his unflagging support and encouragement. I benefited from lively discussion and debate over lunches, dinners, and coffee breaks with Luise White, Doug Howland, and David Gilmartin. I am also grateful for the many suggestions made by Marshall Brown, David Brownlee, Thomas Callaghy, Akhil Gupta, Michael Katz, Gary Marx, Thomas Schwartz, and Steve Wermiel. Tony Cino was an invaluable research assistant. Peter Meyer, chair of the History Department at North Carolina A&T State University, generously arranged the research leave that allowed me to accept the Wilson fellowship.

A large part of the material that makes up the book was presented at conferences and invited talks in the United States, Holland, Germany, Great Britain, and Canada. Those who heard these presentations and made helpful suggestions are too numerous to list here. But I am especially grateful to Tani Barlow, Ellen Basso, Chris Bayly, Greg Blue, Carol Breckenridge, Sandra Buckley, John Calagione, Paul Cohen, Chris Connery, Pamela Crossley, Ralph Crozier, Richard Davis, Ken Dean, Prasenjit Duara, Mark Elliott, Ben Elman, Grace Fong, Jay Geller, John Hay, Ronald Inden, Carl Jacobson, Thomas Lamarre, James Lee, Donald Lopez, Donald Lowe, Brian Massumi, James Millward, Rana Mitter, Susan Naquin, Dan Nugent, Stephen Nugent, Nick Pearce, Bill Pietz, John Pemberton, Vince Rafael, William Rowe, Nathan Sivin, Regine Thiriez, Nicholas Thomas, Naoki Sakai, Lyman Van Slyke, Hans van de Ven, Jing Wang, Jeffery Wasserstom, Robin Yates, Anand Yang, Ernest Young, and Angela Zito.

I have also been fortunate to have had supportive colleagues at the University of North Carolina at Chapel Hill. They include Jane Danielewicz, Marisol de la Cadena, Peter Coclanis, Larry Grossberg, Lloyd Kramer, John Mac-Gowan, Lou Perez, John Pickles, Della Pollack, Richard Soloway, Margaret Wiener, and Gang Yue. A number of graduate students have also read and commented on various parts of the manuscript. They include Mariola Espinosa, Jennifer Heath, Lai Lili, Eric Millen, Eduardo Restrepo, and Michele Strong-Irwin.

Marshall Sahlins always provided provocative questions that opened new areas of research, and Frederick Wakeman was never without a word of encouragement. Bruce Doar deserves special thanks for having not only provided intellectual stimulation, but the booklet of photographs that inspired the title of this book. Lydia Liu has on more than one occasion kindly shared her work in progress. Portions of her forthcoming manuscript parallel topics taken up in parts 1 and 2, and develop themes skirted here in marvelously detailed analysis.

Ken Wissoker, editor-in-chief at Duke University Press, supported this project well before much of it was on paper and shepherded it through its various stages of production. The wonderful staff at Duke, including Christine Dahlin, Pam Morrison, the book's production editor, and the design group, also deserve a good deal of credit for their professionalism and their meticulous eye for detail. It was my pleasure and delight to place myself in their hands.

Parts of this book were published in other forms in journals and edited volumes. Sections of "Making China 'Perfectly Equal,'" *Journal of Historical Sociology* 3.4 (1990): 380–401, appear in chapters 7 and 8; "Leaving a Brand on China: Missionary Discourse in the Wake of the Boxer Movement," *Modern China* 18.3 (July 1992): 304–332, in chapters 7 and 8; "An Imperial Nomad and the Great Game: Thomas Francis Wade in China," *Late Imperial China* 16.2 (1995): 1–22, in chapter 5; "The Scandal of Inequality: Koutou as Signifier," *Positions* 3.1 (1995): 97–118, in chapter 3; "Loot's Fate: The Economy of Plunder and the Moral Life of Objects 'From the Summer Palace of the Emperor of China,'" *History and Anthropology* 6.4 (1994): 319–345, and "Looting Beijing, 1860, 1900," pp. 192–213 in Lydia Liu, ed., *Tokens of Exchange* (Durham: Duke University Press, 1999), in chapters 3, 4, 7, and 8; and "The Archive State and the Fear of Pollution: From the Opium Wars to Fu-Manchu," *Cultural Studies* 12.2 (1998): 234–264, in chapters 5 and 10. I appreciate the many insights and suggestions made by the reviewers for these publications.

Virtually every sentence was read, re-read, and commented upon by Judith Farquhar. For that I know I am an object of envy. Such dedication is part of the conversation that we embarked on some 20 years ago. It continues in these pages, and has become part of our everyday life. How else to account for her appetites for loot at the dinner table and after dark?

BPP	U.K., House of Commons, British Parliamentary Papers on China, Irish University Press edition
B&W	Black & White
CC76	China No. 1 (1876)
CC77	China No. 3 (1877)
CC91	China No. 3 (1891)
CC92	China No. 1 (1892)
CE	Celestial Empire
CESM	Correspondence relative to the Earl of Elgin's Special Missions to China and Japan, 1857–1859
CRAC	Correspondence Respecting Affairs in China, 1859–1860
FO	Foreign Office Archives, Public Record Office, London
FRUS	Foreign Relations of the United States
ILN	Illustrated London News
IOR	British Library and India Office Records, London
JNCBRAS	Journal of the North China Branch of the Royal Asiatic Society
LW	Leslie's Weekly
NAM	National Army Museum, London

NARA	United States National Archives and Records Administration, Washington
NCH	*North China Herald*
OCA	Oberlin College Archives
USMHI	United States Army Military History Institute, Carlisle, Pennsylvania
WO	War Office Archives, Public Record Office, London
YHTLS	Zhongguo shehui kexueyuan jindaishi yanjiu suo "Jindaishi ziliao" bianjizu, eds., *Yihetuan shiliao*
YHTYDSSYL	Li Wen-hai et al., eds, *Yihetuan yundong shishi yaolu*
YMY	*Yuanming yuan*
YWSM, XF	*Chouban yiwu shimo, Xianfeng chao*

MAP I. East China Coast

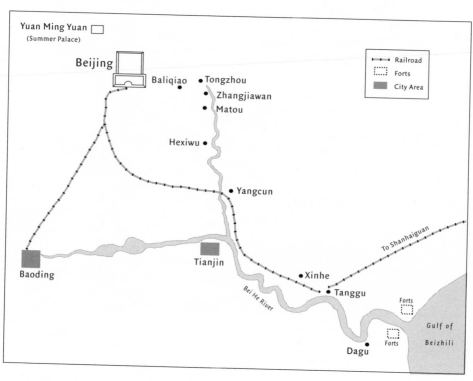

MAP 2. Invasion Route from Dagu to Beijing, 1860 and 1900. Rail lines were built in the 1890s.

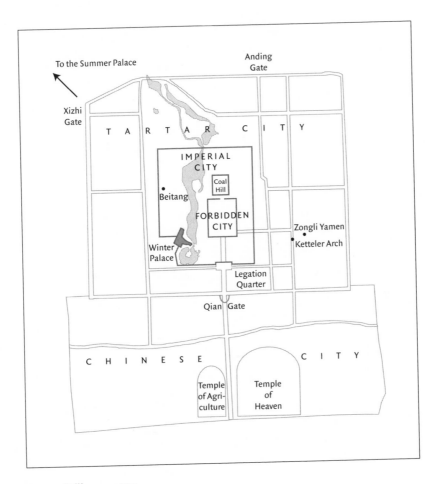

To the Summer Palace

Anding Gate

Xizhi Gate

TARTAR CITY

IMPERIAL CITY

Coal Hill

Beitang

FORBIDDEN CITY

Zongli Yamen

Ketteler Arch

Winter Palace

Legation Quarter

Qian Gate

CHINESE CITY

Temple of Agriculture

Temple of Heaven

MAP 3. Beijing ca. 1900

. . . .

CHAPTER 1

Introduction: Imperialism, Colonialism, and China

THE TITLE OF THIS BOOK was inspired by a gruesome scene of public executions that took place in Beijing, China, in the autumn of 1900 (fig. 1). This photograph, along with three others, was published in a booklet by the Visitors' Inquiry Association in Brighton, the popular beach resort on England's south coast. On the cover, black letters against a deep red background proclaim *Unique Photographs of the Execution of Boxers in China*.[1] When I first opened the slim booklet to this image, my eyes were drawn to and almost as quickly repelled by the beheaded bodies in the left foreground. As my gaze moved from foreground to background, I scanned the living bodies of a crowd pressing around another execution in progress, and it became possible to identify individuals and note differences. If one is somewhat familiar with photographs taken by Westerners in nineteenth-century China, the loose-fitting and unadorned clothes of most of the crowd may be familiar—this is the unmistakable dress of the *laobaixing*, the common folk of China. Other Chinese

1. I am indebted to Bruce Doar for making a gift of the booklet to me in 1991. As he recalled at the time, he had purchased it in Australia a few years earlier, where it carried the unmistakable signs of once having been in a public library.

THE EXECUTION.

1. Execution scene. Source: *Unique Photographs of the Execution of Boxers in China*, ca. 1901.

individuals in fancier uniforms cluster around the next victim of the executioner's sword. These are probably local police and government officials, responsible for carrying out the executions mandated by the foreign armies who suppressed the Boxer movement. As my gaze continued along this line to the left, it was suddenly arrested by an anomaly: three figures in uniforms quite different from the clothing of the others. At the time, I assumed that they were members of the British India army, soldiers of the Raj, who, along with units from seven other powers, occupied Beijing in the wake of the Boxer Uprising of 1899–1900.[2]

A scrutiny of the other photographs in the booklet suggests that they were taken at Caishikou, a marketplace and public execution ground in the Outer,

2. According to Ross M. A. Wilson, curator of Dress and Insignia, Canadian War Museum, Ottawa, the three soldiers, all sergeants, were probably in the Royal Horse Artillery. Personal communication, 1 March 1993.

or Chinese city of the Qing capital, Beijing. The images record one instance of public executions of reputed Boxers. The one reproduced here is among many I later found in American and European archives that show Western military forces and diplomatic officials witnessing local executioners beheading purported Boxers.

Yet, identifying the source of the photograph and my initial observations of it do not yet explain the title of this book. Where do the English Lessons lie in these public executions reminiscent of those of Europe's ancien régime? What sort of pedagogical project, if any, can be found in this picture? Who are the students?

Given the source in which the photograph was printed, one group of students may have been the Brighton tourists who purchased the booklet. It was through media like this that English citizens learned about "civilizing missions" and the punishments of "savage" peoples who transgressed against "civilization." But the picture also reveals traces of another sort of lesson, one barely visible on the tattered paper bearing Chinese ideograms pasted to the pillar on the right. Much like those still to be found on telephone and light poles in contemporary Chinese cities, this one is an advertisement. In Chinese, it announces English-language classes available at a nearby school (Yingwen xuetang).

Juxtaposed to the execution scene, this posting provides an inkling of another sort of pedagogical project, one designed to teach natives how to behave in a white man's world of new and unfamiliar relations of power. It also signifies the complicated relationship between the forceful presence of European imperial troops in China and Chinese people who might consider learning English as a second language. There are probably other meanings that can be teased from it as well, but regardless of the interpretations that might be proposed, the advertisement itself embodies a kind of visual reminder of a historical fact: imperialism was always more than guns and goods; it was also a cultural process involving resistance to and accommodation of forces or entities attempting to achieve hegemonic control over specific geographic spaces. To be directed from the execution ground to the language class was to trace one kind of passage along the colonial divide separating Westerners from the "inferior" races of Africa and Asia. The kind of lessons learned in the English class was, perhaps, the softer side of empire, the side that coaxed and seduced others to participate in what was sometimes imagined as a joint enterprise. The harder side of empire lies to the left of the pillar, encoded in the violent dismemberment of those who defy the language of civilization and its stern rule of colonial law.

In the chapters that follow, these two sides of imperial pedagogy, the violence of arms and the violence of language, are explored. Guns not only force compliance, they also persuade. Words and images do not simply persuade, they also coerce. Although the Qing Empire was beset by multiple Western powers in the second half of the nineteenth century, the focus here is on Great Britain, whose diplomatic and military agents often thought of imperialism and colonialism as pedagogical processes, ones made up of teaching and learning by means of gun and pen. This was especially the case in China, where warfare and treaty making marked critical moments of British imperial pedagogy. It will be useful, therefore, to begin with a broad sketch of Anglo-Chinese conflict, beginning with the first Opium War (1839–1842) and ending with the Boxer Uprising of 1900, the occasion for this particular photograph of executions.

Euroamerican Imperialism in China

The initial Western military assault on the Qing Empire began in 1839 and resulted in an unprecedented opening of China to Euroamerican diplomatic, economic, and cultural penetration. Great Britain went to war with China because Qing government officials had seized and destroyed Indian opium. The opium belonged to English merchants who intended, in defiance of Qing law, to sell it in China. This Chinese government offense against private property and "free" trade was, however, only the most immediate cause of friction between the British and Qing Empires.

The deeper issue had to do with the desires of British diplomatic and commercial agents to open China to greater intercourse with an expanding British Empire. This was, of course, not a situation unique to China; in many other areas of the world the British and other European powers had similar objectives. What distinguished Qing China was its long-standing success at maintaining control over its coastal trade and of allowing local officials to manage foreign relations. British government officials wanted direct access to the Qing emperor and his government, preferably through the establishment of a legation in Beijing. Commercial agents wanted an end to the government-sanctioned monopoly guild of Chinese traders, the Co-hong, which Qing emperors had created for managing all European trade at the single port of Guangzhou (Canton). This system, merchants complained, had been established without negotiation or consultation; its "restrictions" were all the more onerous because these same merchants were convinced that China's population was also interested in greater intercourse with the outside world — ready, as it were, to buy more than opium from European traders. The free trade convictions of British diplomats and merchants ultimately served to justify the use of force against the Qing and resulted in a whole new order of "foreign relations" between China and other powers, which quickly came to include France, the United States, Russia, Germany, and eventually Japan.

Principal instruments for creating the new order were treaties, usually couched in terms of promoting "peace, friendship, and commerce." Through these legal documents, the Qing government was forced to grant Westerners the host of rights they desired in China. The first of these was the Treaty of Nanjing, which ended the Opium War of 1839–1842. The agreement abolished the Co-hong, ceded the island of Hong Kong to Great Britain in perpetuity, opened the ports of Guangzhou, Amoy, Fuzhou, Ningbo, and Shanghai to Western trade, and approved the permanent residence of foreign consuls and their families in these treaty ports. In a supplemental Treaty of the Bogue in 1843, Qing sovereignty was limited in these newly opened ports through three additional provisions. The first stipulated that British consuls could try their own subjects for crimes committed in China; that is, Euroamericans in China enjoyed "extraterritorial" legal rights. Second, the British were given the right to fix customs duties on their imports into China; they were set artificially low in the treaty itself.[3] Third, Britain received most-favored-nation status, which meant that any privileges given to other powers would automatically go to the British without negotiation. The U.S. and French governments rushed in behind the British and concluded their own treaties in 1844. In addition to all the stipulations of the British treaties, the U.S. Treaty of Wanghsia called for revision in twelve years, and the French Treaty of Whampoa included the right to propagate Catholicism.

When the initial treaty settlement expired in 1856, the representatives of Euroamerican powers attempted to open discussions on treaty revision. The Qing government, however, was reluctant to accept fresh limitations on their sovereignty. Another war resulted in a British and French victory and the de-

---

3. The rate was 5 percent of value on Western imports into China. At the time, rates as high as 40 percent were not uncommon in other parts of the world, including the United States. See Hsü 1990: 168–193 and Wakeman 1975: 120–141 for discussions of treaty provisions and the events of this period.

struction of the emperor's Summer Palace (see chapters 2 and 3 for a fuller discussion). The treaty concluding the second Opium War in 1860 granted ten additional treaty ports, freedom of movement for Christian missionaries throughout China, and the right of the treaty powers to establish embassies in Beijing. In addition, China was required to pay indemnities to cover the cost of both wars.

Following the loss of a second major war with European powers in twenty years, the Qing government took action to strengthen itself. Various internal reforms were carried out and leaders attempted to transform the Qing military by acquiring new technologies from the West. As is discussed in greater detail below, these efforts proved to be only marginally effective. Qing influence in Southeast Asia was severed as a result of limited military successes against the French in 1884–1885. A decade later, the shortcomings of the self-strengthening efforts were graphically demonstrated when Japan defeated the Westernized Qing army and navy. By the end of the nineteenth century, Great Britain, France, Germany, and Russia had clearly defined spheres of influence on Qing territory and some observers could seriously discuss the possibility that China would soon be carved up into separate European colonies (fig. 2). This scenario seemed so likely, in fact, that the U.S. government, which in the past had been quick to take advantage of European military successes against the Qing, now called for an "Open Door" in China so that all of the powers would have an equal opportunity to exploit the China market.

Whether or not the American initiative in 1898–1899 stayed the hand of the other powers remains an open question. What is clear is that a Chinese reaction to Euroamerican encroachment soon materialized in the form of the Boxer Uprising, a popular movement supported by elements within the Qing ruling elite. In the summer of 1900, the Boxers and Qing imperial forces assaulted the legation quarter in Beijing and the foreign enclaves in Tianjin. The powers dispatched expeditionary forces, quelled the uprising, and dictated a draconian peace (see part 3). In the wake of the Boxer defeat, the dynasty again attempted to reform, this time directing its attention not only to technological Westernization, but to political reorganization. These efforts proved, however, to be too little and too late. In 1911 the Qing emperor and his imperial government, the primary objects of British pedagogy, ceased to exist as functioning political entities. They were replaced by the Republic of China, a nation-state modeled after those to be found in the West and Japan.

2. Russia carves up China. Germany, Japan, the United States, and France await their portions, while Great Britain is off dealing with the Boers. *Le Monde Illustré*, 28 July 1900.

Assessing Western Imperialism in Nineteenth-Century China

It should be clear from this account that the Euroamerican assault on China had a major impact on the direction of Chinese history. Yet, precisely what that impact was and how to interpret it remains an issue today. For much of the early part of the twentieth century, most Westerners living in the treaty ports of China viewed the use of force against the Qing as a necessary and positive good (Bickers 1993a). Although often repelled by such attitudes, Chinese were attracted to the new military technologies and their underlying sciences, both of which had graphically demonstrated the sources of Western wealth and power and the causes of China's weakness. By the 1920s, Chinese nationalists and communists, the latter of whom would also see the Western assault as an instance of the development of international capitalism, could agree that the West had caused unjustified hardship to the Chinese people and irreparable damage to China as a nation. At the same time, they could also credit Western aggression and semicolonialism with awakening a new spirit among the Chinese and fostering a nationalism determined to end the unequal treaties that had been imposed by force on the Qing. This broadly based nationalist awakening was met with defensiveness or outright hostility by many Europeans and Americans inside and outside of China in the 1920s and 1930s (Cohen 1997: 251–254; Bickers 1999: 143–144).

Yet, hostility was not the only reaction to Chinese nationalism. In the United States, for example, another train of thought emerged that was based on notions of American exceptionalism. In this case, the exception was that the United States had not established concessions in China as the Europeans and Japanese had done, and had stood up for China at the high tide of Western encroachment with its Open Door Policy. Other Americans could point to the long-standing missionary enterprise in China, which, through its evangelical, educational, and medical efforts, was unselfishly helping to improve the condition of Chinese life. Taken together, these benign American activities were understood to constitute a special relationship between China and the United States.[4]

Scholars in the United States, perhaps influenced by notions of American exceptionalism, in turn developed their own understanding of the Western

---

4. The special characteristics of U.S.-China relations from a U.S. perspective are laid out in *The China White Paper* 1967: 1. For a comprehensive analysis of the "special relationship" and its impact on U.S. foreign policy regarding China, see Hunt 1983.

presence in nineteenth-century China. Foremost among these historians was John K. Fairbank, who sought to steer a course between the "extremes" of Chinese nationalism and European reaction. A pioneer in the study of modern Chinese history, Fairbank shifted the historical focus from imperial warfare and hard-won "rights," staples of historians of the British in China (e.g, Eames [1909] 1974; Morse 1910–18), to Western contributions to the modernization of China, particularly those made by missionaries. In addition, he turned attention to new institutions, such as the Imperial Maritime Customs service (IMC), that had been created by the "treaty system," itself a vehicle for "modernizing" Chinese foreign relations and facilitating China's entry into "the family of nations." In the case of the IMC, Fairbank (1957, 1968) argued that the customs was one among many joint products of Sino-Western cooperation that emerged after the conflicts of the opium wars, and he coined the term "synarchy" to identify these. Fairbank and his followers also spoke of "China's response to the West," highlighting the processes by which a "Sinocentric" world order was undermined and cooperative programs of opening to the outside world were inaugurated. In this framework, Fairbank not only tended to erase imperialism and colonialism from the China scene (Barlow 1993: 238–247), but also argued (not unlike Karl Marx) that the Western encroachment into China had produced a positive and necessary good: it awakened slumbering Asian societies and stimulated them to throw off their stagnant past.[5]

Over the past two decades, critiques of the Fairbank approach have emerged, most taking issue with the notion of a static East as the passive recipient of stimulus from a dynamic West. This new historiography can be organized under the rubric of what Paul Cohen has termed "China-centered" history (1984: 153–155). In contrast to Marx and Fairbank, China-centered historians have delved deeply into Chinese historical archives to locate Chinese agency in dynamic processes of change covering much of China's history (e.g., Wakeman and Grant 1975). In the case of the period from the first Opium War to the Communist Revolution of 1949, there are now detailed studies of the role of individual and collective actors from various strata of Chinese society in making the new urban centers of the treaty ports (see

5. For Marx, the agency of change was European industrial capitalism; for a discussion of the fragmentary writings by Marx and Engels on Asia and China, see D. Lowe 1966: 15–29. In Fairbank's (1958: 147) case, the main stimulus came from the Christian missionary enterprise in China.

relevant articles in Elvin and Skinner 1974; Wakeman and Yeh 1992; Hao 1970, 1986; Cochran 1999, 2001; Tsin 1999; Lee 1999; H. Lu 1999). In many instances, historians have identified businessmen and entrepreneurs, some with ties to overseas Chinese communities in Southeast Asia, who competed effectively in a number of spheres with Euroamerican businesses in China. Still others have identified an extended history of Chinese imperialism and colonization in Inner Asia and in areas along the borders between China and Southeast Asian countries, particularly during the Manchu-led Qing era, and rightly wonder how to deal with this phenomenon in relation to European encroachment in the nineteenth century.[6]

This "discovery of history in China" has been an extremely salutary shift, but it has also tended to place Qing China's relations with Western powers into the background, while the West seems to have become an ever more reified historical agent whose features and characteristics no longer require careful analysis. To demonstrate this point, let me consider two products of the China-centered approach that are particularly pertinent to this book. In their exemplary scholarship on the Boxer movement, both Joseph Esherick (1987) and Paul Cohen (1997) have succeeded in humanizing the Boxers while reconstructing histories of the Boxer Uprising unparalleled in Euroamerican China studies. In Esherick's case, the purpose is to clarify the origins of the Boxer movement, a task that he approaches as a kind of Popperian falsification project. Voluminous evidence is systematically worked through to make two key points. First, the Boxers were not just another popular uprising; rather, they were unique in the history of Chinese sectarian movements. Second, they were not an antidynastic rebellion, but a protest against Western incursion into rural China. The task Cohen sets himself builds on this careful social history to extend beyond a purely narrative history of the Boxer events. He presents a more detailed alternative by attempting to recover a sense of what the experience of those events might have been like for actual participants. In the process, he seeks to demonstrate how the Boxers have been mythologized in both China and the West.

In addition to producing a rich history of the Boxer movement, these two studies share historiographic goals; that is, they seek to address methodological issues specific to history as a discipline. For Esherick, the goal appears to be to demonstrate that Chinese archives and secondary materials

6. Qing Central Asia is discussed in greater detail in chapter 6. Recent studies of south and southwest China include Rowe 2001: 417–426; Hostetler 2001.

can be brought together to produce a wholly new view of the Boxer move-ment; these same materials can also serve to critique earlier Westerncentric accounts of the Boxers. There are obvious implications for the study of other popular movements in settings of cross-cultural conflict, particularly during the period of massive European expansion near the end of the nineteenth cen-tury. In Cohen's case, the effort to develop multiple histories of the Boxer Up-rising results in an extended meditation on the historian's craft, with frequent consideration of what makes for reasonable and balanced interpretation. Yet, whether one considers the subject matter of the studies or the historiographic contributions each makes, it seems safe to say that both scholars treat the Western presence in China as a known entity. This is more or less the same West with which Fairbank and his students dealt. And although historical research is nuanced now by a more critical stance regarding Western imperi-alism, the focus remains firmly on China. Neither scholar has broken with the China-West binary that has animated much of the discussion of Western im-perialism in China, nor have they placed the actions of Euroamerican nations in China into a global context. It is as if Fairbank's insistence that colonial-ism did not apply in the China case has precluded any comparison between, for example, the east coast of China and British and French establishments in South and Southeast Asia, or in Africa.

The absence of a comparative framework is, however, only part of the issue posed by China-centered approaches. It is equally significant that Western practices have remained relatively unproblematic. Excesses of violence, for example, are recognized, but no interrogation is made of the particular kind of warfare practiced in China and of its possible links to imperial warfare in other settings. Nor are questions asked about the "China" that nineteenth-century Europeans assumed they were acting on or responding to. Where, in other words, did this China come from? How was it produced and maintained as an object requiring certain kinds of care, management, and tutelage? In the absence of questions like these, there is a real danger that Western imperial-ism in China will be seen as little more than an unfortunate by-product of an era essentially characterized by rapid technological and scientific progress, some of it resisted, but all of it eventually salutary.

Global History and the Question of the Western Penetration of China

One purpose of this study is to place developments in China within a broader global framework. Of particular interest, in this respect, is the fact that many observers at the end of the nineteenth century could think of European activities in China in terms of partition and colonization. Even though such a carving up did not materialize, the fantasy of a China partitioned, much as Africa had been in the 1880s, points to the international and transregional context in which developments in China took place. With only a few exceptions, the countries involved in the forceful penetration of China were also the ones constructing colonial empires in Africa, Asia, and the Pacific. In these regions, as in China itself, European nation-states, the United States, and eventually Japan were competing with each other at the same time that they were breaking down local resistance to their presence. Between 1860 and 1914, these powers divided up and redistributed about one-quarter of the earth's surface among themselves. Great Britain increased its already large empire by some 4 million square miles, France by 3.5 million, and Germany, Belgium, and Italy added around a million square miles of territory each. Russia and Holland consolidated their positions in Central Asia and Indonesia, respectively, and the United States and Japan seized approximately 100,000 square miles of territory from older empires (Spain and China; see Hobsbawm 1989: 59).

To distinguish it from empire building of the past—or, in our case, from Qing Empire building in the eighteenth century—this spectacular division of the globe in the second half of the nineteenth century has often been identified by historians as the new imperialism. What sets this era apart from earlier periods of imperial history (e.g., the Roman, Ottoman, Mughal, and various Chinese Empires) was not only the extraordinary number of political entities engaged in the process of making empires or the number of European monarchs who styled themselves emperor, but the unprecedented combination of new transportation, communication, and military technologies with industrialization, urbanization, and expansive capitalism within Europe. A scientific and technology-driven economic boom had transformed Western and parts of Central Europe from rural, agricultural societies into urban, industrial ones, and reordered European nation-states in the process. By the middle of the century, a new state apparatus appeared on the European scene that took as its task a standardization of its own population into a disciplined, manageable labor force and an augmentation of its external possessions as sources of raw materials to fuel development and keep pace with other powers. Similar processes were underway in the United States and Japan. The competition among European nation-states traversed the globe, appropriating territories not only for their resources but because they lay adjacent to or along transportation and communication routes. Expansion also spawned a new Euroamerican culture, built on "scientific" notions of white racial pre-eminence, novel theories of national and civilizational development (e.g., social Darwinism), and civilizing missions. Europeans and Americans of the new imperial era dreamed of ending "savagism" and "barbarism" among "heathen" peoples through revealed religion and technological superiority (Adas 1989). The sheer energy and audacity of this vision and the mobilization capacities of the new imperial states seemed to overwhelm everything in their path.

Coastal China was unavoidably sucked into this global historical process, but in ways different from those to be found in other colonial settings. No European power, with perhaps the exception of Russia, ever actually considered a political takeover of China, although on at least one occasion Great Britain was in a position to attempt such a feat. China was neither conquered and colonized by a single European power nor divided into separate entities directly controlled by one or another power. Rather, for a combination of reasons—the size of the Qing Empire, its enormous population, and a lingering sense that China was slumbering and would someday awaken to reclaim greatness[7]—European powers chose to manipulate, modify, and work through existing political authorities in China.

It is the argument of this book that to realize this indirect form of influencing Qing China, a pedagogical project was undertaken, one that was itself a form of colonization. European diplomats and advisors to the Qing government proposed to teach the Qing elite and the Chinese people in general through various means of coercion and enticement how to function properly in a world dominated militarily and economically by European-based empires. Great Britain, the prevailing European imperial power in China through the fall of the Qing Dynasty in 1911, took the lead as principal tutor to the Qing regime.

In focusing attention on the pedagogy of imperialism, I neither seek to revive analysis of China's response to the West, nor am I interested in producing a more symmetrical view of Qing foreign relations.[8] Instead, the fundamental objective is to reopen the study of Euroamerican imperialism in East Asia

7. Or, as Napoleon Bonaparte was said to have put it, "Let the Chinese dragon sleep, for when she wakes she will astonish the world" (cited in Hibbert 1970: vii).

8. The notion of a symmetrical view is something I explored in Hevia 1995b. The point was not to unify the Qing and British accounts of the Macartney embassy to China, but rather to keep them distinct so that their particular features could be explored in greater detail. A further elaboration of this method can be found in Hevia 1998.

and to clarify the nature of colonialism in nineteenth-century China. To accomplish these tasks, this book takes up sources beyond the conventional boundaries of diplomatic and economic history. My hope is to suggest ways of supplementing and reconsidering a China-centered approach and of bringing imperialism and colonialism back into the discussion of the nature of China's modernities.

Some may find that the Chinese side of the story is not adequately represented in these pages and that, as a result, Chinese agency is once again being obscured. Certainly, European and U.S. sources predominate throughout, but it is also the case that, as in other colonial situations, local resistance and accommodation at many levels—from ordinary people in cities, towns, and rural hamlets to Qing officials and the Manchu Court—profoundly shaped the strategies and tactics deployed by Western powers. Europeans did not act against passive objects, and their records of encounters with various social strata in China between 1839 and 1901 make that perfectly clear. In the treaty ports, for instance, Chinese businessmen were often so successful that one British consul observed that they were the real merchants and the foreigners merely "commission agents."[9] Similar observations could be made about the Qing Court, particularly with respect to several of the topics taken up here. For example, although the Treaty of Beijing (1860) provided Europeans with access to the throne, the Qing elite very deftly managed to avoid direct contact between European diplomats and the emperor; only one official imperial audience was held before 1896 (see chapter 5). Another example involves the "Great Game" between Russia and Great Britain in Central Asia. The various moves and countermoves by the Russians and British make little sense without recognition of the Qing commitment of men and material to maintaining control over Tibet and Qing Central Asia, including Mongolia and the provinces of Qinghai and Xinjiang (see chapter 6).

These and other examples of Chinese agency are addressed below; the main focus of this study remains, however, on the actions of European powers, especially the British, in China. It is one of the key premises of this study that the interpretation of those activities has been restricted by the ana-

---

9. See Nicholas Hannen to the Earl of Rosebery, 10 May 1893, United Kingdom, House of Commons, *British Parliamentary Papers* (hereafter BPP), vol. 18: 196–197. Thomas Medhurst was one of the first to point to Chinese merchant control of treaty port trade; see Medhurst to Sir Rutherford Alcock, 24 August 1869, BPP, vol. 2: 368. Similar observations were made by Byron Brenan in a report on the state of British trade in China to Lord Salisbury, 15 October 1896, BPP, vol. 20: 193–228. Also see Murphy 1974; T. Rawski 1970.

lytical categories brought to bear to evaluate the Western impact. The emphases to be found in Marx and Fairbank are instructive on this point. For Marx, the primary analytical framework was economic/material, and China's transformation was understood primarily through the lens of the impact of capitalism. For Fairbank, the emphasis was placed on the mental, as opposed to material, impact of the West. The Western onslaught undermined indigenous intellectual traditions and their cultural manifestations, making them untenable and leading to a rejection of tradition and the construction of a new hybrid culture that could support modernization. The difference in emphasis between these two interpretations of the Western impact in China should be obvious. However, the question is not whether interpretations that emphasize economic materialism or cultural processes are more or less plausible ways of explaining or erasing imperialism and colonialism. Rather, what is striking is the precedence or priority given to one or the other in determining historical processes. Indeed, it seems unnecessarily constraining to posit that economic development is the most important factor for explaining historical change. Much the same could be said about intellectual change, which becomes all the more problematic when, as in Fairbank's case, culture is placed wholly on the side of the mental and then opposed to the material.[10]

As an example of the limitations of the interpretive positions of Marx and Fairbank, we might consider the movement of various kinds of material objects through different imperial formations. Objects given to Qing emperors by foreign embassies, often glossed as "tribute," offer a case in point. In a Marxist interpretation, tribute items would be understood as part of the "Asiatic mode of production," an appropriation by a ruling elite of an economic surplus (1973: 472–473). In contrast, Fairbank found little or no economic value in tribute. Rather, its significance lay in how tribute functioned to reproduce Sinocentrism and hence, Chinese culturalism (Fairbank 1942). Neither interpretation pays particular attention to the objects themselves, to the relationship being fashioned through them. As I have argued on another occasion, tribute is glossed in Chinese-language sources as local products (fangwu), that is, things specific to the kingdom of the ruler who presented them to the emperor. The emperor, in turn, bestowed things from his kingdom on the other ruler. This exchange of precious objects was understood to forge a political relationship between the Qing emperor, as the superior, and

10. This is, of course, only one way an idealist version of culture has been used in China studies; see Farquhar and Hevia 1993.

the other ruler, as inferior, the purpose of which was nothing less than the mutual undertaking of the cosmic-moral ordering of the world. The objects themselves and their specific movements, I would argue, cannot be reduced purely to economic or cultural value (Hevia 1995b: 128–130). Rather, they are performative gestures in that they had a role in producing political and even natural relations.

Or one might consider plunder or looting a fundamental aspect of virtually every Western military campaign in nineteenth-century China and one, as we shall see in chapter 4, that included the theft of objects once given by European monarchs to the emperor of China. Is looting an exclusively economic phenomenon or is it a manifestation of, in this case, Western cultural patterns? The choice between the two becomes even more difficult when complex British legal codes governing plunder, and their complete absence in the case of the French, are added to the mix. Also necessary to address are "traditions" of military campaigns, which for the British derived from the recent history of military conflict in India, and assertions about universal human nature or the nature of the behavior of different classes or races of soldiers. Then there are the objects plundered, most of which were taken from the collections of Qing emperors or from the aristocratic elite of north China, where they had very specific meanings for collectors. As soon as they moved into the realm of Euroamericans, these same objects took on new meanings. They could be categorized as prizes of war, as military trophies, as gifts for British and French monarchs, as commodities for sale on the international auction market, as museum pieces, as objects to be put on display at international expositions, as curiosities, and later as high art. Moreover, in each case where new meanings were ascribed to things, they were also accompanied by distinctive forms of practice, including the auction market and its sales catalogues; the exhibitionary complex of museums and international expositions (Bennett 1995; Greenhalgh 1988); and the collection of "curiosities" (Thomas 1991, 1994), each of which is not reducible to either purely economic or ideological interpretations. Nor could these practices be dealt with as exclusively representative of the material reality they reference. Matters are further complicated when one considers the participation of some Qing subjects in looting and in the subsequent sale of plundered objects.

Other examples along these lines could be taken up (and many are in subsequent chapters), but the key point to be made here is that neither the older interpretations that presumed a static China opposed to a progressive West nor the more recent China-centered approach can easily deal with the broad and diverse phenomena of tribute and looting and their multivalent effects. Yet, perhaps more important than identifying the complexities of categories like tribute and loot are the issues raised by addressing them. Such a critique, in fact, points to interrogating reified objects such as "the West" and historicizing them. It also suggests ways of engaging nineteenth-century instances of imperialism and colonialism that might illuminate the complex relationships between global processes and their local manifestations in China. The next section takes up these subjects in turn.

Dereifying "the West" and Bringing China into Colonial Studies

As noted above, one of the things Fairbank and his critics shared was a commitment to the bilateral terms "China" and the "West." The narratives that resulted from this commitment maintained stable meanings for these terms and an assumed relationship between the two. It produced a history in which the West became an increasingly naturalized entity lying outside of historical investigation. This is a rather odd turn of events, particularly when one considers how fruitful and, in many cases, surprising the results of the more recent study of European communities in China have been in raising questions about the unity of the West.[11] Close empirical work is, however, not the only way of destabilizing the West. Another approach is to question the privileged place Europe holds in world history from the eighteenth century forward, especially in claims about the uniqueness of European "civilization" or about Europe as the vanguard of universal historical development and progress.[12] As a number of recent critics have argued, one way of disrupting such presumptions involves denaturalizing or "provincializing" European history, to, as Paul Rabinow (1986) and Dipesh Chakrabarty (2000) have suggested, make European historical development seem strange or local. Whether the focus is on the colonial periphery or the imperial metropole, the most mundane practices of foreign office functionaries, diplomats and colonial officials, soldiers, businessmen, and missionaries should be reappraised and their self-evident features called into question. In the case of this study, such reappraisal involves the close scrutiny of treaties and the way they were

11. See Pelcovits's ([1948] 1969) pioneering study of the British merchant community in China and their conflicts with the foreign office, as well as Bickers 1999 and Scully 2001.

12. For a recent reassertion of European uniqueness, see Landes 1998. Hochschild (1998) provides another way of denaturalizing Europe, telling in great detail the horrors of European colonialism in Africa.

written; analysis of translation procedures and the role of translation on both the hard and the soft sides of imperial pedagogy; military practices of warfare and plunder; and the worldwide production of useful knowledge about China. But this effort will be effective only if, at the same time, the history of the Euroamerican penetration of China is disentangled from the assumed boundaries of the nineteenth-century European and U.S. "formal" empires (i.e., directly ruled conquered territories), as well as from the discrete regional boundaries preferred by contemporary area studies. It is necessary, in other words, to address what was colonial about Euroamerican activities in nineteenth-century China in relation to other colonized settings and in the context of events in the metropolitan centers.

The implications of this larger spatiotemporal dimension makes it possible to circumvent a number of classic frameworks in analysis of the topics taken up here. Rather than viewing Sino-Western contact and conflict as a contest between free trade imperialism and Chinese isolationism, or between tradition and modernity, dereifying a unitary West and placing events on a global scale shift the focus to the political and strategic considerations of various imperial formations in gaining, maintaining, and expanding empires. It also allows us to treat the Qing, British, and Russian Empires, as well as other territorial powers—be they nation-states with claims on noncontiguous regions or various localized political entities—as competing polities, compound or collective agents vying with one another for dominion over or shares in the exploitation of the lands and peoples of Eurasia, Africa, the Pacific, and parts of Latin America.[13] Such collectivities, it must be emphasized, include colonized peoples as active agents in colonial processes.[14] In this study, nothing makes this last point more strongly than the presence of Sikh and Pathan irregular cavalry units in the British expeditionary force to China in the 1860s; of Bengal Lancers in the China relief expedition of 1900; of the Chinese "Coolie" corps that supported the British and French armies in 1860; or of a British-led Chinese regiment from Weihai fighting in Tianjin and participating in the march through the Forbidden City in August 1900!

Dereifying the West also means that Euroamerican expansion and exploitation need not be treated as a unitary or totalizing enterprise, with a central

13. From this perspective, the Qing can be understood as both victims of imperialism in their confrontation with Euroamerican nation-states and as imperialist agent. See part 2 for further discussion.

14. The articles in Cooper and Stoler 1997 provide numerous examples of the ways colonized populations contributed to, as well as resisted, the construction of colonial orders.

intelligence and uniform motives. Colonialism, as Frederick Cooper (1997: 409) has pointed out, was not a set of coherent practices designed to dominate, but a series of "hegemonic projects" that often involved winning the acquiescence of conquered populations. Moreover, it was not simply that various Euroamerican nation-states competed with one another for dominion. Recent colonial studies have demonstrated that no two colonial enterprises launched by even a single imperial power were the same; imperial wars and colonization were neither uniform nor identical in Africa and Asia, nor was their outcome preordained. Colonization was always a messy process, with diverse parties pulling and pushing in many directions at once. Moreover, indigenous rebellion and covert resistance to European rule was a norm rather than an exception, giving rise to many lurid tales of savagery and barbarism among "the natives" and generating the need to closely supervise colonized peoples because they were presumed to be ill-fitted for labor.[15]

Yet, although colonization was disorderly, there were also procedures designed to create order, to link imperial centers and colonial peripheries in rational structures of power and authority. Morever, as many critics of Edward Said's *Orientalism* have emphasized, the East was not a passive recipient of an external coercive regime of power: colonialisms were transformed in multiple encounters, along class, race, and gender lines, between colonizers and colonized (Ahmed 1992; Bhabha 1983; Loomba 1998; L. Lowe 1991; D. Porter, 1983). New social and political forms emerged as a result. To put this another way, the apparently paradigmatic case of colonialism, the India of the British Raj, was unique;[16] moreover, it was itself made up of a wide spectrum of colonialisms, realizing different forms of political, cultural, and economic domination at different moments in time.[17] As one might expect, given the

15. Cooper 1997: 413. The major exception to this view of "native" labor was the "Chinese coolie." See below on the coolie trade.

16. Critics of postcolonial studies have noted the tendency to use the India case as if it could stand as a model for all forms of colonialism. The result is that other histories become subsumed under that of India and the specificity of historical developments in China or the Caribbean disappears. See Parry 1987; Chrisman 1990.

17. This paragraph draws on the excellent state-of-the-field summary on colonialism by Cooper and Stoler (1997: 1–56). Missing from their broad framework, however, are places like China and Japan and discussions of older imperial formations whose structures and history, like that of the Qing Empire, provide alternative visions of power and authority that might be usefully compared to European empires. See Hevia 1993, 1995b and Millward 1998 for discussions of Qing imperialism.

dynamism and diversity of colonial encounters, the nature of the relationship between colonizers and colonized was neither clear-cut nor perfectly stable.

The situation in China through much of the second half of the nineteenth century was as complex as that to be found in settings where European political control appeared to be more formalized. Moreover, as in other instances of Euroamerican and indigenous contact, the China scene presents us with a number of seemingly contradictory developments that defy easy historical interpretation and raise troublesome moral issues. How, for example, do we reconcile the obviously venal opium trade with the well-intentioned missionary activities in nineteenth-century China, particularly when we recognize that both sought to penetrate and reconfigure the same bodies and polity? What are we to make of a use of force that justifies its self-interested violence on the grounds of abstract principles generated from a moral, humanist tradition and that, after World War II, provided the intellectual foundations for a concept of universal human rights? How are we to deal with and interpret direct aggression that claims to stand for the rule of law and presents itself as doing the good work of universalizing that rule? How are we to understand the willingness of some Chinese in this century to reject long-standing cultural beliefs and forms of indigenous knowledge and embrace Western science and political forms at the same time as they claim to be staunch anti-imperialists? How does one distinguish, with reference to whose interests, between the "positive" and "negative" impact of the West in China?

Questions such as these have no simple answers. This is partly because, as the field of colonial studies has demonstrated, Euroamerican empire building was both destructive and constructive: it eradicated old worlds and the ways of understanding those worlds, and made something new in their place. And it did both at an accelerated pace from 1850 forward, sometimes, as was the case in India,[18] disrupting and recolonizing the same region several times over. Moreover, as noted above, nineteenth-century empire building differed from other forms of imperialism in a number of significant ways. One key difference involved the production of knowledge about indigenous peoples and their social practices, knowledge that could then be deployed to manage, monitor, and reorganize populations. Information about others, including vast statistics-generating projects, produced and organized indigenous populations through new forms of record keeping and archiving, while in-

---

18. One could, as Taussig (1987) has attempted to do, make the same case for much of Latin America.

sinuating alien forms of practice into everyday life.[19] These initiatives were complemented by prodigious mapping and surveillance projects that produced novel geographic entities and clearly defined borders where none had existed before. The new administrative territories that resulted reoriented the geographic imaginary of colonized populations, overlaying new structures onto older, cosmic-moral communities. In addition to information gathering and mapping, the new imperialism also included translation projects, some of them on a vast scale, designed to stabilize meaning and standardize many forms of exchange between colonizer and colonized. All of these undertakings relied, in turn, on the technological revolution in transport and communication that transformed much of Europe and North America throughout the period. Steamships, railroads, and the telegraph created a weblike, high-speed interface between an imperial metropole and its colonial peripheries. As a result, resources could be stationed at nodes (staging areas) and, in a crisis, rapidly deployed as needed to other parts of the system. It was possible in 1900 to move whole regiments and their equipment from India to China in less than a month.

These dynamic aspects of the new imperialism were all important in China from 1860 forward (see chapters 5 and 6) and provided coherent links between eastern Asia and other parts of the colonial world. At the same time, however, there were clear local characteristics of Western exploitation in China. Driven sometimes by opportunism, sometimes by defensiveness, and always in competition with other imperial powers, Euroamerican imperial expansion, as Marxist and world systems theorists have argued, resulted in uneven global development.[20] Gilles Deleuze and Félix Guattari, for example, see such unevenness as endemic to what they characterize as the "capitalist machine," a kind of productive apparatus that oscillates between deterritorializing and reterritorializing new zones of contact. The more capitalism

---

19. This process of information gathering is akin to that discussed by Foucault under the term "governmentality" (1991: 87–104).

20. A cluster of terms and concepts surround the notion of uneven development, all of which signal a central debate within Marxism: the colonial question. At its core is Marx's observation about the paradox of capitalism in the colonial setting: it destroys earlier modes of production, yet introduces a revolutionary and progressive form of production in its stead. Others argued that the actual transformations in colonized areas were not totalizing; rather, pockets of earlier modes of production coexisted alongside those introduced by European imperial powers—hence, uneven development. For an overview of the debates on this issue, see Bottomore et al. 1983: 83–85, 498–503.

"deterritorializes," they argue, "decoding and axiomatizing [material] flows in order to extract surplus value from them, the more its ancillary apparatuses, such as government bureaucracies and the forces of law and order, do their utmost to reterritorialize" (1983: 34–35), to recode that which had been decoded. The ancillary apparatuses may be understood as the recovery and redeployment of a host of European cultural, social, and political forms that provided a kind of life-support system for further acts of imperialist deterritorialization.

In the case of China, one could point to specific formations imposed in the treaty ports to sustain the Western presence and produce subjects (some of them Chinese) who could perform continuous acts of decoding and recoding in Chinese settings.[21] Or we might consider commerce and warfare against China as the decoding elements of the apparatus, while the "Treaties of Peace, Friendship, and Commerce" and the treaty port with its many physical structures and institutions can be seen to function as mechanisms of colonial reterritorialization or reordering. These reorderings, in turn, may themselves become sources for further disruptions and recodings. Extraterritoriality provides an instance of this process. While it recoded China's sovereignty, it also produced a series of deterritorializations that penetrated ever deeper into the Chinese body politic, while the ancillary apparatuses of law courts, custom collection procedures, and treaty revision reterritorialized China anew.

Here, deterritorialization and reterritorialization provide a useful way for organizing some seemingly contradictory gestures of the Western presence in China, especially the hard and soft sides of imperial pedagogy visible in the photograph with which we began. At the same time, as Robert Young (1995: 166–174) has argued, one must be cautious about becoming dazzled by the Deleuzian apparatus. It can easily be understood in overly mechanistic and deterministic terms, implying, as Young notes, "too simplistic a grafting of one culture on to another." Preferring to interpret the Deleuzian model of capital as a kind of "territorial writing machine," he offers instead a form of "palimpsestual" inscription and reinscription as "an historical paradigm that will acknowledge the extent to which cultures were not simply destroyed but rather layered on top of each other, giving rise to struggles that themselves

21. As one consul observed, it did not matter that Chinese merchants controlled the transport and resale of British commodities into China's hinterland. The development of trade is "the first consideration" (BPP, vol. 20: 198).

only increased the imbrication of each with the other and their translation into increasingly patchwork identities" (173–174).

The cultural elements that return in this process, however, might best be understood as fragments of the past, invented traditions, grafted onto or insinuated into new formations. Fraternal organizations with medieval rules (the Masons, to take but one instance) appeared in treaty ports Shanghai and Calcutta; Catholic cathedrals displaying variations on Gothic architecture materialized in Beijing, Tianjin, and provincial capitals; and Gordon Hall loomed like a Norman castle in the British concession at Tianjin. New and old military units, some composed of native recruits, were decorated with medieval heraldry, medals, and regalia, and claimed the masculine chivalry of knights errant. Victoria became the queen-empress of the British Empire, ruling over an Indian nobility retooled with European feudal nomenclature. Forms such as the jin-rickshaw appeared, fusing one of the few positively recognized elements of the East, Chinese labor, with Western metal-spoke wheels, rubber tires, and a spring carriage. In this unequal exchange, the form that resulted spread outward and became a staple of the colonial scene in India and Africa.[22] This peculiar array of forms and others like them were mimicked and manipulated by indigenous populations, who added their own elements to the mix, producing what some scholars refer to as "colonial modernity" (Barlow 1997).

These notions of layering, imbrication, translation, and struggle strike me as useful ways for thinking about the movement from opium warfare to treaties of peace, friendship, and commerce, from the violence of warfare to tea parties at the U.S. legation in Beijing with Manchu princesses as guests of honor. They allow us, in other words, to focus on the peculiar nature and specificity of transactions on the China coast, and to recognize that the artifacts of contact—the patchwork entities such as the Imperial Maritime Customs, Fairbank's example of synarchy par excellence, or the new Qing foreign office (Zongli yamen)—were themselves open to an endless series of inscriptions and reinscriptions. Young's observations also suggest that a fundamental condition of the reordered world fabricated by imperial capitalism and its ancillary apparatuses was the demise of discrete cultures (if these ever actually

---

22. Numerous other examples of the process Young identifies might be found by thumbing through the pages of Yule and Burnell's Hobson-Jobson ([1886] 1994), which contains not only Anglo-Indian terms, but terms spanning the British contact zones in Asia.

existed), and the proliferation of fused forms (Latour 1993), both in imperial metropoles and on colonial peripheries. Such patterns of fusion are discernible in China in the middle of the past century and evident at the same time in imperial centers such as London and Paris.[23]

If Young's palimpsestual layering suggests ways to conceptualize the dense and complex interactions played across the structure of colonial authority and domination, it is also helpful when dealing with less colonial situations on the edges or sparsely populated frontiers of empire. The process Arthur Conolly dubbed the "Great Game" (Edwardes 1975: vii; Cheng 1957; Davidson-Houston 1960; Lamb 1960; Morgan 1981), involving the Anglo-Russian strategic warfare across Asia that began in earnest after the British defeated the Sikh armies of the Punjab in 1848, was also a patchwork affair.[24] After a brief flurry of open hostilities from 1854 to 1856 (the Crimean War), the British settled into a war of position designed to contain Russian expansion into Central Asia and protect British interests in the Mediterranean, on the southern edges of Eurasia (i.e., India and Burma), and in the eastern provinces of China. In the Far East theater of operations, the worst-case scenario for British strategists would be the collapse and partition of the Qing Empire, a development that only the Russians would be in a position to benefit from.[25]

The issue that British strategists faced, therefore, involved a difficult balancing act. On the one hand, they sought to make the Qing government more cooperative and compliant. On the other, they hoped that the dynasty would be capable of strengthening itself sufficiently so that it could retain sovereignty over its territory. Looming over these geopolitical concerns were two historical precedents that worried the British leadership. First, they did not want China to become another Ottoman Empire, a weak political entity

---

23. Language is one marker of this proliferation, as Yule and Burnell ([1886] 1994) make clear. Or one might consider "pidgin" English, itself imbricated with a multiplicity of elements that track the movement of decoding and recoding from Africa to East Asia (see Crow [1913] 1973: 11–14 on China). Similar patterns are evident on the edges of empire; see L. Liu's (1995, 1999) discussion of neologisms in Chinese.

24. Known in British imperial history as the Second Sikh War, the conquest of the Punjab extended the British Indian Empire to the borders of Afghanistan; see Byron Farwell 1972: 37–60.

25. T. F. Wade's correspondence to the Foreign Office mentioned the danger of partition; see Foreign Office Archives (hereafter FO), 17/748: 397. On British views of Russian advances, see H. Rawlinson 1875; Boulger 1879, 1885; also see Ward and Gooch 1923, vols. 2 and 3 and the recent study by Hopkirk 1992. On Russian concerns, see Fletcher 1978c: 326–327. On Russian-Chinese rivalries in Central Asia, see Clubb 1971; Paine 1996.

torn by separatist internal tendencies and an object of encroachment by great powers. This dynamic was, in fact, the original theme of the "Eastern Question," the weakening of the Ottoman and other older empires across Asia under the pressure of European expansion east, and the political uncertainty that resulted. Second, they did not want another India, a full-scale colonial enterprise with the capacity to drain British resources. Yet they also wanted to prevent Russian domination of Asia.

As a number of contemporary participants, popularizers of empire like Rudyard Kipling (Kim, [1901] 1981; A. Wilson 1977: 43), and recent historians have observed, the Anglo-Russian rivalry in Asia was widely imagined on both sides as a contest of wits. Played out in that vast expanse of territory stretching in an arc from the Amur River region of Manchuria in the northeast to Afghanistan in the southwest, the Game required, according to Henry Rawlinson, a "vigilant and scrutinizing eye" (1875: 203), capable of gathering and evaluating information in order to plot British and Russian moves and countermoves. At the same time, however, even though the British and Russians might have operated as if they were engaged in a bilateral contest, neither could avoid dealing with the Qing Empire itself, which had conquered parts of Buddhist and Islamic Central Asia and turned Tibet into a protectorate in the eighteenth century. Failure to understand and take into account Qing commitments in Central Asia would have resulted in strategic miscalculations and erroneous assessments of the forces at work in the region. Great Gamesmen required, in other words, knowledge about lands and peoples similar to that produced in other parts of the empire (see chapter 5). There was, however, a distinct difference between Great Game machinations and the more open and overt power politics in eastern China. The secret nature of Great Game activities required deception, stealth, and the indirect manipulation of local populations. Covert operations on this order involved Englishmen attempting to pass as "natives" and indigenous people trained to operate as British agents. Such mixing or confusion of boundaries invariably generated fears of invisible or barely discernible threats lurking over the horizon. In the British case, such fears ran the gamut from possible invasions of the British Isles (Pick 1993), Russian cossacks descending on China and India, and "Oriental" conspiracies bent on destroying the British Empire. Fantasies such as these generated specters and monstrosities, ones that returned to haunt empires, imperial archives, and the "postimperial" world (see chapter 10). Put in these terms, consideration of the Russian and Qing rivalries in Central Asia opens a space for the consideration of imperial imaginaries, fantasies, and hallucinations about the struggle to maintain and perpetuate empire.

. . . .

To summarize, although there were always differential relations of power involved between European nation-states and other parts of the world, power was neither despotic nor unidirectional. The double movement of expansion (deterritorialization and reterritorialization) created new networks for the multidirectional flow of people, material objects, and ideas, flows that could undermine or support the shifting foundations on which colonial authority was constructed.[26] Colonization was not, in other words, a simple matter of conquest and administration; all colonial settings were informed by a dynamic interaction between colonizer and colonized. Resistance and accommodation appeared in many distinct forms, and fantastical constructs of the capacities of self and others supported and subverted colonial policy. As a result, it is difficult to posit any pure form of colonization or any complete model that could fix our understanding of colonial processes.

Instead, we might consider all the entities produced in the age of empire as forms of semicolonialism—especially that patchwork of patchworks, British India, notwithstanding its canonical status as the colony of colonies. As reterritorialization "machines" of Euroamerican expansion, colonial apparatuses strove to achieve, while never actually realizing, complete domination. They also generated a bundle of contradictions that played themselves out along gender, racial, and class lines in the peculiar institutions created in the contact zones. From this perspective, therefore, China was not outside of the "real" colonial world. Rather, it was a variation on forms that were both present and incomplete in Africa, South America, and South and Southeast Asia. And like these other settings, China was made up of collections of disparate elements generated by specific tempos in processes of deterritorialization and reterritorialization, the breaks, disruptions, and dissolutions of local circuits of power and exchange, and the inscription of new forms. The pulsating, wave-like tempos of expansion that emanated out of Europe were, in turn, conditioned by the multidirectional flows along the nervous system of empire,

26. From this perspective, the apparent contradictions of Western imperialism and colonialism discussed earlier might also be understood as the effects of the palimpsestual layering of histories and the proliferation of hybridized formations generated in contact zones.

those channels of transportation and communication that linked imperial centers to colonial peripheries in ever more complex and accelerated patterns of decoding and recoding. It is these patterns, especially as they were worked out along the eastern rim of the Eurasian land mass, that are the central concern of this study. This book is designed to locate China within, rather than outside of or peripheral to, the globalizing forces that transformed the worlds of the bulk of humankind in the nineteenth century.

But I move ahead too quickly perhaps. This book is not only about history; it is a history. To arrive at that postimperial world, it is organized into three parts. The next three chapters, constituting part 1, begin with a narrative of the events during the second Opium War (1856–1860). The remainder of part 1 explores the processes of deterritorialization and reterritorialization that fundamentally reordered Qing China's relationship with European empires and placed European diplomats in legations outside of the gates of the Forbidden City in Beijing. Part 2 is made up of two chapters that deal with the reordering of China in the decades between 1860 and 1900 and the location of the Qing Empire within the larger global framework of the new imperialism. The third part takes up the occupation of Beijing and north China in 1900 and 1901 in the wake of the Boxer Uprising. Its purpose is not only to explore this final nineteenth-century reterritorialization of Qing China, but to deal with the social and cultural ramifications of Euroamerican imperialism in China. From a close analysis of aspects of the occupation and the dissemination of an authoritative narrative about Sino-Western relations, it will then be possible to draw some conclusions about the nature of colonialism in China and its impact on contemporary China and the world.

PART I

Opium Wars and Treaties

of Peace, Friendship, and

Commerce

. . . .

CHAPTER 2

The Arrow War, 1856–1860

BARELY A DECADE AFTER the ratification of the Nanjing Treaty, the Qing and British Empires were at war again. Designated in Great Britain the second and third China Wars, and more universally, the second Opium War, the conflict extended over a five-year period, from 1856 to 1860, and came to involve French and U.S. military forces as well. There were large-scale engagements in 1857–1858 and 1860 between Anglo-French armies and Qing forces and smaller battles with U.S. and British naval units in 1856 and 1859, respectively.[1] Surrounding the military engagements were heated political debates within Great Britain and China and discord over the actions of Great Britain on the part of U.S., French, and Russian diplomats in China. When the wars ended in 1860 with the defeat of the Qing, the representatives of all of these countries, in spite of their differences, took advantage of China's weakness to complete new treaty arrangements. It is the purpose of this chapter to provide

---

1. The former took place in November 1856. When a U.S. naval vessel was fired on, Commodore Armstrong, the American commander, took the forts near Canton and destroyed 167 cannon; see Morse 1910–18, 1: 432–433.

a brief overview of these events and then in the next two chapters to proceed to a more detailed analysis of their significance.

In the mid-1850s, Great Britain and the United States were attempting to open discussions for revision of the treaties that ended the first Opium War. In a refrain that echoes concerns of the present, both parties sought greater access to China's market. They also sought to resolve an issue left over from the first Opium War: the right of entry and permanent residence in the city of Canton. With internal rebellions dominating the Qing Court's attention,[2] efforts to open negotiations were unsuccessful during the 1850s. At the same time, Great Britain and France were at war with Russia in the Crimea, making it difficult for their representatives in China to engage in much more than a contest of words with Qing authorities. However, when the Crimean War ended in 1856, the British government hoped to break the deadlock by dispatching several gunboats and warships to Hong Kong. When it became clear that Qing officials were unimpressed with this show of force, British Prime Minister Lord Palmerston waited for just the right sort of incident to use as a casus belli. Something on that order arrived in late 1856.

The Arrow Incident, October 1856

On 8 October, suspecting that the lorcha *Arrow*, a small coastal trading vessel registered in Hong Kong and flying a British flag, was involved in illegally smuggling opium, Canton officials impounded the ship and arrested its crew.[3] Convinced that the seizure violated the Nanjing Treaty, Harry Parkes, the British consul, presented a demand to the imperial commissioner (*qinchai daxueshi*) and viceroy of Liangguang, Ye Mingchen, for the immediate release of crew and vessel. Two days later, Ye returned nine of the crew, holding three others as suspected pirates. Parkes refused to accept Ye's conciliatory gesture and escalated his demands. He now wanted a formal apology from the viceroy.

There matters stood until Parkes met on 20 October with Sir John Bowring, governor of Hong Kong, and Admiral Michael Seymour, commander of the British fleet. At this meeting, Parkes proposed that Ye be presented

2. The primary uprising at this time was the Taiping Rebellion, which began in the south. There was also a Moslem rebellion in Central Asia and a more classic peasant rebellion in north China called the Nian; for a detailed overview, see Hsü 1990: 221–258.

3. Like rickshaws, lorchas were a hybrid technology composed of a Western-style hull and Chinese rigging.

with a twenty-four-hour ultimatum to comply with British demands. If Ye did not comply, British naval forces would destroy the barrier forts between Whampoa island and Canton. If this failed to move Ye, then the forts immediately adjacent to the city walls of Canton would be taken and, if necessary, the city of Canton, and the viceroy's official residence would be shelled from gunboats in the Pearl River. Bowring and Seymour agreed, and the next day Parkes delivered the ultimatum. Ye promptly released the remaining sailors but ignored the demand for an apology. He also took the precaution of marshaling all the military forces at his disposal to reinforce the Pearl River forts and established a committee of prominent officials to help him deal with the crisis (Wong 1976: 169).

When the ultimatum expired without Viceroy Ye's apology having arrived, Seymour's forces occupied several of the forts up to the walls of Canton, spiking guns and destroying fortifications. In the face of this onslaught, Ye halted all trade at Canton. Bowring then demanded the right to immediately enter the city. When Ye refused to comply, British gunboats began bombarding, every ten minutes, the viceroy's office. Short of forces and bereft of outer defenses, Ye turned for support to the population of Canton and its hinterland (Wong 1976: 171). But before he could organize resistance, the British stormed the city and took Ye's residence. Fleeing to another part of town, the viceroy answered the British with arguments about the rights and wrongs of the *Arrow* affair. In response, the bombardment was extended to much of the city of Canton and additional forts along the Pearl River were taken. By mid-November, matters had reached a stalemate. Ye had neither the forces nor the military technology to clear the Pearl River of British gunboats. The British lacked sufficient land forces to follow up on the navy's initiatives. Having provoked a crisis, Bowring wrote to Calcutta for reinforcements.

Throughout this early phase of the war, Bowring and Parkes had presumed that British firepower would be sufficient to cause Ye, as well as the civilian population of Canton, to capitulate. It seems, however, to have had the opposite effect, stiffening resistance and mobilizing the population behind the Qing government. At the same time, the failure of this aggressive policy to yield quick results had consequences in Great Britain. Soon after the Hong Kong governor called for additional military units from India, a debate began in Parliament over the China policy of Palmerston's government.

Word reached London of the *Arrow* affair by cable on 29 December 1856. By the end of the first week of January, Admiral Seymour's reports of military action in the Pearl River had appeared in the London *Gazette*. Editorials followed in the *Times* and the *Morning Post* condemning Viceroy Ye, supporting Bowring, and railing against the threat to the treaty rights that had been won in 1840. Other newspapers and opinion journals were less supportive of the government, however. The *Daily News* and *Punch*, for example, argued that Bowring and Parkes had provoked hostilities in the face of efforts by Ye to find a compromise.[4] Writing in the *New York Daily Tribune*, Karl Marx drew a similar conclusion (Torr 1968, especially 11–17, 36–44).

The issues surrounding the *Arrow* were soon broached in both houses of Parliament, and on 3 March a vote of censure was passed. The government fell and elections were called.[5] In the ensuing campaign, Palmerston ran on a platform critical of Viceroy Ye and insults to British honor, advocating war with China. He was returned to Parliament with a majority of eighty-five seats. Even before these results were in, however, Lord Palmerston ordered troops to be sent from India to Hong Kong and dispatched a Crown agent to China with powers superior to those of Bowring.

On 12 April 1857, James Bruce, eighth earl of Elgin and son of the man who had removed the marble friezes from the Parthenon and transported them to England, was appointed as Her Majesty's high commissioner and plenipotentiary to China. The instructions to Elgin identified the following objectives for his mission: (1) reparations for injuries and property losses of British subjects; (2) complete execution of treaty provisions at all Chinese ports; (3) liberation of the trade with China through the opening of more ports and the Yangzi River; and (4) provisions for a resident minister in Beijing. In additional instructions, Elgin was told to seek an agreement for greater freedom of action for Christian missionaries in China. Further, in an effort to ensure the continued flow of cheap labor to Britain's colonies, Elgin was to seek an agreement that would permit the free emigration of all Qing subjects. If the government in Beijing proved unwilling to meet these demands, Elgin, with control over all British military and naval units in China, was instructed to use force on a graduated scale. First, he was to occupy Canton; second, close the Grand Canal; third, shut down traffic on the Yangzi and Yellow Rivers; and fourth, blockade the Beihe or North River leading to Beijing. If the Qing still

4. See a review of the press in Wong 1998: 153–165.

5. On the debate, see Lord Derby's speech and those of others made in the House of Lords on 24 and 26 February in *Hansard's*, 3d ser., vol. 144, cols. 1155–1245, 1310–1388. For the debate in the House of Commons see *Hansard's*, 3d ser., vol. 144, cols. 1391–1485, 1495–1585, 1589–1684, 1726–1850. Hurd (1967: 47–60) provides a concise review of the debate and a discussion of parliamentary factions. Also see Wong 1998: 196–198.

remained recalcitrant, Elgin was given permission to assault Beijing itself. To guarantee sufficient resources to accomplish these tasks, additional naval and military units were dispatched from India and Singapore (*Correspondence* 1859 [CESM] 1–7).

Events in China, 1857–1858

Lord Elgin reached Hong Kong in early July 1857 but was unable to take any immediate action because of a rebellion that had broken out in India (the so-called Sepoy Mutiny). By the end of the year, however, he had sufficient forces at his disposal to proceed and had gained the tacit support of the French, U.S., and Russian representatives in China, each of whom were now willing to follow the British lead to improve their own position in China.[6] Elgin was not without doubts and concerns. He thought the British government's China policy "stupid," particularly insofar as it was a response to the "apathetic arrogance" of proud mandarins who, rather than employing intelligence and realism in their dealings with the representatives of foreign governments, relied on tricks. Moreover, he doubted whether the "wretched question of the *Arrow*" merited the attention it had drawn (Walrond 1872: 209, 211–212, 217, 219).

Elgin soon put aside his misgivings. With the aid of the French ambassador Jean-Baptiste-Louis, Baron Gros, who seems to have tutored him in the "forms and usages of diplomacy" (Walrond 1872: 209), he took a by-the-diplomatic-book approach to the "crisis." On 12 December 1857, he dispatched a written ultimatum to Viceroy Ye listing British grievances and demands and indicated that there would be no discussion or negotiation on these matters. Ye must immediately comply with existing treaty provisions and also agree to open negotiations over treaty revision. If he refused, Elgin explained that it would be his "painful duty to direct naval and military commanders to prosecute with renewed vigor operations against Canton." Ye was given ten days to comply. In the meantime, Elgin ordered Admiral Seymour, who remained in command of British navel forces at Hong Kong, to prepare for action (CESM 95–97).

The viceroy's response arrived two days later. Apparently unaware that he

---

6. In 1856, Peter Parker tried unsuccessfully to negotiate a revision of the U.S. treaty; see Morse 1910–18, 1: 416–418; Swisher 1953: 312–326. The Russians had a similar failure a month before.

was dealing with an ultimatum, Ye proceeded to review events at Canton since the signing of the 1842 treaty and added that some of the British demands, including the right of residence within the city walls and treaty revision, did not exist in the Qing version of the Nanjing Treaty. In the case of the residency issue, Ye noted that Sir George Bonham, governor of Hong Kong in 1849, had acknowledged that there was no such provision in the Chinese copy of the treaty (Fairbank 1953: 279–280). Having established the unreasonableness of British claims, Ye laid responsibility for the current impasse at the door of Consul Parkes. He did, however, provide the British ambassador an avenue of retreat by surmising that the content of Elgin's letter might not be his own creation, but that of some mischievous person in his employ (CESM 94, 121–124). Receiving a translation of the letter the same day, Elgin confided to his journal that Ye's response was "sheer twaddle" (Walrond 1872: 212).

The legal niceties of diplomatic usages disposed of, Elgin ordered an advance on Canton. The attack began on 28 December; by 5 January 1858 the city was in British and French hands and Viceroy Ye had been captured. He was placed aboard a British naval vessel in the Canton harbor and, a month later, in an extraordinary violation of the "forms and usages" of diplomacy, shipped to Calcutta, where he died in captivity (Wong 1976: 193–197). In addition, the archives of the viceroy were seized from his official residence. In the hands of Elgin's linguists, Thomas Francis Wade and Horatio Nelson Lay, the documents therein would become a force of their own in subsequent events.

The conquest of Canton settled the residency issue rather spectacularly. But the many other issues that Elgin had been sent to deal with in a new treaty were still unaddressed. As he prepared for his next initiative, Elgin sought to turn the occupation of Canton to his advantage. The British and French would govern it through a "puppet" regime and use this unusual arrangement as a bargaining chip with the Qing Court. For the next three years, a joint commission, headed by no-nonsense Harry Parkes, reterritorialized Canton through British-style colonial law and order.[7] At the same time, however, the seizure of Viceroy Ye and occupation of the city left Lord Elgin without a respon-

---

7. According to Wakeman (1966: 175), by the end of the occupation, the rural peasants in the Pearl River delta, who found themselves beset by bandits, rebels, and irregular government taxation for several years, came to appreciate the peace brought by the foreign presence.

sible representative of the Chinese government with whom to negotiate. After sending a message to Beijing notifying the Court of his actions, Elgin headed north, stopping at the ports of Fuzhou and Shanghai, where he learned that he had delivered an extremely effective English lesson: his seizure and transport of Viceroy Ye had "produced a greater effect on the mandarins than even the capture of Canton" (CESM 231).

As Elgin sailed up the China coast, the Qing Court remained somewhat uncertain about events in the south. Around the middle of January, the emperor received a lengthy memorial from Viceroy Ye. Dated 27 December 1857, the day before the British and French began the assault on Canton, the memorial outlined Ye's dealings with the U.S., French, and British envoys, indicated problems the British were having in India, reviewed the viceroy's handling of the *Arrow* affair, and outlined his response to recent British demands. Signaling the seriousness of the situation, Ye wondered if anyone could have predicted twelve years earlier that the question of British residence in Canton and treaty revision would lead to the present crisis. Still, he assured the emperor that he would remain vigilant, while cherishing and showing compassion (*huairou*) for the foreigners. Perhaps a combination of strength, forbearance, and understanding would result in the withdrawal of their gunboats. If so, he would transmit the good news to the emperor immediately (*Chouban* 1979 [YWSM, XF] 2: 610–619; Swisher 1953: 334–346). After reading the memorial, the Xianfeng emperor sent an imperial instruction on 17 January to the Grand Council commending Ye (YWSM, XF 2: 619–620).

Views changed quickly, however, once word reached Beijing of British actions. Ten days later, in a memorial bearing the names of all the major civil and military officials at Canton, the Court learned of the fall of the city. These officials placed the blame for the disaster on Ye. The emperor and his councillors were left with the impression that the viceroy's bad management and worse judgment were the primary causes of the calamity. Accordingly, Ye was demoted and the others censured. The Court then contemplated its next move. On 30 March, now in Shanghai, Lord Elgin was informed by Qing officials of the emperor's decision to appoint a new viceroy of Liangguang and was instructed to return to Canton and await the viceroy's arrival. Refusing to be diverted, Elgin responded by charging another violation of the Nanjing Treaty: the emperor's message had been communicated through officials who were not of equal rank to his own. A week later, on 8 April, Elgin and his army embarked for north China.

The Treaty of Tianjin, June 1858

The British and French arrived in the Gulf of Beizhili at the end of April 1858. U.S. Minister William B. Reed and Russian Ambassador Count Putiatin accompanied the armies. On the 26th, Elgin received word that Tan Tingxiang, the viceroy of Zhili province, Wu'er Kuntai, vice chancellor of the Grand Secretariat, and two other provincial officials had been delegated to negotiate with him. At their first meeting, Elgin made it quite clear that he would deal only with officials who possessed the same powers as he himself carried, that is, those of a plenipotentiary, one with the authority to make decisions on the spot, rather than referring every item to his government, and he demanded that they produce the appropriate credentials. According to Thomas Wade (who had the pertinent English and Chinese documents in hand), the powers demanded by Elgin were those possessed by Qiying and Yilibu, the two Qing officials who had negotiated and signed the Treaty of Nanjing in 1842. When Viceroy Tan indicated that no such powers existed in China, Elgin broke off contact and ordered military action to commence at the mouth of the North River.[8] On 20 May, the Dagu (Taku) forts were taken and their guns destroyed. Elgin then moved his base of operations upriver to Tianjin.

With British and French armies poised to advance on Beijing and its insufficient forces, the Xianfeng emperor deputed two higher-ranking officials to proceed to Tianjin and deal with Elgin. One of these was Grand Secretary Guiliang, a Manchu nobleman who, over a thirty-year career, had held numerous civil and military posts, the most recent of which, prior to his elevation to the Grand Secretariat in 1857, was as viceroy of Zhili, the province in which Beijing and Tianjin were located. In addition to his title as grand secretary, Guiliang also was designated an imperial commissioner.[9] The other official was Huasha'na, the president of the Board of Civil Appointments (Libu shangshu). Satisfied with their credentials and impressed with the fact that both officials held positions at the highest level of the Qing government, Elgin opened discussions. Over the next three weeks the details of a new treaty were hammered out and signed at Tianjin on 26 June 1858. At the same time,

8. The U.S. and Russian ministers urged Elgin to accept the credentials of the Qing envoys, which he refused to do; see CESM 304–305.

9. In 1854, he had dealt with the British, U.S., and French envoys who had arrived at Dagu requesting treaty revision; see Hummel 1943: 428–430.

the Qing negotiators completed treaties with France, Russia, and the United States.

The British agreement, usually referred to as the Tianjin Treaty, called for the establishment of diplomatic legations with resident ministers in Beijing and London. In addition, diplomats and consuls were to have the freedom to move at will around either country. At the nondiplomatic level, British nationals gained a number of desirable privileges. New ports were opened to trade on the coast and up the Yangzi River, merchants and visitors were permitted to travel in the interior of China, and Christian missionaries could preach without sanctions. A provision was also made for a tariff conference to be held in Shanghai. When it was completed in early November, the tariff agreement provided for the legalization of the opium trade and fixed a duty on the drug (CESM 426–434). Last, in an article unique to the British treaty, the Qing government was forbidden to ever again use the ideogram *yi*, which the British translated as *barbarian*, in its official correspondence. In a separate annex, China was to pay a 2 million tael indemnity to cover British property losses at Canton and another 2 million taels "on account of the military expenses of the expedition which Her Majesty the Queen had been compelled to send out for the purpose of obtaining redress" (347–355). There remained only the process of formal ratification by each government, which was to occur, according to the final article of the treaty, within a year at Beijing.

With the Qing Court forced to comply with all British demands, Lord Elgin was willing to be magnanimous. While the tariff agreement was being finalized, the Qing commissioners made it quite clear that the resident minister issue remained a serious problem. They pleaded with Elgin to reconsider. As an alternative to the establishment of a British resident minister in Beijing, the Qing government proposed to send a secretary of State, a rank presumably equal to that of a British representative, to deal with Lord Elgin or his successor in any province the British desired. In a letter to the Earl of Malmesbury, head of the Foreign Office, Elgin recommended that the British government accept this compromise. Provided the ratification of the treaty went forward as planned, Elgin suggested that it would be in British interests to have Her Majesty's minister "choose a place of residence elsewhere than at Pekin [Beijing], and to make his visits to the capital either periodically or as frequently as the exigencies of the public service may require" (CESM 405, 408). Any possibility of Elgin's suggestion being taken seriously ended, however, with events at the Dagu forts the following year.

The Dagu Forts, June 1859

Following the defeat of 1858, the Qing government refortified the Dagu forts and constructed a succession of obstacles to block passage up the North River. Meanwhile, in Great Britain, Frederick Bruce, brother of Lord Elgin, was appointed British envoy and given the duty of exchanging ratifications in Beijing. When Bruce arrived in China in May 1859, He Guiqing, concurrently the viceroy of Liangjiang and imperial commissioner at Shanghai, suggested that the ratification procedure occur there. Apparently convinced that he must avoid any actions supporting Beijing's "dogma of universal supremacy and national superiority" (cited in Costin 1937: 288), Bruce refused to deviate from any precedents the British had already set in their dealings with the Qing Court. He would communicate only with a secretary of State, follow the route all British ambassadors had taken to Beijing, and exchange ratifications there as per treaty agreement. Along with a fleet under the command of Admiral James Hope and the new French ambassador, M. de Bourboulon, who also sought treaty ratification in Beijing, Bruce headed north.

When the British arrived off Dagu on 16 June 1859, local officials informed them that the river had been blockaded to prevent a rebel invasion from the south, and requested that Bruce land further north at Beitang and proceed down its river to Tianjin. Apparently convinced that any concessions at this point would be a setback, Bruce ordered Hope to clear the river of obstacles. By the afternoon of 25 June, the British gunboats had opened an initial passage and moved to a position near the forts. At this point, the Chinese guns opened fire with startling accuracy. Four of the gunboats were sunk, two badly damaged, and severe casualties inflicted. The British admiral himself was wounded. Efforts to take the forts by storm proved futile, and by the end of the day the British had incurred 434 casualties, including 89 dead (Fisher 1863: 184-198; Hurd 1967: 181–184; Beeching 1975: 268–272; Hibbert 1970: 242–244).

The victory at Dagu produced a degree of euphoria in Beijing and consternation among the British. How could Chinese forces, who to date had shown no particular ability on the battlefield against European armies, suddenly become so effective? British observers at the scene and in London decided that the Chinese must have had outside help. Some suggested that perhaps the Russians had provided military aid, including expert gunners at the forts. There were, in fact, reports that fur hats had been spotted on the heads of some of the Dagu artillery men. Another popular story identified the commander of the Qing forces, the Mongol general Senggerinchin (Seng-ge-lin-qin),[10] as Sam Collinson, an anti-British Irish adventurer.[11]

As these rumors circulated, Senggerinchin reported the departure of the British battle fleet from the Gulf of Beizhili on 14 July. In the same memorial, he also cautioned that although the British forces had withdrawn, their defeat enraged them. In all likelihood, they would assemble reinforcements and strike north again. It was important, therefore, to remain alert; only if the British were defeated one or two more times would they end their aggressive actions. The Court must also be cautious of the other foreign powers. At that moment, Senggerinchin noted, the U.S. minister, John Ward, was at Beitang preparing to make the journey to the capital to exchange ratifications of the treaty completed the previous year. There should be no provocations or deviations from previous agreements about the ratification procedure. Further, if well treated, Ward might be induced to carry a message to the British asserting the Qing Court's right to an indemnity after its victory at Dagu (YWSM, XF 4: 1499–1501; Tsiang 1929: 81–82)!

The Assault on Beijing, August–October 1860

While the Qing Court contemplated how to make the most of its victory at Dagu, word reached England of the defeat. As more details arrived, opinion was mixed over whether Bruce had taken the right course of action. Some thought he should have accepted the invitation to land at Beitang. Others argued that the right of passage on the North River had been firmly established by Lord Elgin and that therefore it was quite appropriate for Bruce to insist on this route. Even Lord Palmerston's cabinet was divided over the issue, with Lord Elgin, who had been appointed postmaster-general on his return to England, advising against too harsh a response (Costin 1937: 293–300).

As the debate continued, the cabinet was goaded into action by the French. Determined to avenge the honor of France, Napoleon III, the French emperor, announced that he would send a military expedition to China to re-

10. The usual form of the name of this Mongol general in English-language accounts of this century is a transliteration from the Chinese in Wade-Giles romanization: Seng-ko-lin-ch'in (this is how he appears in Hummel 1943). Here I have rendered it in a transliteration system closer to Mongol pronunciation and provided the Pinyin in parentheses.

11. Hurd (1967: 184) and Hibbert (1970: 244) mention this tale, but provide no specific references for it in 1859. It did, however, circulate the next year. Colonel Walker (1984: 179) mentions it in a letter of 24 August.

dress the "insult" at Dagu. An additional incentive arrived when news came of the treatment of John Ward during the ratification of the U.S. treaty. According to reports, Ward had been asked to comply with Qing Court etiquette and, when he refused, had been denied an audience with the emperor. As a result, he exchanged ratifications on the coast at Beitang rather than in Beijing (F.W. Williams 1889: 297–326; Banno 1964: 110–119). Convinced that the Qing Court had reverted to its traditional method of dealing with foreign powers, Palmerston's government resolved to exchange treaty ratifications, by force if necessary, only in the Qing capital.

In the late fall and early winter of 1859–1860, the British and French governments agreed on a joint military expedition. It was to be led by the same diplomats who had concluded the Tianjin treaties for their respective governments, Lord Elgin and Baron Gros. Although the British government was concerned that the expedition not further destabilize the Qing Dynasty (the treaties might be meaningless if the Qing were overthrown by the Taiping insurrection threatening from the south), Elgin was instructed to extract an apology for the Dagu affair and an additional indemnity for the costs of the present expedition. If the opportunity presented itself, he was also instructed to acquire the Kowloon Peninsula on the mainland opposite Hong Kong (Costin 1937: 316). As these plans were being made in Great Britain, Frederick Bruce, on his own initiative, delivered an ultimatum on 8 March to the Qing government from Shanghai: unless British demands were met, there would be war. In response, the Qing Court instructed Bruce to return north without military forces to ratify the treaty. At the same time, the imperial commissioner at Shanghai, He Guiqing, through whom the Court's response was passed to Bruce, was ordered to reopen negotiations on the points in the Tianjin Treaty that the emperor and his councillors continued to find objectionable, specifically the resident minister issue and the indemnity (*Correspondence* 1861 [CRAC] 34–36, 42–43). These efforts proved futile, however; Bruce refused to negotiate over points that he believed had been settled by the Tianjin Treaty.

On 26 June 1860, two years to the day after the signing of the Tianjin treaties and a year after the military engagement at Dagu, the British and French governments jointly announced that a state of war existed with China. Two days later, Lord Elgin and Baron Gros reached Shanghai and assembled their staffs. Once again, Harry Parkes and Thomas Wade served as Elgin's interpreters. Henry Loch was appointed as his secretary. The British and French delegations then proceeded north to meet their military forces, which had already taken up positions in the Gulf of Beizhili ports of Dalianwan and Zhifu, respectively.

In command of the British contingent was General Sir James Hope Grant, a hero of the suppression of the Indian rebellion in 1857 (Farwell 1972: 138–139). Grant had at his disposal eleven thousand men, approximately one-third of whom were Indian army regiments, including Fane's and Probyn's Horse, two irregular cavalry units raised during the rebellion in India. The infantry forces were made up of eight battalions from frontline regiments, including the Royal Scots, the Queen's Royal West Surrey Regiment, the Buffs (East Kent Regiment), the King's Royal Rifle Corps, the Duke of Edinburgh's Wiltshire Regiment, and elements of the Hampshire, Essex, and East Surrey regiments, all of whom had helped in the suppression of the Indian rebellion. There were also contingents of Royal Marine Light Infantry, Royal Artillery, and Royal Engineers. The British forces were complemented by a French army numbering seven thousand. Under the command of General Cousin Montauban, it comprised the 101st and 102nd regiments of the line, the 2nd Cavalry Battalion, two companies of engineers, four artillery batteries, and a regiment of marine infantry (Knollys 1875: 29–31). In addition, assembled in Hong Kong were British and French naval units and a twenty-five-hundred-man Chinese coolie corps, which later distinguished itself in the taking of the Dagu forts (Graham 1901: 170; Walker 1894: 210; M'Ghee 1862: 210).

The joint campaign began with the landing of British and French forces at Beitang on 30 July. With the North River still blockaded, General Grant intended to attack the Dagu forts from the landward side. This strategy posed its own difficulties, however. The entire area along the coast was made up of tidal mud flats, salt works cross-cut with steep-banked canals, and swamps stretching several miles inland. The problems posed by the terrain were soon solved, however, when reconnaissance patrols found a raised causeway stretching between Beitang and Xinho, a small town about six miles up the North River from Dagu. On 12 August, British units attacked Xinho. Although the Tartar cavalry showed "great pluck and perseverance,"[12] Indian irregular cavalry, supported with the new breach-loading Armstrong guns, took the town (Walker 1894: 171–172).

As the British and French were preparing to move on Xinho, the viceroy

---

12. Although it was noted in a number of accounts that the Qing forces were either poorly led or seldom well organized, their bravery drew notice from British soldiers and civilians alike. The quote is from Graham 1901: 162; also see Anglesley 1975, 2: 231.

of Zhili Province, Hengfu, contacted Lord Elgin. Expressing confusion over the purpose of the allied landing, he indicated his willingness to talk. To this and subsequent messages Elgin responded that until the Chinese government complied with Bruce's March ultimatum and the North River was opened to Tianjin, he would continue military operations (CRAC 98, 100, 105–107, 112; Loch [1869] 1900: 47–50). The allied armies were then ordered to advance along roads and causeways that led south to the Dagu forts, which were successfully assaulted on 21 August.[13] After the defeat the previous year, the British army considered the seizure of the Dagu forts important enough for battle honors to be awarded to the units involved; following the campaign, victory medals were struck and regimental flags altered to bear the inscription "Taku 1860."[14] With the loss of the previous year now avenged, the armies reversed direction and marched on Tianjin, which was occupied on 25 August. Soon afterward, Lord Elgin and Baron Gros were notified of the appointment of Guiliang, the negotiator of the Tianjin Treaty, Hengfu, and Hengqi as imperial commissioners.

When Guiliang arrived in Tianjin on 1 September, Elgin thought that perhaps "a little more bullying" might be necessary to complete his mission (Walrond 1872: 349). To his surprise, however, Guiliang indicated that all British demands would be met in full. But when discussion ensued over the next few days among Parkes, Wade, the French translators, M. de Méritens and Abbé Delamarre, and the Chinese contingent, the British negotiators reported that Guiliang and the other commissioners did not hold the same powers as they had in 1858 (CRAC 155–156). Elgin and Gros immediately broke off negotiations, stating that they would refuse any further discussions with Qing representatives until they reached Tongzhou, the terminus point of the North River, located some fifteen miles from the walls of Beijing. Thereupon, the armies resumed their march.

On 11 September, the delegations reached Yangcun, about twenty miles

13. The British accounts published immediately after the campaign all contain descriptions of the battle; see M'Ghee 1862; Swinhoe 1861; Wolseley [1862] 1972. Other accounts appeared in reminiscences published later; see Knollys 1875; Walker 1894; Allgood 1901; Graham 1901; J. Harris 1912; Stephenson 1915. British and Indian army unit histories also have accounts. See Wykes (1968: 81) for a painting of the British flag atop the ramparts of the Dagu fort.

14. See Davis 1887–1906, 5: 134 and Weaver 1915: 191–193, for examples of medal and flag. Complete lists of battle honors are in Leslie 1970: 85–86 and Singh 1993: 133.

from Tianjin, and received a dispatch from Caiyuan, the Prince of Yi, and Muyin, president of the Board of War, who claimed to have the appropriate powers. But Elgin and Gros refused to deal with them (CRAC 161–162). The armies continued their march and arrived at Hexiwu, approximately halfway between Beijing and Tianjin, on the 14th. At this point, after consulting with Grant about supplies and having received a dispatch from the Qing commissioners that accepted all of the allies' conditions, Elgin halted the armies and sent Parkes and Wade to Tongzhou to make further inquiries of Prince Yi (Walrond 1872: 352–353; CRAC 170).

At their initial meeting with Elgin's emissaries, the Qing commissioners produced an imperial decree that gave them full powers to arrange a settlement. In the ensuing discussions, it was decided that a draft convention, which contained the additional provisions in Elgin's instructions, was acceptable. In addition, all agreed that the ratifications of the treaties of 1858 should take place in Beijing. Given the sense that hostilities were now at an end, it was also decided that the allied armies should halt their march about six miles outside of Tongzhou, at the town of Zhangjiawan, and encamp. Lord Elgin would then proceed to Beijing with an escort of a thousand armed men (CRAC 171).

On 17 September, Parkes, accompanied by Loch, Bowlby, the *Times* correspondent, two civilian officials, de Norman and Thomson, and a contingent of twenty-six cavalrymen, delivered Elgin's confirmation of these arrangements to Prince Yi at Tongzhou. As the British emissaries began to discuss final details, they found the atmosphere decidedly altered. The Qing commissioners expressed concern over the number of soldiers Elgin intended taking with him to Beijing and Elgin's insistence on delivering a letter from the queen of England into the emperor's hands (CRAC 172). Unable to resolve these questions, Parkes and his colleagues withdrew and, accompanied by some minor Qing officials, proceeded to Zhangjiawan to mark out the campgrounds for the allied armies. Once there, they found Qing troops in fortified positions and elements of Mongol cavalry scattered throughout the area. Parkes sent Loch to warn Elgin and returned to Tongzhou to complain to the Qing commissioners. According to Parkes's account, Prince Yi told him that the Qing forces would not be withdrawn until peace was settled (229). At roughly the same time these events were transpiring, the Qing Court learned that the Tianjin prefect, Shi Zanqing, was being detained by the British. Prince Yi ordered Senggerinchin to arrest Parkes and his entourage, and the Qing

Court, determined now to fight, placed a bounty on the heads of members of the allied armies.[15]

Elgin's immediate response was to move the army forward to Tongzhou. Following the defeat of Qing forces at Zhangjiawan on 18 September, Tongzhou was occupied on the 20th. The next day, the last major engagements of the war took place east and west of Tongzhou at Zhangjiawan and Eight-mile Bridge (Baliqiao; see Anglesley 1975, 2: 228–231; Knollys 1894, 2: 141–142; M'Ghee 1862: 174–178; Davis 1887–1906, 5: 127–129; Walker 1894: 201–202). After a spirited resistance, Senggerinchin's forces were driven back and the road opened to Beijing. When word of these defeats reached the Court, the Xianfeng emperor and his advisors, including Prince Yi, fled to the Mountain Resort at Chengde, two hundred miles northeast of Beijing. Prince Gong (Yixin), the sixth son of the Daoguang emperor and the younger brother of the Xianfeng emperor, was left behind to seek peace (Banno 1964: 171).

On 22 September, Prince Gong notified the allies that he held plenipotentiary powers and asked for a halt to hostilities (CRAC 175). Lord Elgin and Baron Gros refused to do so until Parkes and the other prisoners were released. In response, Prince Gong indicated that they would be released as soon as peace was made.[16] This exchange was probably an effort on the part of the prince to buy time; so too, perhaps, was his message that it would be impossible for Lord Elgin to deliver the letter from the queen into the emperor's hands, as the emperor had departed Beijing on his annual hunting trip. Fully anticipating an assault on the capital, Prince Gong remained outside Beijing attempting to rally Qing forces, while inside the city a commission of defense was established (CRAC 183–184; Banno 1964: 172–177). When it was clear that the negotiations had again reached an impasse, Lord Elgin and Baron Gros ordered their forces to move on Beijing. On 5 October a headquarters was established at the Western Yellow Temple (Xihuangsi) outside of the Anding Gate on the north wall of the city. At the same time, French and British units continued to push north and west of Beijing in search of the remnants of the Qing army. On 7 October, the French column reached a walled park area they identified as the emperor's Summer Palace, the Yuanming yuan. After rout-

15. See YMSM, XF 7: 2315–2321; Hsü 1960: 102. A draft of this edict was captured by the British at the Summer Palace and translated. Elgin saw it as a reason for the seizure of Parkes; see CRAC 206–207.

16. Communications continued inconclusively on these lines for several days; see CRAC 175–187.

ing the few attendants left inside, the French began to plunder the palaces, and soon elements of the British forces joined in.

As the looting of the Summer Palace progressed, a final ultimatum was delivered to Hengqi: either the Qing forces in Beijing surrendered the Anding Gate to the allies by 13 October, or the walls would be breached and the city stormed (CRAC 188). The day after the ultimatum was delivered, Parkes and Loch were released, but the whereabouts and fate of the other captives remained a mystery. As the deadline of noon on 13 October approached, Prince Gong lodged a formal protest over the sacking of the Summer Palace, for which he demanded compensation, and requested that there be negotiations over the disposition of the Anding Gate (195–196). The allies refused to respond. A few minutes before the deadline, the Anding Gate swung open, and hostilities, for all practical purposes, came to an end.

Over the course of the next few days, the surviving members of Parkes's entourage and the bodies of the dead arrived in the allied camps. Altogether, thirty-six members of the allied expeditionary force had been taken prisoner. After their capture, they had been divided into five groups, with Parkes and Loch, five French soldiers, and an Indian cavalryman making up one group. All of them were returned safely on 8 October. A second group was made up of de Norman, Lieutenant Anderson, and five Indian soldiers of Fane's Horse. Of these, four of the Indian soldiers were returned alive on 12 October and the bodies of the others on the 14th. A third group was composed of three French soldiers and five Indian cavalrymen; one of the former and four of the latter were returned alive on 12 October. Group four included a French officer, Mr. Bowlby of the *Times*, four Indian cavalrymen, and Private Phipps of the 1st Dragoon Guards; only two, both Indian soldiers, survived. The last group was made up of three French and four Indian soldiers, all of whom died.[17] Captain Barbazon of the British army and Abbé Deluc with the French forces were captured separately and believed to have been decapitated after the battle of Eight-mile Bridge. With nineteen dead and several others in serious condition, Lord Elgin considered the treatment of those captured an "atrocious crime" (Walrond 1872: 365).

After lodging a formal protest with Prince Gong (CRAC 216), Elgin conferred with Baron Gros over a course of action. Both agreed that monetary compensation for the families of the dead was essential and that an action to

---

17. The list presented here comes from General Grant's official report to the secretary of State for War, 22 October 1860, in War Office Archives (hereafter WO) 32/8237.

punish the Qing leadership, as opposed to the Chinese people, was required. Because they could not get their hands on those they held responsible (the emperor, Prince Yi, and Senggerinchin), they decided to vent their rage on an imperial palace, but disagreed on which one (Morse 1910–18, 1: 610–611). In the end, Lord Elgin had his way and the Summer Palace was destroyed as a "solemn act of retribution" (Walrond 1872: 366). The razing of the palaces is taken up in detail in chapter 4. Suffice it to note here that the French refused to participate.

After the destruction of the Summer Palace, matters quickly moved to a conclusion. On 24 October 1860, Lord Elgin entered Beijing with an escort of several hundred troops and proceeded to the Board of Rites (Libu), located to the south of the Gate of Heavenly Peace (Tiananmen), just outside the walls of the Forbidden City. There he was met by Prince Gong and together they signed the Convention of Beijing and exchanged ratifications of the Tianjin Treaty. The Convention included clauses that confirmed the right of the British government to establish an embassy in Beijing; extracted an apology for the Dagu "misunderstanding" of 1859; fixed an 8-million tael indemnity; opened Tianjin to trade and ceded part of Kowloon to Great Britain; and legalized the emigration of the emperor's Chinese subjects. In addition, the Convention stipulated that the emperor of China was to issue a decree ordering the publication of the Tianjin Treaty in the capital and in all the provinces of the Qing Empire (Mayers [1877] 1966: 8–10). The next day, Baron Gros entered Beijing to ratify the French treaty, formally ending the second Opium War.

Over the course of the next month, the British and French forces withdrew from north China. The following year, Frederick Bruce returned to Beijing to set up the British legation. Meanwhile, under the direction of Prince Gong, the Qing government established the Office for Managing Affairs with Various Countries (Zongli geguo shiwu yamen, usually shortened to Zongli yamen). From this point forward, diplomatic relations with European countries were in the hands of the central government in the capital rather than imperial commissioners in the treaty ports. Furthermore, following the death of the Xianfeng emperor in August 1861 and a palace coup that placed Prince Gong and the empress dowagers Cixi and Ci'an as regents of the boy emperor Tongzhi, the British found a political entity in Beijing with which they could work (Hsü 1990: 262–266). For the next forty years, with only a few exceptions, a kind of peace prevailed. The nature of that peace is discussed in chapter 5. The next two chapters attempt to make another kind of sense out of the events related here.

· ·

CHAPTER 3

Violence and the Rule of Law in China, 1856–1858

THE NARRATIVE PRESENTED in the previous chapter organized the particulars of the second Anglo-Chinese conflict into a standard historical account, a seemingly straightforward unfolding of events and their results. The critical elements that drove these events were conflict and its resolution through treaties. Treaties are generally thought of as a realm of rational negotiation that produce contractual arrangements with attendant responsibilities as well as benefits. As a process that creates order, the negotiation, signing, and ratification of treaties can be explicitly contrasted to warfare. More important, treaties can be made without warfare. And yet, in a very practical sense, particularly with respect to European activities in Asia and Africa, nineteenth-century treaties are almost unthinkable without warfare. Invariably, outside of Europe, the rule of "international" law had to be imposed through the use of force. It would seem that most of the peoples of Asia and Africa had difficulty grasping the logic of treaties until the necessity for doing so had been imposed with the gun.

This chapter and the one to follow explore the relationship between violence and the rule of law in the context of European global expansion in the second half of the nineteenth century. As discussed in the introduction, the pattern of expansion was one of repeated oscillations of deterritorialization and reterritorialization, the ripping up of older networks of power and the laying down of new ones, a flip-flopping between warfare and the rule of law, between imperialism and colonialism.

In China, the decades between 1840 and 1860 were a period in which this pattern played out as an ever greater penetration of European and U.S. capital into the Qing Empire, as the growth of settler communities along the China coast as far north as Shanghai, and as the pernicious spread of lawlessness linked to the increase in opium smuggling. The effects on eastern China were profound. When combined with pressures on the agrarian economy generated by an accelerated population increase, the Western incursion added to the numbers of Chinese vagabonds, brigands, and "coolies," some of whom rose in rebellion against the Qing, others of whom provided a cheap source of labor for old and new European colonies outside of East Asia. Deterritorialization also created a new entrepreneurial population — some local, others drawn in from the Chinese communities of Southeast Asia — who became involved in commercial ventures and in providing services to the European residents in the treaty ports.

To explore processes of deterritorialization and reterritorialization in detail, this chapter considers four kinds of productive apparatuses that provided European powers with critical routes of penetration into the Qing Empire. These include the opium trade itself, new military technologies that overwhelmed Qing defenses, translation projects that enfolded China into global circuits of exchange, and devices through which a European notion of sovereignty was insinuated into the Qing body politic. Each of these elements can be understood to have a history that is not confined to China. Considered as part of a more general process of imperial deterritorialization, they allow us to ponder their peculiar effects on the China coast in the middle of the nineteenth century.

Deterritorialization, 1858 and 1860

Europeans, we are often told, went to China primarily for commercial purposes, that is, to trade for desirable commodities that were unique to China. Until the middle of the nineteenth century, exchange relations were primarily managed and controlled by Qing government officials and commercial monopolies; tea, silk, and porcelain flowed out of China, while New World silver and eventually opium flowed in. On the European side, chartered companies with exclusive rights to trade, ship, and sell goods dominated commerce with the East. By the late eighteenth century, the British East India Company, well established in India in both a commercial and political-administrative capacity, had come to control the bulk of the China trade with Europe. On the Qing side, the Imperial Court attempted to control trade through managed contact. The "Canton system," as historians came to call it, was designed to limit conflict between Chinese merchants and European traders and, at the same time, tax the trade.

Put into operation in 1759, the regulations created a system of managed trade that was confined to the single port of Canton (Guangzhou). Although Europeans could not establish residence or enter the city of Canton itself, they could carry out commercial transactions for a brief period of time each year. These exchanges were organized through thirteen Chinese monopoly merchants who guaranteed prices and deliveries (Hsü 1990: 150–154). In spite of complaints by some of its agents over these "restrictions," the British East India Company (EIC) became fabulously wealthy. The Qing government also benefited from this arrangement; the inflow of silver enhanced the imperial treasure and there were fewer incidents of conflict between Chinese and foreigners.

This comfortable arrangement did more than simply produce a gratifying bottom line. As production shifted to the cash crop farming of tea and the region's transportation and communication networks became oriented to a center of collection on the coast at Guangzhou, it refashioned the social landscape of the southeastern part of China. With tea, silk, and porcelain collected for shipment to Europe and the Americas, a part of China's labor force and material production was drawn into a previously alien formation: the London-centered transregional economy that linked Great Britain, India, and the China coast.

COMMERCE AND OPIUM

As the British came to dominate trade to China, the EIC hoped to substitute British manufactured goods for silver as the medium of exchange. To the surprise of Company agents and manufacturing interests in Great Britain, however, there was little demand for these goods in China. Eventually, in an effort to balance trade in Asia, the British introduced Indian opium into the equation. And although the Yongzheng emperor banned the sale and smoking of opium in 1729 and the Jiaqing emperor prohibited its import in 1796, opium not only found a ready market in China, but it proved to be an extraordinary mechanism of deterritorialization, one that completely reordered commercial relations between China and Europe. Moreover, as the use of the drug spread, opium smuggling and piracy flourished along the China coast, disrupting older commercial patterns and configuring new ones. Between 1800 and 1820, opium entered China at a steady annual rate of four thousand chests a year, each of which contained around 140–150 pounds of the drug. This volume of imports could pay for all the tea and silk Europe and the United States desired.

The era of balanced books did not last long, however. Two things brought it to an end. First, in Great Britain there was a growing clamor to abolish the EIC's monopoly, which officially came to an end in 1830. At the same time, in China consumption of illegal opium grew to the point that silver began to flow back to Europe, with the British Indian Empire and the British pound sterling the primary beneficiaries. Between 1820 and 1830, the number of opium chests entering China per annum rose to nine thousand. Over the next five years, consumption doubled, and then doubled again to over forty thousand chests on the eve of the first war between the British and Qing Empires in 1839. Opium, as a number of recent scholars have argued, was the product that made the British Empire one on which the sun never set (Wong 1998; John Richards 2002).

At the same time, the Qing government retained its ban on the drug. Distribution of opium therefore required an elaborate clandestine network of transportation and communication services. This network ran parallel to and at points overlapped with "legal" avenues of exchange. If problems arose, they were resolved by bribing Qing officials. Meanwhile, the silver drain from China led to inflation, with attendant social consequences: an increasingly impoverished peasantry in the southeast, social dislocation, crime, and, eventually, rebellion. This wave of corruption—of the population that became opium users, of officials bribed with opium profits, of networks of exchange that evaded local administration, and of a social body displaced from routine production—deterritorialized southeastern parts of China and sent political and economic shock waves that were felt in the very center of the Qing Empire, the imperial capital at Beijing. With the social and productive relations of the southeast reoriented to a transnational marketing system over which it had no influence, the Qing Dynasty faced an unprecedented challenge to its authority and to its ability to ensure that economic activity would both enrich the Court and meet the needs of imperial subjects.

The Qing government reacted much as any other government might under the circumstances: it attempted to bring opium smuggling to a halt. The impact of this action was, as noted in chapter 1, the first Opium War and reterritorialization of monumental and unprecedented proportions in the treaties of Peace, Friendship, and Commerce with Great Britain, the United States, and France between 1842 and 1844 (Mayers [1877] 1966: 1–4, 49–58, 76–83). With a legal foothold and basis of operation established through the combination of warfare and treaty settlement, a second great wave of opium-driven deterritorialization occurred via the newly created Euroamerican residence zones in the treaty ports. These sheltered contact zones became havens for numerous nomadic soldiers of fortune and a host of shady wheelers and dealers. The new arrivals were made up of Chinese, Southeast Asians, Europeans, and Americans, a good proportion of whom engaged in the lucrative business of opium smuggling. Still functioning clandestinely, the opium-operating system spread up the Yangzi River and inland, laying down new networks of relationships as it went and spreading corruption ever deeper into China. By 1850 the number of opium chests imported into China topped fifty thousand per annum. In five years, the count had exceeded sixty thousand and was pushing the eighty thousand level by the end of the decade. This extraordinary extension of opium distribution and use quite literally overwhelmed the networks of Qing imperial governance. Opium had become impossible for the Qing to control.

Opium anarchy had other consequences as well. Although it was apparently the ideal instrument for penetrating into China, and thus beneficial to the British and U.S. balance of trade with China, opium smuggling generated a variety of policing problems for Qing and Western officials. Piracy, for example, became so prevalent that by the early 1850s the British Admiralty resorted to a bounty system as a means to control the sea lanes along the China coast (Fox 1940: 106–128). All such efforts proved to be temporary fixes, however; piracy grew hand-in-hand with the increase of the coastal trade, legal and contraband. According to Rutherford Alcock, British consul at Canton in 1857, the primary cause of the increase in criminal activity was that the treaty ports attracted foreigners of worthless character from all nations who "dispute the field of commerce with honester men, and convert privileges of access and trade into means of fraud and violence." Alcock identified immunity created by extraterritoriality as the main culprit and recommended the creation of a disciplinary regime that would place commerce on a firm and sound footing, eliminate abuses, and clean up the treaty ports (CESM 55–60).[1]

Alcock's analysis cut to the heart of the problem. The opium trade disrupted the "legitimate" commerce permitted by the treaties and created diplomatic tensions: smuggling attracted pirates, which placed noncontraband shipping at risk and drew consuls into uncomfortable relations with local Chinese officials (Fairbank 1953: 335–337; Fox 1940: 118–119). At the same time, the privileged status of the treaty ports encouraged Chinese subjects to avoid Qing authority through various legal mechanisms available under foreign law.[2] In the case of ship ownership and registration, for example, one could pay a nominal fee to register a vessel in Hong Kong and fly the British flag.[3] One could also hire foreign captains among, as Richard Cobden put it, the "loose fish . . . stray person[s], . . . or idle young seamen" hanging around Hong Kong and use them to scare off official Qing scrutiny. This was precisely the case of the lorcha *Arrow*, the ship whose impoundment by Qing officials set off the second Opium War.[4] Chinese-built and -owned, it was registered in Hong Kong and had a British captain named Thomas Kennedy when seized in the Canton harbor. From all indications, Kennedy was just the sort of foreigner referred to by Alcock and Cobden, while the Chinese crew of fourteen contained at least two members reported to be pirates, and the ship itself was probably engaged in opium smuggling (Wong 1998: 43–66).

From this brief synopsis, it is possible to discern the power of opium as a spectacular mechanism of deterritorialization. Saturated with addictive desire on both the traffic and consumption ends, it could constitute a world of proliferating hybrids like the *Arrow* itself. No longer discernible as exclusively Chinese or distinctly foreign, the opium network pushed British and Qing officials alike into unanticipated confrontations and conflicts. At the same time, it would be an exaggeration to see opium as totally unique, as somehow outside of or beyond the legal or more acceptable forms of com-

1. Elgin confirmed Alcock's assessment in a reference to the "outrageous conduct of a certain class of foreign adventurers." See CESM 260 and similar comments on 255, 263, 333, 346.

2. See the discussion in Wong (1998: 3–4), who cites Fortune (1857: 425–426) on this issue.

3. The situation with U.S. ship registrations was no different; see Fox 1940: 128.

4. The quotations are from Cobden regarding the *Arrow* incident: see *Hansard's*, 3rd ser., vol. 144, col. 1400, 26 February 1857.

merce. Insofar as it could create pleasure as well as dependency, opium was not unlike those other addictive substances that shaped the Europe-centered global economy—things like sugar and cocoa or substances that contained nicotine or caffeine. Such dependency-producing "software" reordered or, perhaps better, recoded both bodies and geographic space by cutting into flows of distribution and consumption and redirecting them. As these substances insinuated themselves into the social body and worked their magic, they refashioned desire, orienting it away from local economies and toward transnational marketplaces. This was no less the case in Europe than it was in China, producing, as it were, a joint history of global addictions that confounds the neat distinctions between East and West, while constituting addiction as a universal modern attribute that reconfigures cultural and territorial boundaries.

MILITARY TECHNOLOGY

In comparison to opium, new military technologies deterritorialized Qing China at a markedly swifter rate. Critical in this respect were not simply novel weapons, but new ways of organizing and delivering them. And like the transformation of local and global economies wrought by opium, changes in military hardware were inextricably part of developments in India, inseparable from processes of imperial conquest and colonization there.

Two sorts of technological mechanisms stand out in this respect. The first of these involved the creation of highly mobile land and sea forces, whose governing logic was not numbers, but speed and the shock effect of the overwhelming application of force at a strategic point.[5] On land, light cavalry troops, made up of Indian peoples who had submitted to the British—Sikhs and Pathans, for example—were combined with infantry (Farwell 1989). The latter were drilled into highly disciplined units equipped with the latest firearms. These included newly designed hand-held guns, the accuracy of which was improved by rifled barrels, with speed of fire enhanced by self-contained cartridges or bullets (Headrick 1981; McNeill 1982). When these technologies were deployed in China, the cavalry and infantry forces were not used for lengthy campaigns or long periods of sustained action, but as rapid deployment forces. Remaining closely tied to their system of transport and supply, they were to enter quickly, eliminate local opposition with superior firepower

---

5. On the development and spread of European military techniques, see Ralston 1990 and McNeill 1982.

and mobility, and temporarily seize key objectives.[6] They were also designed to move in under or immediately following a sustained bombardment.

The bombardment was, in turn, delivered by yet another new technology, or rather a combination of several new technologies organized onto a single platform: the gunboat. With a shallow draft, steam driven, and highly maneuverable, gunboats carried cannon and rockets. Unlike sailing ships, they could penetrate up China's coastal rivers, destroy fortified positions along the way, attack walled cities, and terrorize the population (Headrick 1981: 43–57). This is precisely what happened at Canton in 1840 and 1857–1858, where, in the latter case, bombardment had another use as well. Directed against the headquarters of the viceroy of Liangguang, the much detested Ye Mingchen, and against the houses of the civilian population of the city, the bombardment provided dramatic payback for previous insults to Englishmen.

In the North China campaign of 1860, one additional element was added to the mix: the Armstrong cannon, a breach-loading field gun that was effectively service tested in this campaign (Knollys 1894: 161). In addition to its use against the Dagu fortifications at the entrance to the North River leading to Beijing, the Armstrongs were coordinated with mobile light cavalry units. At Xinhe and Zhangjiawan in 1860, these artillery pieces devastated the Mongol cavalry deployed against them, helping to open an uncontested path between the coast and the walls of Beijing (Graham 1901: 166; Knollys 1875: 22, 1894, 2: 139, 161, 168; M'Ghee 1862: 126; Walker 1894: 171–172; Wolseley [1862] 1972: 179).

In both its seaborne and land versions, this military form of deterritorialization complemented the opium regime. Rapid, devastating violence was designed to demonstrate that resistance was futile and to quickly transform opposition into submission. At this level of calculation, technology-driven violence was both instrumental and symbolic. That is, it was both tool and expressive technique—a "measure of coercion,"[7] something to be adeptly applied in doses or measured grades, until the mental universe of the enemy was altered. As such, its effects were not only destructive, but constructive. It inscribed a visible sign of loss—dead bodies, destroyed property, severed or blockaded communication lines—but it also taught lessons. After 1860, the

6. On the British army and its nineteenth-century campaigns in Asia and Africa, see Farwell 1972; 1981.

7. Admiral Keppel to Captain Heneage, 5 November 1868, in orders to obtain redress after an attack on British missionaries at Yangzhou; see *China No. 2* (1869): 41.

Qing government sought to acquire similar weapons and hire Westerners to train their armies to use them. As pedagogy, high-speed warfare thus became an element of reterritorialization, a recoding as well as a decoding apparatus.

TRANSLATION

At first glance, it may seem somewhat idiosyncratic to treat translation as if it were akin to an Armstrong gun, yet, in the era of the Opium Wars, translation procedures may be understood as a special form of violence, one that operated as warfare by other means. British linguists in China often used their privileged position as middlemen between British and Chinese officials or Chinese-language texts to reduce or completely eliminate all linguistic ambiguities between the English and Chinese languages. They strove, in other words, for a universal form of exchange of meaning. The products of this linguistic reduction were then deployed rhetorically to advocate a more aggressive policy in China. Some of its foremost practitioners were men like Harry Parkes, Horatio Lay, and Thomas Wade, all of whom were key figures in translating the written and verbal pronouncements of Qing officials to Lord Elgin.

Two of their most important and effective uses of translation as a weapon in combat between British and Qing officials involved the ideogram *gong*, which the British rendered then, and many still do now, as *tribute*. Not only did this choice of words conjure up visions of Oriental despotism and dependency, but it gave the impression to independent-minded Englishmen of a kind of unequal and illegitimate form of economic exchange. They resented being expected to pay tribute for the right to engage in a restricted form of commercial intercourse. A similar situation arose with the translation of the word *yi* as *barbarian*, particularly because it might just as plausibly have been rendered as *foreigner* or *stranger*.[8] But, as barbarian, *yi* signaled the sort of haughty, high-walled condescension and exclusiveness that was believed to dominate the thinking of the Qing emperor and his mandarins.

The consequences of these translation strategies became most clear in the Tianjin Treaty itself. Article 51 banned the use of the term *yi* forever from

---

8. Several English voices were raised in protest over the narrowness of these translations, including that of Sir George Staunton, veteran of the Macartney mission and translator of the Qing legal code. Peter Thoms had similar complaints. Others, including the opium merchant James Matheson, the Christian missionary W. H. Medhurst, and the British consul T. T. Meadows, insisted that terms such as *gong* and *yi* had but one meaning: tribute and barbarian. See Basu 1993; L. Liu 1999: 131–134.

any official Qing document in which the British were discussed. Further, the British insisted that the ban be published and circulated through official government channels to instruct mandarins throughout the empire and the Chinese public that the British were not to be trifled with (CESM 354, 385). It should not be too surprising, therefore, to find British linguists scouring Qing government communications for words that suggested the superiority of the Chinese emperor over the queen of England, or to see these same linguists at Canton in 1858 and later in Beijing in 1861 publicly instructing the populations of those cities on words they could not use when referring to Englishmen (CESM 164; Rennie 1865, 1: 71–72).

If the translation of individual Chinese ideograms had a profound influence on British actions in China, just as significant was the translation of collections of Qing official government correspondence seized during the 1858 and 1860 campaigns. In both cases, a large cache of documents was placed in the hands of Thomas Wade, future British minister to China, and his team of Chinese helpers, and together they identified and separated out those dealing with the British and the other Euroamerican powers.[9]

In the first instance, the source materials were from Viceroy Ye Mingchen's offices in Canton. Between January 1858 and the signing of the Tianjin Treaty on 26 June, Wade and his group worked on these papers, summarizing a number of them and translating several completely.[10] The results were included in the reports of Lord Elgin and Baron Gros, the French minister, to their respective governments. Portions were published in British parliamentary papers and in the United States public record. Several of the documents also made their way into personal accounts by English participants at the time. The circulation of Wade's translations became, in other words, an important element in how the events of 1857–1860 were represented outside of China as well as among foreigners active in China.

Equally important, the translations of the captured documents played significant roles in the negotiations of 1858. First, they provided ammunition for the British consuls to demonstrate to Lord Elgin that they were not making anything up. The documents showed Chinese mandarins to be as antiforeign,

9. Included was the first treaty between China and the United States, negotiated by Caleb Cushing, as well as letters from President Buchanan to the Qing emperor. Lord Elgin had them returned to the U.S. minister Reed, whose attitude toward the British use of force seems to have shifted from opposition to lukewarm support; see CESM 158.

10. See CESM 152, 221, 234, 270–298; a list can be found on 234. For discussion of the fate of the documents see Pong 1975: 3; Wong 1983: 5–6.

inflexible, and ignorant and fearful of the outside world as British officials on the scene had long claimed they were. Citing the documents, British linguists convinced Elgin that the only effective way to deal with Chinese tactics of obfuscation and delay was to appear to be an "uncontrollably fierce barbarian." Elgin complied with their suggestions in 1858, and he may well have recalled that sage advice in 1860, when he decided to burn down the emperor of China's Summer Palace and contemplated doing the same to the Forbidden City.

In addition to influencing the negotiating strategy of Lord Elgin, the translations were also used against Qing officials as weapons. Perhaps the best example of this involved Qiying, the Manchu official who, along with Yilibu, had negotiated the Treaty of Nanjing in 1842. After British forces had destroyed the Dagu forts, Lord Elgin set up a headquarters in Tianjin, where he was met by two high-level Court officials, Guiliang and Huasha'na. Recall that Elgin had refused to deal with them until they produced imperial seals of office and the same kind of credentials possessed by Qiying and Yilibu, those of a plenipotentiary. Before the credentials and seals arrived, however, Qiying appeared at Tianjin. Fearing that his presence might be a ploy to prolong the negotiations, the British sought a way to get rid of him. Wade produced from among the Canton documents a memorial written by Qiying in 1844 explaining his methods for, as Wade translated it, "soothing and bridling the barbarians."[11] According to Lord Elgin's secretary, Laurence Oliphant, it was decided that Wade and Lay would unexpectedly introduce the memo in the presence of Guiliang, Huasha'na, and Qiying, thus discrediting Qiying and forcing him from the negotiations.[12] The strategy was so successful that Qiying disobeyed the emperor's orders and fled Tianjin.[13] He was soon brought up on charges before the imperial clan court and sentenced to death.

The dilemma in which Qiying found himself was the same the Qing Court itself now faced. Not only could its official documents, the very lifeblood of Qing management and control of its far-flung empire, be used to precipitate a crisis, but their appropriation by Europeans also indicated the extent to which the Court had lost control of its own discursive universe in its dealings with Western powers. As opium worked to corrupt those who memorialized

11. Wade's translation appears in CESM 175–177. For another translation of this famous memorial, see Teng and Fairbank 1963: 37–40.

12. Elgin's reference to its use is in CESM 334; the Wade quote is on 322. Oliphant's account, including the complete text of Wade's translation, is in [1859] 1970: 357–366.

13. For Qiying's account, see YWSM, XF 3: 942–943.

the throne, their memorials themselves were now open to a form of scrutiny and surveillance the nature of which no dynasty in China had faced before. It was not just that the British linguists knew their language; they could take that language and transfer it into another discursive universe where it was effectively "disenchanted" and drained of authority.

For those Qing officials who might not yet have grasped the cumulative impact of this particular form of deterritorialization, the point was driven home in Article 50 of the Treaty of Tianjin. It stipulated that the English-, not the Chinese-language version of the treaty carried its "correct sense" and that the Chinese text had "been carefully corrected by the English original." All future correspondence between the two governments was to follow the same procedure.[14] Thus, at a stroke, the Qing Empire contemplated its subjugation in a language and terminology it neither commanded nor understood. This not-so-subtle shift to "correction" by an alien model also inaugurated, at the same moment, a wholly new form of reterritorialization, one that would take the fruits of decoded Qing sources and recode them within a new language of "international relations."[15]

Before moving on, let me deal with one last example of translation as a mechanism of deterritorialization. In 1860, British forces captured Qing Court correspondence at Hexiwu and at the Yuanming yuan. Like the earlier materials, these documents, according to Lord Elgin's linguists, confirmed the necessity for the use of force against the Qing. But they served another purpose as well. Selected ones were forwarded to the foreign secretary, Lord Russell, and may well have functioned rhetorically to justify certain decisions made by Lord Elgin. For example, an imperial edict captured at the Summer Palace showed the emperor ridiculing the idea that he should receive the U.S. representative Ward in an audience according to Western protocol. Another group of documents captured at Xinho indicated the amounts of bounties placed on the heads of the European and Indian troops invading China, and a memorial from Senggerinchin urged the emperor to leave Beijing so that he wouldn't be forced to deal with the European ambassadors in his own capital. Court edicts urged Qing forces to continue fighting at the same time that imperial commissioners were negotiating with Lord Elgin and Baron Gros

14. CESM 354. The Chinese translation is in YWSM, XF 3: 1014–1023, with the relevant clause beginning on 1022.

15. For analyses of the processes by which Euroamerican international law was translated in China and Japan, see L. Liu 1999 and Duden 1999.

(CRAC 115–124, 205–207, 260–267, 269). As in other cases, these documents also made their way into the publications of Parliament and were summarized in various privately published accounts that, like the account of Robert Swinhoe, the interpreter on General Grant's staff, appeared within a year or two of the expedition.[16]

The ability to authoritatively decode Qing internal documents thus had strategic value for the disordering of China and for the creation of the moral terrain on which Lord Elgin and his aides could ground their actions. The effect of the compression of language into a rigid grid of equivalencies and the use of translated documents as offensive weapons worked to destabilize the administrative reporting structure of the Qing Empire. In a political universe whose operation was geared to the upward flow of information and the downward diffusion of decisions, this contamination of the reporting network was probably as damaging to the Qing imperium as the British gunboats. Meanwhile, as the translated Qing documents circulated through treaty port communities, government agencies in London, and newspapers and participant-observer accounts of military campaigns, they provided incontrovertible evidence to justify British policy in China. That is, they effectively legitimated the European-authored historical record, elevating the actions of Her Majesty's agents in China above the mean and ignoble world of self-interest, greed, opium smuggling, and petty insults onto a plane of righteous conquest and universal benefit. China and the world, Lord Elgin and his advisors were convinced, would both be better off as a result of the British use of force.

SOVEREIGNTY

The way translations of Qing Court documents were deployed to justify and confirm British actions in China also occluded the baser aspects of the Euroamerican presence in China, while thrusting into the foreground the question of sovereign equality among nations. For a number of those involved at the time and later, the issue of sovereign equality became, if not the sole cause of conflict, the primary one.[17] My purpose here is not to dispute either the

---

16. Swinhoe 1861: 312–315; Wolseley [1862] 1972: 243–257. Some of the documents also appeared in General Grant's account of the war; see Knollys 1875: 164–189, 1894, 2: 172–175.

17. This is the line of interpretation that effectively begins with the first British embassy in 1793 and runs down to the "tribute system" model of "traditional" Chinese foreign re-

significance of the issue or the subsequent interpretation of it, but rather to explore how notions of sovereignty and sovereign equality were themselves a significant mechanism of deterritorialization. Further, although these concepts have a dense legal and institutional history in Europe dating to well before the conflicts in China, the dispute between the Qing Empire and European nation-states over the question of sovereign equality had its own historical trajectory. This conflict involved certain ceremonial practices of the Qing Court, namely, what Europeans called the *kowtow*—the scandalous practice of kneeling and prostrating before the emperor of China. Yet, the particular significance given to this act, especially by Englishmen, is difficult to understand without some sense of emerging bourgeois notions of masculinity. Critical in this respect were characterizations of the male body as a signifying agent, one capable of delivering meaningful messages through its movements and gestures.

Ceremony and the Sovereign Masculine Subject · In his mid-nineteenth-century novel *The History of Henry Esmond*, William Thackeray wondered if the Muse of History would ever free herself from the encumbrance of ceremony. Like her sister, the Tragic Muse of Theater, Clio only seemed to busy herself with the affairs of kings, "waiting on them obsequiously and stately, as if she were but a mistress of Court ceremonies, and had nothing to do with the registering of the affairs of common people." Thackeray's concern with histories other than those of monarchy led him to ponder whether "History" would "go on kneeling to the end of time." Or would Clio "rise up off her knees . . . take a natural posture," and thus cease her mimicry of Court chamberlains by no longer "performing cringes" and "congees" and "shuffling backwards out of doors in the presence of the sovereign" (1991: 13–14)?

Of interest here are Thackeray's metaphors for depicting Clio's subjugation and potential liberation, and how the actions themselves are linked to a feminine figure. Taken together, these elements of body disposition and the meanings imputed to them place European pronouncements on the scandalous behavior of the Chinese in a larger social and historical formation. Note, for example, his use of bodily position to distinguish between servility and freedom. Only the subjugated kneel, cringe, bow, shuffle backward. The free stand *upright*. Such bodily postures serve to highlight natural versus unnatural practices, while gesturing toward the transformations under-

---

lations posited by John K. Fairbank. For a more detailed discussion of this genealogy, see Hevia 1995b, chaps. 1, 10.

way in the reterritorialized physical space of an emerging bourgeois world. The kneeling/upright binary resonates with oppositions such as high/clean and low/dirty, distinctions that figure not only social class and the geography of the nineteenth-century city and its residents, but, much like Thackeray's Clio, the feminization of servitude in the figure of the kneeling chambermaid (Stallybrass and White 1986). The Victorian gentleman and maker of empire was just the opposite: stalwartly upright, touching the ground with more than one knee only when wounded or dead at the hands of savage barbarians.

Thackeray's version of kingly Court ceremonial might also be read as satire, a kind of ridicule that displaced nineteenth-century Court ceremony in Great Britain from the realm of political ritual onto a new domain that might be called political theater or, perhaps more precisely, the pageantry of British imperialism.[18] By 1820, it would seem, attacks on courtly ceremony hinged on the fact that human enlightenment exposed such practices as ridiculously hollow shams, mere artifice.[19] And yet, contrary to what utilitarian thought and instrumental reason might lead us to expect, neither monarchy nor ritual disappeared in Great Britain. Instead, foreshadowed by Edmund Burke's unsettling notion that reason unwisely laid bare the mechanism of state power (Eagleton 1990: 58), Court ceremonial and other state rituals went public, and in so doing reclothed power as exhibition (Bennett 1995: 59–88; Greenhalgh 1988: 52–81). In spectacular displays of grandeur, international expositions, celebrations of conquest, royal weddings and funerals, and dedications of monuments, all reported in the illustrated press and celebrated in commercial advertising, representations of state power became objects of mass instruction and consumption (T. Richards 1990). As they did so, a distinction was drawn between the appearance and the reality of power, between what was shown to the public and what was hidden behind a screen—the public face of authority, with its humanistic pronouncements, versus realpolitik. Yet, at the same time, only those political orders in which the two were in reasonable conjunction would be identified in the nineteenth century as Powers.

The relationship between the public representations and the hidden realities of power implied, in turn, a kind of instrumentalism lying behind ap-

18. Other sources making disparaging remarks about Court ceremony can be found in works on the laws of nations; see Vattel 1916, 3: 367, the standard reference for diplomats after the Congress of Vienna; and the remarks of John Adams in Charles F. Adams 1853, 8: 251–259 and of Lord Macaulay cited in Crosby 1991: 57.

19. Cannadine 1983: 101–102. On the lampooning of monarchy in English literature, see also Stallybrass and White 1986, 101–102.

pearances: real power was force or strength capable of disordering, and thus altering, another sovereign order. A political entity that seemed to be based exclusively on representational spectacle or appearances carried little weight in Euroamerican thinking. The almost reverential character of the pronouncements by Lord Macartney in 1793 on the superiority of Asian ceremonial splendor and royal pomp over European courts became literally impossible for his successor (Cranmer-Byng 1963: 123–124, 131). As Lord Palmerston's policies made clear, Britain no longer wished to participate in the "pageantry" of Asia on Asian terms. In India, Southeast Asia, and East Asia, British imperial agents worked to alter the structures of political power either by building new ones on the same ground or by manipulating older ones from an "understanding" of the Asian mind produced by new knowledge.

British pronouncements of superiority over Asia were also related to a second trajectory of historical development. This involved the reconceptualization and standardization of European state-to-state relations through the creation of a uniform code of diplomatic practices called the "Law of Nations" that followed upon the Congress of Vienna in 1820. Ceremonial encounters between the head of one state and the ambassador of another became the primary site for the mutual recognition of sovereignty. Understood as an acceptance of sovereign equality, recognition constituted the rational subjects *required* for the completion of contractual arrangements in the form of treaties. With their multiple articles clearly defining rights, duties, and obligations, treaties also functioned to regulate what had become the partner of European diplomacy on the global stage: commercial exchange. Ambassadors and consuls sought to facilitate the movement of merchants and their goods across the same borders they themselves traversed. And like diplomacy, trade revolved around notions of equality, exchange, and contract arrived at by sovereign masculine subjects.

It was precisely at the site of interstate ceremonial that the new notions of diplomacy and commerce converged with emerging pronouncements about acceptable bodily posture for the bourgeois gentleman. With the Congress of Vienna, the form of proper encounters was thoroughly naturalized and advanced as a desirable universal norm. Ambassadors were to enter the presence of the host sovereign, bow three times in their approach, place credentials or letters of credence directly into the sovereign's hands, exchange pleasantries, and retreat as they had entered. They did not kneel on either one or two knees, and when they bowed their heads, they did so from a standing position, bending at the waist. By the middle of the nineteenth century, this form of sovereign recognition and state-to-state equality was universal,[20] the only significant exceptions being those regions soon to be under European colonial rule, and China and Japan, although the last of these would soon conform to the universal particularism of Europe.

The Problem of China · It was axiomatic for enlightened citizens of nineteenth-century North Atlantic nation-states to assume that despotisms stretched from the Ottoman Empire to the shores of Japan. By midcentury, however, most of these despotisms had to one degree or another been forced to accept European diplomatic forms. China was the chief exception. For, unlike any other "civilized" political entity in the world, the Chinese Empire required all those who approached the emperor to "degrade and humiliate" themselves by performing the kowtow.[21] According to many nineteenth-century Euroamerican male observers, China's Court ceremonies demanded the sort of reverence that was due no human being, only the Christian god.[22]

Because ceremony had already been made suspect in unfolding bourgeois definitions of freedom, honor, and dignity, the kowtow came to stand as an absolute other for the upstanding "free subject" of European modernity. The passionate denunciations of the act by such authorities on international relations as John Quincy Adams and the ridicule of earlier European visitors to China, especially members of a Dutch embassy in 1795 who were reported to have performed the act,[23] suggests that bourgeois actors made an equation among kneeling and bowing before the Chinese emperor, the purported absence of freedom and equality in China, and the lofty pinnacle the emperor of China was assumed to occupy in the Chinese mind. It was generally held that until the emperor was understood to be no more nor less than any other monarch in the world, Euroamericans in China would have to continue to suffer all manner of slights from Chinese mandarins and the population in general. Imperial audiences, understood by representatives of North Atlantic nation-

20. On sovereignty and the impact of the Congress of Vienna on diplomatic regulations, see Hinsley 1969: 275–288, 1986; Jones 1984: 20–21.

21. As Hugh Murray put it, China was a place where "ancient usages" were the very "soul" of government; see Murray et al., 1836–43, 2: 161–164.

22. See J. Q. Adams 1909–10, 43: 295–324, F. W. Williams [1889] 1972: 318; and the conversation between British Consul Thomas Meadows and Zhili Viceroy Li Hongzhang reported in FO 17, 748: 377.

23. See J. Q. Adams 1909–10. Also see John Barrow's ([1806] 1972: 9–15) attack on the 1794 Dutch embassy. Duyvendak (1939: 1–4) chronicles the negative assessment of Dutch behavior into the twentieth century.

states as the site where the emperor's superiority inside and outside China was established, became therefore the key arena for facilitating Chinese acceptance of Western forms of state-to-state intercourse.

Indeed, in the early nineteenth century, no European or U.S. ambassador, with the exception of Lord Macartney in 1793, had ever had an audience with the emperor of China in a form approaching that common in Europe (Hevia 1995b: 97–102, 170–176). Moreover, for observers at the time, the Macartney embassy solved nothing. It was followed not by new forms of intercourse more acceptable to Europeans, but by further humiliations such as those visited on the Amherst embassy and Lord Napier's "melancholy catastrophe" at Canton.[24] Through these instances, as well as the translation procedures discussed above, the kowtow, tribute, and barbarian (yi) provided a cluster of native terms that firmly linked Imperial Court ceremony to notions of Chinese "jealousy" and "exclusionism," that is, to the refusal on the part of the Qing Court to allow fair, open, and equal intercourse with fully self-conscious others.[25] China was increasingly characterized as a despotism in which wealth and commerce were held in contempt. Events leading up to the second Opium War only reinforced these attitudes, and any refusal to kowtow could itself become a heroic symbol of resistance to Chinese aloofness and ignorance.

One example from the 1860 military campaign in north China might suffice to make this point. In a seemingly minor incident, a British private from the "Buffs" (the East Kent Regiment) named Moyse became a legend. Along with some Indian soldiers carrying supplies, Moyse was captured near Xinho by Mongol cavalry and brought before Senggerinchin, the Qing commander, who declared that if they would kowtow, they would not be harmed. This the Indians did, but Moyse refused, declaring that he would sooner die than disgrace his country, whereupon he was summarily beheaded.[26] In a poem by Sir Francis Hastings Doyle, Moyse's uprightness was later immortalized. "The Private of the Buffs" emphasized that even a "poor, reckless, rude, low-born, untaught" English soldier could "stand in Elgin's place" and not shame the English race. This collapsing of class distinctions through the evocation of

24. See Ellis 1817 on the Amherst embassy and J. Q. Adams 1909–10, 43: 305 on Napier.

25. According to authorities such as James Matheson (1836: 1), Chinese exclusiveness could be defined as the penchant to "shroud themselves and all belonging to them in mystery impenetrable—to monopolize all the advantage of their situation."

26. See M'Ghee 1862: 103–105 for a contemporary account. The tale is retold in the regimental history by Knight 1935, 3: 501–502.

race was followed, in the penultimate verse, by clearly defining the import of Moyse's individual act of defiance:

> Yes, Honour calls !—with strength of steel
>> He put the vision by.
>> Let dusky Indians whine and kneel;
> An English lad must die!
> And thus, with eyes that would not shrink,
> With knee to man unbent
> Unfaltering on its dreadful brink
>> To his red grave he went.[27]

It is, in fact, precisely this sort of defiance, registered in the actions of leaders as well as lowly privates, that was understood to be the only way of dealing with the unreason of Chinese arrogance, exclusiveness, and ignorance of the world outside of China. One needed, as Lord Elgin put it, to bully and then stand firm (Walrond 1872: 349, 362–363, 365). The slightest hint of weakness would instantly be exploited and any ground gained would thus be easily lost.

Gunboat diplomacy found its ideological foundation precisely here, at the point where constructions of the upright masculine subject of empire were made to converge with the Euroamerican representations of the characteristics of China's ruling elite. Thus, Moyse's defiance and Elgin's firmness should not be taken as mere bravado in the face of an Oriental menace. Rather, they can be understood as prime examples of the relationship Euroamericans took to exist between the appearance and the reality of power. Chinese shows of force were just that—mere performance. Englishmen, on the other hand, did not bluff or threaten violence. They stated ultimatums founded in law, backed them with military force, and defied others to match such upright principled behavior. This masculine ethos was figured in the valiant and unbent body of the English man. Firmly planted on two feet, this imperial subject deterritorialized and reterritorialized China as feminine (a weak-willed and weak-kneed other) in establishing sovereign equality.

27. See Knight 1935 2: 502–503. Reginald Johnston ([1934] 1985: 205) later testified to the important place the poem played in defining British identity in treaty port China. Bickers (1993a, 1993b) has explored these themes in greater detail.

Reterritorialization: Recoding China, 1858

If opium, military technologies, translation processes, and a masculine ethos yoked to the concept of national sovereignty subverted and ultimately destroyed Qing networks of power and authority, they did so as a means to clear the ground for laying down another kind of network, another series of relationships. This reterritorialization in China established a new order of power, at the center of which was the right of physical presence or residence for Euroamericans in China. In the case of ordinary citizens of North Atlantic nation-states, the condition in question was understood as the right to buy and own property, to build dwellings, and to have them protected by extraterritorial treaty privileges. The original treaty settlements in the 1840s established these rights for the first five ports opened. Only Canton remained a problem afterward, but that was solved by the physical occupation of the city in 1858. But, although these privileges provided Europeans and Americans the necessary legal means to establish a physical presence in China, it did not solve what the British saw as the remaining outstanding issue for placing relations with China on a firm and sound footing. The same privileges had yet to be extended to the official representatives of North Atlantic nation-states.

THE RESIDENT MINISTER ISSUE AND
THE PEDAGOGY OF IMPERIALISM

The Treaty of Tianjin resolved the issue rather sensationally. "For the better preservation of harmony in the future," the parties agreed to the exchange of permanent diplomatic representatives between the queen of Great Britain and the emperor of China. Further, the treaty stipulated that the queen's diplomatic agent could either reside in or occasionally visit Beijing. While there, the British minister was to dwell in a structure maintained by his government. With the right of residence and protection of property established, it was perhaps unnecessary to elaborate further the comportment of the agent who would occupy these premises. Nevertheless, the British insisted that a clause be included stipulating that the queen's representative would not be called on to "perform any ceremony derogatory to him as representing a Sovereign of an independent nation on a footing of equality with that of China" (CESM 347). In his evaluation of the treaty settlement, Lord Elgin was quite clear about the implications of making China perfectly equal. By implicitly banning kowtow and allowing for the right of ministerial residence, the Chinese government had, as Elgin put it, surrendered "some of the most cherished principles of the traditional policy of the [Chinese] Empire." This, he asserted, was nothing less than a "revolution" (345).

Elgin was not far from the mark. Having forced the Qing government to accept European customary practices as "universal" codes of diplomatic conduct, he also got the Qing Court to agree to provide a site for a legation, from which future acts of reterritorialization could be initiated. From the point of view of Elgin and other British diplomatic agents in China, this second concession was crucial if the treaty settlement was to be more than a piece of paper. Or if Great Britain was to avoid having to send military forces into China again.

But, how exactly was the legation in Beijing to continue the revolution? It seems clear from the statements of British diplomatic agents at the time and from the activities of those who later took up residence in the legation (see part 2) that the Beijing legation was envisioned as something more than an agency of diplomacy. That is, given the characteristics of Chinese mandarins as the British understood them, the legation was also to function as a mechanism for altering the Chinese perception of the world and their place in it. In a conversation with the secretaries to the imperial commissioners that was part of the negotiations leading up to the Tianjin Treaty, Horatio Lay stated the issue in terms very much like those that have come down to us as part of the dominant Anglo-American interpretation of the problem of traditional Chinese foreign relations. According to Lay, "China had been led by her past exclusiveness to regard herself as the 'central nation' and her ignorance of the existence of powerful and wealthy countries had made her look upon all people not Chinese as 'barbarians,' beyond the pale of civilization. This was a great mistake, which she would have now to *unlearn*; and she must, however much against her will, henceforth comply with the usages of Western nations, intercourse with whom she was manifestly too weak, physically, to decline" (CESM 326; emphasis added).

Lord Elgin's assessment was perhaps more concise. The problem, as he saw it, was that European and American representatives would have to "treat with persons who yield nothing to reason, and everything to fear, and who are, moreover, profoundly ignorant both of the subjects under discussion, and of their own real interests" (CESM 344). The legation in Beijing would serve, therefore, to inform the mandarins about the outside world and teach them how to calculate, like Englishmen, their own interests. As envisioned by Elgin, the pedagogical project would work itself out along the following lines. First, the minister of Great Britain would be "in direct communication with the officers of the Imperial Government" and could thus "give them advice when required." Second, he could help to alleviate tensions by demonstrating that the British had no "sinister designs" on China, thus dispelling fear bred from ignorance. Third, and perhaps most important, the representative, through his good conduct, would serve to "mitigate the prejudices against foreigners which now influence the Imperial Councils" (346). Forming a kind of charter for Great Britain's legation, these three notions about the advantages of a permanent embassy in Beijing run like a golden thread through the reporting of subsequent British ministers to China.[28] Indeed, teaching the Manchu-Chinese hierarchy where their own best interests lay became one of the primary missions of the British minister to the Qing Court. Even Thomas Wade, who often played the role of the uncontrollably fierce barbarian to the hilt, saw instruction as part of his primary purpose for being there (Hevia 1995a).

But placing a British minister at Beijing did not automatically solve all problems. There was still a question of precisely whom he was to speak to in the Qing government. This issue was addressed in Article 5 of the Tianjin Treaty, another revolutionary clause. It stipulated that the emperor of China agreed to appoint a "Secretary of State" or "President" of one of the six boards of government "as the high officer with whom" the queen's representative would transact business. And these men would do so "on a footing of perfect equality" (CESM 348). Out of this provision was born a new branch of Qing administration, the Zongli yamen, or what the British called the Yamen of Foreign Affairs. Henceforth, Great Britain and the other Western powers would have their own branch of the Qing central government with which to deal. With "perfect equality" achieved, Elgin then set about laying down a new set of legal procedures for commercial intercourse.

THE SHANGHAI TARIFF CONFERENCE
AND THE LEGALIZATION OF THE OPIUM TRADE
The Tianjin Treaty called for a tariff conference to be held in Shanghai as soon as possible after the signing of the treaty. Before it began in early October 1858, Lord Elgin instructed Wade to sound out commercial opinion on tariff

28. Lay's summation of the China problem and Elgin's statement about the function of the embassy became common sense about China. A century later, the attitude can be found in Fifty-five Days at Peking, the 1963 Hollywood production of the siege of the legations during the Boxer Uprising; see chapter 10.

revision, and then he set sail for Japan to negotiate a treaty with the Toku-gawa shogunate.[29] When Elgin returned to China, Wade informed him that most of the British merchants were satisfied with the current state of tariff rates. Nevertheless, Elgin insisted on following through on the treaty provision. Although it is not made explicit in his correspondence why he felt the conference necessary, there are at least three reasons that suggest themselves.

First, the conference would create an opportunity for the British plenipotentiary to meet with high-level Qing officials in a setting much different from the highly fraught atmosphere of Tianjin, where the availability of coercive force was made all too clear to Qing officials.[30] A tariff conference at another site would thus put to the test, at least for the British, the footing of perfect equality established in the treaty. Second, it could reorder the thinking of Qing officials by demonstrating to them the proper sort of give and take to be expected in negotiations between sovereign nation-states. In other words, the conference would educate and train the mandarins in the procedures of such interaction, particularly helping them to see the strict division of ceremony, which established sovereign equality among nations, and the business of diplomacy, which negotiated new legally binding relations between nations.[31] Third, Elgin would have the opportunity to play the pedagogue and teach Qing officials what their interests were.

The tariff conference was important for another reason as well. The rules and regulations it produced gave substance to bureaucratic routines and rituals for many varieties of day-to-day interaction between British and Chinese nationals, the nitty-gritty reterritorializations such as ship docking and customs collection procedures, including the creation of bilingual charts of tariff rates. These formal relations, as they were worked out in the practical development of procedures, could then be extended into other domains of contact. More important, the creation of this conventional paperwork was, in fact,

29. Lord Elgin arrived at Edo on 17 August, where he completed an agreement similar to the Tianjin Treaty on the 26th. English, Japanese, and Dutch versions were produced, with the last of these being considered the "original." It was agreed, however, that within five years, Japanese authorities would make all communications with the British in English.

30. Elgin noted that he strove in meetings with Guiliang and Huasha'na to "remove the painful impressions which our interviews at Tien-tsin [Tianjin] might have left on their minds"; see CESM 404.

31. See Hevia 1995b for a fuller discussion of the relationship between ceremony and business in European diplomatic procedures.

a primary vehicle of reterritorialization, a fundamental way in which an expanding zone of contact between Chinese and Euroamericans was minutely reordered and disciplined (see chapter 5).

Indeed, the final provision of the new tariff called for the creation of a uniform system for conducting trade in the treaty ports. To accomplish this, China was to appoint a high commissioner to superintend foreign trade, who was then expected to choose a British subject to "aid him in the administration of the customs revenue; in the prevention of smuggling; in the definition of port boundaries; or in the discharging of the duties of harbor-master; [and] . . . in the distribution of lights, buoys, beacons, and the like." By means of these very literal and detailed reterritorializations, China's foreign trade was made to conform to Euroamerican standards. The Imperial Maritime Customs, with its British inspector-generals, was born.[32]

Perhaps it is not too surprising, therefore, to find here, at this mundane level of procedure, the reordering of opium itself. For it was in the tariff agreement, and not the Tianjin Treaty proper, that the opium trade was legalized. Under Rule 5 "Regarding certain Commodities heretofore Contraband," the restrictions affecting trade in grains, pulse, sulphur, brimstone, saltpeter, spelter, cash, *and* opium were "relaxed." For opium, relaxation meant that it could be sold openly by foreign merchants in treaty ports, where it would be taxed at the highest rate of any item on the tariff list: 30 taels of silver per picul (133 pounds, as defined in Rule 4 of the tariff). It could, however, be carried into the interior only by Chinese as "Chinese property."[33] On the face of it, this provision appears to have resolved the issue of smuggling. In reality, it simply diffused the problems created in the extraterritorial havens of the treaty ports into the physical space of the entire Qing Empire, where opium could now extend the process of deterritorialization relatively unopposed.[34]

32. The first of the inspector-generals was Horatio Lay, who was appointed by He Guiqing in 1859.

33. CESM 432. The Chinese version is in YWSM, XF 4: 1249. Interestingly, the term used for opium is not *yapian*, but *yangyao*, which can be read as foreign medicine.

34. Although I've scanned the relevant chapters YWSM, XF, there seems to have been no debate within the central government in Beijing on the opium question. A meeting of Oliphant, Wade, and their Chinese counterparts that took place on 12 October 1858 notes that opium was one of nine items on the agenda. When the issue of legalization was raised, the Jiangsu provincial officials expressed no objections, provided the tariff was set high enough to "deter the uninitiated from becoming smokers" and Chinese merchants handled distribution inland; see CESM 400–402. Wong (1998: 415) suggests that He Guiqing may

The signing of the Treaty of Tianjin and the conclusion of the tariff conference in Shanghai did not bring to an end this particular phase of disordering and reordering of China. Instead, after the action at the Dagu forts, the governments of Great Britain and France launched a second major military campaign, eventually dictating peace terms in Beijing itself. The next chapter continues this examination of the deterritorialization and reterritorialization of China by focusing on the looting and destruction of the emperor of China's Summer Palace, the Yuanming yuan. From this analysis, it will be possible to make some general observations about the nature of Euroamerican imperialism and colonialism in East Asia, ones that will help to clarify the pattern of foreign presence in China before the outbreak of the Boxer movement.

---

well have decided himself to include opium in the tariff agreement to generate new revenue to put down the Taiping Rebellion. Another possibility is that Qing negotiators might have thought that a concession on the opium trade would get the British to change the articles in the Tianjin Treaty that the Qing Court found most objectionable; see Hsü 1960: 71–79.

. . . .

CHAPTER 4

Beijing 1860: Loot, Prize, and

a Solemn Act of Retribution

THE FINAL ACT OF THE SECOND OPIUM WAR took place in early and mid-October in and around the Qing capital at Beijing. By this time the emperor and his inner council had fled to the Mountain Retreat for Escaping Summer Heat (Bishu shanzhuang) at Chengde, leaving Prince Gong and the demoralized remnants of Senggerinchin's Mongol cavalry to deal with the allied armies. While Prince Gong contemplated his options, Lord Elgin, from his headquarters in Western Yellow Temple outside of the north wall of Beijing, awaited word on Harry Parkes and the group of soldiers, diplomats, and civilians captured near Zhangjiawan on 17 September. Meanwhile, French forces reached the gates of the Summer Palace on 7 October and began to loot the buildings. Later in the day they were joined by elements of the British army. Not long afterward, Beijing surrendered and Lord Elgin learned of the fate of the captives, which led directly to his decision to destroy the Summer Palace. On 18 and 19 October, forty-four hundred officers and men of the 1st Infantry Division of the British contingent burned the entire palace complex. Within days of the destruction of the palaces, the Tianjin Treaty and the Beijing Convention were ratified, and Euroamerican relations with China were forever altered.

This chapter seeks to use these events as a resource for addressing several interrelated issues. The first and perhaps most important of these involves consideration of a relationship between European imperialism and colonialism in East Asia and in other parts of the world. One such link involves the large number of British civilian and military personnel who were active in China after having served in other parts of the empire. An additional connection concerns plunder in warfare and the nomenclature related to it, in particular, the word *loot* itself.

Intimately linked to British expansion in India, loot entered the English language from Hindi or Sanskrit in the eighteenth century.[1] In either its noun or verb form, it frequently replaced older English words, such as pillage, booty, spoils, and plunder. Yet, because it was firmly embedded in the new lexicon of empire, loot was not, strictly speaking, interchangeable with these terms. Insofar as it related to British imperial adventures in India, East Asia, and later, Africa, it evoked a sense of the opportunities, particularly as "prize" of war, that empire building offered to the brave and daring.[2]

Equally important for our purposes here, the imperial lexicon *Hobson-Jobson*, like Lord Elgin, found the term loot entering common usage in India and China between the first and second Opium Wars (Yule and Burnell [1886] 1994: 519–520; Walrond 1872: 215). As the career of the word suggests, although the events of 1860 signaled a shift in global relations of power, the primary actor and main beneficiary of the change in China's relations with the West was the British Empire. Although French, Russian, and U.S. diplomats and the French army played important roles in these events, it was British agents who not only led the way, but who seemed to be motivated by quite different considerations from their Euroamerican colleagues. Such differences can be accounted for in a variety of ways: in terms of the personalities of individual leaders, on the basis of different national goals, and perhaps even on the basis of the historical antipathy and rivalry among the Euroamerican parties. Here, however, the focus is on the different actions of the Western powers in China as manifestations of their distinct historical trajectories in the development of European global expansion. These distinctions then provide a way of making another kind of sense out of the looting of the Sum-

1. See the *Oxford English Dictionary*, where the first usage is attributed to the *Indian Vocabulary* published in 1788.

2. Opportunities for prize and medals for bravery were used on recruiting posters in Great Britain; see Farwell 1981: 211.

mer Palace and its destruction as a "solemn act of retribution" (Walrond 1872: 366).

"No End of Loot!": The Pleasures of Plunder

Let me begin this investigation with accounts of the plunder of the Yuanming yuan, the emperor of China's Summer Palace.[3] In the first few days after they arrived at this sprawling park at the foot of the Western Hills, the two armies ransacked and looted in a seemingly wild, unregulated frenzy of destruction and theft. The specifics of the pillage of the Summer Palace are, however, open to some conjecture, partly because the leaders of the expedition made no formal reports to their respective governments describing the looting. Instead, they either denied that it existed, blamed each other for starting it, or, as in the case of the British leadership, explained matters that were handled after the fact. Accounts that do address what happened are not, in other words, in parliamentary papers or other public records. Rather, they are to be found in newspaper stories, reminiscences, and collections of letters and journals published between 1860 and 1912. Some appeared in the first books about the 1860 campaign, others exist in private papers, autobiographies, and biographies published well after the fact or following the author's death. Among these sources, there is some dispute over how the looting began and who started it.

On the French side, some versions, including those of General Montauban, Charles de Mutrécy (1862), and Paul Varin (1862), simply note that after the French reached the gardens, sentries were posted and no one was allowed onto the grounds, with the exception of a small patrol that discovered a treasury. Once the English arrived, a commission of officers was set up who were to choose the "most precious objects of curiosity" for the Emperor Napoleon and Queen Victoria. Meanwhile, the treasure that had been discovered was divided with the British. None of these sources mentions looting, except by the British. Moreover, because these French versions were the first to arrive in Europe via telegraph, they initially dominated the newspapers and opinion magazines.[4]

---

3. The quotation in the title of this section is from Graham 1901: 187.

4. General Montauban's report of 12 October was published in the Paris *Moniteur* on 19 December. It was later reprinted by Volontaire au 102e (1861: 112–113) and Bazancourt (1861: 273–275). Also see Varin 1862: 235–239, 242; Mutrécy 1862: 2: 25. In London, the

British sources provide a wholly different picture. Among the first published accounts was one that appeared in the *North China Herald* of 20 October; it emphasized that "indiscriminate looting [of the Summer Palace] had been allowed" by the French command. In the same edition, a headquarters general order from 12 October appeared commending the British army for exercising restraint "when a large amount of plunder was at the mercy of the troops." The *North China Herald* report was supported in publications of the personal papers of Lord Elgin (1872) and General Grant (1875) and by British publications that began to come out in 1862. According to Elgin and Grant, when they arrived at the south gate of the Summer Palace, they found the plunder of the site well underway. Elgin added that Montauban was full of "protestations" and promises that all would be equally divided between the two armies, which, according to Grant, he supported on the spot by promising to provide one of the two " 'joës' [jade ruyi], or staves of office" as a present for Queen Victoria (Walrond 1872: 361; Knollys 1875: 128). Supporting these accounts was the "eyewitness" report of Garnet Wolseley, the quartermaster-general for the British contingent. In his book published in 1862, Wolseley reported that although the French command had posted guards, uncontrolled "plunder and wanton destruction" ensued ([1862] 1972: 224). Forty years later, in his autobiography, he added more detail, recalling that when the British contingent reached the entrance, General Montauban met them and "begged" Lord Elgin not to enter. "I was amused by this," Wolseley recalled, "because at that very moment there were a string of French soldiers going in empty handed and another coming out laden with loot of all sorts and kinds." As he spoke to Baron Janin, a French general, soldiers presented Janin with one or another "curiosities" and one of them placed a small enamel into Wolseley's hand, exclaiming, "Mon camarade, voici un petit cadeau pour vous" (Wolseley 1904: 77–78). These versions were further supported by Colonel C. P. B. Walker (1894: 211), who would soon be put in charge of a prize commission for the British army (see next section), the Reverend R. J. L. M'Ghee (1862: 205–207), and later published accounts of British officers who claimed to be eyewitnesses.[5]

ILN of 20 December 1860: 617 paraphrased the *Moniteur*. Two days later, the *Times* published a complete version of Montauban's report; the ILN followed suit on 5 January 1861. Apparently, it was not until the following March that the Elgin-Grant version of events appeared in Great Britain; see *Blackwood's Magazine* 89 (March 1861): 381.

5. Additional testimony appeared in 1874 when Montauban proclaimed his innocence

A third version of events was provided by Maurice d'Hérrison, secretary and interpreter to General Montauban. In a campaign account published in 1866, d'Hérrison wrote that as the commissioners assigned to select objects for the French and British monarchs carried them into the French camp, the following scene ensued: "French infantry, Englishmen, unmounted cavalry, artillerymen, Queen's dragoons, Sikhs, Arabs, [and] Chinese coolies looked on, wondering when their turn would come. Suddenly, word began to spread through the ranks that the Chinese from the nearby village of Haidian had, along with some of the Cantonese Coolies, begun to scale the wall and enter the palaces. The soldiers rushed the gate, carrying away the sentinels, and spreading through the park." [6]

As suggested earlier, these divergent accounts can be attributed to national rivalries, questions of honor, and criticisms generated then and later about the plunder of the palaces. Neither the British nor the French, it would seem, wanted to be held responsible in the eyes of the other, and if a scapegoat were needed, the Chinese were conveniently at hand. At the same time, the dispute over how the looting began deflected attention from the looting itself. How soldiers looted, what they took, and the overall atmosphere of the scene in and outside of the garden grounds seem to have been of less concern. Lost in the flurry of accusations that followed the sack of the palaces was any sense of the sheer enjoyment and pleasure that it provided for many of those involved.

From all indications, the initial stage of plundering was a raucous affair in a carnivalesque atmosphere. French soldiers, many dressed in Qing imperial robes or "richly embroidered gowns of women" and wearing "fine Chinese hats instead of the French képi" (Wolseley 1904: 77), ran about emptying into their tents sacks filled with jade, precious stones, cloisonné vases, ivory carvings, and watches and clocks of European manufacture, while others attempted to commandeer wagons or carts. The chaos outside the palace grounds was matched by what was going on within the gates of the Summer Palace. The reporter from the *North China Herald* wrote that hundreds of rolls of silk were pulled off shelves in store rooms, some spread indiscriminately on the floors, others used to secure the piles of loot on wagons, and

---

yet again in public testimony in Paris; see letters in the *Times*, 12, 13, 14, and 18 March and chapter 5.

6. This version of events is taken from the English translation of the 1901 Paris reprint of the second edition of d'Hérrison (1886); see 1901: 623–625.

still others sewn together to make tents in the French camp (*North China Herald* [NCH], 20 October 1860). After he surveyed the scene, Lord Elgin commented in his journal that there was not a room "in which half the things had not been taken or broken to pieces" and expressed deep disappointment over the waste that was evident (Walrond 1872: 361–362). Observers spoke of seeing "grand embroideries" torn down for no apparent reason, Frenchmen using clubs to smash things to "atoms," and "wanton destruction" of what could not be carried away (Tulloch 1903: 117; Swinhoe 1861: 306; Wolseley [1862] 1972: 224).

Soon the British forces, officers and men, joined in (Swinhoe 1861: 305–306). Frederick Stephenson, adjutant-general of the British army, wrote his brother that

> the rooms and halls of audience . . . and specially the Emperor's bedroom, were literally crammed with the most lovely knick-knacks you can conceive. Fancy having the run of Buckingham Palace and being allowed to take away anything and everything you liked . . . Large magazines full of richly ornamented robes lined with costly furs, such as ermine and sable, were ruthlessly pulled from their shelves, and those that did not please the eye, thrown aside and trampled under foot. There were large storerooms full of fans, Mandarins' hats, and clothes of every description, others again piled up to the ceiling with rolls of silk, all embroidered, and to an incredible amount . . . All these were plundered and pulled to pieces, floors were literally covered with fur robes, jade ornaments, porcelain, sweetmeats, and beautiful wood carvings. (1915: 272–273)

Faced with this awe-inspiring scene, A. B. Tulloch recalled feeling like "a boy suddenly told to take what he likes in a pastry-cook's shop." He loaded himself and his pony with a collection of jade, the like of which "had probably rarely been seen." On his way back to camp, he passed a detachment of the Sikh cavalry from Probyn's Horse and sang out "Jeldi jow sub jata howinga" (Be quick or it will all be gone; 1903: 117–118). They seem to have taken Tulloch at his word. Soon after, Major Gerald Graham of the Royal Engineers noted in his diary that he had seen a troop of Probyn's Horse riding from the gardens laden with loot. They, in turn, were but one part of a train of carts full of loot being hauled away by Chinese "coolies" and what Graham identified as the "Pekin mob" (1901: 188). In another case, a Lieutenant Harris claimed that he got his nickname, "China" Jim, because he was attributed with having gotten more loot from the Summer Palace than anyone else. In his reminiscence, he recalled that he took a vermillion seal from the emperor's own quarters, along with a golden wire basket and large quantities of silk and satins. He also purchased pearls from French soldiers ignorant of their true value and acquired several valuable old watches of European manufacture. One of these came with a label in Chinese, which Thomas Wade translated for him as having been presented to the emperor of China by Lord Macartney! Harris's real coup, however, was hauling off two large solid gold pagodas worth about £22,000 (J. Harris 1912: vii, 111–122).

Given what has already been said about the high moral tone in which the British and French diplomats conducted their intercourse with the Qing Court, how are we to account for the wanton excess that these reports describe? What are we to make of this carnival-like atmosphere in which British officers and men appeared to have been cheek-by-jowl with French soldiers, "wild" Pathans and Sikhs, and apparently even some Chinese in the sacking of the Summer Palace? Are we to consider looting an aberration, a brief slide from civilized behavior into the sort of barbarism that Europeans often ascribed to non-European peoples? Or was plunder simply an unfortunate side effect of warfare, to be expected under the circumstances? These questions seem especially pertinent because, contrary to what might be expected, the British commander, General Grant, indicated in his official dispatches that had he not taken certain actions (see below), his army would have looted in spite of orders to the contrary (Knollys 1875: 226–227). Why, we might wonder, did the general have so little faith in the moral fiber of his men?

In part, the answer to all of these questions appears to have been based on a widely shared understanding of human nature and behavior. For example, General Montauban's aide, Maurice d'Hérrison, noted that when the "artificial regulations which serve to bind nations as well as armies" are suspended, the remainder was "primitive human nature in all its crudity and absolute surrender to its free instincts." To put this another way, without the constraints of what might be called culture, Europeans turned into savages. Under the circumstances, it was best for officers to be "prudent and patient," waiting for the soldiers to fatigue themselves and return on their own accord to take up their "accustomed yoke" (1901: 625–626). British accounts seem to support d'Hérrison. Robert Swinhoe, a consular official serving as interpreter on Grant's staff, argued that the sack of the palaces afforded "good proof of the innate evil in man's nature when unrestrained by the force of law or public opinion" (1861: 306). Colonel Garnet Wolseley concurred, adding that "human nature breaks down the ordinary trammels which discipline imposes, and the consequences are most demoralizing to the best constituted army" ([1862] 1972: 224–225).

This global answer to the loot question (i.e., human nature) was, however, only the most overt response discernible in the campaign sources. In light of discussion in the previous chapter, another explanation suggests itself. Recall, for example, Rutherford Alcock's description of unprincipled foreigners who disrupted the commerce of honest men in the treaty ports. How different was the behavior of Alcock's culprits from that of soldiers who looted? Moreover, given the close link between plunder and British military adventures in South Asia, the difference between British soldiers and those whom Richard Cobden identified as the "loose fish" of the treaty ports might have been a very difficult distinction for the leadership of the British forces to make. One need only add to this Lord Elgin's own observation that contact with "inferior" Asians seemed to bring out the worst features of British character, or the widely held belief that Indians and Chinese were both obsessed with looting and experts at it,[7] to conclude that this particular reversion to a "primitive" state of human development may have been understood as having a quite specific cause, that is, the contact with Asia and Asians. Such concerns about the "polluting" effects of contact with "inferior races" suggest that the breakdown in military discipline signified by looting could easily have been viewed with a profound sense of alarm.

In this respect, plunder posed a serious threat for maintaining order within the army, which itself was coded by means of a ranked hierarchy and by the absolute distinction drawn between officers and the "other ranks"—the warrant officers, noncommissioned officers, and privates.[8] In his discussion of looting, Wolseley, for example, took great pains to make it appear as if it was only done by common soldiers, not officers. Soldiers, he argued, were no more than grown-up "schoolboys," for whom the opportunity to plunder was a "remarkable event" in a life otherwise spent "under the tight hand of discipline." Moreover, looting afforded a kind of pleasure that lived long in a soldier's memory even if he "did not gain sixpence by it." For years to come,

7. On Elgin, see Walrond 1872: 199, 252. Characterizations of Indians and Chinese can be found in M'Ghee 1862: 166, 210, 212, 216; J. Harris 1912: 89; and Walker 1894: 162, 164. Later, Wolseley (1904: 84) argued that the villagers around the Summer Palace got more loot than the two armies combined.

8. For a discussion of discipline in the British army at the time, as well as the division between officers and enlisted men, see Farwell 1981.

soldiers would recall their exploits as part of their own regimental lore, separate and distinct from the official version of events and the stories told in the
officers' mess ([1862] 1972: 225–227). They constructed, in other words, an
oral history of plunder that cut against the grain of the official story produced
in the dispatches of the diplomatic and military authorities and in accounts
of authoritative eyewitnesses like Wolseley.

Pronouncements like those of Wolseley therefore served a number of purposes. First, they sutured up the wounds looting inflicted on the body of the
British imperial project in China and provided a crucial means for retaining
the high moral ground on which the entire campaign was based, while still
accounting for the plunder of the palaces. Second, Wolseley accorded gentle-
men soldiers and diplomats a rationale for distancing themselves from the
polluting effects of plunder and, in so doing, reconstituted the fundamental class divisions that animated the British army and society. Moreover, by
maintaining clear motivational boundaries between participants, his account
provided a rationale for informed public opinion in Great Britain to rally behind the version of events produced in official dispatches. Finally, by framing
the looting question in class terms, Wolseley provided support for the actions
of the British leadership who ultimately decided to impose the rule of law over
the plundering of the Summer Palace.

From the Excess of Loot to the Order of Prize

Unlike the French, the British authorities had long experience dealing with
the issue of plunder and the threat it posed to order and discipline in an army.
This experience had led to the creation of a body of parliamentary and military
law that established a set of procedures for transforming theft into the rightful fruits of conquest. By the time of the China campaign of 1860, these rules
were so ingrained in the behavior of British soldiers that their looting patterns
could clearly be distinguished from those of the French. As d'Hérrison noted,
for example, the British "arrived in squads, like gangs of workmen, with
men carrying large sacks and commanded by noncommissioned officers, who
brought with them, strange at it may seem, touchstones," the "primitive jew-
eler's tool" (1901: 625). They also seem to have worked in units to haul as much
as possible into the British camp at the Yellow Temple near the Anding Gate.

This orderly pattern of plunder can, in turn, be accounted for on the
basis of certain expectations British soldiers had for sharing in the spoils. At
roughly the same time General Montauban and his staff were waiting for the

loot fever to run its course, General Grant appointed Colonel Walker, Major Anson, Major Wilmot, and Captain Lumsden as prize agents and ordered that all looted objects, with the exception of things purchased from the French (Tulloch 1903: 118; Swinhoe 1861: 310), be turned over to them (Knollys 1875: 193–194). The items were to be put on display and auctioned off immediately for the "general benefit." Officers having small items they wished to keep were allowed to take them to the prize committee on 10 October and have them appraised; they then had the option of purchasing them or placing them in the auction. Proceeds would be added to "Treasure already seized" and distributed in three equal parts: one part to officers and two parts to noncommissioned officers and men.[9] This procedure of plunder, auction, and prize distribution requires some explanation.

BRITISH PRIZE LAW

From at least the reign of Henry IV (r. 1399–1413) an intricate pattern of British legal codes had established that plunder taken in warfare was the legal property of the sovereign. At the monarch's discretion, portions of the plunder could be awarded to the military forces involved (Colombos 1940). For much of the seventeenth and eighteenth centuries, these rules applied primarily to naval captures, but from the reign of George III forward a series of parliamentary laws created procedures for the disposition of plunder taken in land warfare.

Prize law was based on the notion that without the promise of an equitable distribution of plunder, armies would become undisciplined mobs. To avoid such a possibility, authorities treated loot as the natural fruit of victory. They converted plunder, with its threats to order, into prize, the lawful reward of righteous warfare, while transforming the stolen objects themselves into private property. As outlined in parliamentary statutes, the procedures used by the British army for legalizing plunder were as follows:

1. The commander in chief appointed prize agents to organize and take charge of a prize commission. The commander also issued orders to members of the army instructing them to hand over all loot to the commission.

2. The commission inventoried all plunder, arranged for its sale at public

9. See WO 147/2: 1–5. Although apparently all forces were allowed to participate in the auction, the prize money was to be distributed only among those who had accompanied the commander-in-chief to the field on 6 October.

auction after the campaign, kept meticulous records of each sale, and created a prize roll indicating how much money was to go to members of each rank in the force.

3. All records of sales were forwarded to the Royal Hospital at Chelsea, which administered the allotment of prize money and kept the records.

4. A notice was placed in the London Gazette announcing the allotment of prize money.

5. Soldiers or their heirs filed claims at Chelsea and produced proof that they were part of the campaign that had seized the prize. (This was apparently the main way for ordinary soldiers to collect prize awards.)

6. Forms were created for such claims and standards established to prove participation in a particular campaign.[10]

Prior to the invasion of China in 1860, these procedures had been used most recently in the wake of the suppression of an 1857 rebellion in India, claims from which were still being processed when the British invaded China. Unlike the India instance, however, the prize commission formed by Grant held the auction immediately in the field. The participants were the looters themselves and the prize money realized through the sale was apportioned on the spot.

THE BEIJING AUCTION

The day before the auction began, items were put on display in the main hall of the Yellow Temple.[11] Robert Swinhoe described the scene:

> White and green jade-stone ornaments of all tints, enamel-inlaid jars of antique shape, bronzes, gold and silver figures and statuettes, &c.; fine collections of furs, many of which were of much value, such as sable, sea-otter, ermine, Astracan lamb, &c.; and court costume, among which were two or three of the Emperor's state robes of rich yellow silk, worked upon with dragons in gold thread, and beautifully woven with floss-silk embroidery on the skirts, the inside being lined with silver fur or ermine,

10. See Statutes of the United Kingdom of Great Britain and Ireland, 54 George III (1814): vol. 54, 328–351; 1&2 George IV (1821): vol. 61, 210–211; 2&3 William IV (1832): vol. 72, 236–259.

11. Originally built during the Ming Dynasty, the temple became associated with Tibetan Buddhism after the Dalai Lama was housed there during the Shunzhi emperor's reign at the beginning of the Qing. The temple is also famous for a white pagoda erected by the Qianlong emperor to honor the Panchen Lama, who died on the site while visiting Beijing. See Bredon 1922: 224–227; Arlington and Lewisohn [1935] 1987: 238–240.

and cuffed with glossy sable. At the end of the hall were piled immense quantities of rolls of silk and crape of various colors, with several of the beautiful imperial yellow, *a kind prescribed by the Chinese law for the use of his Imperial Majesty alone.* (1861: 311; emphasis added)

The auction itself appears to have been a spectacular affair, one heightened by a rumor that one of the officers was "understood to have an unlimited commission from Baron Rothschild." The bidding was lively and the sale prices high (Swinhoe 1861: 311). Army chaplain M'Ghee noted that jade pieces went for £10–30 and furs for £10–50. One of the emperor's court robes sold for £120. General Grant himself bought several jade-stones, a jade and ruby necklace labeled as tribute from a famous "Tartar chief," and a lapis lazuli carving. As the bidding continued, the thoughts of some turned to sovereigns and leaders: two large enamel vases secured by Major Probyn were set aside for the queen, and a "beautiful gold jug, from which the emperor of China used to pour rose-water over his delicate hands," was purchased by the prize commission and presented to General Grant. And while Colonel Walker and Major Graham complained in letters home that they could not compete in the bidding wars, George Allgood wrote enthusiastically about having purchased the emperor's own seal of state (1901: 59)![12] Others wrote that they had been able to acquire just the right "gift" for each member of their family, especially the female ones (Spence 1969: 76–77; Allgood 1901: 59; M'Ghee 1862: 211).

But the acquisition of desirable objects was not the only reward the army received; there was the prize money itself, which totaled £26,000. With Generals Grant, Michel, and Napier relinquishing their shares, it was divided up among officers and men as follows: first-class field officers, £60; second-class field officers, £50; chaplains, £40; lieutenants, £30; ensigns, £20; sergeants, £7 10s.; privates, £5.[13] Meanwhile, in spite of his grousing, Colonel Walker

12. For other accounts of the auction, see Graham 1901: 189; Knollys 1875: 193–194; M'Ghee 1862: 294; Swinhoe 1861: 311; Walker 1894: 213; Wolseley [1862] 1972: 237–242.

13. The figures are from Knollys 1875: 226–227 and ILN, 5 January 1861: 7. In 1861 the monthly pay of a British soldier was around £1 and that of a sowar or trooper in an Indian army cavalry unit Rupees (Rs) 8. In 1855 the monthly pay of British officers in the Indian army was as follows: colonel, Rs 1,478; lieutenant colonel, Rs 1,157; major, Rs 929; captain, Rs 563; lieutenant, Rs 365; and ensign Rs 311. All figures are from Heathcote 1974: 110, 128, who gives the exchange rate for this period at roughly Rs 10 to the £, and Farwell 59–60, 160.

Prize rolls for this campaign are not in the India Office record collection. There are, how-did not go away empty-handed: he received £350 as head of the prize commission. For their part, although the Indian troops were excluded from these procedures, they were not required to hand over what they had plundered from the Summer Palace to the prize commission (Graham 1901: 188).

With the threats posed by plunder effectively neutralized by prize procedures, the British army could now turn to completing its task of disciplining and teaching lessons to the political and military powers of China. Before turning to a discussion of how this pedagogical project worked itself out, however, it might be worth considering in more detail the relations among plunder, prize, and British imperial politics.

PRIZE AND IMPERIAL SOVEREIGNTY

Although the processes of collection, auction, and redistribution of proceeds might seem at first glance unnecessarily involved, their importance lay in the way they mirrored and mimicked the processes of deterritorialization and reterritorialization that were transforming China's relations with European powers. Like warfare and treaties in general, prize procedures incorporated China and its political order into the regularities of the British Empire in Asia. In so doing, they helped to undermine Qing imperial sovereignty. Central to this process of subversion was the theft and redistribution of objects that could be tied directly to the person of the Qing emperor. Objects redistributed in this way included his imperial robes and armor, jade scepters, throne cushions, seals, and the "Cap of the Emperor of China" (fig. 3), a carved screen "from behind the Emperor's throne," pages from the *August Court's Illustrated Catalogue of Ritual Implements* (Huangchao liqi tushi), which included hand-painted drawings of Court robes of emperors and empresses, and the yellow silk identified by Swinhoe as exclusively for the emperor. There were also various objects taken from the emperor's private quarters, such as a small jade-covered book said to be the sayings of Confucius, a Tibetan ritual vessel erroneously but tellingly identified as the skull of Confucius, and a Pekinese

---

ever, a substantial number of rolls and claims for various military operations that occurred in India before and after the China campaign, especially for 1857–1858. See, for example, the Deccan Prize Money rolls, dated 31 July 1832, in British Library and India Office Records (hereafter IOR), L/MIL/5/326, where the distinctions between British and Indian troops is clear. Indian army procedures for handling loot and the allocation of prize money to all ranks dated to at least the middle of the eighteenth century; see Mason 1974: 205.

3. The cap of the emperor of China. Source: Holmes, *Naval and Military Trophies and Personal Relics of British Heroes*, 1896.

"lion" dog christened "Looty" (fig. 4).[14] In addition to these items, a host of objects of European manufacture were also plundered, a number of which could be identified as gifts previously given to Qing emperors by European monarchs. These included numerous mechanical clocks and watches, one of which, as Harris reported, was supposed to be the very timepiece presented by Lord Macartney to the Qianlong emperor, the cannon that Macartney had brought as a gift from George III (Rennie 1864: 166; M'Ghee 1862: 210; Swinhoe 1861: 331), works of fine art like the "Petitot" acquired by Colonel Wolseley, and a tapestry from the French monarch Louis XIV.

Some of these items, such as the emperor's cap, the "Sayings of Confucius," and Looty, were presented to Queen Victoria. Much like the plundered regalia of South Asian kings that Carol Breckenridge (1989: 203) has described, they took their place with other symbols of the British monarchy, constituting an expanded British imperial sovereignty. In other cases, pieces were deposited in the officers' mess of various of the regiments involved. At these sites, Qing objects were incorporated into regimental his-

14. With the exception of "Looty" and "skull of Confucius," these items are all presently in collections in Great Britain.

4. Looty. *Illustrated London News*, 15 June 1861.

tories as trophies, signs not only of successful imperial campaigns, but of a material link between the regiments and the British Crown.[15] Other objects came to rest at institutions that played significant material and ideological roles in supporting and maintaining the British Empire. The cannon, for example, was "repatriated" to the Woolwich Arsenal, the site where it had been manufactured and where armaments were produced for empire.[16] The tapestry from Louis XIV passed through the Victoria and Albert Museum, that treasure house of empire, and came to rest at the Ashmolean Library, Oxford, where so many statesmen and administrators of empire were trained.[17] Other pieces found their way into the collections of the Victoria and Albert, includ-

15. The officers' mess of the Queen's Royal Regiment and of the Wiltshire Regiment have porcelain and silver trophies. On the former, see Davis 1887–1906, 5: 132; Haswell 1967: 103. On the latter, see Gibson 1969: 86. On battle honors, see Leslie 1970: 85–86.

16. Knollys (1875: 128–129) mentions that they were returned, but no records existed in the Arsenal when I visited there in 1987. However, Kaestlin (1963: 15) indicates that the cannon were catalogued as part of the Rotunda Museum collection, which appears to be a separately administered portion of the Arsenal complex. I am grateful to Aubrey Singer for bringing this source to my attention.

17. Victoria and Albert Museum, Acquisition Records, the Crealock file. I am indebted to Verity Wilson for this source.

5. Reverse of throne cushion, Wolseley Bequest. © The Board of Trustees of the Victoria and Albert Museum. Used with permission.

ing a cloisonné ice chest and a throne cushion [18] as well as other items donated by the self-described nonlooter Garnet Wolseley (fig. 5). Still other pieces found their way into the marketplace, where they were revalued as unique commodities bearing the mark of a foreign ruler (see below). As they circulated through these alien domains, the imperial regalia and precious objects of the emperor of China were reordered as meaningful elements within a new realm of sovereignty, one stretching well beyond the territorial limits of any one nation-state. They were now part of the political economy of an imperial sovereignty that spanned the globe.

As if to emphasize this point, the presence of the emperor's regalia and private property in British hands also stood as material proof of Britain's superiority over the Chinese Empire. As Robert Swinhoe so aptly put it, "Fancy the sale of the emperor's effects beneath the walls of the capital of his empire, and this by a people he despised as weak barbarians and talked of driving into the sea!" (1861: 311–312). George Allgood, an officer on Grant's staff, added that the humiliation of the "proudest monarch in the universe" would have an additional benefit. "The news of the capture of Pekin," he wrote, "will resound through Asia, and produce in India an excellent effect" (1901: 60). In these terms, prize and trophies not only bore the signs of the humbling of China's haughty monarch and mandarins. As a deliberate act of hu-

18. These two items were part of a recent Victoria and Albert Museum show on the Victorian era. I saw them both for the first time in July 2001 while in London. See chapter 10 for further discussion.

miliation, it was an object lesson for others who might contemplate defying British power.

The orderly procedures of auction and redistribution had other effects as well. Recall the earlier discussion of prize law. According to its regulations, all plunder seized in time of war belonged to the British monarch, and the auctioning off of the fruits of plunder ought to have been held at another time and place and the army's share distributed at a later date. This did not happen in China. Instead, General Grant decided to hold the auction on the spot and have the prize shares handed out immediately. In justifying this decision to the secretary of State for War, Sidney Herbert, Grant argued that because his men had seen the French "laden with dollars and sycee [silver ingots]," he had ordered the auction and division of the proceeds and other treasure so that his army would be satisfied and have no reason to either loot or complain (Knollys 1875: 192, 226–227).[19] Thus, prize procedures seem to have had the capacity to deflect and channel the potentially disruptive desires generated by the treasures of the emperor's palaces into peaceable feelings consistent with a moral order of law, private property, and orderly commerce.[20] Moreover, because the distribution of prize money was done on the basis of rank, it also had the practical effect of reproducing the proper structure of the army, while maintaining a hierarchical distinction between British forces and India army units. This last was no small concern; one third of the expeditionary force was made up of South Asians. Among these, the "irregular" cavalry regiments were widely asserted to be virtual experts at looting. Thus, prize procedures helped to demonstrate to Sikhs and "wild" Pathans the disciplinary regularities of their rulers. With the army now sealed off from the polluting effects of plunder, the lesson should have been clear: disciplined forces, not a mob of looters like the French, achieved righteous conquest. In 1900, as we shall see below, Indian soldiers demonstrated that they had mastered the lesson.

Commodification, Royal Exotica, and Curiosities

Through its procedures for converting loot into prize via the market mechanism of the auction, British prize law also transformed signs of Qing imperial

19. Grant later received a response from Lord Russell, who said that given the circumstances, the queen had approved his action; see FO 17/362: 94a–95b.

20. See Grant's General Order of 12 October 1860 in WO 147/2: 7.

sovereignty and royal "exotica" into commodities. The French did something similar, although in a more direct way. In their case, the process of commodification began almost immediately. Recall the French military command's understanding of looting: they would let the "fever" run its course and then begin to reimpose discipline in their army. When his soldiers appeared to have exhausted themselves, General Montauban attempted a novel tack: he appealed to the reason of his men. Moving among them, he pointed out that they would have great difficulty carrying off all they had taken. Furthermore, what would they do if they were suddenly attacked by Qing forces? Who knew how large a force of Chinese might still lie between Beijing and the coast? If attacked, Montauban added, the soldiers might lose everything. According to d'Hérrison, Montauban's approach was quite effective; the French soldiers ceased plundering and abandoned some of the larger and more cumbersome items (1901: 631). More than a few, as British sources indicate, became even more rational; they decided to translate their plunder into ready cash, selling either to the English or to the train of suttlers (private merchants) that accompanied the two armies (Graham 1901: 190; J. Harris 1912: 104, 127; Swinhoe 1861: 310; Tulloch 1903: 120). For British officers and men who were unable to acquire a desirable object at the auction, the French market was a welcome source. In all of this, there were a number of effects or consequences.

LOOT INTO COMMODITIES

The market process transformed things produced in imperial workshops for the use and consumption of the emperor and his Court into objects that could be bought and sold by literally anyone with sufficient capital; they entered, in other words, a world of universal exchange. The shift of imperial treasures from the domain of the ruler to the hands of traders meant, in turn, that what had been relatively sedentary suddenly had the capacity for great mobility. In a very short time, Summer Palace loot found itself moving through markets that included Chinese dealers in and around Beijing, traders in treaty ports, and the auction houses of London and Paris. The emperor's subjects, much to the amusement of some Englishmen, became involved in the market almost immediately. They may have been looters themselves, or they might have purchased looted items from residents of Haidian, the village that lay near the Summer Palace, from the foreign soldiers as they departed the city,[21]

21. Tulloch (1903: 121–122) mentions selling silk to Chinese dealers.

or from the "Pekin mob."[22] Yet, regardless of how they got their hands on the emperor's treasures, the Chinese dealers could also easily have been connected to the large fine arts market of Beijing, located in the area outside of the Qian Gate on streets like Liulichang. Indeed, some British officers found Liulichang—they called it Curiosity Street (fig. 6)—and purchased items like those to be found in the palaces (M'Ghee 1862: 302; Walker 1894: 197; *Illustrated London News* [ILN], 16 February 1861: 142, 147).

Soon, however, the objects moved ever further from their point of origin. As the British and French armies withdrew from north China, some soldiers sold their loot along the lines of transportation and communication used to invade China. The buyers were European traders in the treaty ports, but also Chinese in Tianjin, Shanghai, and, eventually, Canton.[23] When the British returned to Beijing to set up their legation in 1861, David Rennie, the medical officer for the group, claimed that it was still possible to buy Yuanming yuan objects from Chinese dealers. He also noted that an advertisement had appeared in a Chinese-language newspaper in Hong Kong a year after the sack offering Summer Palace loot for sale.[24]

At about the same time Rennie was observing the continued flow of deterritorialized Qing imperial objects in Chinese markets, others appeared on the auction block in London and Paris. The first sale of such items was held by Phillips on 18 April 1861. Among the twenty-one items sold were a pair of "magnificent oriental jars" that fetched £585. The next month Christie, Mason & Woods auctioned off a number of pieces brought by Elgin's secretary, Henry Loch, who had carried his lordship's official dispatches to London. There followed three more sales, in June, July, and December 1861. The June sale contained Summer Palace "Art and Curiosities" that belonged to an officer of Fane's Horse;[25] the July sale included Chinese Court dress, a "richly embroidered cover taken from the Imperial throne," and "the Emperor of China's Great Seal of State." Eight more sales followed between 1862 and 1866 (see table 1 and fig. 7). In Paris, meanwhile, there were approximately

22. On Chinese looting, see M'Ghee 1862: 212; most other British sources also mention it.

23. ILN reported on 13 April 1861: 339 that "a certain quantity of the booty" had made its way to Shanghai and Hong Kong, where it was purchased by the "Celestials themselves."

24. On the "art" market, including the offer of an imperial throne, see Rennie 1865, 1: 289–291, 300–302, 313–314, 324–325. Mention of the advertisement appears in 2: 100.

25. I am grateful to Nick Pierce for sharing this catalogue cover with me.

6. Curiosity Street, Peking. *Illustrated London News*, 16 February 1861.

TABLE I. London Auction Sales of Summer Palace Loot

Date	Auction House	Description and Catalogue Accession Numbers
18 March 1861	Phillips	21 items said to be property of an officer, including Oriental jars that sold for £585 (AN 23.DD)
37 May 1861	Christie, Manson & Woods	"Property of a Gentleman"; handwritten, "Mr Loch Lord Elgin's Sect." 8 items in all (AN 23.N)
12 June 1861	Christie, Manson & Woods	A pair of "curious" altar ornaments. "These are models of the Pagoda in the Winter Palace at Pekin, and were taken from the Summer Palace." (AN 23.N)
5 July 1861	Christie, Manson & Woods	Two lots from officers: 8 items; 23 items, including "The Emperor of China's Great Seal of State" (AN 23.N)
12 December 1861	Phillips	1 item from "A Gentleman of Known Taste and Judgement" (AN 23.ZZ)
13 June 1862	Christie, Manson & Woods	Robert Fortune, 1 item said to be from the Summer Palace (AN 23.XX)
30 June 1862	Christie, Manson & Woods	3 enamels from the Summer Palace and "A Magnificent Incense Burner . . . One of the largest pieces brought to England . . . used as a stove in the Emperor's library" (AN 23.XX)
21 July 1862	Christie, Manson & Woods	Brought by an officer, 124 items including a throne cushion and pair of cylindrical vases "believed to be the finest specimens known" (AN 23.XX)
1 December 1862	Christie, Manson & Woods	Sale by Remi, Schmidt, & Co. of items from the International Exhibition: 2 carpets from the Summer Palace (AN 23.XX)
25 July 1864	Christie, Manson & Woods	36 items labeled from the Summer Palace; not so designated, but under "Carvings in Jade, &c." are silks and furs that "may" be from same (AN 23.XX)

TABLE I. *Continued*

Date	Auction House	Description and Catalogue Accession Numbers
18 May 1864	Christie, Manson & Woods	The Elgin sale. None are designated Summer Palace, but the same sale has items from the 1862 exhibition, including the "skull of Confucius," plus items from 1843 exhibition (AN 23.XX)
14 July 1864	Christie, Manson & Woods	10 items in all, including 2 "European watches" (AN 23.XX)
28 June 1866	Christie, Manson & Woods	3 items: pagoda, bed cover, and necklace (AN 23.XX)

Note: This chart was culled from catalogues of auctions held in the National Art Library, Victoria and Albert Museum, London. The number in parenthesis is the library accession code on each catalogue.

twenty-one sales of Summer Palace loot at the Hotel Drouot between 1861 and 1863.[26]

LOOT ON DISPLAY AND INTO COLLECTIONS

The auction markets of Europe introduced Qing imperial objects into an entirely alien and relatively new representational regime that included public display and private collections. A large number of pieces gathered by General Montauban and his staff are noteworthy in these respects. The items in question were those that Montauban organized as gifts for Napoleon III, where they became part of the Empress Eugénie's Oriental collection at the Château de Fontainebleau outside Paris.[27] First, however, the items were put on public exhibit at the Tuileries in April 1861. They were primarily military paraphernalia and included "the Chinese emperor's war costume," rifles, pistols, swords, daggers, halberds, and saddles. In addition, there were two *ruyi* or imperial scepters, a gilded and bejeweled stupa, a guardian figure with flaming head and tail, a large square covered urn, and a bronze bell. A drawing

26. I am indebted to the generosity of Regine Thiriez for information about the Paris sales.

27. The collection remains there to the present; see Samoyault-Verlet 1994. I am indebted to Craig Clunas for bringing it to my attention, Vincent Droguet for allowing a private viewing in June 1998, and Regine Thiriez for arranging the visit to the château.

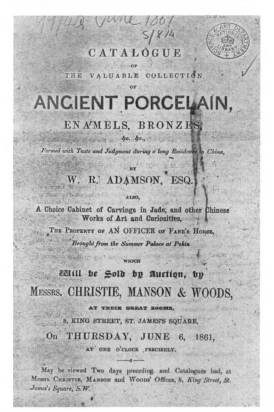

7. Auction catalogue from Christie, Mason & Woods, 6 June 1861, including "Art and Curiosities" from an officer of Fane's Horse.

of this ensemble appeared in the *Illustrated London News* (fig. 8). Capturing the many valences of meaning that the pieces had begun to acquire since their theft, the *News* reporter referred to them as the "booty," "sacred relics," and "curiosities of the Chinese collection at the Tuileries" (ILN, 13 April 1861: 334, 339). A similar, although not nearly as large, display occurred at the International Exposition held in London in 1862 (Palgrave 1862; Waring 1863).[28] Prior to its opening, there was anticipation that the loot of the emperor and empress of the French would take its place beside that reserved for Queen Victoria, all of which would be complemented with the emperor of China's throne (*The Queen*, 18 January 1862: 398). Although none of this actually happened—only a large carved screen taken from behind an imperial throne and the "skull of Confucius" actually turned up (fig. 9)—in conjunction with the

28. Chinese objects had appeared on display in London previously (Altick 1978), but this was the first display of items that had been touched by royalty.

8. The Tuileries exhibition of French loot. *Illustrated London News*, 13 April 1861.

9. The "Skull of Confucius," second from left. Source: Waring, *Masterpieces of Industrial Art and Sculpture at the International Exhibition, 1862*, 1863, vol. 3, plate 291. © The Board of Trustees of the Victoria and Albert Museum. Used with permission.

auction markets, the public displays did serve to fix two critical designations on the emperor's possessions.

The first of these was the designation "from the Summer Palace of the Emperor of China," a phrase that has remained with the objects through future sales and on museum displays almost down to the present.[29] As such, the epithet stood as a continual reminder of the British triumph over China's haughty monarch and mandarins and humiliation of their exaggerated sense of superiority over all foreigners. To put this another way, the presence of the emperor's things outside of his palaces placed a permanent stain on him and his empire. Moreover, the sense of debasement that British actors attached to the possession of the emperor's things was further enriched by generally held notions about Chinese disdain for foreigners. As Wolseley remarked dur-

29. In the late 1980s, it was still possible to see this designation on display tags at the Victoria and Albert and British Museums. Since then, the collection displays have been redone, and all references to the Summer Palace have disappeared.

ing the sack of the palaces and the *Illustrated London News* reporter noted at the Tuileries exhibit, the emperor's treasures were gathered in the "profane" hands and under the "sacrilegious gaze" of "barbarians" and "unappreciating amateurs" (Wolseley [1862] 1972: 224; ILN, 13 April 1861: 334, 339). Thus, the transport of the Chinese emperor's possessions to Europe added another layer of humiliation to a monarch already brought low by the sacking of his palaces. Perhaps here, in the early career of Summer Place loot, we can also observe the central role that humiliation played in the construction and reproduction of European empire in the nineteenth century.

CURIOSITIES, CIVILIZATION, AND THE SOVEREIGN MALE SUBJECT

The second proper name attached to these items was that of curiosities, a designation used in virtually all accounts of looting and one that figured quite prominently in the auction market and public displays. The term itself had a rich history beyond its usage with respect to the emperor's treasures. It had referred, for example, to collections of objects brought to Europe from other parts of the world in the sixteenth and seventeenth centuries and displayed in "cabinets of curiosities" (Pomian 1990; Impey 1977; Impey and MacGregor 1985; Ayers 1985). In this setting, curiosities stood as "singularities" that, because "anomalous," defied classification (Kirshenblatt-Gimblett 1991: 392; Breckenridge 1989: 199–200). By the end of the eighteenth century, the term was used to decontextualize South Pacific artifacts collected by the Cook expeditions and reorganize them into motifs that foregrounded a collector's claims to disinterested scientific inquiry (Thomas 1994). With respect to things Chinese, the term curiosities had been applied to collections that appeared at shows held in London in 1842 and 1847 (Altick 1978: 292–297) and in the China section of the 1851 Crystal Palace exposition, where it seemed to denote the exotic and strange.

While these various senses of the term curiosity may have operated with respect to Summer Palace loot, they were given added weight by the fact that the objects themselves were not produced for export trade or gathered at one of China's treaty ports for a London show. They were, instead, *royal exotica*, which gave them a monetary and collection value, particularly as souvenirs—individual tokens of remembrance—far superior to the sorts of Chinese objects that had previously appeared in Europe. At the same time, however superior their value might appear in relation to other things Chinese, insofar as they could also defy easy classification into known aesthetic categories, labeling them curiosities set them apart from the refined arts of European civilization. This opposition is significant for a number of reasons. It points, for example, directly to the polymorphous nature of the meanings that were being constructed around these objects. At one and the same time, they stood for conquest and humiliation, for fantastic monetary value, and for little or no meaning at all. Curious, indeed. Yet, if the curiosity signaled some kind of absence of meaning, it should perhaps come as no surprise, particularly given that the invasion of China was itself a veritable engine of meaning generation, that over time efforts would be made to fill the curious with content. To gain a sense of these kinds of operations, it is necessary to shift the focus away from the imperial objects themselves to the site where they were found: the Summer Palace.

In virtually all of the descriptive accounts of the Summer Palace, the most detailed of which appear in French, the gardens, palaces, and pavilions were treated as unique works of art. In part, this was because many of the French were aware of the fact that part of the site was made up of European-style buildings, fountains, gardens, and a maze, all of which had been designed by French and Italian Jesuits in the service of the Qing emperors. Given that no one in either of the two armies had been to Beijing before, it is perhaps this knowledge itself that explains how the French and British identified the Yuanming gardens as the Summer Palace in the first place. Be that as it may, when confronted with the gardens, some observers were thoroughly astounded. Maurice d'Hérrison, for example, wrote that "to depict all the splendors before our astonished eyes, I should need to dissolve specimens of all known precious stones in liquid gold for ink, and to dip into it a diamond pen tipped with the fantasies of an oriental poet" (1901: 615–623). Though far less eloquent, Robert Swinhoe was similarly impressed with what he saw (1861: 332–334).

Nevertheless, there were those who, after further inspection and reflection, demurred. And it was precisely the notion of the curiosity that provided the leverage for escaping any temptation to stand in awe of the Chinese emperor. The critical testimony is, again, that of Garnet Wolseley, who once more performed the necessary surgical strike to make sure that there was no seepage of meaning across the great divide of the West and the Orient. More significant, the category of the curiosity allowed Wolseley to situate the Qing Empire and Chinese civilization as inferior to Great Britain and Europe.

Critical to Wolseley's rhetorical strategy was the construction of his encounter with the Summer Palace in a scene like those Mary Louise Pratt has termed the "monarch-of-all-I-survey." Pratt has used this notion to explore the structure of British discovery literature, particularly those moments in which a foreign landscape (presumably those places never before seen by a "white man" and hence, seen by no one of significance) was constituted discursively for the first time. She finds in these writings the creation of an observer position that, through the melding of a language of aesthetics and an ideology of presence, takes possession of that which is observed (1992: 205). There is, of course, an obvious difference in the situation discussed here. The north China plain was neither an "empty" landscape nor one devoid historically of a European presence. Like others in both armies, Wolseley knew that the Summer Palace and its gardens were renowned in Europe; he was also aware that Englishmen had been there before. Indeed, it was a place, he informed his readers, "in which the ambassador of an English king had been insulted with impunity" ([1862] 1972: 226). But if Wolseley could not cast himself as the discoverer of the Summer Palace, he could do something even better: see it as no European had ever been capable of seeing it before.

Wolseley made himself a pioneer through a simple act of defiance. Evoking the history of the kowtow, he walked upright into the Hall of Audience and stood directly in front of the imperial throne, "before which so many princes and ambassadors of haughty monarchs had humbly prostrated themselves, according to the slave-like obeisance customary at the Chinese court."[30] As he turned away from the throne, having quite literally established his own sovereign viewing position, he became the monarch of all he surveyed. The imperial Wolseley could admit, for example, that the overall effect of the Audience Hall was better than his "preconceived ideas" and that each object in the hall was "a gem" of its kind. At the same time, however, "there was nothing imposing in the *tout ensemble*." Chinese architects "seemingly never" strove to achieve a unity of parts that transcended the whole. Rather, "both in landscape gardening and building," Wolseley observed, "the Chinaman loses sight of grand or imposing effects, in his endeavours to load everything with ornament; *he forgets the fine in his search for the curious*. In their thirst after decoration, and in their inherent love for minute embellishment, the artists and architects of China have failed to produce any great work capable of inspiring sensations of awe and admiration which strike one when first gazing upon the magnificent creations of European architects."

30. This and all the quotations that follow in the next two paragraphs are taken from Wolseley [1862] 1972: 232–237.

This "search for the curious," this passion for ornament produced not majesty, but a kind of obsession for the miniature, which in turn led to a second order of failure. Like the grotto at Cremorne, whose "diminutive representations of mountains and rustic scenery" are crowded into small spaces, the Summer Palace (as well as "all other ornamental localities of the empire") has "compressed into every nook or corner, tiny canals, ponds, bridges, stunted trees and rockery." Such comparison led to the conclusion that the Summer Palace "resembles more the design of a child in front of her doll's house than the work of grown-up men."

This reference to the feminine and child-like qualities of Chinese building and landscape architecture was immediately followed by the imputation of another kind of failure. If the living architecture of China was immature, Wolseley asserted, her past architecture was nonexistent. Unlike other great and now dead civilizations, China had failed to produce lasting monuments like those of Egypt, Nineveh, Thebes, Memphis, and even the "long-forgotten races of South America." Accordingly, no one could visit the Summer Palace without being disappointed: "There was an *absence* of grandeur about it, for which no amount of careful gardening and pretty ornaments can compensate."

Wolseley's simultaneous feminization, infantilization, and denigration of the Summer Palace places China in a moral discourse and an economy that defines it as an immature civilization, one lacking anything of superior and enduring quality. Set in this framework, the emperor, his palaces, and his possessions produce a China of absence and failure, a China very much in need of the "social and material intervention" of Great Britain (Pratt 1992: 205). Wolseley creates, in other words, a concise justification for a British pedagogical project in both its destructive and constructive aspects.

The chaotic processes of looting the Summer Palace and transforming its materiality into curiosities might be understood, therefore, as mechanisms of deterritorialization given emphasis by Wolseley's act of defiance before the emperor's throne and through his deprecation of the emperor's precious things. Brought low and disordered by these actions, the Qing Empire could then be reterritorialized in a new role: as the backward student of a British tutor. The tutorials that resulted included punishment and discipline as the necessary grounding on which learning could be initiated.

A Solemn Act of Retribution

Wolseley's discursive maneuvering through the grounds of the summer palace effectively established the position of domination that the British would insist on maintaining for the next half century. At its core was the notion of the political, intellectual, and cultural superiority of the British Empire and Englishmen over China and China's leaders. Its global denigration of all things Chinese was also a virtual mimicking of the attitude that the British had long imputed to the Chinese themselves. This "revered" position of superiority was, in turn, perpetuated by treating any act of resistance, however mild, as an apocalyptic threat to the political order established by warfare and treaty. Due to a degree of Chinese compliance, born of fear, that would have been unimaginable in earlier years, events in the coming decades did not give the lie to these attitudes. The excessive violence and vehement self-righteousness with which China was brought low may well account for that compliance. Nothing exemplifies this combination of British savagery and sanctimony more than the destruction of the Summer Palace; and it, in turn, is difficult to imagine without the position of the elevated sovereign masculine subject that Garnet Wolseley so self-consciously occupied.

The incident that led to the decision to destroy the Summer Palace involved, as noted earlier, the arrest of Harry Parkes, Henry Loch (Lord Elgin's secretary), and their escort near Tongzhou while they were supposed to have been carrying a flag of truce. Lord Elgin and his staff interpreted the arrest and detention as a transgression of "the law of nations" and of the regular conduct of warfare. They also considered it to be a typical act of Chinese treachery and blamed Prince Yi and Senggerinchin personally for what had transpired. No one commented on nor appears to have thought about any connection between the British detention of the Tianjin prefect Shi Zanqing during this campaign or the British abduction of Liangguang viceroy Ye Mingchen in 1858 and the seizure of Parkes and his escort. Nor did anyone give much consideration to the possibility that the meaning of a flag of truce may not have been understood by Chinese forces. Yet, even with these sort of willful refusals to consider the context of the capture of Parkes, what elevated the entire incident onto an almost transcendental plain involved the treatment of the prisoners while in captivity. In Lord Elgin's communication to Prince Gong and in the official correspondence and accounts published shortly afterward, the physical treatment of the captives, visible as signs of "indignities and ill-treatment" on the bodies of the living and the dead, was considered an outrage—it was understood as a transgression of the normal boundary between civilization and barbarism.[31]

More than one account registered shock at the condition of the prisoners when they were returned to the British camp beginning on 14 October. Reverend M'Ghee's reaction was typical: "I never saw a more pitiable sight . . . hardly able to walk, they dragged their legs along and held their hands before their breasts in a posture denoting suffering, and such hands as they were, crumpled up and distorted in every possible way; some with running sores at the wrists, some in which the bloated appearance caused by the cords had not yet gone away, and some were shriveled like a bird's claw and appeared to be dead and withered" (1862: 252).

It soon became clear from accounts of these survivors, all of whom, with the exception of one French private, were Indian cavalrymen mainly from Fane's Horse, that the condition of deformity had been caused by hands and feet having been tightly bound together with wet cords. Trussed up in this way, the captives had been left exposed to the elements and denied food and water for extended periods of time. With circulation cut off to the extremities, flesh swelled and burst, wounds putrefied and became infested with maggots. Depositions taken from survivors and published whole or in part in British parliamentary papers or campaign accounts indicate that all those who died did so as a result of this treatment. The only positive note to be found was in the heroic behavior of Private Phipps, one of the deceased. According to the depositions of Bughel Sing and Khan Sing, as the last surviving European member of his party, Phipps "encouraged the Sikhs in every way he could, until his decease on the 14th day of his captivity." Like Moyse, the Private of the Buffs, Phipps had faced death with the sort of bravery that was the mark of the British soldier "under the most trying circumstances."[32]

The pitiful condition of survivors and the story of Phipps's heroism were further magnified by the mutilated condition of the bodies of the deceased. According to Robert Swinhoe, the dead arrived in coffins with pieces of paper attached to their sides bearing phonetic transliterations in Chinese ideograms of their names. This was, perhaps, all to the good, as the bodies themselves "were found to be in such a state of decomposition that not a feature was

31. The quotation and the reference to barbarism is from Lord Elgin to Prince Gong, CRAC 217.

32. The quotations are from Hope Grant to Secretary of State for War, 22 October 1860, WO 32/8237. Copies of the testimony of the Indian troopers were printed in CRAC 197–198 and in Loch [1869] 1900: 161–165.

recognizable, and it was only by tattered garments" that some were identified. Word quickly spread through the camps, and the mood of the soldiers turned ugly (Swinhoe 1861: 320–321; M'Ghee 1862: 254). Loch recalled that the "sight of the bodies . . . excited general indignation" ([1869] 1900: 160), which, according to Swinhoe, reached a "terrible pitch" (1861: 323). In a letter to French Foreign Minister Thouvenel, Baron Gros summed up the mood of the two camps: "You can well imagine that extreme indignation and rage reigns in the allied camps and that we shall need all the prudence and calm we can command to prevent horrible reprisals from spoiling our cause. There are people who would like to burn Peking and to torture every Chinese mandarin."[33]

Given the general sense of indignation, the desire for revenge, and the central place that the death of the captives occupied in justifying the subsequent destruction of the Summer Palace,[34] one might have expected that the bodies of the deceased would serve as an element unifying the expeditionary force in a common endeavor. To an extent they did, particularly through the burial ceremonies, in which members of both armies participated. Furthermore, most probably agreed with Parkes when, in a letter to his wife of 27 October, he argued that "the treatment of our prisoners was too atrocious to be passed over without exemplary punishment." The difficulty, Parkes added, was "to know what punishment to inflict" (Lane-Poole 1901: 251). Here views diverged greatly.

Major Graham, for example, wondered in his journal why the army did not simply enter Beijing and "sack the palace" (1901: 191). Others, especially the leaders of the two armies, thought that some sort of mark or visible sign of punishment should be left on Beijing, perhaps even the destruction of the imperial palaces (the Forbidden City). As discussions continued, the civil and military leaders of the expedition mulled over their options. They could demand that Prince Gong turn over those responsible for the "high" crime, but the real culprits—the emperor, Prince Yi, and Senggerinchin—were well beyond reach. They could demand an additional indemnity, but that seemed too mild a punishment. They could leave a mark on Beijing, but the city itself had already surrendered and its inhabitants, according to a number of sources, were without blame.

33. Gros cited in Costin 1937: 333; also see Varin 1862: 248–252; Bazancourt 1861: 279.

34. See the reactions in M'Ghee 1862: 221–256; Swinhoe 1861: 303–304, 319–326; Wolseley [1862] 1972: 258–270; Loch [1869] 1900: 102–148, 157–165.

As these options were weighed, Baron Gros seemed to think that treaty ratification overrode all other concerns; therefore, anything that threatened swift completion of that objective, such as continued military operations, was to be avoided. Moreover, the commanders of both armies were bothered by a sudden change in the weather—neither army was prepared to winter in north China—and desired action and withdrawal to the coast as quickly as possible. Equally "pragmatic," the Russian ambassador, General Ignatiev, worried that Elgin's sole goal was "to degrade as much as possible the Chinese government and officials in the eyes of the Chinese people" and warned that a peace based on an overt act of humiliation would work not only against the British, but against all the other powers in China as well (J. Evans 1987: 98–101).

Elgin, however, was only partially influenced by these concerns. In a dispatch to Lord John Russell of 25 October, he justified his eventual decision to destroy the Summer Palace on the logical necessities of empire and on the history of British contact with China and Asia. The former required an action that would create the possibility of future security; the latter was grounded, as noted above, in the British translation of key Chinese terms that exposed the mentality of China's rulers. Underlying this view of China's rulers was a collection of stereotypical ideas about the East, Eastern peoples, Oriental despotism, and what constituted effective action in such an environment. Elgin told Russell, for example, that the low "standard of morals which now obtain in China" would have been lowered even further if he had not dealt with the question of the treatment of captives "as a high crime calling for severe retribution." Such an action, in turn, had to be done in such a way that it would leave a lasting impression if it were to have an effect, one that might even be more binding than the contractual arrangements in the treaty itself. He sought, in other words, something emblematic that would leave a stamp on the minds of China's rulers, one that they would remember and learn from and that would have a direct impact on their behavior.[35]

The razing of the Summer Palace, in Elgin's mind, was the precise act that would have the desired results. As he told Russell, he had "reason to believe that . . . it would produce a greater effect in China, and on the emperor, than persons at a distance may suppose." This was because the Yuanming gardens

35. For a while, he considered having the Qing government build a monument in Tianjin to the dead and compelling the highest-ranking Chinese officials to participate in its dedication. It would have plaques in English, French, and Chinese as a "lesson for future generations." For whatever reason, he abandoned this idea; see J. Evans 1987: 97–98; CRAC 214.

were the emperor's favorite place of residence; its destruction would thus be a "blow to his pride as well as his feelings." It was also the palace where some of the prisoners had been held and tortured; to destroy it would presumably provide some compensation for their suffering. Moreover, the Summer Palace had already been thoroughly plundered: therefore, destroying it would not involve the destruction of many valuable things. Finally, because it was the private property of the emperor and the imperial house, its loss would not be punishment directed at the blameless Chinese people (CRAC 213–215). "The army would go there," Elgin concluded, "not to pillage, but to mark by a solemn act of retribution the horror and indignation with which we were inspired by the perpetration of a great crime" (cited in Swinhoe 1861: 329). As his army carried out his order, Lord Elgin had posted in public places a proclamation in Chinese explaining to the Chinese people the precise cause and reason for the destruction of the emperor's palaces and gardens (Wolseley [1862] 1972: 281).

"A DREARY WASTE OF RUINED NOTHINGS"

"By the evening of the 19th October, the summer palace had ceased to exist, and in their immediate vicinity the face of nature had changed: some blackened gables and piles of burnt timbers alone indicating where the royal palaces had stood. In many places the inflammable pine trees near the buildings had been consumed with them, leaving nothing but their charred trunks to mark the site. When we first entered the gardens they reminded one of those magic grounds described in fairy tales; we marched from them upon the 19th October, leaving them a dreary waste of ruined nothings" (Wolseley [1862] 1972: 280). This passage provides one of the most graphic descriptions of the results of the British army's efforts on 18 and 19 October. And yet, as concise and clear as the passage appears, it tells little about two important aspects of the events: the sheer scale of the undertaking and the way participants justified to themselves and others Lord Elgin's decision. To begin, the destruction of the Summer Palace involved all of General Michel's 1st Infantry Division, which was made up of four British regiments and the 15th Punjabis from India. The combined strength of these units was 143 officers and 4,372 men. Also participating were approximately 300 officers and men of the Royal Engineers (W. Porter 1889 1: 514–515) and several squads of cavalry.

These numbers may seem large, but the site itself was of extraordinary size. What the British and French referred to as the Summer Palace was actually a complex of lakes, villas, landscapes and vistas, gardens, and government offices, the largest part of which was made up of three distinct segments clustered together. These were the Yuanming (Perfect Brightness) garden, often confused for the whole site, the Changchun (Extended Spring) garden, and the Qichun (Beauteous Spring) garden. There were also a number of other, smaller gardens to the south and west of these, including the Wanshou (Birthday) garden, which would later become the focal point of the "new" Summer Palace (Yihe yuan). In addition, the northeast border of the Changchun garden was where the Chinese-rococo-style palaces and fountains designed by Italian and French missionaries were located.[36] Taken together, the gardens covered an estimated 857 acres.[37] Further, although some of the accounts refer to the destruction of the "Yuen-ming-yuen" (or Ewen-ming-Ewen, as M'Ghee delightfully heard it), the actual buildings burned may have exceeded those of the three primary gardens. Colonel C. P. B. Walker's journal entry for 19 October suggests, for example, that the cavalry troop he commanded destroyed buildings right up to the foot of the Fragrant Hills, perhaps including some of the military barracks and temples that were located there (1894: 217). Other accounts mention the burning of villages adjacent to the gardens (Swinhoe 1861: 336; M'Ghee 1862: 283–284; NCH, 7 November 1860).

Reports describing the scale and extent of destruction were coupled, in some cases, with observations of the effects it had on the perpetrators. Characterizing the results as Vandal-like and echoing earlier characterizations of looting, Charles Gordon spoke of the "beauty and magnificence of the palaces we burnt" and called it "wretchedly demoralizing work for an army."[38] Robert Swinhoe was appalled by the "crackling and rushing noise" of the fire as he approached the gardens, and disturbed by the destruction of what could not be replaced (1861: 330). Yet, he was also struck by the way the red flames gleamed on the faces of the men and made them appear to be demons glorying in their task. The sense of pleasure that Swinhoe alludes to here was recorded by a number of participants and was often connected to feelings of satisfaction.

36. Construction had begun during the reign of the Kangxi emperor (r. 1662–1723) and continued well into that of his grandson, the Qianlong emperor (r. 1736–1795). Following a number of southern tours into the Yangzi delta region, the Qianlong emperor had duplicates built of famous scenic sites and gardens from Hangzhou and Suzhou; see Barmé 1996: 118–121. Also see Malone 1934 for a history of the Summer Palace gardens.

37. For maps, drawings, and computer-generated reproductions of some of the buildings and scenic views, see Barmé 1996.

38. The quotation is from a letter to his mother; see Hope 1885: 14; W. Porter 1889, 1: 514–515; Boulger 1897: 46; Spence 1969: 74–75.

Wolseley, for example, argued that this "Gothlike act of barbarism" gave an "unmistakable reality to our work of vengeance" and quite literally awed Qing authorities ([1862] 1972: 279). Some even thought that the British had not gone far enough. In a journal entry, Colonel Walker expressed the desire to burn every government building and house of a known mandarin, the Tartar quarter of Beijing, and the imperial palaces in the center of the city. Further, he regretted that the British did not have the resources to carry away the enormous instrument that gave the Great Bell Temple (Dazhong si) its name. Walker thought it belonged in the clock tower at Westminster (1894: 218–219).

Accounts also acknowledge that the 1st Division did far more than burn the Summer Palace; it also engaged in a second great wave of plunder, one that authorities at the time and commentators later have generally ignored. The 15th Punjabis, for example, were reported to have secured large quantities of gold, with one of their officers supposedly hauling off £9,000.[39]

Yet, at the same time that accounts revel in the scale of the 1st Division's activities, they also expressed a kind of astonishment, bordering on reverence, for the magnificence of that which was being destroyed. This sense of wonder was expressed in an outpouring of descriptive prose about the beauty and expanse of the Summer Palace. Few, perhaps not even Wolseley himself, could look on the scene without a "pang of sorrow" (M'Ghee 1862: 287) or not "grieve over the destruction of so much ancient grandeur" (Grant, cited in Knollys 1875: 205), and this alone may have been enough to stimulate a desire to fix, if only in discourse, an image of what was there before the flames consumed history, taste, beauty, and workmanship. Some observers, perhaps, were aware that it was one thing to make light of their portrayal by the Chinese authorities as barbarians, but quite another to behave like a Vandal or Goth.

Nevertheless, these misgivings did not prevent some observers from attempting to capture the scenery in language like that of a sightseeing tour. Wolseley, for instance, could actually speak of the view from one of the buildings as "charming," and Swinhoe found the area around the Wanshou garden "pleasantly wooded" and the view from a hilltop "most perfect." Major Graham and General Michel had a magnificent view from the top of the White Pagoda in the Fragrant Hills a week after the destruction of the Summer

39. Swinhoe 1861: 331. In his history of the India army, Farwell (1989: 32) argues that the source of the wealth of Probyn's and Fane's Horse, later the 11th and 19th Bengal Lancers, was from China loot.

Palace, and Colonel Walker, from apparently the same place (and while the burning was in progress), praised the view and said he had "seldom looked over a finer country."[40] This is, no doubt, a variation of the master-of-all-he-surveys subject position discussed earlier, but what is stunning is how anyone could see anything through the conflagration and smoke.

These contradictory and, in some cases, seemingly impossible reactions to the destruction of the gardens were accompanied by other peculiar pronouncements. For example, paeans to the beauty of the gardens were paralleled by a tone of disavowal and defiance. These included reminders that the French had been in the garden precincts well before the British, burning some of the audience halls located near the entrance and, as they plundered, leaving behind "little more than the bare shell of buildings" (Wolseley [1862] 1972: 279–280). Henry Loch, who would later deny that Lord Elgin had ever thought about burning the Forbidden City,[41] claimed that nothing of either artistic or scholarly value had been burnt because nothing of rarity was actually kept there by the Qing Court! ([1869] 1900: 168).

By insisting that the gardens came pre-defiled, the British could presumably think about plunder as "salvage" (M'Ghee 1862: 286) and justify to themselves their acts of devastation. If they wavered, there were other means of self-assurance. When he weakened briefly while watching British soldiers set fire to one after another of the garden pavilions, Reverend M'Ghee recalled the mutilated bodies of the prisoners and all regrets vanished. But it was Consul Swinhoe who perhaps best captured the moment. As flames curled into "grotesque festoons and wreaths," twining "in their last embrace round the grand portal of the Palace," as black columns of smoke rose to the sky and red flames "hissed and crackled as if to glorify in the destruction" they spread about, Swinhoe watched with a "mournful pleasure" and "a secret gratification" that the blow had fallen, that justice had been done (1861: 336–337).

How much more forcible a message, Swinhoe seemed to suggest, could the British send to the Chinese government and the people of Beijing? If there were any lingering doubts that the British were sincere and determined in their purpose, the evidence was graphically there in the pall of smoke and burning embers that hung over the gardens, obliterating the sun, casting the

40. The quote from Wolseley is at [1862] 1972: 283; his description is on 282–287. Also see Swinhoe 1861: 332–336; Graham 1901: 196; Walker 1894: 217–218. Graham and Walker are probably referring to the Biyun temple; see Bredon 1931: 322–323.

41. Elgin and Grant had discussed such an eventuality and were prepared to destroy the palaces in Beijing if necessary; see WO 8239.

world around into shadows, and then slowly drifting on the wind and falling like snow showers upon Beijing (Loch [1869] 1900: 170). If the inhabitants of Beijing understood the stern and fearsome justice of the British, how much more so would "the cruel and perfidious author and instigator of the crime" (Swinhoe 1861: 337). The scene of desolation would make the emperor and his mandarins feel "something of the measure of their guilt" (M'Ghee 1862: 288). It was, Wolseley insisted, the only way to strike at the "great vulnerable point in a Mandarin's character": his pride ([1862] 1972: 281).

In the end, therefore, the British accounts invariably arrived at the same point. They cast doubts aside, forgot or trivialized the beauty they had destroyed, and discovered the "real" culprit, the real perpetrator of the crime they were forced to commit. For those who may have had lingering doubts, Chaplain M'Ghee gave absolution; without "a vestige" of the gardens remaining, he wrote, "a good work has been done" (1862: 288–289). There would be no apologies, no regrets. A stern precedent had been set for the future.

Teaching the Paramount Lesson: The Ratification Ceremony

With the Summer Palace destroyed, the primary purpose of the military expedition could now be addressed: the ratification of the Tianjin Treaty. The ceremony itself was carried out within the walls of Beijing on 24 October 1860 and meant to be consistent with procedures used by Euroamerican nation-states in their international relations. But it was also more than this. From the moment it was clear to Lord Elgin and his assistants that it was possible to hold the ratification ceremony in Beijing, opportunities presented themselves for additional acts of humiliation and pedagogy directed against China's rulers. The performance of these actions brought to an end this instance of reterritorialization, but it did so as an expression of imperial, as opposed to nation-state, sovereignty, inaugurating a colonization of the Qing regime, if not its empire as a whole.

SELECTING THE SITE

On 21 October, Harry Parkes, Henry Loch, and a detachment of the King's Dragoon Guards entered Beijing through the Anding Gate in search of an appropriate site to hold the ratification ceremony. They made their way down the narrow streets to the center of town and found themselves in a more open area lying between the Qian and Tianan Gates. Having identified the structures here as the "principal public departments" of the Qing government, Parkes located the Hall of Ceremonies, which apparently had the Chinese ideograms Li bu (Board of Rites) on the door,[42] and with Loch, decided that this would be the appropriate place for the ratification to occur. Given the kinds of spectacular displays of power, the performance of which the British leadership thought particularly effective in the East, Parkes's ability to locate and identify the Hall of Ceremonies was more than a bit of good fortune.

As a linguist, Parkes was particularly attuned to the nuances of Qing Court language and practices. Like other Englishmen, he understood them to be the appearances or symbols of power and authority; indeed, he had spent a good deal of his career attempting to break through these façades and force Qing officials to "face reality." Now Parkes had an opportunity to demonstrate the distinction between apparent and real power, and to do so at sites dense with symbolic meaning for China's mandarins. A similar logic was no doubt at play when Parkes and Loch settled on a place for Lord Elgin and his staff to reside while in Beijing. In this case, they seemed determined to resolve the "city question" at Beijing immediately—there would be no more Cantons. After spotting the roofs of some large buildings in the distance and making inquiries, Parkes indicated that they had found the residence of the duplicitous Prince Yi, and after walking through the buildings and courtyards of the elegant Beijing residence, both agreed that it would make an ideal legation (Loch [1869] 1900: 171–172).

On their tour, Parkes and Loch encountered a group of officials and found themselves with an opportunity to perform the kind of instruction they thought critical, particularly at this juncture. Among the officials, they identified the president of the Board of Punishments. Speaking in Chinese to the "astonished gathering," Parkes told the assembled officials "in the strongest terms of condemnation" of the brutal manner in which the president had treated them. As the president "precipitately retired" from the scene, Parkes admonished him, "When a man takes advantage of the misfortunes of an enemy personally to insult him, then he forfeits the consideration of every civilized nation and deserves to be banished from the society of honest men." The rest of the crowd, according to Loch, "brightened" and made expressions of goodwill ([1869] 1900: 173–174).

These two incidents—locating sites proper for certain acts of discipline and pedagogy and the impromptu public humiliation of a Chinese official— are extremely significant. Both play on a particular aspect of "Chinese charac-

42. See Swinhoe (1861: 346), the only source who mentions this.

ter" the British thought they had astutely identified. The first struck at the purported hollowness of Chinese ceremony and substituted for it performances of real power. The second incident confronted the proud and effete mandarins with moral fortitude and bravery, both of which, when combined with the judicious use of physical force, produced submission. This theory of the Chinese character was commonplace. According to Reverend M'Ghee, "Pride and assertion in the Asiatic must be met in a corresponding manner; and if from a mistaken gentleness you yield to him one inch, he attributes it to fear and impotence on your part . . . and you are obliged again to master him or to leave him alone" (1862: 309). This is, of course, yet another rationale for and justification of gunboat diplomacy.

These perceptions may also be understood as part of a deeply ingrained Euroamerican lore about the fixation of the Chinese on how they were perceived by others around them. A well-placed insult could, as many generations of Euroamericans have learned from reading about incidents like the one involving Parkes and the mandarins (or the British linguists and Qiying), cause them to "lose face," something that appeared to be more important to a Chinese than perhaps life itself. More will be said about this particular "Chinese characteristic" below. Here it is worth noting that if this is indeed a formative moment of the discovery of "face" by Englishmen, it is important to keep the circumstances in mind. The appearance of face-saving and face-losing occurred in a situation of conquest, occupation, and deliberate humiliation. Such circumstances informed the remainder of the choreographed British performance.

PREPARATION

Now that an appropriate site had been selected for the ceremony, it remained for Lord Elgin's assistants to make the necessary preparations. For example, the room where the ratification was to take place had to be arranged in such a way that it demonstrated "equality" between the parties. Moreover, procedures had to be set, documents and credentials vetted, and because a rumor circulated that the Hall of Ceremonies had been mined, the structure had to be carefully inspected. While Colonel Wolseley and some Royal Engineers examined the hall, Parkes and Wade, Lord Elgin's crack linguists, settled "the points of etiquette" (Swinhoe 1861: 344; Wolseley 1904: 84). The latter included establishing the seating arrangement in the hall.

Like other audience halls in Beijing, the Board of Rites was rectangular, with its upper and more inner part on the longer, rear wall and its entrance to the south. According to ritual manuals, for ceremonies held here involving foreign ambassadors, the ambassador and his retinue were placed on the east side of the hall, with imperial officials aligned facing them on the west side. At the upper center of the hall, a table was placed where imperial edicts and the ambassador's credentials were placed.[43] Whether or not they were aware of this particular arrangement, Parkes and Wade positioned the tables and chairs next to each other at the upper end of the hall, where Lord Elgin and Prince Gong would carry out the ratification, with both parties facing the entrance, or south door. Further, they seem to have retained the Qing order in the hall, placing Lord Elgin on the east and Prince Gong on the west. But because extant accounts refer to the location of the British participants as "the place of honor," they may well have interpreted such positioning as a form of appropriation of Qing imperial authority (Loch [1869] 1900: 178; Knollys 1894: 92; Swinhoe 1861: 346).

ENTRANCE INTO BEIJING

Perhaps because of the bomb threat and general concerns that there might be other mischief afoot, the British leaders decided to depute General Robert Napier, commander of the 2nd Division of the army, to post guards from the Anding Gate to the Hall of Ceremonies. Soon after noon, on Wednesday, 24 October, the British ambassador entered the city. Henry Loch described the scene, which was also produced (and reproduced) in a panoramic sketch by the *Illustrated London News:*[44] "[Lord Elgin] . . . was carried in a *chair of state* by sixteen Chinamen dressed in royal crimson liveries; the escort consisted of six hundred men, besides one hundred officers. A body of cavalry led, followed by infantry; the officers who had permission to attend came next, the Head-Quarters Staff in the rear of them, then the Commander-in-Chief with his Personal Staff, and, about thirty yards behind Sir Hope Grant, came Lord Elgin, his horse saddled and led behind his chair, the members of the Embassy on either side of the Ambassador; a detachment of infantry closed the procession" ([1869] 1900: 177; emphasis added).[45]

---

43. See the translation from *The Comprehensive Rites of the Great Qing (Da Qing tongli)* in Hevia 1996: 478.

44. ILN, 5 January 1861: 20–21; Cameron 1970: 357; Hibbert 1970: illustrations following p. 270.

45. Perhaps Parkes and Wade selected a "chair of state." From sketch drawings, this appears to have been a closed sedan chair. See ILN, cited in previous note, and the drawing

As the procession entered the gate of the Hall of Ceremonies, the army band that had been placed in the forecourt struck up "God Save the Queen." Elgin emerged from the sedan chair and was met by Prince Gong, who came forward to greet him.

THE RATIFICATION CEREMONY

Lord Elgin and Prince Gong entered the hall and took up their respective seats on either side. They then commenced the exchange and inspection of credentials. Both sides produced documents that constituted them as the authoritative subjects who could execute the ratification in the name of their sovereigns. In Prince Gong's case, this meant that he had the emperor's permission to affix the Seal of the Empire to the document. The documents conferring plenipotentiary powers having been scrutinized and accepted by both sides, the Convention of Beijing was then signed and the treaties exchanged. In normal state-to-state relations, this should have been sufficient, but according to various accounts, a few more demands were made of the Qing Court. Prince Gong was made to sign a statement that the Tianjin Treaty had been properly executed and the Great Seal affixed, indicating that the emperor accepted all conditions and clauses of the Treaty. This demand may, in turn, have provided the justification for another, the empirewide publication of the Treaty by the Qing government, the translation of which was completed by Parkes and Wade on 7 November, printed, and immediately posted around Beijing (Loch [1869] 1900: 178–179).

With the signing ceremony completed, the British decided to use an unusual technological innovation to capture the moment. Accompanying the expeditionary force since its arrival at Dagu was Felice Beato, an Italian photographer. He now set up what General Grant described as his "infernal machine," the presence of which seemed to shock Prince Gong. He looked at the contraption—Grant claimed it had the appearance of a mortar—"in a state of terror, pale as death," until Lord Elgin assured him that there was no danger (Knollys 1894: 192). Unfortunately for the British and posterity, Beato's photograph did not come out; there was insufficient light in the Hall of Ceremonies.[46] Lord Elgin then rose and departed. In an amiable atmo-

---

entitled "The state entry of Lord Elgin into Peking 1860" located between pp. 192 and 193 in Beeching 1975.

46. On Beato and his photography, see D. Harris 1999.

sphere, Prince Gong saw him off at the top of the front stairs to the hall (Loch [1869] 1900: 179), performing, as it were, the "perfect equality" stipulated in Article 5 of the Treaty of Tianjin.[47]

Thus ended a struggle over the form of intercourse between the empire of Great Britain and the empire of China that had begun with the first British embassy in 1793, continued with the ill-fated missions of Lord Amherst and Lord Napier, and culminated in the third British invasion of China. Certainly conscious of past relations, Henry Loch no doubt felt completely justified in characterizing the signing of the Convention of Beijing and the ratification of the Tianjin Treaty as an incident of world-historical importance. "Thus was happily ended an event," he wrote, "which was the commencement of a new era, not only in the history of the Empire of China, but of the world, by the introduction of four hundred millions of the human race into the family of nations" ([1869] 1900: 180).

And yet, as profoundly important as the leadership of the British forces considered these events, there was at the same time an underlying current of derision, if not contempt for the officials with whom they had to deal. Consul Swinhoe, for example, characterized Prince Gong as "cadaverous-looking" and noted his "timid, sulky demeanour" and "snappish" answers during the ceremony; his retinue, meanwhile, was "dirty and badly dressed" (1861: 348). Chaplain M'Ghee referred to the prince's "sulky dignity" and noted with distaste his horde of retainers of "very questionable cleanliness" (1862: 309). And if the appearance of Qing officials generated a degree of antipathy on the part of British observers, the Hall of Ceremonies itself fared no better. As Swinhoe put it, the place "bore the stamp of neglect and decay of the thousand and one other public buildings in Pekin, and the tapestry that hung from the unceiled roof was of cheap stuff and faded" (1861: 348). But probably the most telling dismissal of the Qing officials and the ceremony came from Major Graham; he wrote in his diary that "the Punjabs thought it a miserable durbar, and that the Chinamen looked like a parcel of old women with no hair on their faces" (1901: 195).

These characterizations of Qing officials and government edifices should come as no surprise, but they do point to one of the unexpected outcomes of the struggle. China did not measure up to one of the dominant fantasies about the Orient: the ostentatious excess of its rulers. Yet, if this was noticed

---

47. Mayers [1877] 1966: 12. A footing of equality *sans* "perfect" is mentioned in Articles 3 and 7.

by the British leadership, it was not registered as a problem at the time. More important for the immediate future was an estimation of the degree to which Qing leaders were learning the lessons Lord Elgin was teaching. A few days after the treaty ceremony, Elgin received Prince Gong in his new residence, the commandeered home of Prince Yi, and had a satisfying conversation with him. The session ended with Beato photographing the prince. This time, the lighting was adequate. The portrait that resulted indicates, if not sulkiness, a degree of trepidation on the prince's face. But perhaps he was still reacting to the "infernal machine," for within a few days Lord Elgin returned the visit and found the prince open and forthright, demonstrating little if any fear of speaking to a foreigner, as Elgin thought common in other officials. Elgin took these signs to be extremely positive. But there was one more lesson he sought to deliver before he left Beijing to put the finishing touches on his mission.

On 8 November 1860, Frederick Bruce, Lord Elgin's brother and minister designate to China, arrived at Beijing. Elgin immediately arranged for a meeting with Prince Gong. At this meeting, Elgin not only wished to pass the torch to his brother, but to do so in a way that the prince would understand as normal diplomatic procedure. As the session opened, Elgin had Parkes explain that "in England the individual who represents the sovereign . . . always takes precedence over all others." Now that Elgin's task in China was accomplished, Bruce would occupy that position. Therefore, Elgin intended at that moment to give up his seat of honor. He then rose and changed seats with his brother, establishing Bruce as the appropriate sovereign masculine subject with whom Qing officialdom would henceforth deal.

The next day, the prince arrived at the British embassy and Elgin had Frederick receive him. Apparently now conversant in "universal" diplomatic forms, the prince engaged in a lengthy and productive conversation with the British minister.[48] Satisfied with his imperial handiwork, Lord Elgin departed the same day for Great Britain.

PRESENTATION IN LONDON

Back in the imperial center, news of the end of the war and treaty ratification, along with appropriate illustrations, appeared in the January editions of the Illustrated London News. The issue of 19 January 1861 provided what was perhaps the most concise report on the victory of the British Empire over the Qing.

48. This and the preceding paragraph are drawn from Walrond 1872: 370–371.

10. Beijing residents reading the treaty. *Illustrated London News*, 19 January 1861.

The front page carried a sketch of a large group of Chinese facing a wall, on which was posted the "Treaty of Peking" (fig. 10). According to the *News*, more copies were posted all around Beijing, where "crowds of astonished natives . . . could scarcely believe their own eyes on beholding such an instance of Imperial condescension." Not long afterward, his work done, Lord Elgin took leave of Prince Gong "with the most cordial respect and goodwill." For his part, the prince had overcome "his morose fit and assumed a cheerful aspect, exhibiting a *teachable and compliant* disposition" (emphasis added).

Just below the China report was another, this one from India. It was an announcement of the creation of a new Indian coinage, one made necessary by the "termination of the East India Company's authority" in the wake of the Indian uprising of 1857. The new coin bore the legend "Queen Victoria" and her portrait (ILN, 19 January 1861: 63–64). Pax Britannica now stretched from the subcontinent to the eastern seaboard of China, and the relationship between the two was on a firmer footing than ever before.

Reterritorializing China, 1861–1900

Introduction to Part II
. . . .

THE SETTLEMENT OF 1860 provided the schematic outline for a new order in Qing China. No longer would representatives of Western powers have to reside at great distances from the center of the Chinese government. Nor would they have to deal solely with provincial officials or other intermediaries in their communications with the Qing Court. A Euroamerican diplomatic presence in Beijing, conceived of as separate and distinct from Qing "tributary" relations with its neighbors, offered the opportunity for diplomats to construct direct and clear communication between the rulers of China and their governments in Europe and North America. Communication would, in turn, now be organized through a wholly new Qing institution, the Zongli yamen. Presumably, to best exploit this opening, the British envoy to China retained the title ambassador extraordinary and minister plenipotentiary so that the Qing would understand that, like Lord Elgin, the minister could make decisions on the spot without consultation with the British government.

Yet, this access to power was built on an odd assumption that, somehow, sovereign equality could be imposed by force of arms, and that benefits would flow in both directions as a result. Nevertheless, with "equality" in place, British officials believed that the Qing elite would see the light and, under well-meaning tutelage, begin to adopt foreign practices as a way of strengthening the dynasty. They would also learn how to calculate their own interests and play by the rules of international power politics. Over the next forty years, the policies and initiatives of British diplomats were premised on the expected behavior of these imaginary Chinese elite actors. At the same time, British leaders also realized that they knew very little about China and that if they were going to transform China's ruling class, they needed to survey and map both China's interior and its vast imperial archive.

Part 2 addresses the issues of Euroamerican imperial pedagogy and knowledge production in China. Chapter 6 places events in China in the context of ongoing shifts in global power relations, deterritorializations triggered by technoindustrial developments that ushered in a new era of European and U.S. imperial expansion, culminating in the colonization of almost all of Africa and much of the greater Indian Ocean world. First, however, this chapter explores the processes that produced new knowledge about China and the new implementation of reterritorializing procedures that resulted. It then examines the effects of these procedures by considering the efforts of the Qing regime to re-form itself on the model of the Euroamerican nation-state.[1]

1. For a more comprehensive overview of Qing reform efforts, see Hsü 1990: 295–386; Wakeman 1975.

CHAPTER 5

. . . .

Constructing a New Order

BRITISH DOMINATION IN ASIA was maintained not simply through control of territory or access to technological instruments, but through the development of comprehensive knowledge about peoples under imperial rule (Thomas Richards 1992: 28). This information empire was produced by field agents who observed local populations, surveyed and mapped territories, and decoded indigenous institutions, producing new objects of knowledge. Through these "investigative modalities" (Cohn 1996: 5–11; Anderson 1983: 163–185) and the mundane operations of processing, cross-referencing, cataloguing, and storing information, colonizers produced an imperial archive, one that had the capacity for transforming imperial into colonial territory —that is, a manageable entity for the exploitation of human and material resources.[1] Supplementing the archival activities of administrators were a number of ancillary apparatuses that were also involved in producing useful knowledge. In the East, these included branches of the Royal Asiatic Society

1. For a study of information gathering in India, see Bayly 1996. For a general overview of the information age of the nineteenth century, see Headrick 2000.

and publishing houses that printed books and journals containing written and visual records of places, peoples, and their artifacts.

Once gathered, information was not only stored locally, but transmitted from the periphery of the British Empire to archival repositories at the imperial center, for example, the Foreign Office, the British Museum and Library, the Victoria and Albert Museum, the Royal Geographic Society, and the libraries of elite universities. At these sites, information could be retrieved for immediate use or catalogued and stored for future consultation.[2] These procedures may seem hardly noteworthy today, but they were highly significant in the nineteenth century. In effect, the great cascade of paperwork produced in the colonies and on the edges of empire quite literally generated completely new objects for analysis, classification, and comparison.

In Beijing and treaty ports such as Shanghai and Tianjin, the effect of this production process was quite profound: it produced a new "China." In other words, the China that Euroamericans thought about and acted on in 1900 was not the same object that Lord Elgin had contemplated in 1860. China had not only been changed internally, but through the accumulation of paperwork during the latter half of the century the proper name China came to represent a different set of objective "facts" to late nineteenth-century foreign observers. How was this possible? How could the bureaucratic routines of collection, processing, and storage produce a new China? It is worth dwelling on these questions for a moment because they help to explain substantive differences in how Euroamericans acted on China and the Chinese well into the twentieth century.

From Paperwork to the Imperial Archive

With a few noteworthy exceptions (Guha [1981] 1996; Cohn 1987, 1996; Bayly 1996), the actual bureaucratic procedures—the paperwork, as opposed to theories about or structures of bureaucracy—that created and maintained the British Empire has received little scholarly attention. But, as Bruno Latour has observed, "paper shuffling" is a "source of essential power" in our world. Why, then, is the paperwork of empire seldom studied? According to Latour, it "escapes attention" primarily because "its materiality is ignored" (1990:55). In his comments on European global expansion from the seventeenth century

2. For a discussion of the form of cataloguing at the British Foreign Office, see Ward and Gooch 1923, 3: 590–591.

forward, Latour observed that the records kept by European explorers and colonial agents also produced objects of analysis, in this case diverse peoples, places, material objects, and commodities. In addition, signs on paper—drawings, text, numbers, and symbols—were superimposed over the material worlds of others, traveled along European communications networks, and eventually were linked through various technologies to centers of collection. At these centers, the inscriptions of field agents made legible to a planning and administering eye things that had been far away and indistinct.[3]

Latour calls these traveling inscriptions *immutable mobiles*, a term that captures two crucial senses of the epistemological object produced in imperial networks. Inscriptions are immutable, first, in the sense that they do not alter their character or degenerate as they travel, and second, in the sense that they can achieve *optical consistency*. That is, inscriptions are presentable, legible, and scalable and thus can be brought into conjunction with other similarly constructed things on two-dimensional surfaces. Examples are Mercator projection maps, charts containing census data, commercial reports, and notes on natural history and human behavior. With real subjects and objects in the world translated onto a flat surface and reduced or expanded in size as necessary, they could now be manipulated through a limited number of representational devices—English descriptive prose, statistics, tables, charts, and maps—and become optically consistent with one another. Once drawings, numbers, and descriptions were arranged on a common surface and in a compatible scale, the immutable could become mobile. Faraway things could be transported on paper to other sites where they could be held in the hands of one person, scanned, reproduced, and spread at little cost throughout the networks of empire. As technologies of empire developed from the sixteenth century forward, it became possible to take instances of one time and space and transport useful aspects of them to other times and other places. At their arrival point or collection sites, the accumulated information allowed work to be planned and man power to be dispatched. It also allowed authority to coalesce at the site where the many immutable mobiles converged (Latour 1990: 26–35, 55).

The collection of immutable mobiles in European archives was not in itself sufficient to explain how small-scale inscriptional practices could lead to large-scale domination, however. For collections to be of use in imperial and

---

3. In developing the notion of networks, Latour draws on Deleuze and Guattari (1983). For further elaboration, see Latour 1993.

colonial projects, they had to be made easily accessible to policymakers. Optical consistency allowed collections to be summarized, cross-referenced, and further reduced in scale. *Harder facts* were made by turning great volumes of paper into less paper: files were made and files of files (Latourian cascades [1990: 40]) — indexes, catalogues, bibliographies, and bibliographies of bibliographies — so that ever more information could be manipulated by fewer and fewer hands. Latour calls the sites where this summing up occurred *centers of calculation* (59). Here cartographers, merchants, engineers, jurists, and civil servants superimposed, reshuffled, recombined, and further summarized inscriptions before storing them for future use. Latour's insistence on following and analyzing inscriptional processes has a number of interesting features. For one thing, it provides a welcome materialist orientation to the definition of bureaucracy, one that moves us away from the "rationalizing mind" of Hegel and Weber to the files themselves. Equally important, his refusal to separate the mental from the material leads him to conclude that the files of empire are actually "totally new phenomena," ones that are hidden from those from whom the inscriptions were exacted (1990: 60).

In redefining epistemology as material practices, directing attention to the fabricated nature of the epistemological objects in the archive, and suggesting that the combination of the two produces a new kind of authority, Latour's work intersects with recent critical scholarship on colonialism. Here it may be sufficient to provide one such instance. In her discussion of British administrative practices in India, Gayatri Spivak (1985) has also questioned the epistemological status of the Western archive. Spivak is interested not only in British efforts to gather information about India, but also in the ways India was reterritorialized. She attends to the practical means by which British inscriptional practices colonized and transformed India — the same process, in other words, that is of concern in China from 1861 forward.

To function effectively on the subcontinent, British agents had to superimpose an alien coding network over India, one that would allow them to gather what they could process as information and put to use in the management of the Indian scene. For example, desiring to tax agriculture, the British administrators transformed complex use rights to land into private property rights, and then mobilized a judicial system to enforce such rights (Cohn 1987: 463–482; Mani 1985). In so doing, they not only indexed the land for calculation purposes, but created a new Indian reality. The "totally new phenomena" that Latour points to were, in effect, fabulous products of the inscriptional-archive project rather than neutral representations of prior "foreign" realities. These readings, or perhaps better, "misreadings" of Indian realities were sustained by the fiction that there was no divergence between the representational regime of East India Company agents (their decoding of India) and that which was represented. Misconstruing colonial administrative fictions as Indian reality, Spivak argues, produced a collection of "effects of the real," the most notable being the proper name "India" itself (1985, especially 129).

If understood as comments about processes of deterritorialization and reterritorialization, of decoding and reordering Asia and Africa, the observations of Latour and Spivak on the epistemological status of the imperial archive suggest that there need not have been any actual fit between the apparatuses deployed and the products they produced, on the one hand, and the human/material landscape into which Europeans ventured from the seventeenth century forward, on the other. Moreover, the disjunction in the archive project could be elided through the fiction that the fit was close enough, that the reality effects of coding procedures effectively described and organized a "stagnant" Asia and a "primitive" Africa. According to Thomas Richards, these sorts of "effects of the real" sustained and generated an imperial imaginary that envisaged the archive as an interface between knowledge and the state. This imaginary then linked information gathering (encyclopedic knowledge of other peoples) to Britain's global preeminence. Understood as an interface, Richards argues, "the archive was less a specific institution than an entire epistemological complex for representing a comprehensive knowledge within the domain of Empire" (1992: 14).

It is precisely this epistemological complex, with its immutable mobiles, networks for generating and transmitting information, its creation of a host of proper names to be used in cataloguing exotic others, and its capacities for transforming and, indeed, assimilating others, that is of critical importance for understanding the nature of the new order imposed on China after 1860. Moreover, by directing attention to this complex, Latour, Spivak, and Richards shift attention away from the correspondence between representations and real objects and from the moral ambivalence of the colonial encounter to the material practices — census taking, map making, ethnographic and natural history description, and the collecting and inventorying of these various inscriptional media — through which the epistemological complex of empire operated.

This understanding of the British imperial archive seems particularly useful when considering the seemingly heterogeneous activities of missionaries, merchants, diplomats, military officials, and fiction writers in settings ranging from direct administration of colonized peoples to less formal arrangements on the frontiers of empire. To put this another way, when the focus shifts to epistemological issues, which would necessarily include the question of translation as well, we can begin to think about British activities in China alongside those in Africa, Southeast Asia, India, and Central Asia without recourse to quantitative categories such as full or semicolonialism, formal or informal empire.[4] And, as in the more prominent examples of European colonization, this focus allows us to note that China also had its paper shufflers, who created particular collections of facts matched by fictions and sustained the collection of these inscriptions with fantasies of total knowledge. British "misreadings" of Chinese realities helped to generate not only a proper name like China, a "Yellow Peril," and even fictional characters such as Fu-Manchu (see chapter 10), but a bipolar Great Game with Russia that elided Qing interests and presence in Central Asia. Equally significant, the specific characteristics of each of these proper names can be understood as effects of the decoding and reordering procedures of the British imperial archive.

Decoding China and Accumulating Useful Knowledge

To understand the decoding procedures deployed by British agents in China, it is useful to remind ourselves that none of the participants in these operations was working completely in the dark. During much of the seventeenth and eighteenth centuries, a substantial amount of European knowledge about China had been generated by Catholic missionaries in the employ of the Ming and Qing Courts,[5] by merchants trading at a limited number of ports on the east China coast (e.g., Morse 1926–29), and by members of diplomatic missions sent to the court at Beijing (Hevia 1995a: 1–22). By the nineteenth century, this kind of information was superseded by a more scientific form modeled after the method of the late eighteenth-century Cook voyages to the Pacific. According to Marshall and Williams, "precise empirical knowledge, such as measurements, statistics, thermometer readings, botanical and zoological specimens, or exact plans" were now considered more valuable than

4. Semicolonialism is a term that has been used in China from Sun Yat-sen forward. Informal empire is a term commonly used in Great Britain; for recent examples, see Atkins 1995; Bickers 1999.

5. See Jensen 1997, especially on the role of missionaries in "translating" important Chinese-language texts into European languages. It is difficult to imagine the identification of the skull of Confucius without the Jesuit contribution to China knowledge.

reflections on the similarities and differences between Asian and European societies (1982: 70, 83; on China, see 45–61, 78–98).

By the 1830s, the trend toward the production of useful empirical knowledge was firmly established in the pages of commercial dictionaries and in the publications of the Royal Society. In China, the British effort to organize knowledge into new empirical categories was spearheaded by the growing number of Protestant missionaries and East India Company officials who, with the aid of native teachers at Canton, began to learn Chinese in the 1820s. In addition to producing grammars, syllabaries, and dictionaries, and translating the Bible into Chinese and the Qing legal code into English, they produced a monthly journal, The Chinese Repository. Modeled after the journal of the Royal Asiatic Society published in Bengal, the editors of the Repository sought to replace the less scientific, and hence suspect, knowledge produced by earlier accounts of China with more exact and empirically based forms, and to do so by drawing extensively on Chinese-language sources. Although they did not expect to find Chinese sources that would rival the arts and sciences or holy writ of the West, they insisted that China's vast and accessible literate tradition provided a convenient entry point for understanding the human and natural environment of the world's oldest living empire.[6] Thus, another archive, the alien archive of China, might prove to be an invaluable tool in the missionary's epistemological project. That assertion echoed down through the nineteenth century as a fundamental organizing principle for all those who followed these pioneers.

When the Repository began publication in 1832, however, the ambitious project outlined by its editors was stymied by the policies of the Qing government. The first and second Opium Wars changed all that. With a Western presence, in and outside the treaty ports, firmly grounded in "international" law, new opportunities presented themselves for collecting and organizing information about China. The decoding of China became centered at sites such as the British legation in Beijing, the various branches of the Imperial Maritime Customs, and the Oriental Society and Royal Asiatic Society chapters established in Beijing and the treaty ports. These institutions may be understood as local centers of collection, each of which produced paperwork specific to its

6. The Chinese Repository 1.1 (May 1832): 1–5. The Repository was published from 1832 to 1851; it included articles on the geography of the Qing Empire, Chinese human and natural history, language and literature, trade and commerce, foreign relations, and beliefs. In addition, the monthly published a steady stream of articles on Chinese character and behavior and on the opium trade and the effects of opium consumption.

function in China. The legation collected data and generated reports on the Qing government's ability to adapt itself to the "norms" of international relations. The Imperial Maritime Customs decoded Chinese weights, measures, and currencies and generated statistics on Euroamerican trade through the treaty ports. Here as elsewhere, British subjects created immutable mobiles and invented ways of more efficiently indexing information on China.

THE DIPLOMATIC CORP AND NEW CHINA KNOWLEDGE

One of the most important sites of knowledge production was the Beijing legation itself. Here Lord Elgin's linguist Sir Thomas F. Wade and others worked with Chinese sources in an epistemological enterprise that produced novel understandings of China's previous diplomatic and commercial exchanges with regional powers. Among those who had established the legation in 1861, Wade remained in China until he retired in 1883, becoming minister in 1871. While there, he put together a significant library of Chinese, Manchu, and Mongol materials made up of 883 works in 4,304 volumes, some of which may have been collected during the looting of the Summer Palace.[7] In addition to being an invaluable tool in Wade's negotiations with Qing officials, the library also served as an important training aid, in China and Great Britain, and as a model for other libraries collecting Chinese-language materials. After his retirement from the diplomatic corps, Wade accepted the first chair in Chinese at Cambridge University, and his library formed the foundation of the University's Far Eastern collection.

Wade divided the library into eight sections: (1) classics and philosophy; (2) history, biography, statutes; (3) geography, travel; (4) poetry, novels, plays; (5) dictionaries, works of reference; (6) miscellaneous, including a number of translations of Christian tracts into Chinese; (7) religion, science; and (8) works in Manchu and Mongol. The collection included all the major ritual texts, numerous commentaries on these and other classic texts, various editions of the Board of Rites Precedents (Libu cili), and the Comprehensive Rites of the Great Qing (Da Qing tongli). There were also dictionaries—Chinese, Manchu, Mongol—and literary concordances, organized by subject, rhyme, and radical; all the great dynastic encyclopedia projects; the Huidian and Huidian shili, or statutes and precedents of the Qing Dynasty; the complete dynastic

---

7. Pauthier (1861: 366) claims that during the looting, Wade selected a number of classic volumes to be shipped to the British Museum. I am indebted to Ann Chayet for bringing this article to my attention.

histories; the descriptive catalogue *Four Treasures of the Library* (*Siku quanshu*); various commentaries on history; Qing Court geographies and accounts of Central Asia, including the Xinjiang *shilue*, written by Songyun, who had been the Qianlong emperor's personal expert on Tibet, Turkestan, and Russia and the same "Tartar" official whom Lord Macartney had found very congenial in 1793 (Cranmer-Byng 1963: 162–163); Manchu translations of the Chinese classics and the *Yiyu lu*, a work on the kingdoms of Central Asia; biographies, memorials, and writings of the Qing Court elite; histories of Beijing; gazetteers from the frontiers of the Qing Empire; and even translations of Western science and mathematics.[8]

It was, in fact, an extraordinary collection; Herbert Giles termed it "a comprehensive library admirably suited to the needs of any ordinary student" (1898: vi–vii). Moreover, having seen the collection in Cambridge, Xie Fucheng, Qing ambassador to Great Britain in the early 1890s, noted that it was not only "remarkable," but made up of many rare items, even more valuable now because of the destruction of great repositories of books in the mid-nineteenth century by Taipings in the Yangtze River valley (Chien 1993: 77), to say nothing of the British expeditionary force at the Summer Palace.

In addition to his library, Wade accelerated the process of information collecting in other ways. For example, he compiled grammars and syllabaries on documentary and colloquial Chinese for training a new cadre of British linguists in the Chinese language. "Student-interpreters" as they were called, learned the northern Chinese dialect, the language of officialdom, delved into the forms of Qing imperial communication, studied exchanges between the legation and the Zongli yamen, and dabbled in local culture. The curriculum involved pairing each student with a Chinese tutor for spoken drills and classroom work on the written script. In the latter case, the course of study involved Wade's own textbook of diplomatic Chinese—the Tzŭ-érh Chi,[9] as it was romanized in Wade's orthography (see below)—the *Jingbao*, or *Peking Gazette*, and a number of novels and histories such as *Dream of the Red Chamber* and the *Record of the Three Kingdoms*.[10] Their training completed, the linguists were then

8. In subsequent years, various donors added additional sources to the Wade collection; see H. Giles 1915 for these additions.

9. The original was published in London in 1867 under the title Wen-chien tsu erh chi (Series of papers selected as specimens of documentary Chinese) and was reprinted in shorter form by Kelly and Walsh of Shanghai, a key publisher of the new China-based knowledge.

10. The routines and training programs of the legation are much understudied. I draw

dispatched to British diplomatic establishments throughout China, where their skills could be used in implementing policy and generating useful, informative reports.

ART HISTORY AND THE MARKETPLACE

At the same time these new forms of knowledge and training emerged, they generated objects of analysis that extended the network of decoding operations in other directions, linking together knowledge, market, history, and the legations as sites of production and collection. One such case involved the creation of new knowledge about objects like those looted from the Summer Palace in 1860. In large measure, these developments were made possible by the unprecedented access to high-quality curios that Euroamerican communities at Beijing and in the treaty ports gained after 1860. As noted above, almost as soon as the British legation opened in Beijing in 1861, David Rennie, the staff surgeon, reported not only the appearance of Summer Palace curios in the local markets but the arrival of dealers and imperial princes at the legation doors with fine objects for sale. This accessibility seemed to pique the interest of legation members, and over the next three decades a number of them were involved in publishing articles that effectively transformed Chinese objects from curiosities into fine arts through the magic of positive knowledge production.[11] Several of these works were produced by functionaries in the Beijing legations, the most significant being those by Stephen W. Bushell.

While a physician at the British legation in Beijing from 1868 to 1900, Bushell collected and wrote extensively on Chinese art, particularly porcelain. Through his study of objects available in Beijing and his translation of the *Tao shuo* (Pronouncements on porcelain),[12] Bushell provided illustrated information on how porcelain was made; accounts of different kinds of porce-

---

here from one of the few first-person accounts, A Student Interpreter 1885: 58–103, which is a chapter entitled "Teachers and Taught."

11. These works included Stanislas Julien's *Histoire de la fabrication de la Porcelaine Chinoise* (1856, a translation of the *Tao lu*), Octave Du Sartel's *La Porcelaine de Chine* (1881), Georges Paleologue's *L'Art Chinois* (1887), Friedrich Hirth's *Ancient Porcelain* (1888), Alfred Hippisley's *Catalogue of Chinese Porcelains* (1890, done for the United States National Museum), Ernest Grandidier's *La Céramique Chinois* (1894), and W. G. Golland's *Chinese Porcelains* (1898).

12. Bushell completed the translation in 1891 and used this source in other publications, but the work was published posthumously in 1910 (see 1977).

lain manufactured over time, sites of manufacture, shapes and styles from particular dynasties; descriptions of types of porcelain that allowed pieces to be more accurately dated; and a bibliography of 105 Chinese sources. He also provided translations of the Chinese dating ideograms to be found on the bottom of pieces. Bushell's efforts made it possible to identify previous errors in writings on Chinese porcelain; sort out the best types of ceramics from particular eras, the evaluation of which was based on Chinese sources and the taste of Chinese connoisseurs; and attach English or translated Chinese terms to the types (e.g., Bushell 1899, [1904] 1924, 1908; Bushell and Laffan [1904] 1907). For the first time, collectors and auction houses were able to put the authenticity of their holdings on a firm footing. At a stroke, Bushell transformed the market, for it was now possible, with an unprecedented sense of certainty, to identify fakes and reward true value. Between 1897 and 1904, Bushell's classification scheme became the standard for public and private collections, including the Walters and Morgan holdings and those of the Victoria and Albert and British Museums.

At the same time that Bushell and fellow legation members were constructing the pertinent categories of Chinese art, the objects themselves were appearing in ever greater numbers in the markets of Beijing and in the treaty ports. By the 1890s, and perhaps earlier, palace eunuchs were bringing curios from the palace collections into these markets (Simpson [1907] 1970: 384) and Chinese dealers sold their wares as a regular feature of Sunday afternoon tiffins at the Beijing legations (Colquhoun 1900: 175–176; Skidmore 1900: 191). These various sales venues were kept supplied by Chinese collectors, who were increasingly forced to sell off treasures because of hardships caused by warfare and political chaos in China.

In addition, foreign art dealers began to appear in Beijing and the major treaty ports, and they seem to have consulted with the experts in the legations. As they bought up valuable collections, newly classified objects found their way into European and U.S. markets. The volume of this traffic seems to have been so great that on her seventh visit to China in 1899, Eliza Skidmore declared that travelers could forget about finding valuable curios in Chinese markets; the best things were on sale in London, Paris, Dresden, Berlin, Weimar, New York, and Baltimore, not Beijing (1900: 197, 200).

Meanwhile, as these developments in China linked Chinese fine arts to urban centers in Europe and North America, Summer Palace loot circulating through the same venues seems to have altered Euroamerican connoisseurial attitudes toward things Chinese.[13] One documented example of such an effect involved the American collector Heber Bishop. According to the preface of a work he commissioned Stephen Bushell to produce for him on Chinese jade, Bishop claimed to have first become interested in collecting jade after seeing a Qianlong-era carved vessel from the Summer Palace. He eventually bought it and several others he found for sale in Europe. Having exhausted the European markets, Bishop then went to Beijing, where he met Bushell and purchased a number of items, including a large collection of jade that dealers had assembled at the request of Court eunuchs as a gift for the empress dowager's birthday.[14] Bishop's coup may stand not only as a prime example of new interest in China's fine arts, but also as an indication of how new knowledge dovetailed with late nineteenth-century markets and desires.

Such changes were also related to the emergence of new sites for producing and circulating knowledge about Chinese arts in East Asia, Europe, and North America and of the opportunities that the deterritorialization of China created for opportunistic collectors. These included not only the exhibitionary order of the public museum and international exposition, but the private sector as well. In Great Britain, for example, the Fine Arts Club of Burlington House exhibited Chinese porcelain in 1878 and followed up with large-scale shows in 1895 and 1896.[15]

Thus, by the late 1890s, there were well-established routes of travel for Chinese art that connected Beijing and treaty ports to the fine arts markets in Europe and North America; an established body of standardized knowledge about various kinds of Chinese art, especially porcelain; and a growing body of authorities on and sites for displaying Chinese objects. Perhaps as a result of these developments, when collectors and connoisseurs consulted newly produced written sources and took advantage of the opportunities to view Chinese art, they no longer spoke of things Chinese as curiosities.

At the same time, however, they might also have fantasized with Eliza Skid-

13. This argument has been put forward by Anna Cocks (1980) and Nick Pearce. Though Pearce's work on this issue remains unpublished, in a recent address at the International Convention of Asian Scholars (1998), he reiterated the point.

14. See Bishop 1900: xiii. Skidmore (1900: 198–199) relates this story, but does not mention Bishop by name. Later, it seems to have taken on the quality of an urban legend; see Morrill 1926: 136–137.

15. Burlington Fine Arts Club 1878: 34, 36; see also 1895 and 1896. The two later shows were done under the aegis of Cosmo Monkhouse, whose own book on Chinese porcelain was prefaced by Stephen Bushell.

more about how they might themselves acquire such pieces. Bishop's cornering of the jade market in Beijing was, by the end of the century, an exceptional action. Yet, Skidmore was certain that hundreds, perhaps thousands of superb art objects lay in the hands of Beijing collectors, who held them off the market because they had no reason to sell. Only "some great political convulsion, the fall of dynasty, a foreign war with another sack of the palaces," she argued, would force collectors back into the marketplace (1900: 196). The kind of event Skidmore seems to have had in mind occurred the following year; it came in the form of the Boxer Uprising and the severe punishments meted out by the treaty powers in retribution.

STANDARDIZATION OF INFORMATION

As various kinds of classifying and cataloguing operations expanded the China portion of the imperial archive and augmented links among government, private institutions, and markets, they also created a number of problems for organizing information. Of particular concern was the vast array of orthographic schemes for transliterating Chinese ideograms into the Roman alphabet. Here, again, the diplomatic corps in the person of Thomas F. Wade played a critical role. In fact, Wade remains best known today for his orthographic efforts, a scheme he devised in the 1870s for standardizing the transliteration of Chinese ideograms. Previous schemes had not only been haphazard, but included efforts to duplicate the different sounds of words in the many dialects spoken on the east coast of China. In contrast, Wade's system was keyed to the language of the Qing Court and its officialdom, the four-tone pronunciation of north China referred to in the West as Mandarin. Later modified by Herbert Giles, Wade-Giles orthography became the norm throughout the British Empire and the United States, where it had a vast effect on enhancing optical consistency among various forms of information about China. Orthographic regularity made it possible to draw together dictionaries, bibliographies, and biographical dictionaries and cross-reference them.[16]

Standardization along orthographic lines in turn encouraged other efforts at systematizing data. For example, well into the 1870s there were no accepted standards for rendering the names of Chinese government offices or the titles of Qing functionaries. William F. Mayers, a member of the British legation in

---

16. Recently, the U.S. Library of Congress and the British Library converted to the romanization system invented in the People's Republic of China known as Hanyu pinyin.

Beijing, published *The Chinese Government* ([1877] 1970) in an effort to eliminate confusion and provide consistency in translation. Drawing on the *Collected Statutes of the Qing Dynasty*, a source in which "every detail of the Chinese polity is anticipated and prescribed for," Mayers included Chinese ideograms and translations for offices and titles at all levels of the Qing bureaucracy.[17] Appendixes dealt with forms of official correspondence between the British legation and the Zongli yamen, the titles in Chinese and English for various kinds of documents, and Chinese renderings of European titles as found in Qing documentary sources.

In another instance, Mayers collaborated with N. B. Dennys and Charles King to produce a guide book to *The Treaty Ports of China and Japan* ([1867] 1977). Remarkable not only for the detail it provided on commercial matters, the guide also afforded helpful information for the ordinary traveler. In addition to steamship time tables from Europe and North America, the treaty port entries included information on accommodation; food prices; shopping districts where one could find curiosities, old coins, "and that class of goods included under the term 'Articles of Vertu' "; interesting sights; local history; city maps; geology and geography of the region in which the port was situated; currencies; import-export statistics; and the Chinese ideograms for local place names, combining, as it were, commercial dictionaries, the returns of the Imperial Maritime Customs, and tourist travel guides. A twenty-six-page bibliography of nonphilological works on China was included. Composed of English-language histories, travel accounts, journals, and translations from the Chinese dating to the seventeenth century, it is perhaps one of the first comprehensive catalogues of European-language sources on China.

There was also a large section on Beijing, one that provides an important link between 1860 and 1900. The authors begin by laying out the route to the Qing capital taken by the allied armies in 1860, relying on the same sources used in chapters 3 and 4 of this study. As they traveled in the footsteps of Lord Elgin and the Anglo-French expeditionary force, they pointed out battle sites such as Dagu, Tianjin, Yangcun, Hexiwu, Zhangjiawan, and Tongzhou. At Beijing itself, the authors drew on a map of the city done by Russian and French surveyors sometime between 1861 and 1866 and entries from previous works on China, as well as observations produced since the establishment of the

---

17. The *Statutes*, a standard official handbook of institutions, titles, and dynastic codes, was edited and revised in successive reigns of the Qing emperors. It is unclear which edition Mayers relied on.

legations in 1861. The map of Beijing is of interest not simply because it over-lay onto the city a new reality created through the technology of surveying. It also established the basic nomenclature for the physical structure of Beijing. Identifying three parts to the city, each of which was bounded by walls, they labeled the northern part the "Tartar" city, nested within which was the Im-perial or "Forbidden City." To the south was an area they called the "Chinese" city. These names stuck. The Forbidden, Tartar, and Chinese cities would not only identify the major divisions of Beijing for Euroamerican visitors well into the twentieth century, but stand mimetically for certain truisms about China, particularly its high-walled isolation and exclusiveness that seemed to sepa-rate the Chinese and their rulers from the progress of the world and give them a false sense of superiority (Mayers et al. [1867] 1977: 464–537). The efforts of Mayers, Dennys, and King might stand, therefore, for the optical consis-tency that Latour points to in projects that draw together disparate elements, combine and reconfigure them, sum them up, and produce in the process a whole new formation of knowledge that effectively transforms or supersedes that which came before.

In other cases, consul-writers updated and expanded the work of their pre-decessors. In 1897, for instance, G. M. H. Playfair revised a third edition of Mayers's *The Chinese Government* and adopted Wade's orthography for it, thus bringing the book "into line with the majority of similar works of reference having to do with China" (Mayers [1897] 1970: iv, ix). In another contribution to optical consistency, Playfair published *Cities and Towns of China* in 1879 (2d ed. 1910), a geographical dictionary with longitude and latitude designations, alternative place names from different dynasties, and Chinese characters and cross-references, all of which was indexed by the Wade-Giles system. Based on an earlier work in French by Biot, Playfair's added a host of new names drawn from articles in *Transactions of the North China Branch of the Royal Asiatic Society.*

Some consuls used the language training and the experience they had accu-mulated working in China to write and teach following their retirement from the consular service. After serving in China from 1858 to 1865, Robert Douglas returned to England, where he taught Chinese at King's College, London, was keeper of the Oriental and Printed Books collection at the British Library from 1892 on, and contributed the section on China for the tenth edition of the Encyclopedia Britannica. Edward Harper Parker was a student-interpreter in Beijing from 1869 to 1871 and served in a number of consular posts until he retired in 1895. Returning to England, he taught Chinese at University

College, Liverpool and Victoria University, Manchester. Both Douglas and Parker wrote books on China, citing in many cases the new sources discussed above,[18] and translated a variety of Chinese works into English. Parker, for example, translated the letter from the Qianlong emperor to George III, a text that became important to nineteenth- and twentieth-century Euroamerican interpretations of traditional Chinese foreign relations (Parker 1886; Hevia 1995b: 232, 238).

These sorts of efforts were augmented by the new institutions created as a result of the 1860 settlement. The Imperial Maritime Customs played a key role in this respect. At its Statistical Department in Shanghai, the commercial transactions of the treaty ports were summarized, usually in annual and decennial reports. The IMC also invented the reporting forms on which its agents inscribed this information, and printed the postage stamps used by the reorganized Imperial Post, an offshoot of the IMC.

GRAMMARS AND HISTORIES

Members of the Customs Service were also instrumental in improving the networks of relationships created by the IMC itself. One of its members, Friedrich Hirth, who published a work on Chinese porcelain, also produced textbooks on documentary Chinese and IMC Chinese-language procedures. Students were systematically guided through reporting forms and introduced to the novel vocabulary then being generated that connected Chinese markets to global networks.[19] A second, enlarged edition of Hirth's textbook was edited in 1909 by C. H. Brewitt-Taylor, commissioner of Customs and director of the Customs College at Beijing. Members of the service also wrote influential works on Chinese history and Sino-Western relations.

The career of Hosea B. Morse, an American who joined the IMC fresh out of Harvard University in 1874, demonstrates how the institutional structures the British imposed on China effectively produced the significant history of China after 1860. Morse published a raft of widely circulated pieces on the Chinese economic sector created by the Euroamerican presence, which was further summarized in his *Trade and Administration of the Chinese Empire* (1908). This

---

18. See, for example, Douglas 1894, which draws heavily on the *Peking Gazette* for original source materials, and Parker 1901.

19. See Hirth 1885–88. A German national, Hirth would later go on to take a chair in Chinese studies at Columbia University and publish numerous works on China. On Hirth, see references to him in Fairbank et al. 1995.

work combined maps, statistical tables, and IMC documents with a narrative history. Morse also made a study of Chinese commercial guilds (1909), and of Chinese currency, weights, and measures ([1905] 1907). The last of these publications sorted out regional variations and provided a basis for future "reforms," to be carried out in many cases by the Chinese themselves.

After he left the IMC, Morse turned his attention to another kind of summary, chronological histories of Sino-British relations. In a multivolume work entitled *Chronicles of the East India Company Trading to China, 1635–1834* (1926–29), he drew on numerous handwritten folio volumes in the archives of the East India Company's London office, reducing their contents to five easily handled printed volumes. A second multivolume project, *The International Relations of the Chinese Empire* (1910–18), sorted out Foreign Office records, parliamentary papers, and memoirs to produce a similar summary and miniaturization. According to Morse's biographer, John K. Fairbank, the significance of these studies was "to establish chronology and try to get the story accurate and consistent." Morse's chronology became, in fact, an international standard—even cold war–era anti-imperialist historians in the Soviet Union and communist China found it indispensable (Fairbank, Coolidge, and Smith 1995: 224, 226).

These many efforts to produce and better organize knowledge were complemented by a rapid growth in the publication of firsthand accounts about China in the post–Opium War era. In some cases, these publications made their initial appearances as oral presentations at the meetings of the Royal Asiatic Society in Shanghai, the site of an extensive library of old and new works on China,[20] and eventually entered the pages of the Society's journal. An index prepared by Henri Cordier in 1876 indicates the scope of the early years of this decoding operation. Building on but vastly expanding the work of *The Chinese Repository*, the *Transactions of the North China Branch of the Royal Asiatic Society* capitalized on the unprecedented access Europeans now had to the land, populations, and institutions of the Qing Empire. In its first two decades of publication, the journal included articles on Chinese law; nautical and meteorological observations along China's eastern seaboard; the natural history of silkworms and birds; cotton and sugarcane production;

20. It contained Chinese-language materials as well as the works on China then being produced by Euroamericans in China. For a catalogue of their holdings see the *Journal of the North China Branch of the Royal Asiatic Society* (hereafter JNCBRAS) 29 (1894) and 30 (1895). Separate catalogues were published in 1909 and 1921.

geology and mineral deposits; music; medical practice and medicines; geography, usually in the form of firsthand accounts of travel into China's interior; history and biography; myths, legends, and folklore; translations of ancient stelae; and information on Chinese manners and customs (Cordier 1876). These individual projects were complemented by ever more ambitious collective ones, like the geological surveys directed by Ferdinand von Richthofen (1877–1912), and involving several researchers. As the scale of the China archive grew, Cordier himself indulged a mania for the index, eventually producing two five-volume bibliographies of Western writings on China and Southeast Asia. In other cases, writers revised and updated their earlier work.

The net effect of these efforts was to construct a uniform referential grid of things Chinese, the legibility of which was enhanced by consistent terminology and standardized orthography of Chinese proper names and concepts. These field-of-knowledge effects made it possible to produce uniform indexing in individual works, to cross-reference works of different authors, and to incorporate ever greater amounts of Chinese nomenclature within a given epistemological object. By the last decade of the nineteenth century, new knowledge and optical consistency had created a whole new China, one that was accessible to a growing English-speaking and -reading audience; organized maps, statistics, and charts; filled in empty spaces in the taxonomy of the imperial archive, China branch; and multiplied the expanse of the British imaginary of China.

Now that signs signified a uniform set of proper names of people, places, and things, more and more people far removed from the China scene could collect "authentic" information and contribute commentary on the Far Eastern question. They could, in other words, look over the shoulder of Arthur Smith as he entered a Chinese village or reflected on the essences of China in his *Chinese Characteristics* (1894).[21] They could follow D. Warres Smith (1900) into the European settlements in the treaty ports of China as he described local conditions and institutions and reviewed the commercial returns of the Imperial Maritime Customs. They could join in the romantic adventures of the Great Game through the firsthand accounts of Francis Younghusband ([1910] 1985)[22] and A. R. Colquhoun (1900). And they could join in specula-

21. For full citations of the works of the authors mentioned in this paragraph, see the bibliography. With only a few exceptions, the bulk of these publications appeared between 1885 and 1900.

22. Younghusband was more than a writer about the geopolitical situation in Central

tions about the Far Eastern Question with armchair Great Gamesmen such as D. C. Boulger (1879, 1885) and Alexis Krausse ([1899] 1973), who analyzed published summaries of the archive project to uncover Russian machinations in eastern Asia and evaluate the condition of the Chinese Empire.

People far from China could draw together these many kinds of information, as the anonymous authors in the Adjutant General's Office of the United States War Department were able to do in 1900, and produce something like *Notes on China.* Prepared for the American expeditionary force at the time of the Boxer Uprising, the *Notes* cited many of the authors discussed above, as well as the *Hong Kong Directory for 1900,* the *Chronicle and Directory for China,* the *Statesman's Year Book for 1900,* British parliamentary papers on China, a report by James Ginnell on railroad development in China,[23] and scholarly journals. Its ninety pages were crammed with statistics on population and railroads, descriptions of wharves and docking facilities, and distances between key cities in north China and their longitude and latitude. There were also entries on the new Qing military forces, some of which were taken from a translation of a Russian intelligence report. In addition, there were maps of Beijing and Tianjin and of the route from Dagu to the capital. The last of these provided a detailed view of the North River, new rail lines from the coast, and notations of key points on the road and river to Beijing. Based on U.S. hydrographic charts, it drew on Bretschneider's map of north China and "other authorities," such as the maps done by the British and French during the 1858 and 1860 campaigns in the region.[24] The *Notes on China* is precisely a collection of immutable mobiles and summarization (the Latourian cascade) discussed earlier. In this case, the capability of the Adjutant General's Office to mobilize the discrete elements that made up the *Notes* allowed the scrutinizing eyes at

---

Asia. In 1904, he led a British army into Tibet, a maneuver stimulated by British fears of Russian advances into the region; see his *India and Tibet* ([1910] 1985) for an account of the campaign.

23. Ginnell is identified as the district engineer of Imperial Chinese Railways. His 1898 report was made to the British and Chinese Corporation, Limited, in London; see U.S. War Department, Adjutant General's Office 1900: 26.

24. The hydrographic charts are numbered 1870, 1871, 1872, and 1873. The first two were based on a French survey of 1858, the latter on a British survey of 1860. They are listed in U.S. Navy, Hydrographic Office 1919: 102, among similar charts of China's east coast. I am indebted to Ridley Kessler of Davis Library, University of North Carolina at Chapel Hill and David Cobb of the Harvard Map Library.

the War Department to plan and deploy actions from a distance and to place in the hands of its operational components the information needed for the exercise.

Thus, as a result of a little less than half a century of dedicated work, Euroamericans could now hold China in the palm of their hand, scan it, claim to understand it, and act on it—an alien empire had been decoded, classified, summarized, and, as a result, was known as it had never been known before. Just what sort of China they had in hand is taken up in more detail at the end of chapter 6. For now, it is important to follow out the practical consequences of these projects as they reshaped China to fit it into global imperial schemes.

Reordering China

The ability to produce new knowledge about China was not exclusively a function of the kinds of inscriptional projects discussed above. Part of the epistemological complex was also linked to the alien institutions that were imposed on the Qing and were remapping the Chinese polity. These apparatuses, made up of missionary, commercial, and diplomatic enterprises, functioned in two ways. On the one hand, they provided secure channels along which information generated by various agents could flow. On the other, through the replication of structures that were identical in the older treaty ports and in newly opened territory, they penetrated deeper into China, selectively reordering locales and linking the resulting formations to global networks.

As has been noted, the Imperial Maritime Customs is the clearest example of this reordering process. Originally created during the Taiping Rebellion, when the Qing appeared on the verge of collapse (Fairbank 1953), the IMC ensured that tariffs on imported goods were collected. After becoming a formal part of the Qing administration in the 1860s, its director, British subject Sir Robert Hart, began to expand its reach. From its unique position as both part of and alien to its host, the IMC did the bookkeeping, printed the identification tags, designed the forms, and generated all the other little bits of paper—examples of which were in Hirth's training course—that captured Chinese and foreign things and allowed them to be exchanged. In addition, the IMC opened new treaty ports; organized China's seacoast on the European navigational model with lighthouses, buoys, and so on; directed the building of port facilities based on "international" standards; and encouraged the spread of its bookkeeping methods into other areas of Qing administration. The IMC also functioned as a teaching instrument. Hart himself sought to demonstrate to members of the Zongli yamen the operations of a contemporary nation-state by drawing on encyclopedic sources such as John R. McCulloch's *Dictionary, Practical, Theoretical, and Historical of Commerce, and Commercial Navigation* (1842).[25] These various efforts were complemented by the IMC's education department, which established the Tongwen guan, a school for training Chinese interpreters of European languages. Under the direction of the American missionary W. A. P. Martin, this unit translated a number of works on international law, political economy, and math and science, as well as Henry Lansdell's *Russian Central Asia*.[26] Its statistical bureau helped to integrate China into the global capitalist economy of the late nineteenth century by generating the returns on trade between China and the West. These numbers represented both the scale of China's new "foreign" commerce and allowed capitalists to plan for further penetration of the China market. It also created an environment in which domestic and overseas Chinese could thrive within the protected enclaves of the treaty ports (Hao 1986; Cochran 2001). By the end of the century, the IMC was overseeing treaty port operations in every major coastal city of China, as far north as the Amur River in Manchuria, deep into central China along the Yangzi River, in the southeast on the West River, and on the borders of Burma and Vietnam. It became so indispensable an agency for the Westernization of China that after the fall of the Qing Dynasty in 1911, the IMC continued operations as the Chinese Maritime Customs (Fairbank et al. 1995; L. K. Little 1975, 1: 3–34; Atkins 1995).

While the IMC was reordering China from inside the Qing administration, other operations sought to link coastal and interior China via the treaty ports to Europe and North America. The missionary enterprise, which combined educational and medical missions with proselytizing, is probably the best-known and most completely documented of these reordering operations. Indeed, missionaries not only broke new ground in physically occupying parts of China beyond the treaty ports, but several, like John Fryer, W. A. P. Martin, and S. Wells Williams, worked either for the Chinese government or their own

25. On the use of McCulloch, see R. Smith et al. 1991: 150. McCulloch originally published his work in 1842 and it went through many editions. For a similar type of work, see MacGregor 1850, which also combined commercial intelligence with statistical summaries of international trade.

26. On the unit, see Biggerstaff 1934–35; a list of translations is provided on 332–333; see also Su Ching 1985: 159–160. On W. A. P. Martin, see Covell 1978: 170–186; Hsü 1960: 125–131. For a critical evaluation of the unit and Martin's role in translation projects, see L. Liu 1999: 142–159.

government as translators and functionaries. Other missionaries founded schools that introduced Western science and mathematics as well as religious subjects to Chinese students (Cohen 1978). Through these agencies and various affiliated organizations, missionaries connected China to a global network of Christian missionary activity.

There were also other organizations, such as the Society for the Diffusion of Useful Knowledge, the Society for the Diffusion of Christian and General Knowledge among the Chinese, and the Young Men's Christian Association, to say nothing of commercial banks, trading firms, and the aforementioned Royal Asiatic Society, each of which reorganized Chinese reality in its own way and connected the resulting forms to global networks. At different points in their lives, Europeans — and, by the end of the century, re-formed Chinese — might touch down at different nodes in these networks, sometimes decoding and sometimes reordering China. H. B. Morse, for example, was a member of each of the associations mentioned above. When he retired to England, he joined the Council of the Royal Asiatic Society, the Committee of the China Association, the Royal Geographic Society, and the Royal Societies Club, serving at times in an executive capacity in one or another of them.

Through these various agencies, parallel or overlapping networks were integrated horizontally, reordering Chinese realities as effectively as the treaties imposed on the Qing. At the same time, the linkages among networks accelerated the accumulation of immutable mobiles and the summarization of information on China. The nodal points or centers of collection in these networks were not only prime sites for the display and circulation of new knowledge, but themselves helped to lengthen networks, making it possible to envision the gradual achievement of comprehensive knowledge about China and the Chinese. But, as should be clear from the earlier discussion of British India, knowledge for its own sake was not the purpose of the imperial project. If knowledge was going to have any value, it had to be implemented, put into use so that the world could be made safe for empire. In China, this meant using new knowledge in pedagogical exercises to prevent another *Arrow* affair or another war like 1860.

Implementations: Teaching Lessons through Diplomacy

From the perspective of seasoned British diplomats like Thomas Wade, if the Qing government was to make sound decisions, the consciousness of its leaders would have to be altered so that they could see clearly the real conditions of international relations and understand the nature of China's weakness. But achieving such enlightenment was no small task, because, as Wade and others observed, the Qing nobility and government mandarins were obsessed with the shadow rather than the substance of power, with appearances instead of hard political realities, with ceremonial form rather than the material manifestations of power (FO 17/748: 8–9, 77, 134). The inability of China's rulers to make clear distinctions between appearance and reality resulted in an irrational fear of the unknown. Rather than grappling with change and facing their fears squarely, they constructed a wall of haughty arrogance and willful ignorance.

These traits had been identified as the central problem of China's elites by a succession of British diplomats, merchants, and missionaries, and this perceived problem had been directly confronted and challenged by British ambassadors from Lord Macartney to Lord Elgin. Although the rhetoric of guns and words appeared to have effected some changes, problems persisted. There was, for example, the occasional nonimplementation or nonenforcement of treaty provisions, the unwillingness of the Qing government to actually set up legations in foreign countries, and the refusal of the Court to grant imperial audiences to Euroamerican diplomats. Full-scale Chinese exclusiveness may have ended, but the high walls were hardly down. The fact that obstructions appeared to remain in place indicated to Wade an obstinate misapprehension of reality on a scale that prevented the Qing Court from addressing constructively China's political and military weaknesses.

How, then, to change minds? One common thread running from Macartney to Wade on this question involved the notion that the Qing Court did not have a clear understanding of the true character of Englishmen. If they did, their attitudes would change and their minds would open to new possibilities. Macartney was certain that he had achieved such mental alterations (Hevia 1995b: 218), but the failure to secure a legation in Beijing meant that the apparent successes of 1793 had disappeared over time. Now, with the establishment of the Beijing legation, the opportunity presented itself for the completion of the task first framed in the eighteenth century. The 1860 settlement provided the necessary conditions for creating a perfect communication, for teaching the Qing Court that their interests coincided with those of Great Britain[27] and that the latter would make a formidable ally.

27. There were a number of Englishmen who made this argument; see Kuo 1978: 515–516.

This pedagogical project[28] was to be carried out by a new breed of British diplomat, the linguists on whom Lord Elgin had relied. They would now direct their talents to helping their counterparts in the Zongli yamen learn the lessons of China's recent difficulties with Great Britain and other Western powers. The teaching would occur in the day-to-day business of diplomacy and would be supported by the new knowledge about China that the linguists themselves and other foreigners were producing. With unprecedented access to Chinese source materials, British diplomatic agents at Beijing could construct a critical comparative framework for accurately assessing the "real conditions" in China. The results could then be used to transform Qing officialdom, to teach the benighted Qing nobility and their Chinese mandarins the lessons of the contemporary international world.

At the same time, however, the dynamics of the situation in Beijing were more complicated than simply a Chinese-British binary. Soon after the British arrived, the French, Germans, Americans, and Russians set up legations, presenting both threats and opportunities to British interests. Wade, for example, was often impatient and alarmist about what he saw as Chinese foot-dragging and complacency in the face of aggressive moves by other Western powers (R. Smith, Fairbank, and Bruner 1991: 174, 295, 303, 319). At the same time, he took the initiative on more than one occasion to instruct the Qing Court on the policies it should be implementing to protect itself and its relationship with the British. In 1866, for example, Wade wrote a memorandum to the British minister at Beijing, Rutherford Alcock. Translated into Chinese by the latter and with a Chinese preface added by Wade, the "Brief Discussion of New Proposals" (*Xinyi luelun*) was sent to the Zongli yamen. In his communication, Wade urged the Qing government to recognize the changing international situation that now placed powers such as Russia, Great Britain, and France on the borders of the Qing Empire. He suggested that China begin a reform process that would include the reciprocal exchange of diplomats (Hsü 1960: 156–158; R. Smith et al. 1991: 288–289). A stronger China would result, and was indeed required, if Russian advances from the north and French ambitions along the Vietnamese border were to be checked. The British would be more than happy to aid the Court in the difficult transition ahead.

28. The diplomats were not alone in thinking that the next task in China was educational. *Blackwood's Magazine* 93 (1863): 59 argued that the Foreign Inspectorate of Customs (soon to be IMC) was a "potent engine for introducing to the minds of the Chinese governing classes Western ideas and practices, political and moral as well as commercial; and a perfect guarantee against any more Chinese wars with Europe."

But if diplomatic practice and negotiation provided an ideal classroom, one necessary component of this strategy remained elusive. The British had yet to secure an audience with the Qing emperor, which was seen as a critical step in creating the proper environment for the pedagogical project to flourish. To bring about an audience with the emperor, the British could rely on the support of the other powers with legations in Beijing. All of them were interested in aligning Qing Court ceremonies with European diplomatic practices and, in particular, wanted to deliver their credentials and communications from their sovereigns directly into the hands of the Qing emperor—to enact, as it were, the "perfect equality" stipulated in the treaties.

However, between 1861 and 1872, Western diplomats were unable to achieve this goal because the reigning emperor, Tongzhi, was a child. In 1873, when the emperor reached his majority, the diplomatic corps saw an opportunity to resolve the audience question and, perhaps more significant, to introduce and educate the Qing on European-style audience protocols (see Rockhill [1905] 1971: 42–44; T. Wang 1971). Having by that time been elevated to the position of British minister to China, Wade played a key role in the discussions that ensued.

Wade broached the audience question in a memorandum to the Zongli yamen in the spring of 1873. Characterizing it as an "instrument of instruction," Wade said the memorandum helped to "educate the Chinese for the question which must be faced" (FO 17/630). Negotiations soon began, the upshot of which was a protocol that governed an audience held on 29 June 1873 (FO 17/748–750).[29] The ministers of Great Britain, France, Germany, the United States, Russia, and Japan were received together at the Pavilion of Purple Brightness (Ziguang ge) in the park to the west of the Forbidden City. There the ministers remained standing while they delivered their letters of credence and congratulated the emperor on having reached his majority. This diplomatic coup seemingly put to rest the central issue that had divided China and Europe for two centuries or more. From the point of view of the diplomats, the kowtow had disappeared from China's diplomatic relations with Western powers and the Qing Court had seemingly reconciled itself to the sovereign equality of nations.

Yet, there is more here as well. Wade's reports to the British Foreign Office on the negotiations firmly locate them in the larger concerns animating Brit-

---

29. For discussions of the audience negotiations, see Rockhill [1905] 1971: 41–42; Morse 1910–18 2: 266–270; T. Wang 1971; Cooley 1981: 86–95.

ish activities in China. The reports are cross-cut with references to Great Game strategic considerations, applications of local knowledge, and ruminations on pedagogical practice. They also provide a good example of the new kind of knowledge Wade was able to produce from his library.

From Wade's perspective, there was a far larger issue at stake than simply an audience with the emperor. If the Qing Court accepted European forms of diplomatic practice, it would be signaling to the Western powers and the Chinese public[30] at large that it recognized the change in its global position and that it no longer desired to make universalistic claims about its own superiority. Such acknowledgment would, in turn, give all the other foreign powers in China a sound reason for retaining their legations in Beijing. Wade thought this particularly important because he was convinced that Russian policy was to keep the missions away from Beijing "not only as corps of observation, but as civilizing influences which may develop China more rapidly than Russia desires" (FO 17/748, 134; also see 14–17).

In the negotiations leading up to the audience, Wade relied on a number of sources to sharpen his rhetorical tactics. He sounded out those who had regular contact with Qing officials such as Robert Hart, W. A. P. Martin, and Thomas Meadows, the British consul at Tianjin. He explored the historical records of British relations with China, particularly accounts of the first two British embassies, those of Lord Macartney and Lord Amherst in 1793 and 1816, respectively (FO 17/748: 9, 13, 339–354, 376–381, 433; 749: 11–14, 22–24). Extensive knowledge of those encounters was important because Wade found that Qing officials were attempting to rewrite the historical record by claiming, for instance, that Macartney had performed the kowtow (three kneelings and nine bows). Wade not only refuted their claims with his sources,[31] but when officials shifted position to argue that the Macartney precedent of kneeling on one knee before the Qianlong emperor should be retained in the forthcoming audience with the Tongzhi emperor, he rejected it. In conversations with Wenxiang, the head of the Zongli yamen, Wade stated that in the present age, it was out of the question for ambassadors to kneel before other sovereigns. Moreover, he added, references to kneeling

30. The concern with the Chinese public's "knowing" of concessions granted by the Qing was widely shared; see FO 17/748, 126; 749, 130; 750, 6–7.

31. FO 17/749: 16. In the case of the Macartney embassy, the rewriting and reevaluating of the historical record was hardly a one-sided affair. See the discussion in Hevia 1995b, chap. 10.

were "offensive" to the foreign representatives "not only as Ministers, but as individuals" (FO 17/748: 345–346).

He also relied on the knowledge he had acquired from the study of ancient and contemporary Chinese-language sources, some of which were official publications of the Qing government. His familiarity with these sources not only allowed him to translate and annotate Qing government correspondence forwarded to the British Foreign Office (see, e.g., FO 17/749: 142–147), but to produce a novel form of reporting that looked much like a scholarly treatise. One important example of this kind of report was entitled "Memorandum on Chinese terms used in the discussion about the Audience," dated 11 June 1873 (FO 17/749: 236–303).

FROM WADE'S LIBRARY TO THE IMPERIAL ARCHIVE

The audience memorandum is an extraordinary document. Among other things, it demonstrates the close links established in British strategic thinking during the latter half of the nineteenth century among scholarship, local knowledge, policymaking, and negotiation with officials like those to be found in Qing China. The research report itself was necessitated, Wade explained, by his efforts to outmaneuver these officials. According to members of the Zongli yamen, the Chinese translation of the audience request made by the foreign ministers had used the character *jin* for audience, which, they explained, referred to one held in the autumn. It being the spring of 1873, Qing officials wanted to defer discussions to comply with the request. Wade's research demonstrated, however, that their interpretation was either a subterfuge, which he easily could expose, or an example of how ignorant Qing officials were of their own historical sources.

Wade's inquiry extended over the range of material in his collection dealing with imperial audiences and rituals. From these sources, the British minister reconstructed a history of the character *jin* with full citations of sources, footnotes, and Chinese ideograms in the margins. Furthermore, he brought the entire issue into the contemporary scene through reference to sources from the Court of the Daoguang emperor (r. 1821–1851) and to the writings of the Qing scholar Ruan Yuan (1764–1849).

In his conclusion, Wade argued that any effort to limit the meaning of the term *jin* to autumn court audiences, particularly when the sources used to do so were questionable ones from the much earlier Zhou period (ca. fifth century B.C.E.), was in error. Moreover, in historical sources whose authenticity was less in doubt, the term itself was never used to refer to audiences at a certain time of year, but audiences between emperors and their officials.

Perhaps more important than this conclusion is what it signified. It showed that a well-trained agent could move among the indigenous population and the highest realms of political authority in China, gain command of significant cultural and historical objects prized by China's ruling class, and turn those objects against them to make a number of tactically significant moves. To Qing authorities, it may have made the point that there were few ways of avoiding the British imperial archive. Pedagogy, it would seem, also involved cutting off any escape routes for those being taught.

Wade repeated these techniques on numerous occasions over his many years in Beijing, continually returning to the venue of diplomacy to move the Qing along into the modern world. Two years after the imperial audience, for example, the British interpreter Augustus R. Margary was killed in Yunnan by local people.[32] Margary had been sent to Yunnan to meet a British expedition from Burma purportedly attempting to open trade routes into southwestern China. Again, Great Game machinations were involved. From Wade's perspective, however, the central issue was that Tianjin Treaty provisions allowing free passage of foreign nationals had been violated, and he was convinced that Chinese officials were involved in the outrage. Because "the antecedent history of foreign intercourse with China" indicated to Wade that the real culprits would probably never be brought to justice (China No. 3 1877 [CC77]: 51), he decided that the incident might best be used as a teaching opportunity.[33] After putting intense pressure on Prince Gong and the Zongli yamen, Wade delivered an ultimatum demanding that the Qing government take responsibility for the incident or he would withdraw the British embassy from Beijing to Chefoo (Yantai) on the north coast of Shantong province. The outcome was the Chefoo Convention, signed by Wade and Li Hongzhang, as China's plenipotentiary, on 13 September 1876 (Mayers [1877] 1966: 44–48; CC77, 64–67).

The first two sections of the Convention dealt with the Yunnan affair and

32. On the Margary affair and the negotiations that followed, see Cooley 1981: 116–35; Morse 1910–18, 2: 297–305; Hsü 1990: 304–305.

33. As with the audience issue, Wade reported the minute details of the negotiations in dispatches to the Foreign Office in London. See China No. 1 1876 (hereafter CC76) and CC77. For Wade's summary reports to British Foreign Secretary Lord Derby, see CC77 51–58, 111–147.

official intercourse, and did so in a way that continued the project of teaching the Qing Court proper diplomatic forms.[34] The Zongli yamen was to present a memorial to the throne—after Wade had reviewed it to ensure factual accuracy—that contained a full account of what had transpired in Yunnan and acknowledged the violation of treaty provisions. The throne was then to issue an imperial decree reasserting treaty rights and a public proclamation stating those rights. The proclamation was to be posted throughout the empire, the occurrence of which was to be verified by British observers under the protection of local authorities. Before the proclamation was distributed, Wade was to inspect it to be certain that the correct lesson was being circulated to local officials and the Chinese population (CC77: 85–88, 93, 96, 102, 104–106). In addition, the Qing Court was to send an apology mission to Great Britain bearing an "Imperial Letter," the text of which Wade was to approve prior to the departure of the mission (90–91).

Procedures such as these were not only significant at the time, but set a precedent for later "agreements," including the Boxer protocol of 1901. In addition, they bring into sharp focus the peculiar notion of "perfect equality" put into practice by British diplomats in China. The direct intervention into Qing Court affairs by a British minister who spoke without need of direction from his own government and this same minister's insistence on approving the Court's communications to his own ruler did more than undermine Qing sovereignty. These actions constituted the Qing in colonial terms. The emperor of China had become much like "native" princes under British "indirect" rule.

In addition to dealing a severe blow to Qing imperial sovereignty, the Convention also required that the Zongli yamen begin discussions with the foreign ministers in Beijing over a code of etiquette for intercourse between foreign officials and representatives of the Qing government. These discussions were to include both procedures in China and at foreign capitals. Implicit in this clause was the insistence that the Court would now complete its Tianjin Treaty obligations to establish permanent embassies abroad. Indeed, the apology mission to Great Britain was to do just that.

Finally, there was one extraordinary provision added in a separate article

---

34. Other clauses dealt with a number of outstanding issues, including commercial matters; the tax on opium was to be increased, new ports were to be opened and foreign settlements clearly defined, and taxes on foreign goods were to be collected only at ports of entry. These provisions were, however, placed at the end of the Convention.

at the end of the agreement. The British were given authorization to send a "Mission of exploration" into Qing Central Asia with the object of journeying through Tibet to India. The route was not specified, but it would be either via Gansu and Kokonor or through Sichuan. The Zongli yamen was charged with making the arrangements for the mission, creating the passports, and notifying Qing officials in Tibet of the British plans. Thus, it would seem, the Great Game was removed from the realm of imaginary speculations and secret communications and codified as a formal part of British relations with China.

Learning Lessons, Passing Tests

The settlements of the audience question and the Yunnan affair might be seen as the high point of British reterritorialization efforts in nineteenth-century China. In 1877, these English lessons were capped by the establishment of a Chinese embassy in London. With a Tongwen guan translation of Charles de Martens's *Guide Diplomatique* (*Xingyao zhichang*) in hand, the Qing apology mission, headed by Guo Sungtao, arrived in London in January 1877.[35] On 8 February, Guo and his entourage presented the emperor's letter of apology to Queen Victoria in a formal audience at Buckingham Place. Thomas Wade was in attendance, along with three assistant secretaries from the Beijing legation, A. R. Hewlett, W. C. Hillier, and Halliday Macartney, a descendent of Lord Macartney. They were joined by Lord Derby, the Grand Chamberlain the Earl of Caernarvon, and Master of Ceremonies Sir Francis Seymour.

As it turned out, however, there was one hitch prior to the audience proper. It would seem that having read de Martens, the Qing officials wanted to make certain that they should perform three bows when entering the queen's presence. According to Liu Xihong, the vice envoy, the Chinese delegation queried Wade the day before the audience, but he claimed he was uncertain about the procedure. They then asked Master of Ceremonies Seymour, who was equally vague. Liu assumed that they were being tested to see if they could carry out the ceremony properly; it was, after all, identical to the proceedings of 1873 before the Tongzhi emperor and was no different from what European diplomats had been accustomed to for over one hundred years.

If indeed the Qing delegation was being tested, Wade must have felt gratified when his pupils performed admirably. After three bows, Ambassador

---

35. The account that follows is taken from the diaries of Liu Xihong and Zhang Deyi, which are translated in Frodsham 1974: 118–121, 155–157.

Guo and his retinue arrived in front of Queen Victoria and the ambassador proceeded to read the letter from the Qing Court in Chinese. After he concluded, Halliday Macartney read a translation of the message aloud in English. Guo then presented the letter to the queen and she passed it to Lord Derby.

Through these seemingly minor gestures of protocol, the Qing monarch was brought down from his high pinnacle of superiority as imagined by the British and transformed into one among other Oriental rulers who paid homage to the Queen Empress Victoria, the ruler of the greatest empire the world had ever seen. Over the course of the next two years, the Qing government established legations in Paris, Berlin, Spain, Washington, Tokyo, and St. Petersburg. By the 1870s and 1880s, some Qing officials, intellectuals, and merchants, drawing on recent translations of international law and practices within the treaty ports, began to push for institutional reform that would eliminate the portions of the treaties that were increasingly understood as infringements on "national sovereignty." [36] It would seem that China had at last been made perfectly equal.

Pedagogy and Westernization

The transformation of Qing external relations that the audience with Queen Victoria represented was but one of the changes that the dynasty reluctantly acceded to. On other fronts, English lessons seemed to have another kind of effect: they energized elements within the Qing elite to a clear-eyed assessment of the enormous military technology gap that had opened between China and Great Britain. Prominent officials such as Zeng Guofan, Li Hongzhang, and Zuo Zongtang (each of whom had played a significant role in putting down rebellions against the Qing), midlevel officials in coastal provinces, and observers in treaty ports concluded that the European challenge was unprecedented in China's history. They argued that it was essential for central government officials to learn the intricacies of international law and diplomatic practices and for the Qing to shift resources to the acquisition of the powerful weapons with which European powers had humiliated the dynasty (Kuo 1978: 496–497; Hao and Wang 1980: 156–172).

After Zeng Guofan's death in 1872, Li Hongzhang and a small group of

36. Specific treaty provisions targeted were those involving extraterritoriality, most-favored-nation, and tariff regulations; see Hao and Wang 1980: 194–197.

like-minded officials took the lead in efforts to renovate Qing land and sea forces through the transfer of technology and the introduction of technical education. The "self-strengthening" group pursued these goals in the face of frequent opposition from other powerful figures among the Qing elites (Kuo 1978: 529–531; Hao and Wang 1980: 172–188)[37] and without a coordinated centralized plan or sufficient resources to carry out their projects. Yet, much was accomplished.

Initially, drawing on the revenues of the Imperial Maritime Customs under Robert Hart's management (Kuo 1978: 514), the self-strengtheners were able to pursue a number of courses. They bought arms from European weapons dealers; built arsenals, with the help of Western advisors, at Tianjin, Shanghai (the Jiangnan Arsenal), Nanjing, and Fuzhou to manufacture ships and guns; set up army and navy training schools and brought in foreign experts as instructors; and sent missions abroad for training in science, mathematics, and engineering (J. Rawlinson 1967; Biggerstaff 1961; Kuo 1978: 520–525, 537–542; Hao and Wang 1980: 170; K. Liu and Smith 1980: 248–250, 257–258, 266–268). At the Fuzhou and Jiangnan arsenals, translation bureaus, not unlike the Beijing Tongwen guan directed by W. A. P. Martin, were created and eventually expanded into engineering schools (Kuo 1978: 525–529, 531–537). These institutions benefited, in turn, from contact and cooperation with secular education projects undertaken by Euroamerican missionaries (Cohen 1978: 576–580).

The first major test of these efforts occurred during the Sino-French War of 1884–1885, with mixed results. Although Qing land forces held their own along the Vietnam border and on Taiwan, the French navy destroyed the Fuzhou shipyard (J. Rawlinson 1967:109–128). Thereafter, the Qing regime took a more active part in directing technological development. A Naval Department was created and funds raised through foreign loans. Pressure was put on provincial authorities to remit taxes (K. Liu and Smith 1980: 254–255). But fiscal shortages continued to affect both education and technology transfer, and opposition within the government slowed or undermined programs. Moreover, the self-strengtheners found it difficult to create an institutional structure that would best use and reward those trained in new skills. Yet, in spite of these difficulties, foreign intelligence gatherers found much to praise

---

37. These conflicts also involved factional struggles around the Qing throne and the efforts by Empress Dowager Cixi to ensure that no one group became strong enough to challenge her position; see, for example, Kuo 1978, 505–506, on Prince Gong.

in the Qing effort. On the eve of the Sino-Japanese War, some of these experts thought that China was ahead of Japan and even predicted a victory for the former if the two ever went to war.[38] From this perspective, it would not be difficult to conclude that English lessons had taught the Qing not only the proper sort of intercourse with powerful Euroamerican nation-states, but how to transform itself into a power like them. More important, perhaps, the British insistence that Qing interests and their own were fundamentally the same and that Qing Westernization would be mutually beneficial seems to have created the kind of ally a succession of British diplomats had hoped for. Yet, as much as these developments seemed to point to the success of the soft side of British pedagogy, the deterritorializing effects of global forces were undermining these apparent gains.

38. See K. Liu and Smith 1980: 245, 268–269 and the sources they cite, which include assessments by U.S. and British military observers.

CHAPTER 6

The Qing Empire in the Era of

European Global Hegemony

QING "SELF-STRENGTHENING" EFFORTS were not wholly a result of British tutorials; they were also part of an effort to address the many challenges the dynasty now faced as a result of internal changes within the empire. The Manchus had come to power in China in 1644 as a result of civil war and the collapse of Ming authority. Over the next half century, the Manchu elite worked to restore order, consolidate their own position, and create a political structure that would allow them, as alien conquerors, to remain in power. Early Manchu emperors were especially adept at accomplishing these tasks, and by the early eighteenth century had consolidated Qing authority over the territories that made up the Ming Empire. But China proper was not the only arena of Manchu ambitions. From the late seventeenth century forward, the Qing emperors strove to establish themselves as overlords of all of eastern Asia. By the middle of the eighteenth century, the Manchus dominated Mongolia and much of central Asia and had established themselves as the sole patron of the dominant sect of Buddhism in Tibet (the dGe-lugs-pa, headed by the Dalai and Panchen Lamas). The result was the largest, wealthiest, and most populous empire ever created on the eastern Eurasian land mass. Qing leaders had accomplished this enormous task by combining conquest with adept coalition politics among rulers who acknowledged their supremacy both inside China proper and on the new frontiers of empire.[1]

By the beginning of the nineteenth century, however, the empire and its coalitions showed signs of stress. Unprecedented population growth in China placed significant pressure on the economic and political system, while fiscal crises and poor administration creating unrest among the subjugated populations of Central Asia suggested that Qing power was in decline. Rebellion within China brought Qing weakness into sharp focus. The mid-nineteenth-century Taiping Rebellion and outbreaks of armed resistance in many parts of Central Asia demonstrated that Manchu military might had waned. Ultimately, the Taiping was suppressed by Chinese armies raised and trained by Chinese officials of the Qing Dynasty, and a new political accommodation was reached between the Manchu ruling house and the Han Chinese majority. Chinese officialdom backed the restoration of the dynasty's authority; in return, Chinese officials at many levels of the governmental hierarchy would dominate the fiscal life of the state. Yet, even in this position of weakness, the dynasty did not abandon its commitment to the larger empire. In the 1870s, Qing forces retook Central Asia and solidified what would become, in the age of European global hegemony, the borders of the Chinese nation-state.

It is within this dynamic of shifting relations of power affecting China and Central Asia that the global challenges the Qing imperium faced should be placed. Those challenges were, in turn, exacerbated by a historically unprecedented overseas expansion of continental European nations and the United States, the results of which were the colonization of almost all of Africa, the Pacific, and much of Asia. Often referred to as the "new imperialism," the effects of this expansion on China were profound. Not only was Great Britain's position as the primary articulater of Euroamerican interest in China challenged by these developments, but the demands that were made on the Qing Court changed as well. There was less interest on the part of the Western powers in the kind of imperial pedagogy that had been involved with treaties of friendship and commerce. Instead, the new imperialists wanted exclusive concessions involving spheres of influence, territory, railroads, and finance and a host of special privileges. English diplomats and merchants saw these developments as a threat to Britain's unique position in China and hegemony over the region. And although they were concerned about rivals such as France

1. On Qing rulership in the eighteenth century, see Hevia 1995b: 29–56; Crossley 1999; Elliott 2001; Millward 1998; E. Rawski 1998; Zito 1997.

and Germany, it was Russia that appeared to pose the greatest threat to British interests throughout Asia.

This chapter addresses some of the issues involved with the new imperialism and its impact on the Qing Empire. Rather than attempting a comprehensive analysis, my purpose here is to expand on themes already encountered in earlier parts of this study. These include the shifting ground of Qing relations with other powers, Euroamerican understandings of the nature and condition of Chinese sovereignty and the Chinese people, and the changing British assessment of the Russian threat to their empire. In each of these domains, I explore the relations among developments within China, the Euroamerican production of knowledge about China, and the fantasies that were generated as the two converged and diverged. The following sections take up these issues in turn, beginning with a discussion of economic change in Europe and its global implications.

The New Imperialism, Colonial Expansion, and Qing China

In the decades leading up to the beginning of the First World War in 1914, sovereignty over approximately one-fourth of the earth's surface was redistributed, with Great Britain increasing its colonial territories by around 4 million square miles and France by some 3.5 million. In addition, new colonial powers appeared on the scene. Germany acquired over 1 million square miles of territory, Italy and Belgium just under 1 million each, and the United States and Japan around 100,000 square miles each (Hobsbawm 1989: 59).

This new imperialism fundamentally reorganized global relations of power and authority in novel and far-reaching ways, generated in large measure by the ruling ideologies of the imperial powers. These included the social Darwinist or Spencerian notion of the survival of the fittest. Fitness was linked to imperial expansion in a simple formula: only those peoples capable of conquering others would continue to exist; those unable to meet the stringent demands of the modern world would eventually disappear. As Lord Salisbury, the British prime minister, put it in 1898, the world had become divided between "living" and "dying" powers.[2] Supporting this harsh vision of history were new theories of racial difference, backed up by science, that readily supported assertions of Euroamerican racial superiority and white

---

2. Cited in Kennedy 1987: 195. See Langer's ([1935] 1965: 85–96) still useful discussion on the transposition of biology to politics.

supremacy (Gould 1981). A third pillar of this ideological structure was the idea that scientific technology was the highest achievement of civilization (Adas 1989: 199–236, 292–342). The products of all human civilizations were now to be measured by the standard of technological complexity, and graded accordingly.

The privileging of science and technological advance was connected, in turn, to the transformations under way in Europe's national economies—the movement from commercial-agricultural economies to ones based on mass production, capital-intensive heavy industry, and urbanization. Yet these developments, as Eric Hobsbawm has emphasized, were fraught with contradictions. For one thing, the period between 1860 and 1900 was one of general economic recession punctuated by periodic booms. In this unstable atmosphere, the leadership of most nations in Europe abandoned the anarchy of free trade liberalism and threw up protectionist barriers around their industrialized sectors. Yet, it was also a period of rapid economic growth fueled by phenomenal technological change that saw, by the first decade of the twentieth century, British industrial power eclipsed by that of the United States and Germany. In addition, the industrial growth of smaller powers throughout Europe suggested that Britain's dominant economic position would be challenged on many fronts, even while Britain retained and indeed expanded its hold over global finances, insurance, and shipping. London remained the undisputed center of the global financial system (Kennedy 1987: 194–249; Hobsbawm 1989: 34–66).

How, then, did imperial adventure and colonial forms of power fit into this contradictory mix of rapid technological advance and economic instability? There are at least four elements in the pattern of economic change that connect it to imperial expansion. The first of these, and perhaps the most obvious, was the emergence of a global economy in the nineteenth century, whose deterritorializing and reterritorializing mechanisms integrated ever more remote areas of the world into its forms of practice. These processes were accompanied by the thickening and extension of communication networks along which capital, goods, and people moved between more and less developed areas of the world.

At the same time, expansion was not a unified, single-stranded process. Rather, it was one driven by the rivalries and contradictions *within* national formations and *among* European powers for resources and markets outside of Europe. The result was colonization, an ancillary apparatus of expansion whose agents were both democratic and authoritarian nation-states. Regardless of their political structure, states became colonial empires and hereditary rulers became emperors as they strove to protect the industrial enterprises and businesses based in their territories, to open markets overseas for their nation's products, to provide their entrepreneurs with privileged access to industrial raw materials (unexploited quantities of which could be found outside of Europe and North America), and to open new lands for the settlement of growing populations.

The second key development, and one clearly related to the first, involved the synergistic relationship that emerged among technological change, corporate capitalism, and expansive European nation-states. This relationship was probably best exemplified in the communication, transportation, and armaments race among the European powers. Critical here was the appearance of what William McNeill (1982: 262–306; Headrick 1981) has identified as the first modern military-industrial complexes, the close interaction between private armaments producers and national governments. In much of industrialized Europe, these changes meant a sometimes difficult transition to professional armies and a greatly expanded arms procurement industry that demanded levels of public expenditure for military "necessities" unheard of in the past. These developments also led to a vast expansion in the powers of states, particularly in their capacities to mobilize and command their resources and populations.

The third development was related to the means or methods necessary for ensuring the security of the commercial, governmental, and military institutions that were being established to support and realize empire around the globe. In the case of Great Britain, for example, strategic thinking involved protecting existing possessions from incursions of other imperial powers as well as expanding into new territories to create buffers. This emphasis accounts for the various methods the British used to play the Great Game with Russia, which by its very nature was defensive, that is, protecting the frontiers of India and the transportation lines between India and the British Isles. Once the Suez Canal opened in the 1860s, such defensive-mindedness led to the creation of British spheres of influence around the canal and the acquisition of strategic spots from Gibraltar to Egypt and beyond. The predominance of steam power by the 1880s, moreover, required supplies of coal and coaling stations along transport lines. These sites too needed to be controlled and protected.

Because of the fact that it was enmeshed in this seaborne network of communication and transportation, China could not help but be affected by these global developments. And there were good reasons for China's involvement, at least from the point of view of competitive Euroamerican nation-states. With its enormous population of purportedly industrious and acquisitive people, China was imagined by some as the ultimate solution to the problems of the business cycle. Technological change and industrial growth across Euroamerica had led to production gluts and shrinking profits. If all of China could be opened to free trade, Chinese consumers might single-handedly be able to absorb the industrial world's surplus production. What more incentive did anyone need to justify and encourage an ever deeper penetration into China's interior?

As the treaty port system replicated itself along the coast of China and along inland waterways like the Yangzi River, more and more of China was linked to global commercial networks. These same networks also introduced alien political, economic, and cultural forces, ones that, wherever they touched down, had the capacity to destabilize the local scene. By the 1880s, the relatively consistent deterritorialization processes generated by British political and economic expansion between 1820 and 1860 had given way to an increasingly unstable process governed by capitalist business cycles of boom and bust and by rivalries among the European powers. These changes placed new pressures on the older agricultural-commercial and new treaty-port-based economies of China. Thus, even as China was being more firmly integrated into the British imperial marketplace, as British China policy was being tied closely to the fate of India both economically and geopolitically, counterforces—infringement by other powers on Qing territory, Anglo-Russian rivalries in Asia—were undermining British diplomatic efforts.

Just as had occurred with the first treaty settlement in 1842, the Tianjin and Beijing agreements of 1860 reterritorialized China and simultaneously opened the door to another wave of deterritorialization. The privileges that Europeans and Americans enjoyed inside treaty enclaves and at the points of contact they had with the Chinese market continued to attract free market advocates of various stripes, many of whom found extraterritoriality a convenient loophole for operations that would have been of questionable legality outside of the China scene. As before 1860, the interests of state and those of commerce did not always coincide. The Chefoo Convention negotiated by Thomas Wade and Li Hongzhang in 1876 is a case in point. Recall that this was the agreement that settled the Margary affair and sent a Qing apology mission to London. Other parts of the agreement addressed outstanding issues concerning British trade in China. Merchant firms successfully blocked ratification of the agreement on the grounds that it did not outlaw the regional tariffs on foreign goods (lijin), which most merchants thought violated existing treaties, and did not provide sufficient guarantees against future antiforeign actions on the part of Chinese officials. Nor, they argued, did the agreement provide adequate measures for furthering the commercial penetration of China (Pelcovits [1948] 1969: 125–130). Opposition did not come solely from commercial quarters, moreover. The government of British India, which had come to rely heavily on the opium trade with China to balance its own imperial books, opposed provisions to increase the opium tax. Meanwhile, the other foreign powers in China were disturbed by Wade's unilateral action in negotiating the Chefoo Convention, perhaps because he himself had opposed a similar move by the French chargé d'affaires only a few years before (Hsü 1990: 305; Cooley 1981: 72–77).

Thus, by the end of the 1870s, it seemed that the united front forged to meet Qing recalcitrance was beginning to unravel. At the same time, the competition among nation-states for markets and territory encouraged leaders to think in terms of protected or sheltered zones of economic activity. Given Western views of Qing sovereignty, the specter of partition, of the dividing up of eastern China into separate zones of foreign domination to protect hardwon treaty rights, became conceivable and feasible.

The State of Chinese Sovereignty and the Condition of China

In making China perfectly equal in 1860, the British had hoped that the Qing monarchy would abandon the silly illusion that the emperor of China was superior to other monarchs in the world. The kowtow signified the crux of the problem, but now that it had been forcefully banished from interactions between the Qing Empire and Euroamerican nation-states, any claims to superiority ought to have followed it into oblivion. But that was not quite what happened after the establishment of the legations in Beijing. For one thing, the 1873 audience proved to be of little consequence. In 1875, the Tongzhi emperor died and was succeeded by the child emperor Guangxu. Once again, there was no sovereign to address and, thus, no opportunity to fully realize routine state-to-state relations.

Other members of the diplomatic corps agreed that although the 1873 audience was welcome, its import and effects were ambiguous. Recall that it had taken place in the Ziguang ge, a building that astute sinologues had identified as the place where earlier Qing emperors had received tribute envoys from vassal states. If audiences were to be effective, most observers argued, the site where they took place ought to clearly separate the past from the present. Even the many efforts of the Guangxu emperor to accede to European demands, which included a new audience venue (the Wenhua Hall, inside the east gate of the Forbidden City) and the emperor standing to receive communications from envoys in his own hands, was ultimately not the perfect expression of equality that many of the ministers sought (Rockhill [1905] 1971: 45–48; Ball 1893: 46–47). Until they could be received in one of the central audience halls of the Forbidden City in a European-style audience, diplomatic observers in Beijing understood any other audience form to indicate a residual, unresolved sign of the Chinese emperor's claim to universal dominion. To put this another way, any gesture on the part of the Qing that smacked of a sense of superiority and antiforeignism or that appeared to preserve a domain of specifically Manchu-Chinese sovereignty untouched by the global imperial order was treated with derision by European diplomats.

The inconclusive outcomes of the continuing struggle over competing notions of sovereignty were reflected in other forms of disorder that now beset the Qing realm. To be sure, part of the problem was directly connected to the precarious position of Qing emperorship in the wake of the Taiping uprising. Not only had power become more diffuse and decentralized, but Qing authority over local officials had been seriously eroded. The post-Taiping political scene had witnessed a steady devolution of power from the center to the province level. As the internal tariffs (lijin) on domestic and foreign goods suggested, localities levied taxes over which the central government had little or no control. Prominent governors-general such as Zhang Zhidong, Liu Kunyi, and Li Hongzhang, though openly loyal to the Court, built regional power bases that stood as challenges to central authority.[3]

Such decentralizing tendencies were also evident among the foreign powers. The year after Thomas Wade retired to his chair at Cambridge, British domination over Euroamerican political activities in China came to an abrupt end. In 1884, France went to war unilaterally with the Qing Empire, not to defend or extend treaty privileges, but to seize territory on the southern bor-

3. The extent to which centrifugal forces were undermining the loyalty of high officials and creating quasi-independent bases of power has been much disputed by historians. See, for example, the discussion in Wakeman 1975: 163–168, 263; K. Liu 1978: 477–482.

ders of the Qing realm. In spite of some successes on the battlefield, the Qing were effectively forced to accept French colonization of Vietnam. More important, perhaps, the crisis with France led to the fall of Prince Gong and the cashiering or demotion of the grand councillors and the chief officers of the Zongli yamen linked to the prince (Eastman 1967). For good or ill, the leadership that had worked with Wade during the quarter-century after the second Opium War was gone. A decade later, China was at war with Japan. Although Qing forces were better equipped and trained than in the past, the results were even more devastating. Japan took Taiwan and Korea became "independent" and thus open to Japanese colonization. The clear weakness of the Qing military and the apparent failure of many efforts on the part of the Manchu and Chinese leadership to Westernize its military forces opened the door to a new chapter of aggressive military-political penetration by the powers.

Quite literally on the verge of partition, the Qing were forced to grant long-term leases to Great Britain and Germany in Shandong province, to Russia on the Liaodong peninsula, and to France on the Fujian coast. The powers, it would seem, were willing to work unilaterally to gain territorial footholds. But, perhaps more important, the British objective of assimilating the Qing as allies for their own geopolitical concerns in Asia lay in disarray. Indeed, after 1895, the British acted like any other predator, and thoughts of a Qing-British partnership were eclipsed by great power politics. China was now the sick man of Asia (fig. 11), and "informed" opinion wondered what would stand in the way of the Russian tsar's ascending the throne in Beijing and mobilizing the largest military force the world had ever seen (e.g., Krausse [1899] 1973; Colquhoun 1900).

The combination of the decay of Qing authority within China and the aggressive actions of the Western powers produced a crisis of unique proportions. It was further exacerbated by the ambitious reterritorialization efforts of the British that came in the wake of the second Opium War. The extension of treaty ports deep into China's interior, each one of which carried extraterritorial privileges for foreigners, placed larger and larger numbers of Western merchants, missionaries, and consuls in the midst of populations still grappling with the aftereffects of the Taiping Rebellion, the most costly domestic war, in both human and material terms, in Chinese history. As before, existing networks of relations were disrupted and new ones laid down. Conflict was quite literally impossible to avoid: as Westerners clamored for their treaty rights and privileges, local Chinese were both resentful and suspicious of the intentions of their uninvited guests.

11. "How the Russian Bear Threatens China." *Leslie's Weekly*, 6 April 1901.

From the beginning of the 1880s forward, anti-Westernism[4] and opposition to Christian proselytizing simmered, sometimes erupting into violence, as in the Tianjin Massacre of French missionaries (1870), which invariably led to diplomatic confrontations in Beijing (*China No. 3* 1891 [CC91]; *China No. 1* 1892 [CC92], especially the formal protests of the ministers, 86–92). At the same time, this accumulation of disasters appeared to observers to have little impact on the thinking and behavior of China's rulers. Following the Sino-Japanese War, the Great Gamesman Valentine Chirol was taken aback that "nowhere in Peking could the faintest indication be detected of a desire to apply, or even a capacity to understand, the lessons of the recent war." He concluded that "a more hopeless spectacle of fatuous imbecility, made up of equal parts of arrogance and helplessness," was "almost impossible to conceive"

4. I use this term rather than antiforeignism or xenophobia because resentment was quite clearly directed at Euroamericans, not others, and was based on clearly demonstrable causes.

(1896: 9). The sense that the dynasty was perhaps beyond redemption gained additional validity when, in 1898, the young Guangxu emperor's efforts at reform were thwarted by a palace coup and the aged dowager empress Cixi emerged, yet again, as the power behind the throne.

At the end of the nineteenth century, to many outside observers the situation in China seemed to have changed little since 1860. The dynasty still appeared to be living in the "fantasy world" Thomas Wade had identified. Shadow still appeared more important than substance, attitudes of superiority and aloofness were more common than frank awareness that the Court and Qing officialdom had nothing to feel superior about. Neither military defeats, loss of sovereignty, nor Russian encroachment seemed to spur the Qing to take the steps necessary to ensure their own survival. With the mass of evidence now readily at hand in Beijing, London, Paris, and other capitals, interested observers waited for some final dose of reality to bring the entire edifice down. The Qing was a "degenerate empire," as Eliza Skidmore (1900: 1–12) put it, where everything, if not dead, was at least comatose. The dragon, as many were wont to say, was asleep, slumbering away seemingly impervious to the wake-up call made daily by the Western powers.

Qing Central Asia

This bleak assessment of the Qing requires qualification, however.[5] As we have seen, foreign evaluations were primarily conditioned by events in and around the eastern seaboard of the empire. In the second half of the nineteenth century, as well as later, judgments were based on calculations of the ability of China's leaders to measure up to standards imposed by the Western powers, and they continue to come down to us in those terms, particularly among postimperial observers often obsessed with "modernization." Yet, it was also the case that none of the imperial formations with which the Qing had contact were — even if we could decide on a definition of the term — wholly modern. The gap between China and the West tended, on the whole, to lie in the realm of commercial and military technologies, not necessarily in methods of organizing and ruling empires. Nowhere were the British and Manchus closer in their thinking or methods than in relation to Central Asia. It is perhaps worth dwelling on this proximity for a moment, because it will

5. This section relies heavily on the works of Joseph Fletcher (1978 a, 1978b, 1978c) and James Millward (1998).

help to clarify the complex political dynamic that allowed the Qing to appear to some observers to be adapting to change, and to others as hopelessly out of step with contemporary trends.

From the late seventeenth century forward, the Qing geopolitical objective in Central Asia was to ensure that no leaders or groups would arise capable of forming military coalitions to overwhelm Manchu hegemony in the region. The primary concern for the Qing leadership was Mongol khanates, the leaders of whom claimed descent from Genghis Khan and historically close ties with the Dalai and Panchen Lamas of the dGe-lugs-pa sect of Tibetan Buddhism. They could thus serve as a rallying point for Mongol unification. In addition to this Mongol-Tibetan alignment, there were other khanates scattered along the Silk Road and in Central Asia that drew authority not only from purported genealogical links to Genghis Khan and his descendants, but from their links to pious Islamic saints. Unlike the Mongol khanates, the Muslim groups were not conceived by the Qing as a direct threat to their rulership over their empire. Instead, the problem was the possibility of the creation of independent kingdoms on the western edges of the imperium, thus politically fragmenting regions that had been hard-won in a succession of military campaigns launched by the Kangxi, Yongzheng, and Qianlong emperors in the 1670s and 1750s (Perdue 1996; Millward 1998: 27–32; Barfield 1989: 277–294).

Yet the Qing elite were also aware that they could not deal with the western territories as if they were China proper, where they retained the Ming bureaucratic structure while monitoring it through a secret palace memorial system and, eventually, a parallel oversight structure termed the Grand Council. To manage Central Asia, the Qing created a new arm of governance, the Lifan yuan (Ministry of Outer Dependencies). Originally established in 1638 to deal with eastern Mongol khans who had submitted to the Qing, the ministry eventually had responsibility for all Central Asian affairs and Russia (Mancall 1971). It had trained linguists and created its own imperial archive of critical information on the peoples of the areas it oversaw (Chia 1992). This information system involved dictionaries and grammars, and research was conducted into history, religion (particularly Tibetan Buddhism), geography, and the genealogies of important personages in Central Asia.

Not unlike the British in India, the Qing used a number of political, economic, and cultural techniques designed to prevent the emergence of a challenge to their rulership. These included granting noble titles and perquisites to loyal khans (i.e., indirect rule), creating buffer states, patronizing religious organizations, and incorporating the military units of loyal khans into their own army. In Mongolia, the Manchus organized seven large khanates and several smaller ones (Fletcher 1978a: 48–58). Like Indian reservations in the United States, each Mongol group was confined to its designated pasture land, while the khans themselves had individual relations with the Manchu ruling house, whose leader, the emperor, they acknowledged as kaghan or great khan. This divide-and-rule strategy was complemented by Qing patronage of the dGe-lugs-pa sect and of monastic communities in the khanates. Throughout the nineteenth century the number of Mongols taking vows rose to between 40 and 60 percent of the adult male population. With the bulk of the male population in monasteries and Mongolia's economy dominated by Chinese merchants, Mongol threats to the Qing evaporated.

This was less the case, however, further to the west. After conquering areas beyond Gansu province and establishing a protectorate in Tibet at the end of the eighteenth century, the Qing set up a form of indirect rule in a vast area renamed Xinjiang or New Dominions, which was managed partly by the viceroy of Shaanxi-Gansu and partly by military governors at specific cities. Xinjiang comprised two large basins surrounded and divided by high mountain ranges, the Altai on the north, the Tianshan in the center, and the Kunlun to the south. The northern basin, known as Zungaria, opened on the west to the steppe-lands of south central Russia. These vast grasslands extended into Mongolia, providing grazing lands for nomadic sheep herders and for horse cavalry armies like those of the Mongols. Nestled in the western edge of the Altai range was the Yili River and the city of Kulja or Yili, south of which the Muzart Pass provided an entry point into the second basin, the Tarim. Known in Turkic as Altishahr, this was the land of the fabled Silk Road, two legs of which skirted the basin itself, the Taklamakan Desert, which was dotted by the oasis cities of Hami, Turfan, Kucha, and Aksu on the north, and on the south, Dunhuang, Yarkand, and Khotan. Yarkand and Khotan were, in turn, connected commercially, via passes in the Karakorum range, to Ladakh and the Indus River Basin, the region of British India referred to as the Northwest Frontier and the Punjab, including Kashmir and Ladakh. Anchoring the western edge of Altishahr, where the two legs of the Silk Road diverged, was the commercial center of Kashgar, which was connected by passes through the Pamir Mountains to the Ferghana valley and the caravan cities of Kokand, Tashkent, Samarkand, and Bukhara further to the west (Fletcher 1978a: 58–59).

From a geopolitical perspective, of particular interest in this topography are the river valleys and mountain passes that linked Qing Central Asia to the Russian and British Empires: the Yili region in the north, the Silk Road passes through the Pamirs, and the Karakorum Pass. This was the landscape of the Great Game in Central Asia, a terrain that provided passageways for commercial and political intercourse and for fantasies about protecting and expanding empires through exploitation of the Central Asian trade routes. The mountains themselves provided superior cover for rebel groups, warlords, and bandit gangs who preyed on the caravan trade. For much of the two centuries preceding the establishment of the Qing in 1644, empires and smaller kingdoms rose and fell, with pastoral nomads of the steppe grasslands or hill peoples vying for dominion with agricultural-commercial-based authorities in river valleys (Lattimore 1940; Barfield 1989). Although Islam and Tibetan Buddhism did little to alter the overall cyclical pattern of political power shifts, they did introduce new elements to the mix, ones that changed the ways in which power and authority could be constituted. Whether they were khans, amirs, or cakravartin kings, rulers had a duty and an obligation to protect religious communities, create the conditions for the extension of the teachings of these communities, foster the study and reproduction of canonical texts, and protect and patronize sacred sites (e.g., mountains and shrines).

In the Islamic communities of Altishahr, other dynamics were also at work. In addition to the religious establishments of mosques and schools, Sufi brotherhoods (tarikats) and saintly families (khojas) provided leadership in communities and oversaw the protection of sacred sites, including the tombs of holy men. The tarikats and khojas could also become focal points for anti-Qing movements in Xinjiang. A case in point was a Naqshbandī tarikat known as the Makhdūmzādas, the Āfāqī branch of which, under Burhān ad-Dīn, went into exile in Kokand when the Qing conquered western Altishahr in the eighteenth century. From roughly 1820 to 1870, several generations of Burhān ad-Dīn's descendents, alone or in concert with other forces, launched jihads against the Qing to reclaim the region. According to some sources, the Qing reimbursed Kokand annually to keep the Makhdūmzādas in check. Seeking special trading privileges at Kashgar, the Kokandi seem to have held up their end of the bargain only when it suited their immediate purposes (Fletcher 1978a: 74–76, 87–90, 1978b: 360–375, 385–395; Millward 1998: 25–36). At one point the Qing attempted to appease Kokand by acceding to an agreement, the commercial provisions of which, as Joseph Fletcher (1978b: 375–385) pointed out, included many of the elements present in China's first "unequal" treaty with Great Britain in 1842. Nevertheless, in spite of these concessions, neither the Āfāqī jihad nor Kokandi ambitions disappeared, and the incursions into Altishahr continued into the 1870s. The situation might have continued to oscillate between greater and lesser Qing commitment of resources in the region if not for two developments.

The first of these involved the rebellions in eastern China, the Taiping and the Nian, that began in the 1850s (Kuhn 1978; K. Liu 1978). It took the dynasty well over a decade to restore order, at an enormous cost of human life and treasure. As a result, there were limited resources available to maintain Qing control of other parts of the empire or, as was the case in Xinjiang, meet the challenge of the ongoing Āfāqī jihad. Moreover, other groups unhappy with Manchu-Chinese rule rose in rebellion. In Yunnan and in the Shaanxi-Gansu regions, these included Chinese Muslims with long-standing grievances against the Qing (K. Liu and Smith 1980: 212–221). By the 1860s, the Qing presence in all of these areas had been seriously undermined and would require a major effort to restore the dynasty's control.

The second element that altered the political dynamic of the region was the growing British and Russian presence in the areas bordering Xinjiang and the resulting decline in the power of Central Asian khanates. As early as the first Opium War, rumors had circulated in Beijing that the British might be courting the Āfāqī (Fletcher 1978b: 387). Whether or not this was true, the British had been sending fact-finding expeditions into the region for some time, a process that accelerated after the Sikh Wars in the 1840s and the British occupation of the Punjab.[6] These missions not only explored various routes for opening up British trade with Xinjiang, but found a well-established and growing Russian presence in the region.

Russian interest in Central Asia and Qing Xinjiang was part of the general expansion across Asia of the tsarist empire that began in the mid-sixteenth century (Clubb 1971: 9–29). Trade and border agreements had been made with the Qing in the seventeenth century and the Russians had been given permission to set up an ecclesiastical mission at Beijing, which continued to function well into the nineteenth century (Fletcher 1978c: 318–319, 324). Unlike their relations with European powers, the Qing organized those with Russia through the Lifan yuan, the same unit that managed Central Asian affairs. After the first Opium War, the Russian government sought additional trade

6. See Hopkirk 1992, who discusses many of the missions. The British also trained Indians, known as the "pundits," to carry out such surveys; see 329–332.

concessions. The result was the 1851 Treaty of Kulja, which opened Yili and Targabatai in Mongolia to trade and placed a Russian consul in Yili. During the second Opium War, the Russian representatives in Beijing, ostensibly acting as mediators in the dispute with Great Britain and France, made even more spectacular gains. The 1860 Treaty of Beijing opened the entire northern and western frontier of the Qing Empire to Russian commercial and political influence. Ultimately, the Qing ceded territories to the north of the Amur and east of the Ussuri Rivers in Manchuria, the latter of which provided a warm water port on the Pacific at Vladivostok, a key Russian goal (Fletcher 1978c: 329–350).

In spite of these British and Russian advances on the borders of their empire, or perhaps because of them, the Qing, with substantial backing from Han elite, remained firmly committed to retaining Xinjiang. By the late 1860s, however, this was no mean task. The Āfāqī jihad continued under Buzurg Khan and one of his generals, Ya'qūb Beg. In a series of campaigns beginning in 1867, Ya'qūb conquered much of Altishahr, usurped the khan's position, and established his own khanate. With Xinjiang no longer in Qing hands, the Russians moved quickly to occupy Kulja on the pretense that they were protecting their borders against Muslim raids (K. Liu and Smith 1980: 221–225). As a hedge against further Russian advances, the British government in India opened discussions with Ya'qūb. By 1872, the new khan had recognition and commercial treaties with both the tsarist and British Empires (Hsü 1990: 318–319). With the Qing still reeling from the effects of the Taiping Rebellion and the ongoing Nian Rebellion in east central China, the British and Russians appear to have decided that the Qing presence in Central Asia was at an end.

Yet elements within the Qing leadership were not willing to lose Xinjiang. The suppression of Muslim rebellions in Gansu and the reconquest of Xinjiang would, however, take a decade (1867–1877), and involve foreign loans to finance the effort, a major foreign policy debate, and the reconceptualization of Qing Central Asia. The Court appointed Zuo Zongtang, a highly decorated veteran of the Taiping wars, as the viceroy of Shaanxi and Gansu, with instructions to restore order in the two provinces. In 1868, Zuo launched a systematic five-year campaign that culminated in the reduction, with the use of Krupp field guns, of the last Muslim stronghold at Suzhou (K. Liu and Smith 1980: 225–235). He then turned his attention to Xinjiang.

Before he could begin his campaign, however, Japanese forces occupied Taiwan, precipitating a policy debate over where military resources should be directed: to coastal defenses to deal with the multinational maritime threat, or to the reconquest of Central Asia? Each side in the debate presented cogent and well-reasoned arguments. The advocates of maritime defense, led by Li Hongzhang, organized their views around four key points: the proximity and hence vulnerability of Beijing to the coast, the cost and uncertainty of victory in Xinjiang, the economic unproductivity of the western regions, and the future cost of retaining Xinjiang against hostile neighbors to the west and south (Russia and Great Britain). They also argued that a focus on maritime defense would not be a renunciation of lands conquered by the great emperors of the Qing, but simply a prudent move under the circumstances. Advocates of frontier defense were led by Wenxiang, the head of the Zongli yamen, and Zuo Zongtang. They countered that not only was the northwest frontier critical to the defense of Beijing, but the greater immediate foreign threat to the dynasty came not from an invasion of a European power on the east coast but from Russian expansion on the northern and western frontiers. Arguing much like their British tutors, they differentiated Russia from other Western powers on other grounds as well: that the ambitions of the latter in Asia were primarily commercial, whereas Russia's, especially after the treaty settlement of 1860, were territorial in nature (Hsü 1965b, 1990: 319–321). In addition, although not fully articulated in the debate, the frontier defense group (and perhaps even some of the others) reflected an interest in Xinjiang that, as James Millward (1998) has argued, indicated a subtle shift in perception regarding the western regions of the empire. Until the middle of the nineteenth century, most Han literati saw the west as a wasteland bereft of civilization, an attitude that was reinforced by the Qing use of the area as a place for exiling disgraced officials (Waley-Cohen 1991). Now, however, perhaps because of the Court's policy of encouraging Han migration westward as a way of alleviating population pressures, some Chinese officials, including Zuo, began to view Xinjiang as part of China and advocated its transformation into a province (Millward 1998: 245–251).

In the end, although the Court did not give up naval development, the arguments about Xinjiang's strategic importance and the Russian threat carried the day. A substantial portion of the funds that were used to finance the Xinjiang campaign, moreover, were acquired in a novel way, through loans from the Hong Kong and Shanghai Banking Corporation, which floated bonds in the treaty ports to raise the capital.[7] By 1877, Xinjiang was retaken and Ya'qūb

---

7. Robert Hart notes that he invested 100,000 taels in the bonds; see Fairbank, Bruner, and Matheson 1975, 1: 251–252.

Beg was dead. In 1884, at Zuo's recommendation, the Qing Court made the region into a province, with a civil administration like other provinces and a capital at Urumchi in Zungaria. There remained, however, one piece of unfinished business left from the chaos in Xinjiang: the Russians remained at Kulja.

In 1878, the Court dispatched a mission to St. Petersburg, at the head of which was Chong-hou, a Manchu with substantial administrative and diplomatic experience, including a position in the Zongli yamen. As superintendent of trade at Tianjin, he had negotiated a number of treaties with minor European powers in the early 1870s, led the apology mission to France after Catholic missionaries were killed in Tianjin, and participated in the 1873 imperial audience negotiated by Wade. His knowledge of the New Dominions and the geography of the Yili area, however, apparently was limited. In the negotiations that ensued in Russia, Chong-hou regained Kulja, but at the expense of ceding to Russia much of Yili, including the strategic Muzart Pass, and committing the Qing to a 5 million ruble indemnity. When word of the conditions of the treaty reached Beijing, there was an uproar. Matters were made worse when Chong-hou unilaterally signed the treaty and returned to China without imperial authorization. Led by Zuo Zongtang, the vast majority of Qing officialdom urged the Court to reject the treaty, even if it meant war with Russia (Hsü 1965a).

As both sides prepared for hostilities, the Court dispatched a second mission to Russia, this one led by Zeng Jice (son of the great statesman Zeng Guofan), who was then minister to Great Britain and France. Assured by the British Foreign Office of unofficial assistance, Zeng arrived in St. Petersburg determined to regain the lost territory. After six months of negotiations, the Treaty of St. Petersburg was signed in February 1881. It returned Yili to Qing control and set the Russian indemnity at 9 million rubles. For both Qing officials and foreign observers, Zeng's diplomatic coup suggested a turning point in Qing fortunes, a situation that was somewhat confirmed four years later in the war with France. In spite of the fact that the Qing lost the Fuzhou arsenal and shipyard, its forces were able to defeat the French along the Vietnamese border and hold their own against French assaults on Zhejiang and Taiwan (Hummel 1943: 48, 246, 527).

The Qing success at regaining Xinjiang, their adroit dealings with Russia on the Yili matter, and the reasonable showing of Qing forces against French aggression all suggest that the dynasty was far from moribund. Why then, we might wonder, were assessments of the Qing so harsh? Certainly, Japan's defeat of China in 1894–1895 was a major reason opinion turned against the

Qing. But those events seemed, for many observers, simply to reinforce what was already known about China's capacity to transform itself. Those evaluations were, in turn, grounded in the racial classification schemes and typologies that had come to dominate thinking about Chinese character and conditions.

China Knowledge, Racial Discourse, and Chinese Characteristics

At the end of the nineteenth century, as discussed in the previous chapter, Europeans and Americans had accumulated a mass of information about the historical and contemporary condition of China. Through many individual projects, the vast territory that constituted the Qing Empire had been opened to the scrutinizing eyes of historians, linguists and philologists, philosophers, geographers, and political economists. Out of this assemblage of data had come a new China, one built on readings of local archives and on firsthand experience in Chinese cities, towns, and villages. Yet, it would be somewhat misleading to approach this body of China knowledge as if it were produced in a circuit involving only China and the West. In the process of coming to a new understanding of China, observers ranging from missionaries such as Arthur Smith to travel writers like Eliza Skidmore drew on methods and techniques developed in other colonial settings to organize their "data" and inevitably made comparisons, usually on the basis of racial typologies, between the Chinese and other peoples of the world. As such, the new literature on China can partly be understood as an element within a broad discourse on race and civilization common in industrialized Europe and North America. This is important to bear in mind, primarily because knowledge about Chinese people, particularly as it related to what were identified as common and uniform characteristics of the race, had practical effects, ones that determined, in a number of instances, Euroamerican reactions to the events of 1900, decisions about how the Chinese should be punished for crimes against civilization, and ultimately the shape of the final settlement after the Boxer Uprising.

For this reason, it is worth reviewing the Euroamerican notion of race that circulated inside and outside of China at this time. The term itself has a long and complex lineage in the West, an extensive discussion of which is beyond the scope of this study. Of greatest significance here, however, is the transformation the concept of race underwent in the second half of the nineteenth century. Until around 1860, race had been used for some time as a designation for a population understood to be of common descent or origin. In this form, race was often employed in the retrospective reconstruction of the history of a particular nation. At the same time, the distinctive features or characteristics of races—this is, how to account for different physical features of various kinds—were usually explained as a result of variations in climate or environment.

This definition of race was displaced in the latter part of the nineteenth century. As the result of the growth of the natural sciences and their broad diffusion through Western societies, race came to designate more fixed biological characteristics, ones that were measurable and common to an entire population understood to be part of a particular, rigidly bounded group defined in quasi-biological terms. As Robert Miles has explained in his study of the race concept, "Science purported to demonstrate that the biological characteristics of each 'race' determined a range of psychological and social capacities of each group, by which they could be ranked" (1989: 31–32; Stocking 1968). Thus, race was not simply a descriptive term. It also was a way of organizing and evaluating and ultimately was a guide for acting on whole populations of the world. When race was welded to European expansion, the concept provided both a rationale or explanation for why white men ruled over Africans, Indians, and Asians (and not the reverse) and a justification for that rule. To put this another way, the science of race provided a framework in which white supremacy was naturalized and normalized.

The consequences of these developments remain of profound importance today and continue to influence global relations among peoples. This is in large part because European expansion was in most respects catastrophic for the non-European peoples subjugated by Euroamerican colonial powers. The people of China, particularly those along the eastern seaboard, were no exception. Western privilege in treaty ports was grounded on white racial superiority, the content of which constructed the Chinese as an absolute racialized other. By the 1890s, the Chinese people, in spite of linguistic and cultural differences among themselves, were understood to be a single population with uniform characteristics.

These characteristics, moreover, were known; that is, like other areas of knowledge production about China, the Chinese themselves had been analyzed. The result was their placement into a position on a universal scale, the simplest form of which was a color hierarchy of white, yellow, and black, or Caucasian, Mongolian, and Negro. This ranking was reinforced by a number of equally simplistic schemas. So, for example, brain size might be correlated with civilization. Larger brains meant higher, more advanced civilizations;

smaller, less advanced; and still smaller, savage. Another form of ranking was recapitulation theory, the idea that the adult member of an "inferior" group was the developmental equivalent of an earlier age of a superior group. On this line of reasoning, adult Negroes were assumed to be like Caucasian children, and Mongolians were the equivalent of Caucasian adolescents (Gould 1981: 40, 114–116). These gross generalizations were then buttressed by specific features or characteristics attributed to subgroups within the major classes.

For immediate purposes, what stands out in these rankings is the consistent placement of Mongolians at an imaginary midpoint between the "most" and "least" advanced peoples. This in-betweenness may help to explain the often mixed nature of the characteristics imputed to Asiatics and, in particular, to the Chinese. From 1840 forward, the steady stream of studies of China discussed in the previous chapter included numerous analyses of Chinese character. Some of these drew on earlier conceptions, which, as Miles (1989: 33) indicates, did not so much disappear as become incorporated into the discourse on race and remain relatively stable for representations of the Chinese. But, as the evidence on character accumulated, what became clear was that the Chinese were a bundle of contradictory tendencies.[8] "Chinese character and conditions"[9] included "flexible inflexibility," ignorance and the capacity for willful misunderstanding, and honesty along with wiliness, craft, and inscrutability.[10] Most of all, the Chinese were industrious and capable of working incredibly long hours without fatigue, and yet China was stagnant, asleep, and clearly in decay. Indeed, the polar oppositions that made up Chinese character led Ronald Hall, who surveyed this literature in the 1930s, to note that a conclusive book on Chinese characteristics had yet to appear, in part because the authorities seemed to cancel one another out.[11]

8. In his study of Western imperialism, Kiernan (1986: 159–164, 170–174) noted the odd contradictions that made the Chinese the best of the nonwhite races and a "yellow peril."

9. I take the phrase from D. Z. Sheffield in a letter to Judson Smith, 27 September 1900, an understanding of which was often used by missionaries to justify their advocacy of the use of sterner measures against the Chinese; cited in M. Young 1968: 188 and Miller 1974: 274.

10. These are truisms confirmed by many observers of Chinese character. See A. Smith 1894 (from whom the quotation is derived); Ball 1893: 91–103. They were also readily available for incorporation into encyclopedic projects of the late nineteenth century; see, for example, Ridpath 1893, vol. 7.

11. Hall [1931] 1966 offers a clever juxtaposition of the contradictions in expert testimony of those who lived in China for an extensive period of time.

Be that as it may, the contradictions of behavior characteristic of the Chinese race, well documented and testified to by a wealth of first-person observations, could account for the problems in Sino-Western relations as well as for the arrested development of the Chinese. Chinese energies had either become frozen or misdirected into channels where the distinction between appearance and reality, or shadow and substance, as Thomas Wade had pointed out, became wholly confused. This particular development produced by China's isolation and stagnation had in turn led to the emergence of what many, by the end of the century, identified as the chief Chinese characteristic, that is, the Chinese notion of "face."

It is difficult to overstate this "discovery" or exaggerate its importance. Face not only played a major role in conditioning Western behavior in China in the late nineteenth and early twentieth centuries, but has continued to function as a causal factor or explanatory element for analysts and historians of China. More important for this study, the analysis of face was one of the products of the epistemological complex of the imperial archive, China branch. Face quite literally emerged as an object of investigation in the late nineteenth century and was filtered through the writing of the American missionary Arthur H. Smith. At the time one of the most widely read experts on Chinese behavior, Smith defined face as "an integral part of both Chinese theory and practice," one in which "realities" (echoing Wade) were far less import than "appearances." "If the latter can be saved," he explained, "the former may be altogether surrendered. This is the essence of the mysterious 'face' of which we are never done hearing in China. The line of Pope might be the Chinese national motto: 'Act well your part, there all the honour lies'; not, be it observed, doing well what is to be done, but consummate acting, contriving to convey the appearance of a thing or a fact, whatever the realities may be." Smith added that the Chinese were constantly caught up in the process of gaining, preserving, or losing face. In so doing they frequently had to act in an "arbitrary and violent manner," "fly into a violent rage," or otherwise use "reviling and perhaps imprecatory language." Such behavior was essential for indicating to the "spectators" of the "drama" in which the individual was "at the moment acting" that he was "aware just what ought to be done by a person in his precise situation." Not to do the proper thing would be to descend from the stage or "lose face."[12] The language here is important, for in

12. Cited in A. Brown 1904: 37–38. In Arthur Smith's 1894 text, the first chapter is aptly titled "Face." Hayford (1985: 153) notes that the book was widely read through the 1920s.

Smith's version of face, the Chinese treated all the world as a stage on which appearance was all, reality insignificant.

This "Chinese characteristic" was presented as an accurate representation of Chinese social behavior, and it has come down to us largely unquestioned in that form. For our purposes here, however, the point is not whether face was (or is) an actual organizing category in Chinese practices, but rather the central place it holds in a Western discourse on the Chinese.[13] The China lore of missionaries such as Smith constituted face as a singular attribute of the racial other, while denying that Westerners themselves were concerned with face or appearances, or that their discursive practices might actually produce face. Constructing the Chinese in these terms (making their objects of analysis, as it were, responsible for the illusions of face), Westerners could then use this knowledge to manipulate the China scene. Moreover, as we shall see below, face could be used to justify a host of violent, ritualized actions perpetrated by Euroamericans against Chinese and things Chinese on the grounds that Chinese face had to be confronted, discredited, and destroyed.

Thus, by the end of the century, there was in place a substantial "sociology" of the Chinese, enmeshed within a broader discourse of race and fleshed out with specific elements unique to the Chinese. The upshot of this growth in knowledge was a virtual collapse of the optimism about productive engagement with the Chinese that had been evident in the thinking of British ambassadors from Lord Macartney to Lord Elgin and in the pedagogical project that even a skeptic like Thomas Wade could promote in the latter part of the nineteenth century. Few Englishmen now thought that the Qing leadership could be taught to move along a constructive path of reform, one that would integrate China as a willing partner into a British-dominated Asia. Along with many other foreigners in China, the British believed that the Qing Court had not changed very much at all; it remained antiforeign, aloof, and dis-

---

Mackerras (1989: 51) notes its continued influence into the 1970s. Smith's work mimics the anthropology of the time, particularly in its widely disseminated popular form of using imputed physiological traits to establish racial hierarchies. For a discussion of Smith's influence on Lu Xun, see L. Liu 1995. On the popular anthropology of the time and its dissemination in American society, see Rydell 1984.

13. For a linguistic analysis of multiple Chinese expressions translated as "face," see Kipnis 1995.

connected from the realities of global power politics. Inside and outside of China, the Far Eastern Question remained unanswered and, given the number of new powers and interests on the scene, was more complex than forty years earlier. Moreover, no amount of Qing success or lesson learning seemed to answer those aspects of the Far Eastern Question that dealt with Russian ambitions in the region.

State of the Game

British efforts in western Asia had temporarily checked the Russian advances and prevented the latter's acquisition of a warm water port on either the Mediterranean or the Persian Gulf. Those successes had also served to redirect Russian energies eastward, toward eastern Asia, Siberia, the Caucasus, and Central Asia (fig. 11; Fletcher 1978c: 335–337). Spearheading this expansion were not only Russian armies, but railroad lines. From the 1860s forward, Russian rail construction converged on the Tashkent-Samarkand region from the Caspian Sea port of Krasnovotsk, skirting the northern border of Afghanistan, which itself contained a route through the Khyber Pass into British India and terminated, ultimately, in Andijan in Ferghana. The upshot of this advance was the Russian conquest of Kokand in 1873 and the consolidation of a tsarist empire in southwestern Asia that stretched from Azerbaijan in the west to the Pamirs and Ferghana in the east. Another Russian rail line pushed eastward through Siberia. In the mid-1890s, the construction had reached Lake Baikal and, as a result of an agreement with the Qing in 1896 to lay track across Manchuria, extended to Vladivostok by 1905 (Hopkirk 1992: 438, 502; Clubb 1971: 119, 123). It was Russian railroad construction, in particular, that concerned the British. According to one Great Gamesman, these events effectively shifted "the centre of gravity . . . of the whole political world" (Michie 1893b: 635). Brute power seemed capable of altering the rules of the Great Game, rules that had hitherto been based on stealth, intelligence, and deception.

Some even imagined that Russian rail power might counter British naval preeminence. In the vast expanses of Asia, with its numerous mountain ranges, the key factor for dominance might be railroads that made it possible to supply large military forces across inhospitable terrain. Such possibilities generated fantasies of catastrophic proportions for British interests in Asia (e.g., Krausse 1900b: 196–217). Further fueling British anxiety was the alliance between Russia and France in 1894,[14] the consequences of which, when projected eastward, conjured visions of a serious rail-driven threat to British interests in China. French occupation of much of southeast Asia opened the possibility of a rail advance into southern China as well, while Russian moves into Manchuria threatened encroachment from the north. Squeezed between these two powers was the Yangzi basin, the primary sphere of British interests in China (Langer [1935] 1965: 390–393; L. K. Young 1970: 40). Indeed, the threat appeared so obvious that even Alfred Thayer Mahan, the American naval officer best known for his writings on sea power, expressed concern over Russian railroads across Asia. In a series of articles published in 1899 and 1900, Mahan argued that Russia was a kind of natural expanding organism, the spread of which threatened to engulf Asia and could be limited only by a strong land-based counterforce to hem it in. In this case, the British Empire, stretching from Suez to eastern China, was the best power positioned to do this. But Mahan, like his British counterparts, wondered if British resources and will would be sufficient (1899–1900, 1900).

It was precisely this geopolitical imaginary that stimulated panics beyond the usual race-based Russophobia, which had long depicted the tsar as an Oriental tyrant and his Cossack armies as ignorant, brutish barbarians bent on Hun-like pillage. In contrast to this simplistic view, many of the most prominent writers on the Eastern Question in Great Britain, while acknowledging the significance of race, argued that contemporary Russian expansionism was a historical phenomenon dating back to Peter the Great. What was insidious about it was the consistency of Russian purposes over time and a perceived willingness to use any means at hand to achieve imperial ends. For writers such as Alexis Krausse ([1899] 1973) and Archibald Colquhoun (1898, 1900), it was the patience and deliberate effort of the Russians, while British policymakers twiddled their thumbs, that was cause for alarm.

At the extreme end of this line of reasoning was a nightmare vision of the demise of the British Empire, one that was centered for its plausibility on earlier British writings about China. Rediscovered in the 1890s and much cited by the "realist" Russophobes was Thomas Meadows, who had been a British consul in the middle of the century and had authored several works on China. In one of them, Meadows predicted that, left unchecked, Russian expansion into the Far East would not only place the tsar on the throne of

14. For an analysis of the machinations that resulted in the alliance, see Langer [1935] 1965.

China, but provide the man power to push all of the European powers out of Asia. Giving this argument further credence in the 1890s was the conviction that the Russians themselves were more Asian than European and thus had a natural affinity with the Chinese. It was absolutely essential, therefore, for the British to impose themselves between the two to ensure that such an unholy alliance would never materialize (see Hazeltine in Boulger 1900: 533; Colquhoun 1898: 350–351).

These views of the Russian threat were openly voiced in publications in Great Britain and India in the last two decades of the nineteenth century. Each Russian advance, each concession wrested from the Chinese, and each sign of possible Russian-French collusion to the disadvantage of the British brought a new panic (Hopkirk 1992: 418–425). Russian moves also sent some of the important authors in the genre across Eurasia by land to see for themselves. When they returned to London, they issued dire warnings about the Russian threat to British interests and to the continued existence of the Qing Empire.[15] Such alarmism can also be found among British colonial officials. Even before he became viceroy of India in 1898, Lord Curzon expressed fears about Russian expansion and rejected the view that little could be done to stem its inevitable tide.[16]

Yet, precisely what the thinking was of the political leadership in London was another matter. There were, of course, those in a succession of cabinets who feared the Russians, but by the end of the century another view came into focus. The tsar's empire was powerful, to be sure, but it was hardly an industrial and technological giant. This meant, in part, that it would not be easy for the Russians to break out of British containment along the southern rim of Asia. Moreover, the diversion of Russian energies to the east (i.e., Siberia and Manchuria) had relieved pressures at other points, particularly the northern frontier of India (L. K. Young 1970: 41–42). Why not encourage the development of a greater Russian presence in the Far East, but do so through an agreement that defined the "spheres of preponderance," a phraseology preferred by Lord Salisbury, the British prime minister? As long as no existing agreements were thereby negated and China retained its territorial integ-

---

15. Michie 1864, and his later pieces for *Blackwood's Magazine* such as 1893a and 1893b. Also see Colquhoun 1898; Chirol 1896.

16. Curzon 1967; Gillard 1977: 172. Also see the articles by Swettenham, Lady Lugard, Holdich, and Chirol in Goldman 1905, where dire pictures were drawn of Russian threats to the British Empire throughout Asia and the tropics.

rity, a clearly defined and delimited Russian presence in the Far East could benefit Great Britain (Langer [1935] 1965: 468–469). The British government floated this idea in 1898, arguing to the Russians that their contrary positions in China effectively cancelled each other out. If the two could come to an understanding, it might make each more effective in the geographical regions of China they deemed most important. The upshot was something like an understanding achieved in 1899. In an exchange of notes, Great Britain agreed not to seek a railroad concession north of the Great Wall, and Russia would do likewise in the Yangzi basin (Krausse [1899] 1973: 387–388). However, the agreement did little to silence criticism of the British government as ineffectual in the face of Russian provocations.

Among the more outspoken members of the anti-Russian front in London was Alexis Krausse, who made a career of studying the Far Eastern Question. In the 1890s, he published several works on the subject, including *China in Decay* ([1900a] 1973) and *Russia in Asia* ([1899] 1973). When the Boxer Uprising broke out, new editions of each appeared and he was also contracted to write *The Story of the Chinese Crisis* (1900b). In the last of these, Krausse pointed out that the 1899 railroad agreement had already been violated. The Russian government secretly held the majority shares in a concession issued to a Belgian consortium for a Beijing-Hankou rail line (1900b: 143).

Like the other realist Russophobes, Krausse emphasized the consistency of Russian purpose and the danger to the British Empire should the tsar come to occupy the throne of China. But he went further than others in finding the basic fault of British policy in efforts to create "buffer states" in central Asia while promoting the "open door" in China. This explicit criticism of Great Game strategy led Krausse to call for a clear-sighted understanding of the limits of British power, which meant neither withdrawal nor despondency over the inevitability of Russian success, but a practical awareness that Britain needed allies to stem the Russian advance. Half a century before George Kennan's pronouncements on the Soviet Empire, Krausse argued that containment would buy the necessary time to allow the internal contradictions of the Russian Empire to produce its own collapse ([1899] 1973: 319–322).

Krausse also went to great pains to contrast Russian policies in Asia with those of the British, finding in the former a determination and sense of purpose that the latter seemed to lack, perhaps a reference to those in Great Britain who opposed empire. Among the many contrastive examples that he took up was one involving the Russian willingness to use punitive force in Asia, often massacring thousands in the process. Rather than seeing this as Russian barbarism, however, Krausse argued that it was a calculated policy, one understood by Russians and Asians alike to be an effective tool when dealing with the Asiatic mind. As preparation for some views to be discussed in the next chapter, it is perhaps worth quoting Krausse on this issue in detail:

> It is pointed out by Russians that England's idea of punitive expeditions is quite erroneous. It is . . . a fatal error to retire in Asia. If you wish to impress an Asiatic, you must adopt the means suited to his understanding. The Asiatic is cruel, grasping and relentless. He does not understand the principle of mercy, and it is useless to exert it towards him. If it is necessary to advance into an Asiatic country to make an example of its people, it is mere folly to retire, for retirement is construed into defeat, and the withdrawal of a conquering army is regarded as an admission of its inability to remain. Yet it is this policy which has been repeatedly indulged in by England, and each repetition has injured her interests the more. ([1899] 1973: 278)

Krausse was not alone in his racism, of course, and in a manner of speaking, nothing in this passage is particularly shocking. What must be borne in mind, however, is that this statement is more than a justification for the use of violence. It is consistent with a uniform Oriental character produced by the "science" of racial classifications and new knowledge generated in colonial settings. When conflict erupted in China in 1900, it was this unitary Asian subject to whom Europeans and Americans would direct their lessons. On this occasion, however, the emphasis would not be on enticing the Chinese into becoming cooperative subjects, but rather on the hard side of imperial pedagogy. According to General Adna Chaffee, commander of the U.S. China Relief Expedition, "immediate and unfailing" punishment was what was needed to restore and maintain order in China.[17] In an age of European global hegemony and competing empires, there would be no shortage of punishments meted out to recalcitrant others.

17. Cited in Hunt 1979: 529; also see A. Smith 1901c: 869.

Making China Perfectly Equal

Introduction to Part III

. . . .

The violence that has ruled over the ordering of the colonial world, which has ceaselessly drummed the rhythm for the destruction of native social forms and broken up without reserve the systems of reference of the economy, the customs of dress and external life, that same violence will be claimed and taken over by the native at the moment when, deciding to embody history in his own person, he surges into the forbidden quarters.
—Frantz Fanon [1963] 1966

IN 1900 PEASANTS IN NORTH CHINA, claiming for themselves the violence that had been visited upon them by Euroamerican penetration, surged into the "forbidden quarters" of missionary stations, railroad rights-of-way, and the legation quarters in Beijing. The Boxer Uprising of 1900 was one of many spontaneous attempts by ordinary people to end the disruption to their lives created by Western imperialism and colonialism. The uprising had been set off by a convergence of forces and events, including the political impotence of the Qing Dynasty, socioeconomic dislocations of the population of north China, the economic ambitions of Western companies (especially mining and railroad firms, whose activities in rural China were seen as disruptive to the natural cycles of Heaven and Earth), drought and bad harvests, rivalries among the Great Powers, and friction between Westerners and Chinese on a variety of fronts. As in other cases, the uprising achieved only minor success, but it forced many Chinese and foreigners to rethink the nature of Western enterprises in China.

For representatives of the powers, the uprising, though a shock, provided an unusual opportunity for altering, once and for all, Qing notions of imperial sovereignty and for teaching the Court and its subjects a hard lesson on the consequences of resisting the Euroamerican presence in China. For China's educated elite, the uprising demonstrated more clearly than ever the bank-ruptcy of the Manchu Dynasty and, in some cases, of monarchy in China. After 1900 the question for most informed Chinese was not whether the dynasty would survive, but how long it would be before it was overthrown. For ordi-nary Chinese living on the north China plain, the uprising meant a year-long occupation of Zhili province—the area in which the Qing capital of Beijing was located—that included mass slaughter, collective punishments, and po-litical and economic anarchy. For missionary groups, by contrast, the uprising indicated that there might be definite boundaries to their civilizing mission.

The three chapters that make up this section deal with the punishment of north China by the powers, the year of occupation, and the effects rather than the events of the Boxer Uprising itself. The history of the Boxer movement, the killing of Chinese converts and Euroamerican missionaries, the siege and the relief of the legations at Beijing, and the settlement that followed, has been told many times. Most recently, Joseph Esherick (1987) and Paul Cohen (1997) have provided comprehensive accounts of these events that draw from the wealth of documentation and historiography now available in China, as well as in Euroamerican archives. Their work provides an essential foundation for the remainder of this study. My concerns, however, are somewhat different from theirs. I seek to explore the effects of the processes of deterritorialization and reterritorialization generated by European and U.S. global expansion in the second half of the nineteenth century. My themes, therefore, are those discussed in previous sections: the relation between warfare and technological change, between knowledge production and pedagogy, and between competing and conflictual imperial imaginaries (e.g., the Great Game versus conceptions of national or racial destiny). My purpose is to address what happened in the wake of the Boxer Uprising as the result of a complex interaction between the sociopolitical situation in China and the many contradictions inherent in Western expansion, contradictions that, as shown in the final chapter of the study, generated effects that linger into and shape the present.

One major reason the events of 1900 continue to reverberate today involves the enormous expansion of media coverage of them, coverage that fundamentally altered reception and understanding of Chinese history in Europe, North America, and in China itself. By 1900, wholly new mechanisms of information processing were in place to exploit the story on a scale that had been unimaginable in 1860. Vastly expanded transportation and communication systems linked the east coast of China into a global steamship and railroad network capable of rushing reporters to the scene in two to three weeks. Submarine cables across the Pacific and through the Indian Ocean made it possible for newsmen to communicate by telegraph with Europe and North America at high speed. New printing technologies, particularly ones able to accommodate illustrations, packaged and delivered the sensational developments in China at a velocity and in a form that made information itself a spectacle, allowing for a vast expansion of vicarious audience participation in events. And with so much new information audiences were not entirely predictable in their responses.

12. Guinea Gold advertisement. *Illustrated London News*, 11 August 1900.

These new technologies and the networks of relations in which they were nested made it possible to capitalize almost immediately on breaking news. The Guinea Gold advertisement (fig. 12) appeared in the 11 August 1900 issue of the *Illustrated London News*, three days before the relief of the legations (ILN 17.3199, 1900: 213). Part of its significance lies in the way rich colonial references—cash crops (in this case, tobacco), maritime empire, native labor, native troops, and the suppression of rebellion—draw links between imperial capitalism and the policing of "rebellious," non-European populations. A similar pattern of event exploitation is evident in commercial advertising in the United States. In a few cases, advertisements were linked to maps of the theater of operations in China and military actions, which included detailed drawings of the route from Dagu to Beijing and, in the case of one printing company, a place where a business advertisement could be inserted directly onto the map. But whether or not one considers the Guinea Gold and the U.S. maps advertisements, their main significance may lie in the fact that they exist at all, that events in China could so easily be enfolded into mass media and commercial enterprises by drawing on rich colonial imagery and lore to create a sense of the interconnectedness of here and there, nation and empire.

Added to this burgeoning network of print capitalism were the dramatic elements that the event itself offered for exploitation. There were reports of missionaries having been killed—men, women, and children—which were not only sensational news, but recalled other instances of atrocities committed against whites in the colonial world. In addition, contact with the legations in Beijing ceased after the telegraph line to Tianjin was cut in July. In Great Britain, this situation immediately brought to mind events in South Africa, where Boer armies lay siege to the towns of Kimberly, Ladysmith, and Mafeking (Pakenham 1979), the last of which had been relieved just a few weeks before contact was lost with the Beijing legations. With the fate of the hundreds of other missionaries in China and members of the legations uncertain, the relief expedition took on epic proportions precisely because it was fed by speculation and fantasies of Oriental cruelty. Some newspapers drew on their own archives to remind readers of the nature of that cruelty and to presage the kinds of punishment in store for the Boxers (fig. 13).

It was into this novel media climate that news from north China entered. Newspaper reporters were present from the moment the allied armies landed at Dagu. Their accounts of the campaign, including vivid descriptions of looting and, in some cases, of atrocities committed by allied soldiers not only appeared in their own newspapers, but were picked up by others in the treaty ports and in review magazines in Europe and North America. In addition, some accounts from 1860 were republished, including that of d'Hérrison, and comparisons between the two campaigns were immediately made (Read 1900).[1] Even if these reports contained no aspersions, they gave a sense of the sheer breadth and scope of plunder and of the scale of the violence. Before turning to these subjects, however, it might be helpful to provide a brief overview of the beginnings of the Boxer Uprising and its immediate consequences.[2]

In the late summer and fall of 1899, an extended period of drought and famine brought extreme distress to the agrarian population of the north China plain. Much of Zhili, Shandong, and eastern Shanxi provinces were affected, and as the conditions worsened, farmers and townspeople wondered why the spirits of the land had abandoned them. Adding to the general so-

1. Republications included Henry Loch's ([1869] 1900) account of events in 1860; George Allgood's (1901) diary made its first appearance.

2. The most comprehensive and concise overview of the Boxer Uprising is Cohen 1997: 14–56.

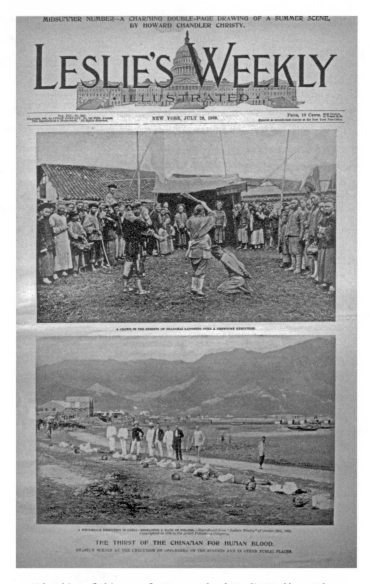

LESLIE'S WEEKLY
ILLUSTRATED

NEW YORK, JULY 28, 1900.

A CROWD IN THE STREETS OF SHANGHAI LAUGHING OVER A GRUESOME EXECUTION.

A WHOLESALE EXECUTION IN CHINA—BEHEADING A GANG OF PIRATES.

THE THIRST OF THE CHINAMAN FOR HUMAN BLOOD.
GHASTLY SCENES AT THE EXECUTION OF OFFENDERS ON THE STREETS AND IN OTHER PUBLIC PLACES.

13. "The Thirst of Chinamen for Human Blood." *Leslie's Weekly*, 21 July 1900.

cial malaise brought about by disastrous weather conditions were other problems, which in many cases were man-made. In particular, there was the growing presence of European and American missionaries and small but vocal communities of Christian converts in rural areas. The continued drought exacerbated tensions between these communities and led to the outbreak of a popular anti-Christian and anti-Western movement in north China (Esherick 1987). In 1898 and 1899, Boxer groups attacked Christian converts and some mission stations, but the movement remained local, mostly in western Shandong province.

Notices of Boxer activity began to appear in foreign newspapers in the fall of 1899, and in December S. M. Brooks, a British missionary in areas where Boxers were active, was killed. In a dispatch to London in early January, Sir Claude MacDonald, the British minister, identified a "secret society" called the "Boxers" as the chief culprits in the unrest (Cohen 1997: 44). Soon afterward, the ministers of each of the legations filed formal protests with the Qing government, which expressed regrets but took no action. Over the next few months, as reports of Boxer activities increased, the foreign ministers protested what they viewed as the government's refusal to deal with the situation. In mid-May Boxer activity exploded in Zhili province, just south of Beijing on the rail line to Baoding. The Catholic church in Gaoluo village was destroyed and over thirty families of converts killed. In an effort to halt further violence, Qing government forces moved in to suppress the movement, but the Boxers killed the official in charge. Attacks along the Beijing-Baoding and Beijing-Tianjin rail lines then followed in rapid succession.

Meanwhile, uncertain how to proceed and divided by pro- and anti-Boxer elements within the government, the Qing Court did nothing. By the end of May a rising tide of anti-Westernism, fueled in part by reports of the arrival of foreign soldiers in the Zhili region, made it virtually impossible for the Court to suppress the movement. Early June saw several Europeans killed by Boxers, and larger and more numerous groups began operating between Beijing and Tianjin. As the middle of the month approached, the legations sent a call for help to the coast. On 13 June British admiral Edward Seymour set out with a multinational force made up primarily of sailors and marines, intending to protect the legations. A few days later, about halfway to Beijing, the expedition was halted in an engagement with Qing forces and Boxers and retreated to Tianjin after suffering heavy casualties. The legations were now cut off from the coast.

Meanwhile, in two separate incidents a few days apart, the secretary of the

Japanese embassy, Akira Sugiyama, and the German minister, Baron Clemens von Ketteler, were killed by Qing soldiers when they ventured out of the legation quarter. On 20 June, Qing forces and Boxers opened fire on the legations and a siege began. It lasted until 14 August. On 16 July 1900, the London *Daily Mail* printed a dispatch from a special correspondent in Shanghai reporting that legations had been overrun and the entire foreign community massacred.[3] A memorial service was immediately planned for St. Paul's Cathedral, London.[4]

Even before this erroneous account reached Europe and North America in July, Great Britain, France, Germany, Austria, Italy, Russia, Japan, and the United States mobilized forces and dispatched them to China. The goal was to rescue the besieged diplomatic corps,[5] if possible, and to punish China for this affront against "civilization" and "international law." Count Alfred von Waldersee, a German general close to Kaiser Wilhelm, was given command of the international relief effort.[6] The invading armies took the same route that British and French troops had used in 1860. By all accounts, the fighting was brutal. Much of Tianjin was destroyed and many of the villages on the line of march were so heavily damaged that, when he arrived in China in late September, Waldersee characterized the route from the coast to Beijing as "a terrible state of devastation" (Waldersee 1924: 216). There is no accurate count, but certainly several thousand Chinese soldiers and civilians died. On 14 August, after a little over two weeks of actual fighting, the allied forces stormed Beijing and relieved the besieged legations.

The Western powers then set about exacting retribution for what an American newspaper referred to as the "yellow terror" or "yellow horror" (see *Leslie's Weekly* [LW] 28 July 1900, 25 August 1900). Punitive expeditions were launched into the Beijing hinterland and public executions of accused Boxers became commonplace on the streets of the Qing capital. All of Beijing and much of Zhili province were plundered. Needless to say, Skidmore's (1900) prediction that chaos would bring a wealth of Chinese art onto the market proved to be

---

3. *The Graphic* (7 July 1900) also printed the story.

4. The service was not held because of doubts over the veracity of the *Daily Mail* report, stimulated in part by the release of a cable from the U.S. minister at Beijing, Edwin Conger, that the legation was besieged but yet to be overrun; see Fleming 1959: 134–137.

5. The story of the seige has been told many times, both immediately afterward and more recently; see, for example, Fleming 1959; Hoe 2000.

6. Waldersee did not actually arrive in China until well after the relief of the legations, at which time he had difficulty asserting his authority over all the armies.

the case. But the Boxer "convulsion" did much more than simply open the floodgates of the art market. It also led to a reordering of China's relations with the powers that exceeded in scope and punitiveness any of the treaties previously imposed on the Qing Dynasty. For all intents and purposes, Qing kingship ceased to exist after the final agreement was implemented. China was left with an enfeebled imperial political system that, under the weight of political and trade restrictions and saddled with enormous indemnities to each of the powers, was virtually incapable of regeneration.

. . . .

CHAPTER 7

A Reign of Terror: Punishment and Retribution

in Beijing and Its Environs

IN THE AFTERMATH OF THE RELIEF of the legations, the armies of the eight powers, including Japan, launched another kind of warfare, one directed at "symbols" of Chinese sovereignty and civilization.[1] Unlike the conflict in 1856–1860, in which a transgressive Imperial Court could be seen as separate from the more reasonable Chinese people, the offenders appeared for the first time to be everyone in China. Thus, symbolic warfare was not confined to Beijing. In Baoding and Taiyuan, where missionaries had been killed, Europeans and Americans blew up city walls and gates and destroyed temples. Far from being merely random acts of aggression like much of the looting, rape, and murder in which allied forces also engaged, retaliation outside of Beijing was designed to negate or overwhelm imputed Chinese beliefs, many of which were seen as directly responsible for what was described by one missionary as the "Yellow Crime" and by another as that "awful catastrophe that cast its shadow over the whole world" (Coltman 1901; Reid 1901, 1902). The victors

1. Historical studies of events in and around Beijing after the relief of the legations are rare. Hunt (1979), however, has dealt with aspects of the U.S. occupation.

aimed, therefore, to do more than merely retaliate; they also wished to teach the Chinese lessons for the future so that such a disaster would not recur.

These two sides of symbolic warfare—the retaliatory and the pedagogical—are, of course, very similar to the kinds of activities undertaken by the British in 1860, specifically, the destruction of the Summer Palace and the formalistic ratification of the Tianjin Treaty. The difference now was not simply the numbers and varieties of foreign forces operating in China. The various retaliatory actions were grounded in the knowledge of "Chineseness" that had been produced over the previous decades, including a conception of what Chinese people were capable of understanding, lore about Chinese characteristics, and a distinct sense of the superiority of Western civilization bred from a generation of colonial rule in Africa and Asia. In addition, the actions of the allied forces were also intended, at least by some, to incorporate Chinese people into a Christian moral universe of "retributive justice" and to leave an unforgettable "brand" on the land and its inhabitants. Such action was presumed to be necessary if international law was to be honored by the Qing and if missions were to be reestablished in areas where they had been destroyed.

At the same time, organized violence was also staged for an effect that extended beyond China and the Chinese. The various acts of punishment were meticulously recorded, appearing in European and American books, newspapers, periodicals, journals, and the illustrated press. In the last case, the illustrations were either drawings, engravings taken from photographs, or photographs themselves. As in 1860, the camera was present, but by now it had become pervasive. The 1900 generation of photographers brought with them a whole new array of photographic technology, ranging from the Kodak reloadable camera to the complex apparatuses employed by civilian and military professional photographers. There was also a motion picture camera, and aerial photographs were taken from balloons. The use of photographic technology added a unique dimension that went well beyond Felice Beato's 1860 documentary record. In 1900, actions were staged for the benefit of the camera, transforming punishment into a performance of power, a spectacle for viewers in North America and Europe to share. It should be borne in mind, therefore, that although all of the photographs are not reproduced in this study, it would be possible to illustrate virtually all of the themes that emerge in the history constructed below.

Frames of Reference: Disorderly and Orderly Punishment

On 14 August 1900, the day the legations were relieved, Lancelot Giles, one of the besieged Europeans, wrote his mother about the euphoria that came from having been saved by the allied forces:

> We are actually at last relieved!!!!!!!!! It was a moment of a lifetime, and can better be imagined than described. Shakings of hands galore! Sikhs patted on the back! Grimy gunners hugged! . . .
>
> That afternoon I went with the party who cleared the wall, to the Ch'ien [Qian] Gate. Some Chinese soldiers ran out in the yard below the gate and started firing at us. They were shot. Two Maxims were fixed up on Ch'ien Gate and turned on a stream of people who were hurrying across the inner Palace yard. About fifty to seventy rifles were turned on them too . . . Any amount slaughtered. Every day looting parties go out and get what they can. I have done some splendid looting already. You wait and trust to me, before you speak. Cannot write more at present, as the excitement is something frantic; and it is difficult even to sit at a table. (1970: 177–178)

Giles's frenzy, his coupling of slaughter and looting, is apparent in many other accounts. While soldiers and civilians turned their guns on the fleeing inhabitants of Beijing, a host of plunderers descended on the city.

Yet, even as this seemingly random and pleasurable violence was targeting Chinese bodies and objects, the diplomatic corps and military leaders were designing a campaign of deliberate punishment, the features of which were intimately linked to their understanding of the Chinese mentality. The punishment was planned, in other words, to cause China's rulers and the Chinese people to lose face. In the case of the monarchy, humiliations began with the actual entry of the allied forces into the imperial city. Arthur Smith, our expert on face, noted that the center door of the Qian Gate, the one reserved exclusively for the use of the emperor, was blown open by Western guns, the equivalent, he added, of "a Great-Wall-of-China obliterated at a blow" (1900: 498).

In addition to entering the many courtyards and halls of the Forbidden City, foreigners humiliated the Qing monarchy by sitting on thrones to be photographed (fig. 14), going into the private apartments of the emperor and empress dowager, bivouacking U.S. and British troops at the Temples of Agriculture and Heaven, respectively, using the grounds of the Temple of Heaven for playing field hockey (fig. 15), photographing the 16th Bengal Lancers in

14. French Minister Pichon and entourage on the throne in the Qianqing palace, Forbidden City. *L'Univers Illustré*, 21 December 1900.

15. British officers and India army soldiers playing field hockey at the Temple of Heaven. Courtesy United States Army Military History Institute.

full dress at the Temple of Heaven (fig.16), and stationing "swarthy" Sikh guards at its gates, which one observer, apparently quite alert to issues of race, saw as a fitting humiliation of the Chinese Empire.[2] In addition, the British removed the tablets from the Manchu ancestral hall in the Forbidden City and sent them to the British Museum (A. Smith 1901b, 2: 548; S. Smith 1901: 133; Broomhall 1901: 12). Not to be outdone, the French and Germans appropriated the astronomical instruments from the Beijing observatory and shipped them to Paris and Berlin (e.g., Conger 1909: 177; Fleming 1959: 252). Each of the powers also seized Zongli yamen records of their legations, which one observer characterized as a thorough "humiliation" of the Qing Empire (S. Smith 1901: 138), and held them hostage until there was a peace settlement.

Other acts of humiliation were directed at the Chinese people as a whole. The British, for example, blew a hole in the massive city walls of Beijing—

2. See, for example, Martin 1900: 138; Steel 1985: 63, 65, who mentions playing field hockey and polo on the grounds of the Temple of Heaven. On "swarthy" Sikh guards as humiliation, see S. Smith 1901: 132; A. Smith 1900: 498.

16. 16th Bengal Lancers in dress uniform at the prayer hall, Temple of Heaven. Courtesy of the Director, National Army Museum, London.

17. The "Great British Gate" through the outer wall of Beijing. Courtesy United States Army Military History Institute.

the "Great British Gate," as one wag dubbed it—for the purposes of running a railway into the Temple of Heaven (fig. 17), the construction of which included the deliberate defiling of a Chinese cemetery.[3] All of the powers seemed keen on burning Buddhist books, in part because they believed "Buddhist superstition" probably lay behind the Boxer Uprising (Lynch 1901: 146–147). Because it was part of Euroamerican lore that walls and gates were the proudest symbols of a Chinese city, destroying them, as was done in Tianjin and in places were missionaries were killed, was seen as a fitting form of collective humiliation.[4] At a more mundane level of everyday practice, the U.S. army routinely punished Chinese for petty crimes in their occupation zone by cutting off queues (U.S. National Archives and Records Administration [NARA], RG395, 943, 25 September 1900). In addition, the Qing palaces and the homes of Manchu nobles and other wealthy Beijing residents were looted, rummaged through, and sometimes commandeered as residences for the occupying armies.

Once Beijing had been adequately subjugated, the armies of the powers used the central north-south avenue leading to the Forbidden City—a space they believed had always been reserved for the emperor—for their own parades and reviews.[5] Perhaps the most conspicuous use of such space occurred in early 1901, when Queen Victoria died. On 2 February the British held a memorial service within the Forbidden City at the Meridian Gate. An altar was placed near the central doorway of the Gate (fig. 18), with the Union Jack draped across it, and contingents from all the occupying armies participated (Conger 1909: 195–196; Steel 1985: 86).[6] Photographs of the proceedings were taken from atop the wall looking down on the gate's forecourt, a viewing position unimaginable in the past. This placement and document-

3. See Conger 1909: 187; A. Brown 1904: 197. Steel (1985: 88) refers to the hole made in the wall for a rail line as the "Great British Gate." Vaughan (1902: 149) heard that the railway would be continued right up to the legation quarter.

4. See A. Smith 1901b, 2: 522; S. Smith 1901: 130; Martin 1900: 138. On Tianjin, see A. Brown 1904: 197. Similar procedures were followed in towns where Christian missionaries were killed.

5. Conger (1909: 195) mentions the forces "vying with one another in their Grand reviews." A review was held when Field Marshall Waldersee arrived on 1 January 1901 and another celebrated the German emperor's birthday; see Steel 1985: 80, 83. J. Wilson (1912, 2: 534–535) describes an American parade on 3 October 1900 that traveled up the central avenue and marched to the tune "A Hot Time in the Old Town Tonight."

6. A program of the memorial service is in NARA, RG395, 906, box 4.

18. Memorial service for Queen Victoria, Meridian Gate, Forbidden City. Courtesy United States Army Military History Institute.

ing of the British monarch in absentia in a space reserved for the emperor of China suggests that the powers were also intent on erasing, once and for all, any real or imagined Qing claims to universal kingship. The so-called Son of Heaven was to be made mortal through the *disenchantment* of his earthly domain and the overlaying onto it of new orders of meaning.

These two sides of punishment—frenzied attacks on Chinese people and their possessions and calculated acts of desecration and reinscription of things held to be of special significance to the Chinese—formed a regime of retribution depicted as fully justified and justifiable to any who might question it. They also generated unpredictable responses among those who carried them out and those who witnessed them. Reactions ranged from triumphal gloating to disappointment and disillusionment; from firm resolve to mete out harsh sentences to guilt and sorrow for Chinese suffering. Underlying and informing these responses were a variety of conflicting beliefs, ranging from the contradictory elements to be found in Old versus New Testament Christian morality, to tensions between international law and the selfish interests of individual nation-states, and the simultaneous attraction and repulsion many Euroamericans felt toward the Chinese people. This play of differences began with the desecration of the Qing imperial palaces, the Forbidden City.

Staging Punishment: "Rending Asunder the Veil of Mystery"

The Forbidden City, as Westerners usually called the palace complex in Beijing, appears in contemporary accounts as a thing of mystery, the "holy of holies," the most "sacred" place in all of China for the Chinese (the quote in the title to this section is from Carter 1917: 203). These accounts constructed the palace complex as dark, closed off, and self-contained. At the same time, the residents of the city, the emperor and his Court, must have been ignorant of its incompleteness, for it was also presented, in a widely shared misapprehension, as a place where no "white man" had stepped before.[7] Henry Savage Landor, who had already accumulated a number of "first white man" trophies in his career, heard from General Linievitch, commander of the Russian forces, that he would be "the first Englishman — in fact, the first Anglo-Saxon — that can claim the privilege," and Private William Crishton of Company M, 9th U.S. Infantry wrote his mother with a similar tale.[8] For white men to breach its walls, open its doors, and step into the Forbidden City was, therefore, to place race and nation at the very center of a place purportedly off-limits to both. It was also to foreground violation and desecration as a fitting punishment for the emperor of China. Moreover, the introduction of white men into the Forbidden City would expose its secrets and mysteries to the light of reason and, as word spread, would serve to teach the Chinese that their high-walled exclusionism was misguided.

The process of penetration, pedagogy, and desecration began on 18 August 1900, when U.S. cannon blew open the gates leading up to the Hall of Supreme Harmony. However, after consultation among the military commanders of the allied forces, General Adna Chaffee, commander of the U.S. forces, de-

7. One of the few exceptions seems to have been James Ricalton (1901: 309), who recalled the Dutch embassy of 1795.

8. According to the 1906 edition of *Who's Who*, Landor had a number of white-man-firsts. The quotation is in 1901, 2: 361 and repeated on 211, 365, and 382. Also see A. Brown 1904: 197; Broomhall 1901: 12; Conger 1909: 169; Lynch 1901: 156; Steel 1985: 25; Daggett 1903: 103; Butler 1933: 77. The Crishton letter is in USMHI, Spanish-American War Era Veterans Survey, China Relief Expedition, 9th Infantry.

cided to halt further action and withdraw. The majority of the diplomatic corps were much disappointed by this decision. They succeeded in reversing matters within a few days.

Arguments for and against entering the Forbidden City, if not actually occupying it, were based primarily on the diplomats' perceptions of the Chinese mentality. Brigadier General A. S. Daggett of the U.S. army provides the following account of the debate:

> Some argued that if the city should be left undisturbed, the Chinese would believe the gods had intervened and prevented those sacred pavements from being polluted by the tread of the hated foreigner. It was therefore thought best to occupy or at least enter the city, for the purpose of breaking down their superstition and teaching these people that they were at the mercy of the allies.
>
> On the other hand, it was said that the city had never been entered by the white man; that its invulnerability against the foreigner, superstition though it was, was so deeply imbedded in Chinese sentiment that to break and shatter it would crush the spirit of the Chinese, and that they might not recover from the blow. They might not be able to negotiate terms of peace with the Powers nor pay an indemnity. China might be partitioned. The former opinion prevailed. It was decided that the city should not be occupied, but that a column should pass through the main street from the south to the north gate.[9]

The Triumphal March thus agreed on was held on 28 August and included military contingents from the eight nations as well as the diplomatic corps.[10] The contingents from the eight armies marched up the central avenue leading through the Imperial City, making a point of passing through doorways understood to be reserved exclusively for the emperor. As they marched, photographers took pictures. Some cameras were placed directly above the cen-

9. Daggett 1903: 106. Daggett's account is the only one I have found that gives competing points of view in these terms. Others note only the majority reason for entering the city. See Carter 1917: 202; Butler 1933: 77. Landor (1901, 2: 358) writes that after the assault on the Imperial City was halted, "pigtailed busybodies" spread stories that the foreigners were too weak to have continued further. The Triumphal March was decided on as necessary to maintain Western "prestige" and "give China a lesson."

10. Russia entered first with 800 soldiers, followed by Japan, 800; Great Britain (India Army), 400; United States, 400; France, 400; Germany, 250; Austria, 60; and Italy, 60 (U.S. War Department 1901: 500).

19. Triumphal March entering the Gate of Heavenly Peace (Tiananmen). Courtesy United States Army Military History Institute.

tal passageway at the Gate of Heavenly Peace (Tiananmen) and the Meridian Gate (Wu men), so that the photographs taken at these posts are perfectly centered, adopting, as it were, the view reserved for the emperor and his court (fig. 19). Other photographs were taken at ground level and show the marching columns advancing on the center line to the next hall (fig. 20). These photographs, not unlike the full-dress portrait of the 16th Bengal Lancers at the Temple of Heaven, created a documentary record of events that had great significance, particularly for the British, in the history of China's relations with the West. Emphasizing this historic moment, the march was followed with a twenty-one-gun salute by British artillery. "The occupation in force of the innermost shrine of Chinese exclusiveness," General Stanley Smith explained, "was now completely accomplished. Thus was added the final touch to the punishment of Peking" (1901: 140).

The Triumphal March, whether presented as pleasure, humiliation, or desecration, was, in turn, informed by an identification of things that, like African fetishes, the Chinese held to be invested with mystical powers. As Daggett's account and other sources indicate, British and American actors

20. American contingent, Triumphal March, forecourt of Grand Harmony Hall (Taihedian), Forbidden City. Source: Landor, *China and the Allies*, 1901.

on the scene were concerned to take advantage of this unprecedented opportunity for combating Chinese "superstition." But as Daggett also indicates, assaulting Chinese beliefs and causing a massive loss of face held its own dangers. If the monarchy was brought too low, it might collapse. There was concern, therefore, that the Imperial Court might be so demoralized by "barbarian" pollution that there would be no Chinese sovereign with whom to negotiate. Who, then, would guarantee the payment of indemnities? Who would sign the treaty? Who would restore order? Would the partition of China be necessary to protect the lives and property of Europeans and Americans? Such questions circulated in the foreign community with additional urgency after the sacred veil had been rent and the secrets of the Forbidden City had proven more astonishing than any fantasies.

DRAGONS, DUST, AND DISILLUSIONMENT: INSIDE THE FORBIDDEN CITY

Although this was certainly not the initial entry of Europeans into the Forbidden City, it was probably the first time those styling themselves "white men" or Anglo-Saxons had done so. There was, in other words, no shortage of "historical consciousness" concerning the entry of the Western powers into the Forbidden City. Since the establishment of the legations in 1861, no European or American diplomat had ever been allowed to enter the central audience halls of the palace complex, let alone the private quarters of the Court that flanked and stood to the rear of the great halls. Some admitted that they had a longing to enter the "forbidden spot" (Conger 1909: 169; Mrs. A. Little 1901: 502). Now the whole palace complex lay open to penetration; its secrets were finally going to be exposed to the world (Simpson [1907] 1970: 316–317).

What did the invaders find inside? Many accounts begin by noting that it was devoid of Chinese people; there were only several hundred eunuchs who looked "dejected and doleful" or had "stolid faces" that expressed "hatred and contempt." But few were interested in the inhabitants of the palaces; it was the buildings themselves and their material content that drew the most notice. Sarah Pike Conger (1909: 169), the wife of the U.S. minister, found imperial splendor in the city, and journalist George Lynch reveled in its "gorgeous rottenness and decay most royal"; others were less impressed. Lynch acknowledges that there was "a shroud of dust, dirt and decay" over everything" (1901: 157, 161). Courtyards were overgrown with weeds, carpets in halls were thick with dust, and the palaces themselves did not appear very splendid. As Count von Waldersee later added, the palaces were in "absolutely shocking condition," which led him to conclude that a monarchy that tolerated such a state of decay could not possess great wealth.[11] Smedley Butler later recalled that the emperor's palaces were bereft of the much anticipated Oriental splendor: "The rooms were filled with uncomfortable-looking furniture. There were not gold, silver and precious jewels, only some gold pillars. The men investigated these gold pillars with the tips of their bayonets, only to find them covered with thin gold leaf. As we swung out of the north gate, we were filled with contempt for those Chinese rulers who were satisfied to live in musty, old palaces" (1933: 77–78). Others found rooms full of mechanical toys, clocks, and music boxes of European manufacture, but few Oriental articles of clear value. H. B. Vaughan of the India army, after recalling that one British general wondered why the Chinese were not all mad, "what with making dragons and incessantly looking at them," wrote that he "had expected something so very much better" (1902: 141–143). Disillusionment and anticlimax, according to Lynch, diminished the thrill of violating the "holy of holies" (1901: 156; Landor 1901, 2: 378–379).

It was as if the palaces had been pre-defiled.

11. Waldersee 1924: 224. Waldersee visited the Forbidden City for the first time on 23 October.

For the thoughtful, the condition of the Qing palaces raised immediate issues. Colonel J. T. Dickman of the U.S. army was disappointed at the "exhibition" as a whole and saw in it a metaphor for the problem of China that the allies now faced. As he put it, "The glories of the place have long departed and the puny imbeciles of to-day do not even keep clean the massive works of art left by their ancestors. The filth and decay prevalent in the heart of the sacred palace are a fair index to the condition of the celestial Empire" (NARA, RG395, 913, no. 33). As if this were not bad enough, compounding the problem was the fact that the emperor himself was absent. He and the empress dowager had fled when the allied military forces had stormed Beijing. Now that white men had entered the sacred precincts, W. A. P. Martin, for example, saw this as a difficult problem, arguing that certain birds whose nests had been intruded upon never returned to them (1900: 139).

But the problems posed by the visible decay of the Chinese Empire would have to be dealt with on another day, and left to the diplomats. There was still much pleasure to be taken from even decaying palaces. As they moved through the private apartments, officers and diplomats filled their "capacious" pockets or sacks with a few "souvenirs."[12] As they walked through the rear gardens of the palaces, passing the not-quite-human eunuchs who offered them tea, cakes, and "Huntly & Palmer Biscuits,"[13] many perhaps contemplated the massive amount of wealth that still lay behind the walls of courtyard houses in this still imperial city.

"A Carnival of Loot"

If the physical state of the imperial palaces shattered fantasies of Oriental opulence, the contents of the palaces and the houses of the city's inhabitants were far less disappointing. Almost immediately after the relief, members of the eight armies, diplomats, and missionaries turned to looting (Allen 1901: 231). The *Sydney Morning Herald* called the mad scramble for plunder a "carnival of loot" (cited in Nicholls 1986: 111), and W. A. P. Martin spoke of a riot "in the midst of booty" (1900: 134). These characterizations suggest that the sack of Beijing was similar to what had occurred at the Summer Place forty

12. See, for example, the *Shanghai Mercury*, 1967: 108; Lynch 1901: 159–160; Landor 1901, 2: 379.

13. See Daggett 1903: 108; Landor 1901, 2: 380; Lynch 1901: 158, who also mentions dried and crystallized fruits.

years earlier; that a loot fever gripped the armies and Euroamerican civilian population in Beijing, and a wild orgy of plunder ensued. Moreover, many accounts agree that few if any were immune from the loot fever. Several British accounts claimed that their arch rivals in Asia, the Russians, were the worst of the looters,[14] but Bertram Simpson later argued that he and his compatriots had been made "savage" by the loot fever and that there were no restraints on anyone ([1907] 1970: 334, 349, 354). Lady Claude MacDonald, wife of the British minister, was reported to have been at the head of one looting expedition and to have exclaimed, after having already filled eighty-seven cases with "valuable treasure," that she "had not begun to pack" (Sharf and Harrington 2000: 222–223; see also Fleming 1959: 243; Pearl 1967: 151; Hoe 2000: 196). Even those who resisted temptation eventually succumbed. Polly Condit Smith, a siege survivor like Martin, recalled that when offered a sable fur coat, she turned it down. Soon after, she accepted a tortoise shell bracelet inlaid with pearls, explaining that her nerves could not stand a repetition of the coat incident (Hooker [1910] 1987: 189–190).

Yet, as much as the initial stages of this second looting episode at Beijing resembled the frenzy of its 1860 predecessor, there were certain differences. For one thing, no Garnet Wolseley emerged to keep looting safely contained as an attribute of the lower ranks of soldiers. Further, the loot itself did not have attached to it the aura of a proper name, such as "from the Summer Palace of the Emperor of China." Given the self-righteous conduct of Euroamerican diplomatic and military personnel in China, particularly as it was articulated through rhetoric that demanded "retributive justice" for "savage" and "barbaric" Boxer assaults on Christian missionaries and defenseless legations, this is something of a surprise. One would expect to find references in museum collections or other displays of artifacts to the Forbidden City, or Beijing 1900, or the Boxer episode. But only a few items so labeled seem to have surfaced in London, then or later.[15] Nor were there sales of Beijing loot in London and Paris auction houses comparable to those of the 1860s. The reasons for this are, perhaps, not too difficult to discern. First, as Eliza Skid-

14. S. Smith 1901: 128; Steel 1985: 59; National Army Museum (hereafter NAM), 6902/3, no. 2: 20, diary of Lieutenant Colonel Gartside-Tipping.

15. I have found only two references to sales of 1900 loot in England. CE, 6 March 1901 noted that a British private had sold some items through the Stevens house. In 1913, Stevens sold a Chinese drum said to have been captured by the 39th Regiment at Beijing during the Boxer Rebellion. See National Art Library auction house catalogues, 23.ZZ.

more (1900) had indicated the year before, there was a ready market for Chinese art in Europe, where auction houses and museums had already begun to adopt the nomenclature of Stephen Bushell and other experts. Second, looting in 1900 was a major point of contention and public debate in China, the United States, and Western Europe. Just why this was the case is dealt with in greater detail below. Here it is important to note that because of the controversy surrounding plunder, many accounts are more concerned with limiting discussion of looting or constructing justifications for it, rather than, as in 1860, celebrating it.

Nevertheless, it is possible to piece together enough material to compare the two looting episodes. Consider, for example, the physical geography of looting. In 1860, it was more or less confined to the area in and around the Yuanming Gardens or Summer Palace. In 1900, it included all of Beijing, the new Summer Palace, and virtually every city and town of Zhili province. Along the line of march from the coast, Tianjin and Tongzhou seem to have been picked clean. Moreover, unlike in 1860, when plundering lasted two to three days, looting in 1900 began with the occupation of Tianjin in late July and stretched well into October in Beijing. Outside of the Qing capital, it continued even longer as punitive expeditions were mounted in various parts of Zhili province.

At the same time, there were certain similarities to 1860. As before, much was broken and destroyed as soldiers searched for bullion (Waldersee 1924: 221; Seagrave 1992: 367). In the face of this onslaught, the Chinese inhabitants who remained in the city attempted to protect themselves by crudely fashioning Japanese, English, French, and U.S. flags in hopes that by flying them they would be spared. Others posted notes in European languages or asked soldiers to write notes to the effect that they had already been looted. In other cases, "blackmailers" made signs indicating that a property was owned by a European.[16] But, regardless of whether householders posted notices indicating that they had already been looted or flew the flags of the invaders, according to Bertram Simpson, "jeering looters" often tore both down and gave no quarter.[17]

16. Simpson [1907] 1970: 326, 339, 341–346, 349; Stewart 1908: 238–239; Lynch 1901: 162–163; S. Smith 1901: 128; Steel 1985: 55; Vaughn 1902: 120–121; NARA, RG395, 934, 25 September 1900. One enterprising individual charged hefty sums for making flags and posting notices; see F. Brown 1913: 177–178.

17. According to Seagrave (1992: 366), a student interpreter referred to Chinese who put up signs as "grovelling curs."

In Beijing, the period of unregulated plunder lasted for several days. During this time, the Japanese army, which seems to have had a fairly good sense of priorities, located the Qing treasury and made off with its store of bullion. By the end of August, however, serious attempts were being made by some of the allied commanders to control or manage looting in the capital; the general sense was that unless some order was restored, the Chinese markets for food and fuel necessary for maintaining a lengthy occupation of the city would not materialize (NARA, RG395, 944, 12 September 1900; G. Barrow 1942: 64). As they had done before, the British army took the lead in systematizing loot by setting up a prize commission. Echoing General Hope Grant in 1860, the British commander, General Gaselee, explained in a report to the War Office that he had been compelled to set up the commission to maintain the "contentment and discipline" of his forces "under the demoralizing conditions of this particular campaign" (Stewart 1908: 241–242). At the same time, he claimed that he was "unacquainted with the rules under which prize funds were established after Delhi, Lucknow and Pekin 1860."[18] This may indeed have been the case, yet Gaselee seems to have had at least a passing acquaintance with the practices of the British army in India and China a half century earlier and with the often ambiguous rules on plunder to be found in military law and army regulations,[19] for he had little difficulty putting together a prize committee that apportioned shares on the basis of rank and race. Indian sol-

18. Recall the rules for prize commissions discussed in chapter 4. According to a British War Office report of 1903 (WO 33, 6338), investigators found only a few instances of prize funds actually being allocated in any military actions from the Crimean War forward. This led them to conclude that prize was "a thing of the past." It had gradually been phased out and replaced by a cash gratuity for hardship and campaigning. This might also explain why Gaselee expressed doubts and confusion over invoking prize procedures.

19. The War Office's *Manual of Military Law* (first edition 1884), in a section entitled "The Customs of War," noted that the seizure of scientific or art objects was "incompatible with the admitted restrictions" of depriving the enemy of war-making resources and "could only be justified as a measure of retaliation." Within a page, however, the editors acknowledged that officers should attempt to prevent pillage *and* noted procedures, identical to those found in prize law, for dealing with its results. At the same time, they indicated that the regulations therein were compiled only for the use of officers and had no official authority; see U.K. War Office 1887, 311–313. This is the second edition. The sections cited here are the same in the third and fourth editions of 1893 and 1899. Army regulations were no less ambiguous. *Queen's Regulations and Orders for the Army* (1868: vol. 2, 186) forbade plunder and indicated that officers had a duty to prevent it; no mention was made of prize money. In contrast, the *King's Regulations and Orders for the Army* (1901: 50) contained a section on prize, noting that it was the property of the Crown and therefore subject to acts of Parliament.

21. Auction at the British legation. *The Graphic*, 15 December 1900.

diers were given one share less than British soldiers of equivalent rank, and native officers, regardless of rank, were held to be the equivalent of British warrant officers (WO28, 302: 28–29).

The fund itself was raised through the public auction of booty brought in by authorized "search parties" and held on the grounds of the British legation, pictures of which were published in London illustrated newspapers such as *Black & White* and *The Graphic* (fig. 21).[20] By 22 August the sales of plunder appear to have become a daily occurrence and word of them had spread to other units. As in 1860, they were lively affairs and, at least in the first days, included the British generals as well as Sir Claude MacDonald, the British minister. In addition, there were members of each of the regiments of the British contingent, including native soldiers of the India army, Japanese, U.S., and German soldiers, legation members, and even Chinese traders (Lynch 1901: 177–180). In his autobiography, William Oudendyk, a Dutch diplomat, provided one of

20. Remarkably, *Black & White* printed a photograph of the sales at the British legation as early as 20 October 1900. The caption claimed that the items were "found in deserted homes." The same issue contained a drawing of axe-wielding soldiers "looting a mandarin's house in Pekin" (p. 644). The drawing from *The Graphic* appeared in the 15 December 1900 issue on p. 885.

the few detailed accounts of these proceedings. At the British legation, in front of MacDonald's residence, he wrote:

> A collection of Chinese things lay spread out on the tiled floor, from silks, furs to blackwood furniture and antique bronzes. All the legation people, amongst them Lady MacDonald sitting on a chair, and a number of other English men and women thronged around this display of valuable articles, taking them up and examining them and discussing their age and merit. There was an atmosphere of happiness and enjoyment. A sergeant held up each article in turn, and the bidding was lively, but the prices were low, there was evidently a glut in the market. An officer noted down sums in a register, the proceeds going to his regiment's prize fund. While this was going on two Chinese mule carts drove in escorted by some Indian soldiers under an officer. They were heavily loaded with more Chinese valuables destined for auction. This had a bad influence on the bidding. (1939: 107–108; also see Hoe 2000: 374)

Although there was a much larger pool of buyers than in 1860, the bidding, as Oudendyk suggests, was moderate, with many valuable items, particularly furs, going for a few dollars.[21]

Even so, General Norman Stewart suspected that the foreign residents and legation members—the "knowing ones," as he called them—probably got even greater bargains (1908: 256). Later, residents of other treaty ports and, eventually, curio shop owners from Shanghai and Hong Kong, some of whom were reported to have commissions from European auction houses and art dealers, and dealers from the United States arrived to participate (*Celestial Empire* [CE], 19 November 1900: 617; Waldersee 1924: 231). One report indicates that the viceroy of India, George Curzon, sent £1,000 to Guy Hillier at the British legation in Beijing to "invest in curios" (Pearl 1967: 151). Moreover, as replacement troops filtered in, they too had the opportunity of acquiring valuable Chinese curios. Just as Eliza Skidmore predicted, they seemed to come from the "ends of the earth" to join in the plunder (1900: 196). By mid-October, the auctions, which had been held daily except Sundays for almost two months, had generated a prize fund of more than $50,000 (*Peking and Tientsin Times*, 18 October 1900).

---

21. In contrast to the accounts of Lynch and Oudendyk, Gartside-Tipping complained that the prices were too high; see NAM, 6902/3, no. 2: 22. Meanwhile, Edmond Backhouse saw the fur market of 1900–1901 as a banner one; see Lo 1976, 1: 201.

Eventually the fund rose to $330,000. When divided up it yielded $27 per share, with the lieutenant general commanding receiving 10 shares; general officers, 8; field officers, 7; captains, 6; subalterns, 5; warrant officers and native officers, 4; British NCOs, 3; native NCOs, 2; British soldiers, 2; and native soldiers, 1.[22] The allotment was, as Sir Claude MacDonald later argued, orderly, fair, and moderate (CE, 22 April 1901: 4). It also had the added virtue, as had been demonstrated in 1860, of drawing a distinction between the British forces and those of the other countries—from the "crude" Russians to the "thorough" Americans[23]—involved in the expedition. Morever, as before, it reproduced the army by order of rank and sealed it off from the moral chaos of plunder, while maintaining a clear distinction between white Englishmen and Indian native soldiers. This last distinction was now racial, but without, as the British liked to believe, pejorative connotations. It was, instead, the natural order of things as the British had created them in colonial India. The China relief force, made up almost wholly of native troops from India army units, had been transformed from the wild plunderers of Fane's and Probyn's Horse, active in 1860, to the "martial races of India," who as such had a rightful place in the ordering processes of empire (Farwell 1989: 179–190). That a native officer did not receive a share equal to that of a British officer (or any of the other equivalent ranks, for that matter) was not so much a statement of inferiority as a means for making clear who was the ruler and who the ruled.

Regardless of whether they understood the full import of the British "system," others were impressed with it. The correspondent for the Paris weekly L'Ilustration called it "procèdent systématiquement" (12 January 1901: 19), and Arthur Smith, the American missionary, thought it "scientific" in comparison to the behavior of other armies, who seemed on the whole (with the possible exception of the Japanese units; see below) to have no method at all (1900: 497). Reports continued well into October 1900, often implicating the Russian forces, of daily mule trains hauling the plunder from Beijing. Even the American soldiers, who often appear in accounts as virtually immune to temptation, became involved in looting. Leslie Grove wrote his wife, "Our rule against it is utterly ineffectual & those who disobey do so with impunity

22. NCH, 24 April 1901: 784. In 1995, I found a reference in an India Office catalogue to a Prize roll for China 1900. Archivists were unable to locate it, however. I am grateful to Frances Wood for trying.

23. These are Waldersee's characterizations. He discusses national patterns of looting in 1924: 219.

& get many interesting articles thereby" (U.S. Army Military History Institute [ISMHI], Grove Correspondence, 22 August 1900).

It was not until 21 September, in fact, that General Adna Chaffee, the U.S. commander, acted. Faced with open violation of U.S army general orders in time of war,[24] Chaffee followed the British lead by ordering that all loot be called in and auctioned off. But instead of creating a prize fund with auction proceeds, he erased any references to plunder. His officers auctioned off "captured property" and created a Public Civil Fund that was used to pay a portion of the cost of the U.S. occupation of Beijing in the coming year.[25] Such propriety on Chaffee's part also resulted in one of the few recorded cases of the return of a looted object. In May, the general returned to Li Hongzhang, Qing plenipotentiary at the peace negotiations, a silver spoon received by the latter as a souvenir when he had visited Niagara Falls in 1896.[26]

These formal measures for dealing with plunder were accompanied by the emergence of "extemporized" and "extremely picturesque" street bazaars (CE, 19 November 1900: 617). As in 1860, individual French soldiers took the entrepreneurial lead. Bertram Simpson recalled that on entering the French camp, soldiers produced little *objets de vertu* from their pockets and tunics. They were willing to sell these items cheaply because rumor had it that all loot was soon to be confiscated by officers. Meanwhile, British soldiers, contrary to orders, were selling items in their camp, and soldiers from India army units opened up shops on Beijing streets (Simpson [1907] 1970: 372, 374–375, 415–416). With Chinese merchants and Western missionaries also participating in the sales, business was apparently brisk. Some buyers even wrote home to let their wives know of their good fortune.[27]

24. According to J. Wilson (1901: 389), it is General Order No. 100, written by Professor Francis Lieber in 1863.

25. For sources related to Chaffee's decision, see NARA, RG203, entry 4, pp. 54–56; Chaffee's letter of 8 March 1901 is in RG395, 898, "Letters Sent, 1900–1901"; and the Office of Finance, *Ledgers of Emergency Fund Account, 1898–1909*. The China relief expedition section indicated that loot was transformed in Washington into "Money received from auctions sales of captured property in China, Special order no. 36, Gen'l. Chaffee."

26. NARA, RG395, 898, no. 554, 16 May 1901. According to G. E. Morrison, the *Times* correspondent in Beijing, Victor von Grot, a Russian in the IMC, had purchased "tens of thousands of taels worth" of curios and intended returning them to the emperor and empress; see Lo 1976, 1: 174–175. The French government also refused to accept the items sent by General Frey; see *L'Illustration*, 29 December 1900: 406.

27. Stewart (1908: 257) mentions the Chinese shopkeepers. Chamberlin (1903: 101–102) told his wife he had purchased Chinese goods from missionaries. Grove purchased

While soldiers and civilians bought and sold plunder in various quarters of Beijing, army commands set their sights on collecting trophies for their nations and regimental headquarters. In the British case, this included gathering captured European-manufactured field guns and shipping them to London, Edinburgh, Sidney, and Dublin (IOR, L/MIL/7/16765, p. 11). Meanwhile, the 4th Prince of Wales' Own Gurkha Rifles made off with a temple bell and a block of stone from the Great Wall of China. After being inscribed "China 1900," the stone was placed in the walls of the regimental headquarters in India (R. MacDonnell and Macauley 1940: 228). Boxer and Qing imperial army banners and flags were other favorite forms of trophy. For their part, U.S. forces shipped samples of Chinese weapons, Boxer flags, and a statue of the Chinese god of war, Guandi, to the recently established trophy room at West Point.[28] In addition, two of the units involved, the 9th and 14th Infantry Regiments, incorporated yellow dragons into their insignias and took new nicknames, the "Manchus" and "Golden Dragons," respectively.[29]

In these and other ways, the meanings attached to Summer Palace objects were easily transposed onto 1900 loot. They could stand for the orderly reconstitution of armies (in this case, the British and U.S. contingents) while highlighting the differences between disciplined and undisciplined forces. They could also act as signs of humiliation, of taste and discernment, of the triumph of civilization over barbarism, and of military trophy collecting and regimental "heritage." Yet, as much as there were commonalities in the meanings attached to 1860 and 1900 loot, there were also a number of discernible differences.

In addition to now being able to characterize their thefts as inflicting a loss of face on the Chinese, it is possible to identify a more sophisticated approach to plunder among some of the looters. Officers in the Japanese army, for example, were especially interested in Chinese art and antiquities, and even issued guidelines to soldiers distinguishing various grades of plunder,

---

some things from Chinese dealers and felt better about it; see USMHI, Grove Correspondence, 11 October 1900

28. NARA, RG395, 944, Circular 4, 24 September 1900. Chamberlin (1903: 119) mentions the war god and something labeled as such is in McFarland (1929: 41), which also contains other Boxer trophy. Also see Leonard 1944, where the Boxer items are grouped together.

29. See the Web sites www.perso.hol.fr/~nguiffen/manchu.html and www.25thida.com/14thinf.html, accessed 16 February 2002.

ranging from those for the Japanese imperial household, to those for display in museums and schools and for military trophy (Sand 2000: 654). Although he makes light of it, George Lynch, a reporter on the scene, observed that "when offered a china cup or saucer, the correct thing to do is to look at the mark at the bottom as if one understood what it meant, and shake the head" (1901: 170). What people were looking for were imperial reign date ideograms, known from publications such as those of Bushell, that provided authenticity and indicated the value of objects. Although Lynch did not understand what the symbols meant, those privy to the vast amount of scholarship on Chinese art produced in the Beijing legations were indeed "knowing ones." After observing that legation members were "in full cry in the appropriative hunt," a reporter for the *London Daily Express* added that "they had a decided advantage over the relievers, inasmuch as they were familiar with localities and the whereabouts of precious things. They got in 'on the ground floor'" (cited in CE, 14 January 1900: 55–56). The report might have added that along with Lady MacDonald, they headed straight for the private residences of the Qing nobility.[30] On one social occasion, Leslie Grove explained to his wife, the Reverend and Mrs. Reid gave him a number of small items they had taken from the palace of Prince Li (USMHI, Grove Correspondence, 9 September 1900). In another noted case, Herbert Squiers, secretary at the U.S. legation, left Beijing in September 1901 with what was reported to be several railway cars filled with Chinese art.[31]

This shift in the understanding of the value of Chinese objects was matched by other novel forms of plunder. Perhaps the most controversial of these involved Christian missionaries, who, like the Reids, engaged in the looting of Beijing and its environs. In some cases, missionaries were reported to have seized the homes of imperial princes and the wealthy of Beijing and sold their contents (see Simpson [1907] 1970: 374; Steel 1985: 56; Martin 1900: 135). Miss Georgina Smith, a British missionary, was reported to have assembled

30. Personal journals indicate as much; see Hoe 2000: 316, where the palace of Prince Chun is mentioned, and Seagrave 1992: 367, where Prince Tuan's residence is noted.

31. The report appeared in the *New York Times*, 3 September 1901; cited in Seagrave 1992: 368. Not everyone, however, thought that there was anything special about the Beijing loot; a piece in CE (19 November 1900: 617) argued that most of the objects could be gotten in any good curio shop. What is remarkable about these observations is not so much the author's criticism of the caliber of the loot, but that there were standards and market knowledge to draw on.

"wonderful treasures," which she sold off from late August forward (Hoe 2000: 322).

These "fire sales," ostensibly in the name of raising funds for destitute Christian converts, were accompanied by retributive expeditions into rural areas where missions had been attacked and destroyed. Led by American missionaries, these operations were initially conducted with the cooperation of U.S. forces. The first seems to have occurred on 20 September, when a patrol of the 6th Cavalry, accompanied by the Reverends William Ament and Robert Coltman, entered a village outside the capital. Ament identified signs of Boxer activities, and after speaking with a group of Chinese Christians, sanctioned their looting of several of the homes in the village. Captain Forsyth, the commander of the unit, objected, insisting that the property be returned or he would immediately go back to Beijing (NARA, RG395, 913, no. 19). Incidents like this one led some of the higher officers in the U.S. command to surmise that they were being used by the missionaries (U.S. War Department 1901: 512).

The fact that they had no legal leg to stand on and that their activities bordered on extortion did not seem to deter the missionaries. Unwilling to give up military protection, they tried another tack. They requested support through the U.S. legation for troops to accompany missionaries on what were supposed to be fact-finding tours. However, on one of these, E. G. Tewksbury immediately began to collect bullion in one of the villages they entered. Bothered by the fact that there was no procedure for determining the responsibility of individual villagers, Lieutenant P. W. Guiney asked Tewksbury for an immediate accounting of what was being collected. The Reverend demurred, saying he would send a record to the U.S. legation. Guiney reported the exchange to the adjutant general, and this seems to have brought the military escorts to an end.[32]

Paralleling the missionary activities in rural areas were punitive expeditions designed to collectively punish communities. These expeditions involved the destruction of property as well as extortion and looting. As armies swept through villages, they created an enormous amount of chaos in their wake. One result of this disorder was the emergence of roving bands of rob-

32. NARA, RG395, correspondence involving Tewksbury in 906, box 1 and box 2, and 943. Subsequently, Tewksbury did send an account to Conger at the legation, but in addition to assessments for property loss, it included a demand for the villages in question to build new chapels and set aside land to support the missions.

bers made up of Boxer remnants and persons displaced by six months of warfare in the region. In a case noted in December, some of these groups were reported to be carrying the flags of one or another of the allied forces and "levying tribute upon and plundering villages."[33] In other instances, deserters from the allied armies engaged in similar operations;[34] in one case, American soldiers were reported to be leading bands of looters (Waldersee 1924: 262–263). One of the most spectacular such incidents involved two U.S. privates who forced several Chinese men at gunpoint to hold up a village outside Tianjin. As the wagons were being loaded, a French patrol caught them in the act. With the testimony of the commandeered Chinese as evidence, the two were tried, convicted, dishonorably discharged, and sentenced to twenty-one years at Alcatraz (NARA, RG395, 944, 5; 906, box 4).

Enterprising operations like this one, though exceptional, were by no means isolated. It is impossible to tell how many instances of theft and extortion went undetected or unreported, but at least one case later surfaced to provide some hint of the variety of activities to be found even among the otherwise well-disciplined British. In 1926, a story circulated about the theft of two golden bells from the Temple of Heaven by officers of the 16th Bengal Lancers. Claiming them as trophy, the officers had spirited them off with other objects ostensibly destined for the officers' mess. Sometime around 1905, they decided to melt down one of the bells and divide the spoils, but one of their number objected, claiming the share allotted to him was insufficient (IOR, L/MIL/7/16819). Of interest here is not simply that the story of the bells came to light, but what it tells us about initiatives outside of the legal channels of prize procedures. It is perhaps indicative, therefore, of the enormous scale of the plunder of Beijing and Zhili province, a scale that to this day defies easy reckoning because, with the exception of trophy, it is difficult to discern where the vast majority of the loot finally came to rest. Knowing this, it should be difficult indeed to look at any piece of Chinese porcelain or Qing imperial regalia in the great museums of France, the United States, and Great Britain and not think about the sack of Beijing in 1900.[35]

33. NARA, RG395, 898, 472, order to Captain Forsyth to be on the lookout for these bands, dated 17 December 1900. See also 968, reports dated 17 December 1900 and 19 January 1901.

34. In WO 32, 6417, Colonel Grierson's staff diary reports that a band of sixty Sikh deserters were marauding in the countryside; see entry for 10 January 1901. See also NARA, RG395, 968, 18 April 1901.

35. This is particularly the case with the Metropolitan Museum of Art in New York,

Rough Justice: Executions, Punitive Expeditions,
and the Punishment of Baoding

Death was a constant presence for Chinese and Westerners alike in the summer and fall of 1900. It came in numerous forms and there were an equal number of reactions to it (Cohen 1997: 173–208). Euroamericans, missionaries and their families, perhaps 270 people in all, were probably the most prominent among those who died. But there were also several thousand Chinese Christian converts and the hundreds of combatants and noncombatants killed in the brutal fighting that took place between Dagu and Beijing. Many of these dead never found a proper grave and became, as the Chinese believed, hungry ghosts haunting the north China plain. There was also an uncountable number of suicides, young Chinese women fearful of rape and whole families who killed themselves rather than face the fearsome monsters of the foreign armies. And then there were mass slaughters perpetrated by allied soldiers, like the one on the Qian Gate described by Lancelot Giles (1970).

In most of the cases where allied soldiers killed Chinese people, there was little or no apparent concern about whether they were Boxers. In fact, in one incident involving a U.S. patrol, the officer in command ordered their Chinese guide to reconnoiter the countryside ahead of them from the top of a village hut's roof. Almost as soon as he got up there, he was mistaken for a Boxer and shot by a member of the patrol (NARA, RG395, 913, no. 19, 20 September 1900). Cases like these were aptly summarized by General Chaffee: "It is safe to say that where one real Boxer has been killed since the capture of Pekin, fifty harmless coolies or laborers on the farms, including not a few women and children, have been slain. The Boxer element is largely mixed with the mass of the population, and by slaying a lot one or more Boxers might be taken in" (cited in Lynch 1901: 84).

Chaffee's observations do not mention certain disturbing features, found in other accounts, of these slayings. Henry Savage Landor recorded "a disgusting bit of cruelty" that took place at the U.S. camp (the Temple of Agriculture in the southern part of Beijing). A person suspected of being a Boxer spy was taken before an officer, who told his subordinates to do with him what they "damned please." According to Landor, the American soldiers, "misunderstanding" their officer's intent, kicked and punched the hapless cap-

which seems to have received a number of donations from Herbert Squiers; see Seagrave 1992; 368–369.

tive. Then, in what might be called a spirit of international cooperation, a passing French soldier shot him in the head and a Japanese soldier "stomped" on the "poor devil." With his skull now crushed but demonstrating "amazing tenacity of life," the victim had his clothes ripped off as soldiers searched for the charm that all Boxers were supposed to have on them. Finding nothing, hundreds of soldiers lingered over him for nearly an hour, his agony stimulating "roars of laughter" among them. We may wonder about Landor's attribution of such cruelty to a misunderstanding and question his claim that the incident he so graphically described was "painful" to most U.S. officers, who were usually "extremely humane" and "extravagantly gracious" to the enemy. But he does make it clear that silence on the part of officers over incidents like this one was taken "as encouragement" by the lower ranks (1901, 1: 364–365). There was a sense, among some at least, that the Chinese were getting what they deserved.

Indeed, into September, all Chinese people appeared to be fair game. George Lynch reported that in the German sector, officers used torture during interrogations and immediate execution by firing squad afterward, eighty-three of which had occurred in the previous week alone (1901: 143–144). Although it is unclear how many were slaughtered in this manner, the Germans were not alone in the use of firing squads. In other cases, suspected Boxers were beheaded or strangled by members of the Japanese army. Summary "justice" was meted out, according to General Stewart, through September and into the middle of October (1908: 267, 283).

By then there were indications that the killing was having unanticipated effects on the executioners. According to a paymaster named Wynne in the Australian contingent of the British Empire forces, firing squad soldiers were "growing callous." He attributed this to what he termed "the Eastern education." "Until you can bring yourself to regard the Chinaman as something less than human," he explained, "considerably less, you are at a disadvantage" (cited in Nicholls 1986:104). Wynne's statement draws attention to what soon became a concern for the commanders of the British and U.S. contingents: the apparent alteration to the soldiers' sensibilities that "the Eastern education" suggests. Those involved in this more routinized form of killing were compelled to dehumanize the Chinese if they were to carry out their business. This is not an unusual feature of colonial aggression directed at a non-white population, but given what has already been said about English lessons, there is something unusual about "the Eastern education." It would seem that Wynne and the other executioners had begun to mimic a well-known feature

222 · ENGLISH LESSONS

of Chinese character: a complete absence of sympathy for human suffering
(A. Smith 1894: 196–197). If soldiers failed to learn this lesson, Wynne tells
us, they were at a "disadvantage." The solution to this dilemma appeared at
roughly the same time as Wynne recorded this disturbing emergence of "Chinese characteristics" in white men. The problem was solved by having Chinese
swordsmen execute supposed Boxers in a form of capital punishment taken
to be common in China: beheading (see below).

This form of execution, however, was primarily directed at individual Chinese in and around Beijing. To collect larger numbers of suspected Boxers, the
allies launched "punitive expeditions" into Zhili province. Operations began
almost immediately after the relief of the legations and extended well into
the next year (one of the last apparently occurring at the end of April 1901
near Hexiwu). In late August, for example, the U.S. 6th Cavalry, under Captain William Forsyth, attacked the South Park (Nanhaizi), a Qing hunting
preserve, where they engaged a group of Boxers, burned a village, and seized
rice stores and cattle (NARA, RG395, 913, no. 12, 29 August 1900). The Germans launched a similar campaign two weeks later that killed an estimated
250 suspected Boxers in Liangxiang county, southwest of Beijing.[36]

Although concern over hidden Boxer groups would remain a justification
for at least some of the expeditions, by mid-September forays into Zhili province became a spectacular form of retributive justice. Violence was directed
at the Chinese people themselves, who, unlike the population of 1860, were
no longer considered innocent, but collectively responsible for the siege of
the legations, deaths of missionaries, and destruction of Western property.
This orientation was, in itself, a significant change, one that earlier British
diplomats such as Lord Elgin might have found objectionable. For one thing,
actions like punitive expeditions tended to mimic the Chinese notion of collective responsibility. Indeed, it was precisely the Euroamerican rejection of
such Chinese legal notions that had led to the creation of extraterritoriality
in China following the first Opium War. Few, however, seemed to recall this
history. Instead, they sought ever more creative forms of collective punishment.

36. See Li, Su, and Liu (1990: 329–330), who use English, French, Russian, German, and
Chinese sources to reconstruct the occupation of Zhili. Also see *Yihetuan shiliao* (hereafter
YHTSL), 1981, 1: 104, 118, 122, 148, 150, 196, 205–206, 374, 411; 2: 802–803. The *Yihetuan
yundong shishi yaolu* (hereafter YHTYDSSYL) 1986 offers a chronology of events from 1896
to 1911 and includes a number of entries concerning the activities of allied forces in rural
areas; see especially 1 October 1900.

One of the more popular of these was to strike at Boxer superstition by attacking the physical sites where their rituals occurred. One of the earliest examples of this sort of symbolic warfare was a joint British, German, Japanese, and U.S. expedition launched on 16 September to the Western Hills near the Summer Palace. Its target was the Bada temple complex, which was supposed to contain a large group of Boxers. Near the temple, the British and U.S. legations had established summer residences some years earlier, the former on Mt. Bruce, named after the first British minister, the latter on Mt. Burlingame, named in honor of the U.S. minister. Perhaps because of this, George Lynch facetiously referred to the entire operation as a "punitive picnic" (1901: 214–215). When the units converged on the temples, they found the legation residences destroyed and evidence of a Boxer presence, but no actual Boxers. The British commander, General Barrow, thereupon asked permission in the name of Sir Claude MacDonald from General Wilson, leader of the U.S. contingent, to blow up the white porcelain pagoda, a structure that stood at the rear of the Lingguang temple (Arlington and Lewisohn [1935] 1937: 301). Having actually visited the temples in 1885, Wilson was taken aback by the request, which seemed to him to be made in the spirit of "barbarism," and asked Barrow what would justify such an act. "His reply," Wilson recalled, "was still more amazing, for he explained . . . that if the Christians did not destroy this famous Chinese temple, the Chinese, who had destroyed many missionary churches, would conclude that their gods to whom the Pagoda was dedicated were more powerful than the God of the Christians." At this, Wilson dissolved the joint operation, telling Barrow that he must pursue this course alone. As the Americans withdrew the next morning, the British destroyed the pagoda.[37]

Temples were not the only objects of assault by the allies. Untold numbers of ordinary Chinese villagers and their villages were also targets. Lieutenant C. D. Rhodes made an extremely vivid report, one that reads eerily like accounts from the Vietnam War, of an incident that took place near Yangcun. Claiming that they had been fired on, a force of German, French, and Italian soldiers punished the villagers. Soon afterward, a company of the U.S.

37. J. Wilson 1912, 2: 527–530; NARA, RG395, 913, no. 20; U.S. War Department 1901: 509–512. Also see Li et al. 1990: 330. Wilson clearly did not understand the logic of symbolic warfare, but perhaps this was because he was puzzled by the necessity for punitive operations. Instead of roving bands of Boxers and besieged missionaries, Wilson found that "peace, order and industry" prevailed "as though there had been neither violence or war in the land."

6th Cavalry, traveling with a doctor, entered the village, treated the wounded, and recorded the account of the villagers. Claiming that they had fired on no one, the elders in the village explained that when the soldiers approached, the younger villagers fled into the surrounding fields. This left the old and the very young in the village. The foreign troops proceeded to shoot or bayonet six of them and then burned several houses, killing at least one child. Rhodes was convinced the entire incident was perpetrated by a soldier firing at dogs and that the others simply responded to the sound (NARA, RG395, 913, no. 29). Such incidents were repeated all along the line from Tianjin to Beijing.

When allied forces were convinced that Boxer activity emanated from a particular town or village, the results could be devastating. On 19 September, the villages of Guanyin and Yiba in the Western Hills were destroyed and over a hundred purported Boxers killed. The next day, a joint force attacked towns near the Beitang forts and killed a number of people. At the end of October, German, French, Italian, and English forces burned and looted towns throughout the province, destroyed temples, and killed over a thousand people. Some of these units ransacked and plundered Xiling, the Qing imperial tombs west of Beijing, and Dongling, or the Eastern Tombs. Others seized Shanhaiguan at the extreme eastern end of the Great Wall, and Qinhuangdao, an island that they would eventually convert into a port for large ships (Li et al. 1990: 331, 334, 345–346, 365, 383). The goal of these activities seems to have been to clear Zhili province of Qing civil and military authorities until a settlement was reached. Their effect, however, was to eliminate local authorities, and hence local policing activities in many areas, adding greatly to the general chaos in north China. The allied reign of terror continued into the winter of 1900–1901. In December, a French punitive expedition destroyed two thousand homes in Sulu county and killed over a thousand people in and around Shenzhou. In February 1901, German forces engaged Qing units at Yongqing, Canzhou, and Guangcheng, killing over thirteen hundred and extorting funds from local officials. The expeditions extended into April, with harassment and extortion in addition to outright slaughter. Over one hundred perished in an engagement at Zhangjiakou (Li et al. 1990: 372, 376–377, 385–386, 390).

THE BAODING EXPEDITION, OCTOBER 1900

Probably the most spectacular of the punitive expeditions was the one directed at Baoding prefectural city, ninety miles southeast of Beijing, where eleven adults and four children of American and British missions had been slain. The expedition took on emblematic significance for Western military leaders and missionaries because it embodied the kind of retributive justice and symbolic warfare generally agreed to be the most effective against the Chinese. The expedition was made up of two columns, one from Beijing under the command of General Gaselee and the other from Tianjin, commanded by General Bailloud of the French contingent. Totaling over six thousand men, there were French, German, Italian, and British units, including a company of Australian engineers. Captain Grote Hutcheson of the 6th Cavalry represented the United States, and the Reverend J. W. Lowrie, a member of the American mission at Baoding, joined the force as one of the interpreters.

The two columns arrived at Baoding on 20 October and an international commission was set up to determine the circumstances of the deaths of the missionaries. Primarily relying on Chinese witnesses, the commission heard that on 1 July 1900, one group had perished in Boxer attacks on mission stations. Included among these was the Reverend Pitkin, whose head was severed and delivered to the prefectural yamen. A second group, made up of three women, two men, and one child, were held for a time in the Qisheng'an temple, the Boxer headquarters, and then removed from the city, beheaded, and buried in shallow graves outside the southwest corner of the city wall. The commission also heard the testimony of the Green family and Miss Gregg of the China Inland Mission. According to T. J. N. Gatrell, an interpreter with the expedition, the evidence they gave "went a long way toward bringing" the local Qing officials to justice (1901: 149–150). On 27 October, the international commission ruled that Qing officials were complicit in the deaths and sentenced Tingyong, the prefectural treasurer, Guiheng, commander of the Manchu garrison, and Wang Zhangui, colonel of the Chinese garrison, to be put to death "by the Chinese method in vogue for criminals—beheading."[38]

Before these sentences were carried out, however, suspected Boxers and the city of Baoding itself were punished. German soldiers rounded up several men, took them outside the city, made them dig their own graves, and summarily executed them (Nicholls 1986: 90). After the commission had collected its evidence, General Gaselee ordered the Qisheng'an temple, where the missionaries had been held before their executions, and the Chenghuang temple, the seat of the city god, blown up (NARA, RG395, 913, no. 36). The destruction of the first temple might be understandable, but by also blowing up the

38. See the account of Captain Grote Hutcheson in NARA, RG395, 913, no. 36 and U.S. War Department 1901: 461–476. See also A. Brown 1904: 208; Li et al. 1990: 366.

22. Execution of a Qing official at Baoding. Also shows destruction of the city wall and temple. *The Graphic*, 5 January 1901.

city god temple, the British commander indicated that the kinds of warfare commonly practiced against rebellious native populations in Britain's colonies would be extended to China; the things that gave the Chinese people and their culture distinct identity would be destroyed. As Arthur Brown reported, two of Baoding's gate towers were also destroyed and a section of the southeast wall, near where the missionaries were believed to have been executed, was blown up (1904: 210). In carrying out these actions, the British, according to Arthur Smith, left "a brand upon the provincial capital" that had witnessed official crimes (1901b, 2: 611). Over the next several days, as the Tianjin column returned to its base, other brands were also administered. Villages all along the return march were looted and burned, and portions of city walls were blown up (Nicholls 1986: 90–91). Not long afterward, the Qing officials at Baoding were punished. On 6 November, Tingyong, Guiheng, and Wang Zhangui were taken to a spot near the southwest corner of the city wall, "as near as practicable to the place where the missionaries had been beheaded, and there in the presence of all the foreign soldiers, they themselves were beheaded" (A. Brown, 1904: 209; fig. 22).

As it turned out, this was the only case in which Qing officials were directly punished by the powers. But this was not the only reason these executions were noteworthy. As far as can be ascertained, it was apparently also the first time a "Chinese" form of execution was sanctioned by the allies. Moreover, in its details, the form mimicked the execution of British and American missionaries. As such, the decision to employ a Chinese form of capital punishment against mandarins (and, eventually, suspected Boxers) suggests an economy of vengeance that went beyond the blowing up of Confucian and Buddhist temples to strike at native superstition. In an unprecedented fashion that quite literally deterritorialized Qing political authority, the executions established a perfectly equal exchange, one that made Qing officials wholly accountable for their actions in Euroamerican terms.[39] And it did so in a framework that demonstrated the capacity of the judges to decode an indigenous form of punishment and turn it back against the natives.

The "justice" meted out in Baoding established one other precedent. The executions were themselves staged as a public spectacle, in which foreign soldiers not only bore witness to the punishment of the guilty, but were able to view, for their own enjoyment, the peculiar and "barbaric" customs of the natives. A reporter from the *Sydney Morning Herald* described the scene as a "Bland Holt kind of execution," referring to the spectacular stage productions of an Australian entrepreneur, and added that the French and Germans impressively "stage-managed" the whole affair:

> A large open space, empty but for the guards stationed at each entrance and at each platform in the center. A bugle blast, a roll of drums, the even tread of marching men, and 3000 troops filed in, and placed themselves around. Another flare of bugles and roll of drums—enter the victims and the executioners. The chief bows low to the victims, then to the audience, in the matter of an acrobat about to perform a difficult feat. The assistants do likewise, and throw themselves into statuesque postures . . . Another signal, and the first victim was forced to his knees, two assistants held him firmly by the shoulders, a third seized his pigtail, a fourth handed his axe to the executioner, and he balanced it carefully, raised it slowly to his shoulder, lowered it till the edge touched the bare neck, and left a scarlet mark. Once, twice, and he swung it with all his might. There was a spurt of blood, a few convulsive movements, and the

39. As a means for ensuring that officials do their utmost to prevent attacks on Euroamericans, this was a proposition long advocated by those on the scene. Charles Denby (1900: 2486), former U.S. minister, repeated the mantra on this occasion.

man with the pigtail tugged savagely, the threads of hair parted and it
was all over. (cited in Nicholls 1986: 90)

There is no other record of how the audience reacted, but it seems clear from
the Herald report that the form of execution hit a resonant note. It was, after
all, done on a scale that was not far removed from the staged reenactments
of colonial warfare common in Great Britain and North America by this time.
Such exhibitions, be they at the Belle Vue Gardens, Manchester, England,[40] in
wild west shows, or at international expositions, performed colonial conflict
as a spectacular staple of popular culture. But even if the connection between
public spectacle in Europe and the all-too-real enactments of retributive justice performed in China was not made by all participants, one thing was fairly
clear: after what transpired in Baoding, the punishment of the "guilty" was
less likely to make soldiers callous or to have their actions mistaken as in any
way comparable to those of savage Boxers and their benighted rulers. After
all, the executioners were now native Chinese, and the form of punishment
was thought to be an appropriate way to address the Chinese mentality. As
Count Waldersee noted in a letter to the kaiser on 3 November, the entire
Baoding affair was "exercising a moral influence of far-reaching importance"
(1924: 226).

From this point forward, the execution of putative Boxers was to be me-
diated by forms that had presumed cultural significance for the Chinese. At
a public execution ground in Beijing and on the grounds of the Temple of
Heaven, the staging of Boxer executions, with large numbers of soldiers,
missionaries, reporters, and photographers in attendance, became a "hid-
eously commonplace"[41] part of the occupation scene, extending well into
1901 (fig. 23). At the beginning of March, for example, Private Charles Wafer,
Co. D of the U.S. 9th Infantry, wrote to his mother and sister about witnessing
executions in the British camp. Although he claims they made him sick to his
"stumack," he stayed to see seven people get their heads cut off. Indeed, he
was so impressed with the executions he was sure that the guerrilla warfare
in the Philippines would cease if the United States would carry out a few executions (USMHI, Spanish-American War Survey, 9th Infantry, Wafer letters

40. Belle Vue Gardens had begun to stage reenactments of British imperial battles in
the 1850s; see Mayer 1992.

41. The phrase is from Sidney Adamson, special correspondent for Leslie's Weekly, who
provided one of the few detailed accounts of the executions occurring in Beijing; see the
issue of 18 May 1901: 484.

23. Public execution with allied soldiers observing. Courtesy of the Director, National Army Museum, London.

dated 5 and 6 March 1901). Private Wafer may not have been able to spell, but he shared with Waldersee and others an understanding of the stereotypical Oriental mind.

But the pedagogical force of a form of punishment understandable even to a barely literate private in the U.S. army was perhaps of less significance than what the procedure itself signified. It moved executions out of the realm of summary and arbitrary acts of punishment by allied forces and reterritorialized China through a legal-rational procedure, comparable to that of British prize law, where soldiers prone to mimicry could be shielded from the polluting effects of Chinese characteristics. A legal framework had been rolled into place to try Boxer suspects and have them executed by their own compatriots (fig. 24).[42] In an atmosphere in which questions had begun to be raised about the behavior of allied forces, this was no small matter.

42. In January 1901, a Chinese criminal court was established in the American sector with the power to execute those convicted of Boxer activities, looting, and rape. See NARA, RG395, 944, no. 3 and 911, General Order 3.

24. Boxer trial, Reverend Gilbert Reed fourth from right. Courtesy Library of Congress.

Civilization and Barbarism

The armed intervention of the Western powers into China in the summer of 1900 was justified on two grounds. The first was international law, which protected the diplomatic corps and the legations, as well as the person and property of foreign nationals in another country. The violation of the sanctity of the legations, the destruction of foreign property, and the loss of life made China liable for sanctions and restitution. These were hard and fast rules, ones that had been imposed regularly in China and in other parts of the world by European powers from 1840 forward. The second justification was somewhat more nebulous than the majestic nobility of a universal code of international behavior, but no less important for imperial and colonial actors. This was the notion of a *mission civilisatrice*, a "White Man's Burden," in which representatives of Western civilization had a responsibility to address and reform the barbarism of less civilized populations in other parts of the world.[43] The British had been engaged in something like a civilizing mission in China for some time. As we have seen, they organized that project as a pedagogical one in which they would teach China to be a responsible member of the international community. The Boxer uprising not only brought this project up short, but indicated anew the latent "barbarism and savagery" inherent in the Chinese people.

Yet, the presence of such savagery, though something of a surprise—the Chinese were, after all, supposedly stagnant and slumbering—could be addressed in much the same way as in other colonial situations; it simply required, as Alexis Krausse pointed out, the will to punish and a firm hand in meting it out. Public executions, the destruction of temples and city walls, and triumphal marches were all designed to teach lessons that would presumably pull Chinese civilization up from its downward slide. If they needed an additional moral sanction to justify their use of force, the powers found ready allies among Christian missionaries in China. The Reverend William Ament argued, for example, that "if you deal with the Chinese with a soft hand they will take advantage of it" (cited in M. Young 1968: 191; see also Miller 1974). Reverend Hykes of the American Bible Society added that, practically speak-

43. There is a wealth of material on this subject, the pervasiveness of which forms the critical target of Edward Said's *Orientalism*. For thoughtful discussions of the historical and historiographic issues surrounding the connection between European colonialism and civilization discourse, see Adas 1989; R. Young 1990, 1995. Critical anthropology has taken on this subject in a variety of ways; see, for example, Fabian 1983; Rabinow 1986.

ing, "the Chinese understood no other form of the display of power" (*Shanghai Mercury*, 1967: 79). Their position was reinforced by Arthur Smith, who explained that punishment was simply "a recognition of the indisputable and ominous fact that an Oriental interprets Occidental concession of what is, according to Oriental ethics, outside the pale of concession, as fatal weakness, and of that weakness the Oriental will take immediate and fatal advantage, as indeed he is now doing with signal success" (1901b, 2: 869, 726).

Although such arguments were repeated by others familiar with the Chinese and had firm support in treaty port and European newspapers, there began to emerge a sense among some observers that there was something disturbing about the level of retributive violence involving executions and plunder. Dissonant tones of concern appeared first in private journal entries and letters to loved ones. Waldersee, for example, thought that the actions of the powers were hardly an advertisement for Christian civilization, adding that there had been nothing like it since the Thirty Years' War or the plundering campaigns of the French in the days of Louis XIV (1924: 232). Speaking specifically of looting, General Stewart noted in his campaign diary that during the march through the Forbidden City, objets d'art "were lifted." Although he thought that it was perhaps best to keep "eyes front" and confine comments about such matters to the officers' mess, he was clearly disturbed by reports that even women from the diplomatic corps may have been involved. Moreover, even the orderly prize procedures of the British army appeared to provide no solace, leaving him to conclude that he was "beginning to hate the sound of the word 'loot.' If you happen to pick up an article which seems good, and for which you have paid the price you are at once asked 'Where did you loot that?' Even those who ought to know better seem to doubt your honesty. Life under such conditions is a bit degrading" (1908: 252).

Stewart's sense that the honesty and integrity of Europeans and Americans, even officers, was under scrutiny is borne out in other sources, some of which acknowledge participation in the opportunities available to obtain Chinese objects, while privately expressing moral doubts about the conditions of acquisition. For example, Leslie Grove, a U.S. army chaplain, initially wrote his wife of the grand opportunity at hand to acquire valuable Chinese curios. However, as he became more fully aware of the extent of the looting, the American missionary involvement in it, and the degree to which plunder was made acceptable through prize sales, Grove, like Polly Condit Smith, had moral qualms and decided to stop buying plundered objects at the British auctions. He also became convinced that missionary complicity in looting would cause a severe blow to their cause (USMHI, Grove Correspondence, letters of 22 August; 9, 13 September; 11, 16 October 1900).

Grove's instincts were right. In Shanghai, for example, that bastion of foreign privilege and treaty rights, the *North China Herald*, expressed concern at early reports coming from Tianjin. Recalling 1860, when looting had been "authorized" as a means of "punishment of the Peking Government," the editors seemed perplexed by the plunder of private, as opposed to government, property in Tianjin: "It will be a shock to the modern sentiment of the civilised world if such orgies . . . are to be the regular thing. Wherein will the much-boasted civilisation of the West appear if such deeds are the outcome of it? Our troops have come to do a necessary duty. They have to get the upper hand of a savage and sanguinary enemy, to whom murder and pillage are but the incidents of an ordinary day's work. It is to exterminate this demon, *not imitate him*, that the United Powers of Europe have sent troops, and we shall be much mistaken if the plunder of civilians in the shameless manner depicted does not raise a howl of execration from one end of the civilised world to the other" (8 August 1900: 277–278; emphasis added).

Of import here are three elements that would become central to many other critiques of looting. First, and perhaps most important, was the problem looting posed to civilization. Could one be civilized, or claim the superiority of the West, if one looted? The second, and related element, was the issue of mimicry: How could the powers retain the moral high ground if they slavishly copied the behavior of savages? Third, looting appeared to have occurred innocent of any sense of shame; this was not only akin to the practices of the uncivilized, but invited criticism from throughout the civilized world. When reports arrived in Shanghai of a repetition of the loot "orgy" in the Qing capital, the paper added one more element to the mix: it referred to the sack of Beijing as a "scandal" (NCH, 12 September 1900: 542).

As the *Herald* predicted, when word reached Europe and North America of the carnival of loot, it caused a sensation.[44] The *London Daily Express* observed that once the mission to China was accomplished, "civilization" ought to "have the grace to blush" (cited in CE, 14 January 1901: 56). In an editorial, the *Review of Reviews* (22, 1900: 52) argued that the news from China was "calculated to make Europeans hang their heads for shame." Pointing to looting,

---

44. The U.S. Congress passed a resolution of inquiry that was sent to the secretary of War, Elihu Root. See House of Representatives, 56th Congress, 2nd Session, vol. 2, 4213, Report no. 2358.

loot sales in the British legation, and Russian massacres in Manchuria, the editorial concluded, "We have flung aside the garb of civilization, and are acting like our piratical ancestors in the days of the Vikings. Civilization is but skin deep, and the restraints that conscience endeavours to place upon the human brute have snapped under the strain of events in China."

Other newspapers, journals, and books echoed the *Daily Express*'s sense of a scandal. In France, *La Vie illustrée* ran a critical photo-essay on the looting of Beijing, complete with pictures of looted items and sales at the Italian legation (fig. 25). There was also a picture of a guardian lion taken from the Qing Ancestral Temple, dispatched to France by General Frey and, in an apparent fit of embarrassment, sent back to China by the French government (1 February 1901: 283–300)! Robert Hart, the head of the Imperial Maritime Customs, noted that a bit of temptation placed before a European easily led to a "retrogression to barbarism"; he worried that "for a century to come Chinese converts will consider looting and vengeance Christian virtues!" (1901a, 1901b: 87–89). According to James Ricalton, a photographer on assignment for Underwood and Underwood's stereoscopic world tours (see chapter 8), Li Hongzhang, the eminent official and Qing representative to the peace conference that would produce the Boxer protocol, was also puzzled by the behavior of members of Western civilization. After consulting the "mosaic decalogue," Li suggested that "the eighth commandment should be amended to read, Thou shalt not steal, but thou mayst loot" (Ricalton 1901: 233). Li's criticism was all the more telling because it indirectly pointed to Christian missionary involvement in the looting.

Similar patterns of outrage are discernible in publications in Japan and the United States. In the former case, reports of looting were accompanied by allegations of the complicity of the military high command and Japanese businesses in the plunder, and charges of a government coverup. In November 1901, the Japanese newspaper *Yorozu Chōhō* published a detailed list of the kinds of things looted and charged that although Lieutenant General Yamaguchi Soshin issued explicit orders forbidding plunder, this was merely a façade behind which he and his subordinates hid their activities. According to the paper, "Whenever they witnessed looting by enlisted men or junior officers, they exclaimed angrily that it was a disgrace to the military [then] . . . they hauled the loot to divisional headquarters, where especially valuable items were distributed among the bigwigs while the remainder was disposed of in a manner convenient to maintaining a show of appearances. For example, a portion of the loot was held on to until merchants entered Beijing, then en-

25. The pillage of Beijing. *La Vie Illustreé*, 1 February 1901.

trusted to them so that the [military] could be said to have clean hands, forever maintaining appearances" (5 December 1901). The *Yorozu Chōhō* kept up
its spirited attacks against the army high command into 1902, with the eventual result that General Yamaguchi and General Manabe Bin, commander of
the 9th Infantry Brigade, were forced to resign, providing the only two clear
cases of repercussions from the looting scandal.[45]

In the United States, by contrast, the primary issue was not military, but
missionary involvement in looting, the earliest reports of which appeared
in the *New York Sun* under the byline of Wilber Chamberlin. But what elevated the missionary question into a cause célèbre was an interview, published on Christmas Eve 1900, that Chamberlin conducted with the Reverend
Ament, in which missionary looting was fully justified (cited in M. Young
1968: 191). The logic of Ament's argument prompted a response from no less
a figure than Mark Twain, one of the leading critics of U.S. expansion into
the Pacific. In an article entitled "To the Person Sitting in Darkness," Twain
wrote a scathing critique of missionary morality and linked it to U.S. activities
in the Philippines. Twain's caustic indictment in turn generated a defensive
apologetics on the part of the American Board of Commissioners for Foreign Missions. Both Gilbert Reid and Judson Smith claimed that missionary
looting was "high ethics," and added that American missionaries had looted
only to provide money for the relief of Chinese Christians, a proposition that
Twain gleefully shredded in his response.[46] Somewhat at a disadvantage in
this exchange, missionary leaders nevertheless attempted to influence opinion in China: Arthur Smith joined Reid and Judson Smith in writing letters
to the *North China Herald* justifying missionary actions and criticizing Twain
(27 March 1901: 602–603; 3 April 1901: 660–661; 19 June 1901: 1193–1194).

Whereas missionaries and their critics appear to have been bounded by the
discursive regularities of a Christian moral universe, other critics attempted
to mobilize history and international law to make their arguments. This was
the case with John MacDonnell. In a piece that appeared in the *Contemporary
Review*, MacDonnell (1901) discussed the history of British prize laws, arguing
that rather than acting as a deterrent, laws, because they gave a dispropor-
tionate amount of a prize fund to officers, encouraged common soldiers to

45. Cited in Middleton 2001: 14–15, 19. Following their resignations, both officers were
subsequently promoted and awarded the Order of the Rising Sun.

46. For the Twain-missionary exchange, see Twain 1901a, 1901b; J. Smith 1901; Reid
1901, 1902; Ament 1901a, 1901b. Also see Favier 1901; *Literary Digest* 23.2 (1901): 36–37.

loot more. He based this conclusion on the report of an 1864 parliamentary commission on army prize procedures, a source that investigated instances of prize dating back to 1807, including the Napoleonic War campaigns and campaigns in India (*Report of the Commissioners* 1864). Although it did not outlaw plunder, it did recommend that share allotments be made more speedily and that the scale of distribution be made more equitable among the ranks of soldiers. Whether or not the recommendations were actually implemented remains unclear. What was significant for MacDonnell was that a new body of international law on warfare had emerged since 1860.

Following France's defeat by Prussia in 1871, many European countries looked to professionalize their armies by integrating new organizational and weapons technologies into them, reforming their armies and improving their officer corps.[47] Over the same period of time, the rapid change in military technology led to discussions concerning the establishment of international standards for the conduct of warfare. The result of these discussions was the Hague Conventions of 1898 and 1899, the second of which dealt with rules for land warfare. Plunder and the seizure of private property were outlawed without qualification (Bevans 1918–30, 1: 260). All of the nations that invaded China in 1900 were parties to the convention, as was the Qing government.[48] Although these developments did nothing to prevent another instance of looting in Beijing, they do point to a kind of international reterritorialization of the practices of warfare that could not but have an effect on the way events in China in 1900 were interpreted.

In MacDonnell's case, the criticism was obvious: the "letter and the spirit of the Hague Convention" had been violated in China. As he put it, the theory of the convention was "all that could be desired." So what had gone wrong? MacDonnell pointed directly to the question of race. In dealing with "Oriental nations," he noted, when opportunity presented itself, "the old outrages were repeated." Those outrages were, in turn, deeply rooted in the practices of the British army in India and sanctioned by prize law, with the result that they continued to produce the most extreme examples of plunder to date.[49]

47. In Great Britain, several parliamentary commissions recommended reform and re-organization of the army, and these changes began to be implemented by the 1880s.

48. Formal ratifications were delivered at the same moment the looting of Beijing was underway. See Carnegie Endowment 1914: 2–4.

49. J. MacDonnell 1901: 444–452, especially 446–450. Also see *Review of Reviews* 22 (1900): 52.

MacDonnell was not alone in pointing out that Hague Conventions had been violated by the powers. But plunder, as we have seen, was not the only issue. The *North China Herald*, for example, pointed to a number of specific violations concerning "Rules and Usages of War." These included the atrocities committed by Russian forces, the punitive expeditions launched by the powers, the theft of the scientific instruments in the Beijing observatory, and the "charity from loot practiced by some American and British missionaries" (24 April 1901: 784). Like the *Herald*, George Lynch was also disturbed by the violation of the Hague Conventions and, like MacDonnell, he was bothered by the level of violence directed at ordinary Chinese people by allied military forces. Drawing attention to the mass beheadings of suspected Boxers by Japanese soldiers, the rape of women and the bayoneting of children, German torture of suspected Boxers, and the mass suicides that occurred in a number of Chinese villages, Lynch wondered what "fears" had driven these actions. His conclusion was that the West had mistaken speed for progress, which was "propelling us like a herd of Gadarene swine over an abyss of God knows what." Western civilization, he concluded, was "merely a veneer over savagery" (1901: 303, 311–317).

Some would balk at describing that savagery as "too grewsome [sic] for presentation" (Lucas 1990: 184), whereas others would use it as an occasion to deromanticize modern warfare. This was the case with E. J. Dillon (1901), whose "Chinese Wolf and the European Lamb" turned reporting of the war on its head. The piece was a litany of the executions, slaughter, and all other manner of atrocity committed by the allied forces. The catalogue ran from July into September and drew occasionally for emphasis on the graphic interviews about German atrocities published in the *Bremer Burger Zeitung* and the *Frankfurter Zeitung* in October and November. Dillon concluded his piece with the following question: "Why should cultured and more or less truth-loving people persist in speaking of the glorious work of civilising China, when it is evident that they are ruining her people and demoralizing their own troops besides?"

Dillon's query remained unanswered, but his insistence on not turning a blind eye to Western atrocities provided ammunition for others. Thomas F. Millard, an old China hand, charged in *Scribner's Magazine* that the allied insistence on revenge was criminal. "Seized with a vertigo of indiscriminating vengeance," he wrote, "the powers are trifling with the peace of the world. Events such as the months of September, October and November brought to China have carried war back to the Dark Ages, and will leave a taint in the moral atmosphere of the world for a generation to come" (1901: vol. 29, p. 194).

These critical interventions into discussions of how to interpret the actions of foreign powers in China are significant; they indicate that neither the events that transpired there nor the way they were understood by European, American, or Japanese people existed in a vacuum. The larger context involved the way individuals or groups within each of the nations involved explained and justified expansion into other parts of the world. As we have seen, in the case of Euroamericans, issues of racial difference, especially the link between race and the progress of civilization, was a central element in the ideological construction buttressing positive assessments of colonialism. Directly and indirectly, race was not far from the thinking of either critics or apologists for the actions of the powers in China. Moreover, race was a continual undertone throughout the campaign and the occupation of Beijing. The Japanese soldiers, for example, were lauded for being the exception to Orientals in general. Count Waldersee thought that the German army should not be called on to "fight against heathen races"—it was bad for morale and discipline (1924: 234). In other cases, there were open altercations between India army soldiers and soldiers from other countries. The situation became so severe that at one point Colonel J. M. Grierson was convinced that contempt was being shown the British due to their having "practically no white troops" among the occupation forces.[50]

Yet, regardless of how one interprets pronouncements, one cannot avoid being reminded of the central racial issue of empire. Were whites, as Paymaster Wynne and Count Waldersee suggested, altered by contact with lesser races? Was "the Eastern education" simply another name for racial degeneration through contact? And, perhaps most important, how was it possible for the pedagogical project to be reversed? Such questions existed in a far broader context than the China coast and are probably most evident in widely diffused apprehensions about atavistic primitivism in the last quarter of the nineteenth century.[51]

As a kind of repressed element within bourgeois sensibilities about the stark division between the civilized and the savage, such concerns focused

50. See WO 32/6413, 6422, 6423, 6425, 6426, 6427, in which Grierson discusses various incidents involving the India army troops.

51. Hobson (1901), for example, pointed to it in his discussion of jingoism; cited in Pick 1993: 113.

not only on "racial" mixing, but on the possibility that contact with "inferior" civilizations or peoples would awaken latent desires or primitive remnants in the European psyche. Mainstream media, scientific journals, popular fiction, and dissident literature during this period were rife with such concerns (Brantlinger 1988: 227–254; Gilman 1985; McClintock 1995: 49–61; Stoler 1991: 72–88). Thus, when real events such as the extreme violence directed against Chinese or the sacking of Beijing exceeded rational expectations and seemed to converge with fiction, tropes from the latter were readily available for representing the meaning of European and American behavior in terms other than a triumphalist narrative of civilization overcoming barbarism. And, although there was not a thorough inversion of meaning, insofar as atrocities and plunder could serve as signs of degeneration, it was more difficult to construct the events of 1900 in the clear terms of European moral superiority that had dominated the constructs and rationales of the 1860 invasion.

Moreover, the chaotic violence of retribution and revenge that swept across north China after the relief of the legations was a challenge even to the sensibilities of those with long experience in disciplining unruly native populations.[52] The situation became such that by December 1900, Colonel Grierson, serving as British representative on the international staff commanded by General Waldersee, felt compelled to explain to the German commander, Lieutenant Colonel Gündell, that Zhili province would degenerate into anarchy if the Germans were "to kill on sight every Chinaman who bore arms for the civil power" or flogged and cut off the queues of mandarins, as had been reported (WO 32/6415, diary entries of 20–29 December 1900). This sense of excess, of having overstepped some boundary between civilization and savagery, was, in other words, a very real issue for both observers and observed. There was, to put it simply, an enormous gash in the body of Western self-perception, a cut that would require both triage and expert suturing. China would have to be reordered yet again so that the problem of barbarism within the civilized could effectively be suppressed.

52. In the spring of 1901, Colonel Grierson, citing the 250 years of British experience in the East, lectured the Germans on how to conduct warfare in Oriental countries. See WO 32/6423, letter dated 2 April 1901.

CHAPTER 8

Desacralizing Qing Sovereignty, 1900–1901

THE SUPPRESSION OF THE Boxer Uprising led to a reterritorialization of China on an unprecedented scale, one that operated not only to establish a new order of foreign relations, but to resolve the contradictions of the barbarism lurking within civilization. This chapter and the one that follows explore three discrete but interrelated zones of activity in which agents of Euroamerican imperial powers reordered China and performed the ideological suturing necessary to occlude Western barbarism. One of these zones was in the arena of international relations. The legal-rational procedures of international law were brought to bear, and through negotiations a settlement was imposed on the Qing government. A second area of action was within an international exhibitionary culture, the features of which served to produce China as an archaic and backward spectacle for Euroamerican consumption. The third arena of activity involved ideological efforts to produce an unambiguous meaning for the events of 1900. Critical to such production was the creation of an authoritative narrative, one that circulated in a variety of venues, including the formal memorialization of the "victims" of Chinese "savagery" (see chapter 9). In each of these realms of meaning production, the moral crisis related to Euroamerican atrocities and plunder was effectively resolved by displacing them onto other, less threatening formations so that, much like the disenchantment of Qing rulership, their unique specificities were dissolved. In their place appeared confirmations of the peculiar behavior of racialized (i.e., Chinese, Asiatic, or Oriental) others and the congenital antiforeignism of the Chinese.

Reterritorialization 1901: The Final Protocol and the New Imperial Audience Format

In the fall of 1900, the ministers of the Western powers found themselves in a unique position to punish China for transgressions against international law and to resolve issues dating back to the treaty agreements of 1860. To address these matters, the powers composed a joint note, the final form of which contained twelve demands, all of which were included in the *Final Protocol* signed on 7 September 1901 (Foreign Relations of the United States [FRUS] 306–339). The note was delivered to the Qing government on 22 December 1900 and, the following day, Prince Qing (Yikuang), head of the Zongli yamen, and Li Hongzhang, viceroy of Zhili province, delivered documents certifying their plenipotentiary powers.[1] Thereupon, negotiations formally began.[2]

In his report on the ensuing peace conference, William Rockhill, the U.S. representative, summarized the goals and objectives of the powers under "four principle heads": (1) punishment of the "authors" and those guilty of actually participating in the "antiforeign massacres and riots"; (2) indemnification for property losses sustained as a result of the riots; (3) adoption of measures so that such outbreaks could not recur; and (4) the improvement of relations, "both official and commercial," with the government of China and with the Chinese people (FRUS 4–5).

The first two headings—punishment of the culprits and indemnities for losses—targeted the Chinese government and succeeded in further eroding

1. See FRUS 58–60. The note expanded on a French and an Anglo-German list of demands on 4 October and 23 October, respectively; see FRUS 26–27, 31. The plenipotentiary powers of Prince Qing and Li Hongzhang are in FRUS 61 and seem to have caused little difficulty.

2. The most comprehensive history of the conference remains Kelly 1963, which makes clear that there was not always a consensus of opinion among representatives of the powers. In addition to the mutual suspicion among the negotiators, substantial criticism was leveled against them by observers who saw them as novices dealing with a wily Court; see Lo 1976, 1: 141–202, especially William Drummond's comments on 163.

Qing imperial sovereignty. The Chinese government was forced to execute, degrade, or otherwise punish its own imperial princes and officials, an extraordinary demand by any standard of international intercourse, even as European nation-states understood such standards. It also forced the Qing to acknowledge their errors by requiring the posthumous rehabilitation of officials who had opposed the Court's policy regarding the Boxers and had, as a result, been executed. As for the indemnity, it was unprecedented in scope and draconian in implementation. Over the next forty years, a succession of Chinese governments was saddled with payments for which they were required to commit all of their maritime and domestic customs revenues, as well as the revenues of the state salt monopoly.

Yet, as impressive as these strictures were, they form only part of the final protocol and remain relatively explainable as stemming from the interests and asymmetric powers of nation-states. The other two headings to which Rockhill referred—security for the future and the improvement of relations—indicate that punishment and restitution were only two of the concerns that animated the diplomats. The ministers were also determined to ensure that any future "antiforeign" outbursts in China would be nipped in the bud and that the foreign community, be they diplomats, businessmen, or missionaries, would be adequately protected. The protocol accomplished these tasks by making officials of the Qing regime personally responsible for antiforeignism and by reducing the stature of the emperor of China. In the realm of relations between sovereign nation-states, and in relation to an emerging world of figurehead rulers in European "spheres of influence," the emperor of China was to be little more than a mere symbol of an archaic form of power.

Given the many different kinds of purposes and interests that Rockhill identified as operating in the Final Protocol, it is perhaps wise to approach this text with a degree of caution, to treat it, in other words, as a far from transparent document. Such caution is justified, moreover, because the protocol did more than resolve matters of immediate concern; it also addressed, as Rockhill hinted, a number of issues that had been at the core of the struggle between the Qing Empire and the North Atlantic nation-states for much of the nineteenth century. Because of its importance, the provisions of the document are dealt with in some detail here to tease out its operating system and expose its mechanisms of power.

The prologue of the document begins with the names of the plenipotentiaries of each of the twelve sovereign nation-states who were parties to it: Germany, Austria-Hungary, Belgium, Spain, the United States, France, Great

Britain, Italy, Japan, the Netherlands, Russia, and China. Following the list of names of the representatives and their nations, the document cites the authority on which each article of the protocol is based. In so doing, it establishes the technique by which the articles of the treaty are made legitimate and binding. The protocol accomplished its legitimacy by cross-referencing the demands of the powers to the documented acceptance of those demands by the Chinese sovereign, that is, the emperor of China as the head of state. So, for example, the prologue ends by citing the "joint note" addressed to the "government of China" of 22 December. It then signifies the Qing acceptance of the note by referring to an imperial decree on 27 December, which is then presented in full in Annex 1 of the protocol. This procedure is repeated for each of the twelve articles of the protocol, "giving effect," as one official British publication put it, to the terms of the joint note (Norie [1903] 1995: 499–507).

The articles of the protocol are similar in substance and order of presentation to the twelve clauses of the note. The two might, therefore, be usefully read together, particularly because they are not quite identical. The joint note markedly differs from the protocol in that it—rather than the protocol—lays out the conditions and circumstances of the existence of both. In other words, the joint note provides the rationale on which its demands are grounded and the ultimate justification for each of the clauses in the *Final Protocol*. It does this by situating both in the following context: "During the months of May, June, July and August of the present year, serious disturbances broke out in the northern provinces of China, and crimes *unprecedented in human history*, crimes against the law of nations, against the *laws of humanity* and *against civilization*, were committed under peculiarly odious circumstances" (FRUS 59; emphasis added).

I have added the emphasis in this opening passage to provide some sense of the way the powers collectively decided to frame the conflict. Moreover, because missionary writers would later present matters in similarly hyperbolic terms, it is important to recognize that the dominant narrative framework for the events of 1900 was firmly situated within diplomatic as well as popular formations. Such was necessary, in fact, because although the powers were within their rights, as they defined them, to claim compensation for losses inflicted on persons and property during the conflict, they also intended to impose a moral judgment on the conduct of the Qing regime. China first had to be situated beyond the pale of civilization—the Boxers were no ordinary local rebels, this was no ordinary military action—and the Qing represented as having removed themselves from normal international relations, before the Court and the Chinese people could be readmitted, at the sufferance of the powers, to the "family of nations."

The *Final Protocol* addressed this rite of passage from barbarism to civilization in three ways. First, it insisted on formal apologies for the actions taken by Chinese against foreigners. Second, it dictated the punishment of those held most responsible for those actions. Third, it created a new kind of relationship with China, one that authorized novel physical and institutional structures to support the Western presence in China. All of this was, in turn, made to appear as if the powers or the particular elements of the protocol had the full cooperation and support of the Qing regime through the citation process mentioned above.

Formal apologies were of two kinds. Articles 1 and 3 stipulated that the Qing government was to dispatch an ambassador from "His Majesty the Emperor of China" to their "Majesties" the "Emperor of Germany" and the "Emperor of Japan" bearing expressions of regret on his part and that of his government for the "assassinations" of Baron von Ketteler, the German minister, and Mr. Sugiyama, a member of the Japanese legation. The delegation to Germany was to be led by an imperial prince, in this case, Caifeng, the Prince of Chun. The Japanese delegation was to be led by Na Tong, "vice-president of the Board of Revenue." Translations of the relevant imperial edicts were contained in Annexes 2 and 9.

There are two points to be made about the content of these articles. First, note that the names and titles of the Qing ambassadors are written into the protocol; not only were the ambassadors to be publicly known, but attention drawn to their ranks and administrative positions. An effort was made, it would seem, to guarantee that someone of sufficient rank present regrets. Presumably, any apology could be understood as sincere—rather than, for instance, "face-saving" or a mere "appearance"—only if made under these conditions. The second feature of the articles is that they characterized the killings of the two diplomats as assassinations. In addition to the political connotations of the term, it also carries a pejorative sense of a crime committed on an unsuspecting victim through secret and devious means, a crime, in other words, that itself reflected contempt for the laws of humanity and civilization.

Complementing the apology missions to Germany and Japan was another form of expression of regret, one that was designed to leave a visible sign, or, as Arthur Smith had suggested, an indelible brand for all to see. The Qing government was to construct a "commemorative monument" on the site where Baron von Ketteler had been killed. According to Annex 3, at the decision of the emperor of Germany, the monument was to be an archway that spanned the entire street where Ketteler died and was to be built from *new*, not used material. In addition to the Ketteler memorial, the Chinese government "agreed to erect an expiatory monument in each of the foreign or international cemeteries which were desecrated" and tombs destroyed (Annex 10). It was left to the discretion of the particular legations to settle the details concerning the monuments.

In addition to building new memorials, an older monument that was supposed to have been destroyed by the Boxers was restored. This was the monument in the Russian cemetery to the sacred memory of the British soldiers, civilians, and India army troopers who had been "treacherously seized in violation of a flag of truce on the 18th September, 1860, [and] sank under the inhuman treatment during their captivity." These dead included, it will be recalled, the immortalized Private Phipps. The Qing Court was required to put up a new monument, with the same legend and a kind of footnote stating that this "stone replaces the original memorial destroyed by the Chinese in June 1900" (Arlington and Lewisohn [1935] 1987: 237–238).

More will be said about monument construction in the next chapter. Here it is worth noting that for the British in China the historical continuity between 1860 and 1900 was made clear and "permanent." But it was also the case that this inscription was hardly intended for the ordinary Chinese who might contemplate antiforeign activity like that of the Boxers. Surely the British did not expect many "Chinamen" to be able to read English. What the footnoted monument suggests, therefore, is that there was more than one imagined audience to be taught lessons — Englishmen who might come to China in later years, for example, to remind them of the sacrifices of their predecessors.

That Chinese could kill Westerners and attack Christian missions was, however, not a novel development. In this case, however, the culprits were identified as being in the highest councils of government—the heads of bureaus, grand secretaries, governors of provinces, and so forth—holders, in other words, of the highest civil service degrees in China, the literati, the cream of China's elite, often referred to as mandarins. Here, then, was an opportunity to make examples so that others would learn the consequences of antiforeign outbursts. It was also an opportunity to settle old scores with generations of mandarins who frustrated Euroamerican ambitions in China.

But this was not all. It was not simply that a group of Qing officials were treated as if they were the leaders of a rebellious tribe on the frontiers of empire. At the head of the list of those slated for punishment were three imperial princes of the blood. Two of them, Caiyi, Prince Duan, and Cailan, Duke of Fuguo, were grandsons of Daoguang, the fifth emperor of the Qing Dynasty. The third, Caixun, Prince Zhuang, the ninth person to hold this hereditary princedom, was a descendant of the Kangxi emperor, the second ruler of the Qing.[3] Conventionally, it has been the norm to refer to these noblemen and officials as xenophobes, that is, as Chinese whose hatred of all foreigners was of such an extreme nature as to be almost irrational.[4] Executed imperial princes and high officials would, in other words, provide object lessons of the consequences of such "irrational" thinking. At the same time, others would learn that their life might depend on performing the policing functions mandated by the treaty. Those not devoted to protecting the interests of foreigners faced possible execution.

In the end, however, even the chastened Qing Court was unwilling to submit fully to the demands of the powers, and a compromise was struck. Article 2 condemned only Caixun to death, and he was allowed to commit suicide. Caiyi and Cailan were to be banished for life to Xinjiang. In addition, Ying Nian, president of the Court of Censors, and Zhao Shuqiao, president of the Board of Punishments, were ordered to commit suicide, and Yuxian, the governor of Shanxi, Ji Xiu, president of the Board of Rites, and Xu Zhengyu, former vice president of the Board of Punishments, were condemned to death. Others were posthumously demoted in rank, and an unspecified number were to receive punishments once their complicity was determined. These actions were confirmed by imperial edicts in Annexes 4 through 6, and the capital punishments were to be verified by Qing Court-appointed witnesses. In addition, Xu Yongyi, Li Shan, Xu Jingzheng, Lian

3. None of the three princes is accorded a separate biography in Hummel 1943, but they are mentioned in those of others. For Caiyi and Cailan, see 393–394. For Caixun, see 926.

4. In addition to the citations in the previous note, see, for example, Esherick 1987: 306. It should be borne in mind, however, that it was the aggressive actions of the Western powers in China, not a kind of generalized or pathological aversion to foreigners, that precipitated the crisis. The princes and the officials who supported them were the descendants of emperors and upholders of an imperial sovereignty that had been battered and humiliated not by generic foreigners, but by the representatives of Euroamerican nation-states and empires.

Yuan, and Yuan Zhang, all executed by the Qing Court for protesting the "outrageous breaches of international law," were posthumously rehabilitated by an imperial edict of 13 February 1901 (Annex 7).

With procedures now established for making a clear demarcation between good and bad mandarins, the powers extended the principle of punishment to the literati class in those regions where antiforeign incidents had occurred. In all cities "where foreigners were massacred or submitted to cruel treatment," the official examinations for those wishing to hold office were to be suspended for five years. The decree affected approximately fifty prefectural and district towns in six provinces and Manchuria (Annex 8). Further punishments included a ban on the importation of armaments and arms manufacturing equipment for two years and an indemnity of 450 million Haiguan taels (approximately three times the annual revenue of the government), which included an elaborate amortization and payment scheme, and official exchange rates for the various currencies at the time the protocol was signed (Articles 5 and 6, and Annexes 11 and 12).

Having clearly laid out procedures for apologies and punishments, the protocol then took up the institution of a new order, beginning with the security of the foreign legations. In perhaps the most ironic element of the settlement, the powers decided to build their own high walls of exclusion, ones that were to surround a greatly expanded legation quarter bounded on the north by present-day Chang'an Boulevard, on the south by the preexisting city wall, on the west by the Qian Gate Eastern Boulevard, and on the east by Chongwen Gate Inner Boulevard. On the map included with Annex 14, these streets are identified as Stewart Road (N), the Tartar Wall (S), Gaselee Road (W), and Ketteler Strasse (E). In this quarter, according to Article 7, the Chinese were excluded from the "right to reside," and the area itself was to be made "defensible." Further, each power had the right to maintain "a permanent guard in the said quarter for the defense of its legation."

The legations would also be defended by establishing clear and secure lines of communication between Beijing and the coast. The Dagu forts were to be razed (Article 8), the navigation of the North River (Beiho, Article 11a) improved, and various strategic points occupied by military forces of the powers, including Tianjin and Shanhaiguan (Article 9). In addition, Qinhuang island was to be occupied and a port facility built to accommodate transport vessels and warships. Article 11 also stipulated that the Huangpu River at Shanghai was to be improved, and provided details for making the river more accessible to larger foreign ships (Annex 17). This, it might be added, was the sole element in the protocol related directly to commercial issues.

A second aspect of the new order was the promulgation throughout the empire of edicts detailing the steps taken to punish those responsible for crimes "unprecedented in human history." In addition, Article 10 stipulated that local officials were to be held responsible in their districts for the treatment of foreigners and the enforcement of treaty rights. Failure to comply with this edict would result in immediate dismissal, "without the possibility of being given new functions or new honors." In other words, officials who did not stamp out anti-Western activities were liable to lose their government positions, a form of punishment that Europeans had been advocating in China for over half a century. This article also targeted the general population. Chinese people were prohibited "forever, under pain of death," to join any antiforeign society (edicts in Annex 15 and 16).

Last, the protocol addressed issues regarding the conduct of Qing foreign relations. The Office of Foreign Affairs, the Zongli yamen, was abolished and replaced by the Ministry of Foreign Affairs (Waiwu bu), which, according to Article 12, took "precedence over the six other Ministries of State." Thus, the foreign representatives made clear that the most important business of the Qing government would henceforth be its relations with the eleven foreign powers who signed the protocol.[5] Unmatched in the organization of their own governments, the elevation of China's foreign relations established an almost perfect symmetry with the commitment the Qing was forced to make of all its customs revenues for the retirement of the indemnity.

This clear and unprecedented infringement of Qing sovereignty concluded with one final insult. The powers had stipulated in the joint note of 22 December that the procedures for Imperial Court audiences for the reception of foreign representatives was to be determined "in a manner" that they would lay out for the Court (FRUS 59–60). The results appeared in Annex 19 and resolved once and for all the audience question, the "long and hard-fought battle between Chinese and Western etiquette" that, for many Euroamericans, dated to time immemorial (Rockhill [1905] 1971: 8). Annex 19 deserves careful consideration, therefore, and not simply because of its historic im-

5. Imagine the howls of derisive laughter if a foreign power told the U.S. Congress that the State Department would henceforth be the preeminent branch of the government of the United States.

portance. It was here, at the level of the formalized routines and rituals of international relations, that Qing sovereignty was thoroughly and conclusively reordered.

ANNEX 19 OF THE FINAL PROTOCOL: "MEMORANDUM ON THE CEREMONIAL TO BE FOLLOWED IN SOLEMN AUDIENCES"

The solution to the battle over "etiquette," as the ministers saw it, was to impose a court ceremonial that they would write themselves to ensure that there was not the slightest hint of Chinese arrogance. But as they turned to the audience question, the diplomats faced two problems. It was not only that the Chinese emperor did not fit neatly into a standardized view of a monarch, even of the retooled "Asiatic" sort that had appeared in Japan and Siam near the end of the century.[6] The emperor was still, for all intents and purposes, a despot—a living representation of an archaic form of government, dealings with which had always been problematic. Moreover, China was an "Oriental despotism," whose chief feature in the past had been a preference for "shadow" over "substance" and "jealous" and "deceitful" relations with European powers. The collective Western experience—the imperial archive created by over a generation of observers that was embodied in the records of the legations and in the works on China's past (see chapter 5)—argued that without significant structural change, Qing despotism would simply revert to its natural form. It might be necessary, therefore, to include elements in the audience ceremony that would not normally be found in other settings.

The second problem had to do with the existing conditions of this particular despot. Having been confronted with the objective fact of his palaces, the ministers knew that by any standard of how despots ought to live, the Chinese emperor failed to measure up to the fabled excesses and extravagance of the Orient. Moreover, the current Qing emperor was emperor in name only. His own well-intentioned efforts at reform in 1898 had led to a conservative backlash, restored the dominant position of the empress dowager, and ultimately resulted in the antiforeign Boxer movement. Thus, the emperor had to be not only restored to power, but also quite literally refashioned. He had to be reconstituted as a monarch, perfectly equal to other monarchs, who, of his own free will, would do what the Western powers wanted done, that is, like the

---

6. Anderson (1983: 27) argues that by the late nineteenth century Western notions of monarchy had become a "semistandardized" model and had been accepted by a number of countries, including Thailand and Japan.

26. German minister carried in large chair to Qianqing palace. Source: Mumm, *Ein Tagebuch in Bildern*, 1902.

Meiji emperor in Japan, conform to Euroamerican diplomatic practices and provide a responsible agency for the implementation of treaty agreements.

The diplomats faced a delicate balancing act as they tried to achieve their goals. Actions sanctioned by them had already humiliated the monarchy. Thus, they would have to not only bring him down from his perch of high-walled exclusionism, but elevate him to a position befitting a monarch who represented the sovereignty of his nation. The process of elevation was not without its own ambiguities, however. The final audience protocol seems to have had past slights figured into it and the books balanced. For this reason, it is cited here in full, with a number of the most significant elements italicized.

1. *Solemn audiences* to be given by His Majesty the Emperor of China to the Diplomatic Body or to Representatives of the Powers separately shall take place in the palace hall called "Ch'ien-ch'ing Kung" [Qianqing gong].

2. In going to or coming back from these solemn audiences the Representatives of the Powers shall be *carried in their sedan chairs* as far as outside of the Ching-yun gate [fig. 26]. At the Ching-yun gate they will get out

27. German minister carried in small chair to gate of Qianqing palace. Source: Mumm, *Ein Tagebuch in Bildern*, 1902.

of the sedan chair in which they have come and will be carried in a little chair [fig. 27] as far as the foot of the steps of the Ch'ien-ch'ing gate. On arriving at the Ch'ien-ch'ing gate the Representatives of the Powers shall get out of their chairs, and shall proceed on foot into the presence of His Majesty in the Ch'ien-ch'ing Kung hall. When departing the Representatives of the Powers shall return to their residences in the same manner as that in which they arrived.

3. When a Representative of a Power shall have occasion to present to His Majesty the Emperor his *letters of credence or a communication from the Head of the State* by whom he is accredited, the Emperor shall cause to be sent to the residence of said Representative, to bear him to the Palace, a sedan chair with *yellow trimmings and tassels,* such as are used by *princes of the Imperial family.* The said Representative shall be taken back to his residence in the same manner. An escort of troops shall likewise be sent to the residence of said Representative to accompany him going and returning.

4. When presenting his letters of credence or communications from the Head of the State by whom he is accredited, the Diplomatic Agent, while bearing said letters or communications, shall pass by [way of] *the cen-*

tral openings of the Palace doors until he has arrived in the presence of His Majesty. On returning from these audiences he will comply, as regards the doors by which he may have to pass, with the *usages already established* at the Court of Peking for audiences given to Foreign Representatives.

5. The Emperor shall receive *directly into his hands* the letters and communications above mentioned which the Foreign Representatives may have to hand to him.

6. If His Majesty should decide upon inviting to a banquet the Representatives of the Powers it is well understood that this banquet shall be given in one of the halls of the Imperial Palace and that *His majesty shall be present in person.*

7. In brief, the ceremonial adopted by China as regards Foreign Representatives shall, in no case, be different from that which results from *perfect equality* between the countries concerned, and without any *loss of prestige* on one side or the other.[7]

Clearly, "equality" and "prestige" are among the overriding concerns evident in Annex 19. Leaving aside the syntactic peculiarity of Article 7 (what sort of agency is implied in "results from . . .".?), a reading of these articles raises at least two questions: What perceived problems were being addressed? and What was to be gained by codifying ceremony in such terms? I address these questions by considering the following features of the Annex: (1) the site of audiences (i.e., Ch'ien-ch'ing Kung; hereafter the Palace of Heavenly Purity, Qianqing gong) and the doors through which foreign representatives were to enter the emperor's presence; (2) the apparent distinction drawn in Articles 2 and 3 between two kinds of audience; (3) the sedan chairs in which Western representatives were to be carried to audiences and the places where they were to alight; and (4) the stipulation in Article 4 that the emperor "receive directly into his hands letters and communications."

The Audience Hall and Entryways · The site of audience stipulated in the treaty, the Palace of Heavenly Purity, is the first of three innermost halls within the Forbidden City. It is located on the center line extending north-south through the palace complex and is north of three outer halls among which the south-

---

7. MacMurray 1921, 1: 307–308; FRUS 338–339. The United States negotiated a new treaty in 1903 that embodied elements of the protocol. The ceremonial toward the diplomatic representative of the United States was to be that "observed toward the representatives of nations on a footing of equality, with no loss of prestige on the part of either" (*China White Paper* 1967: 418).

ernmost, the Supreme Harmony Hall (Taihe dian), was known by Westerners to be the site where China's tributaries were received in audience (Landor 1901, 2: 381–382). The Palace of Heavenly Purity was part of an innermost set of buildings in which the imperial family lived and where emperors in the past had conducted the day-to-day business of the empire. Why, therefore, was this palace selected over other possible sites?

Recall that since 1873, when Court audiences for Western diplomats were formally altered to exclude the kowtow, the sites for audiences had been in halls that were within the Forbidden City, but not in the great halls positioned on the central north-south axis of the city. On these occasions, diplomats stood before the emperor and exchanged courtesies, presented their credentials, and delivered communications from their government, although not directly into the emperor's hands (Rockhill [1905] 1971: 41–48). Although such procedures were perceived as an improvement over earlier forms of audience, the fact that they did not occur in one of the primary audience halls of the Forbidden City was considered a slight as well as an assertion on the part of the Court of its unaltered superiority, in spite of its defeats on the battlefield.

The Palace of Heavenly Purity, therefore, had a number of appealing features. It was on the central axis and more inner than halls such as the Supreme Harmony Hall. As such, the Palace of Heavenly Purity made it possible for the powers to be distinguished from China's tributaries as well as to transcend what was considered a humiliating past. Moreover, because it was on the north-south center line and had three entrance doors—one on the east, normally used by court officials; one on the west, normally used by military officials and, under certain circumstances, foreign representatives; and one in the middle reserved for the use of the emperor[8]—it offered opportunities for making additional reordering statements. It was the center door that Western diplomats insisted on entering, especially when they presented their credentials or communications from their head of state. When doing so, they would follow the established usages of European diplomatic practice, common since the eighteenth century: they would bow at the threshold, midway in and before the foreign sovereign, and repeat the procedure when exiting.[9]

8. Rockhill [1905] 1971: 44. In the 1873 audience, foreign representatives had to enter through the west door. Presumably this continued to be the case until 1901.

9. See chapter 3. Rockhill ([1905 1971: 44) indicates that this procedure was followed in

At the time, however, there was more at work here than merely bringing Chinese practices in line with those of "international" codes of diplomatic protocol. By entering via the center space reserved for the emperor, a space already violated by the Triumphal March, for example, the representatives of the powers were intent on reterritorializing "traditional" imperial practices, inscribing onto Qing ritual forms (carefully studied by Wade and others) a style of audience that had no international history, strictly speaking, but was simply the forms peculiar to European Court ceremonies. Its effect was clear, however; it placed the emperor on a level of equivalency with European sovereigns, binding him, as it were, to other, similarly constructed monarchs. Thus, any metaphysical claims to superiority Manchu emperors might have made in the past would be precluded by the new order. By seizing the space previously reserved for the emperor, the powers (in their terms) effectively "desacralized" or "disenchanted" the emperor and his palaces while transforming the emperor himself into a legal person, a head of state.

Two Kinds of Audience · Article 1 distinguishes between audiences given for the "Diplomatic Body" and audiences for individual representatives. According to a communication from the Spanish minister B. J. de Cologan to the Chinese plenipotentiaries in April 1901, the powers wanted separate sites for audiences: general audiences in the Supreme Harmony Hall and individual audiences in the Palace of Heavenly Purity (FRUS 189). This demand would seem to contradict the interpretation offered above concerning the desire on the part of the powers to enter the innermost palaces of the Court. Indeed, such an interpretation is made even more questionable by the fact that the Chinese plenipotentiaries insisted that both kinds of audience be held in the Palace of Heavenly Purity.

It seems, however, that the representatives, drawing on a wealth of knowledge about Qing practices produced by Thomas Wade and other early sinologues, were trying to distinguish between Imperial Court assemblies at fixed times of the year (e.g., New Year's day, the emperor's birthday) and special audiences in which they might deliver their credentials or communications from their government. In other words, the diplomats appear to have been

---

1873. A protocol for what is apparently the first audience held following the ratification of the Boxer treaty indicates that bows were to be made at the threshold of the Palace of Heavenly Purity, one a few paces in and one before the throne; see USMHI, Nial Vass Napier, Co. B, 9th U.S. Infantry, n.d.

attempting to organize a hierarchical relation between more and less important ceremonials by instantiating a hierarchy of audience halls. For the more
important business, that concerning international relations between sovereign nation-states, they wanted to be in the inner sanctum; for the peculiar
customs of the natives, they were willing to participate at a site that they apparently understood as the usual one and as less significant for their own
purposes. Moreover, by moving inward toward the "home" of the emperor
for the "real" business of diplomacy, representatives of the powers presumably wished to make the point that they, and they alone, were in a position to
address imperial sovereignty on a common level. If this is, in fact, the case,
then it betrays a certain assumption implicit in these demands. For what the
protocol accomplished was to impose a notion of political authority in which
sovereignty was assumed to be unitary, exclusive, and evenly spread across
a bounded terrain, which was then *represented* in the physical person of the
monarch.

Hitherto, this notion of sovereignty had been unacceptable to the Qing.
Manchu sovereignty was built on principles of a graded hierarchy organized
around a high center and low peripheries, and of the inclusion of the powers
of other kings within the rulership of the emperor.[10] What can be discerned in
the protocol is an effort to manage and discipline the body of the emperor, a
body that, in the past, had resisted being circumscribed and fixed in its movements in the terms acceptable to Euroamericans. Much the same could be
said about the insistence in Article 6 that the emperor be present in person
for banquets given to representatives of the powers. Presumably, the option
of flight exercised by the Xianfeng emperor in 1860 and the Guangxu emperor
in 1900 would no longer be possible. Instead, like a European monarch or the
head of a republic, the Chinese sovereign would perforce be available for the
important moments of interstate ceremonial.

Sedan Chairs · The process of desacralizing and disciplining the person of
the emperor was further encoded in demands about the kind and style of
sedan chairs in which representatives of the powers were to be carried and
the location at which they wanted to alight from these chairs. Two messages
from Minister de Cologan to the Chinese plenipotentiaries in April and May
indicate that the powers had resolved that they should be conveyed directly
"before the hall in which they shall be received by the Emperor" and that they

10. For a discussion of Qing sovereignty, see Hevia 1995b: 123–124, 217.

desired to be carried in sedan chairs in the "Imperial color," meaning yellow, the color of the Qing Dynasty (FRUS 189, 191). After concerted opposition from Chinese officials, who pointed out that only the emperor rode in yellow-covered chairs and that only the generational superiors of the emperor could be carried directly before the hall, a compromise was reached (FRUS 190–192; Rockhill [1905] 1971: 49–50). Rather than being deposited directly before the Palace of Heavenly Purity in the sedan chairs that had carried them from their residence, representatives of the powers would switch to smaller chairs, like those used by the father and uncles of the emperor, at the Jingyun Gate and be carried to the Palace of Heavenly Purity in them. The larger chair that carried them from their residence to the Jingyun Gate was to be green with "yellow trimmings and tassels."[11]

Seemingly trivial, this battle of the chairs tells us a good bit about the nature of the struggle taking place. For their part, the powers bent their efforts to reordering the Manchu imperium as a recognizable monarchy, while at the same time appropriating certain prestigious signs of the "unreformed" Qing emperorship as a way of preventing the newly constituted monarch from reascending to his remote perch within the high-walled city. The Chinese plenipotentiaries, on their side, struggled to resist reordering, at the same time attempting to encompass the powers in what remained of the ordering processes of the Qing imperium. In the context of this sort of struggle, statements about perfect equality and no loss of prestige appear to be euphemisms.

Presenting Documents · Article 5 indicates that the emperor shall receive communications directly into his own hands. This is another reference to unacceptable Chinese diplomatic procedures. During the Qing Dynasty, as earlier, credentials were not presented in Court audiences, but to officials of the Board of Rites (Libu), who reviewed them and translated them into Chinese. Europeans found this procedure distasteful because it undermined their notion of the unity of sovereignty and its representation in the person of the sovereign. After all, their credentials carried the imprimatur of their own sovereign, whom they themselves represented, and it was thought only proper that another similarly constructed sovereign have physical contact with these docu-

11. See FRUS 280. The chair appears similar to the one Prince Heinrich, brother of Kaiser Wilhelm, was offered when he visited Wuhan in 1899; see Morse's discussion in Fairbank et al. 1995: 152.

ments. To do otherwise would have been to accept the possibility that their own notion of sovereignty was particularist rather than universal, as they not only claimed but were forcefully asserting in the protocol.

. . . .

Taken as a whole, these alterations to Court ceremony form a rather peculiar set, one that simultaneously inscribes an idiosyncratic Euroamerican view of diplomatic ceremony over that of the Qing Imperial Court while also maintaining certain features that can be found only in Imperial Court ceremonial. Moreover, the audience protocol imposed this hybridized entity onto sites and circumstances alien to them. To talk, then, of "perfect equality," as Article 7 does, is to pile fiction upon fiction. Not only did the emperor exist, much like Fu-Manchu after him, as a demon of the Euroamerican imagination, but Western diplomats also created a monarch who was more like a puppet than the equal of his Western counterparts.

Nothing, perhaps, made this point more clearly than the citation by the diplomats themselves to their resolution of the audience question. In his *Diplomatic Audiences at the Court of China* (1905), a revised update of an article that had appeared in the *American Historical Review* in 1897, William Rockhill published the new audience protocol and accompanied it with photographs he had taken in the Forbidden City, effectively citing (and siting) the halls and gates named in the text with those visible in the photographs. They are labeled as follows: (1) Ching-yün Gate, *Where Ministers take "Palace Chairs"*; (2) Ch'ien-Ch'ing Gate, *Where Ministers alight from and take "Palace Chairs"*; and (3) Ch'ien-Ch'ing Kung, *Where Diplomatic Audiences are Given*.[12] In a similar vein, the German diplomat Mumm von Schwarzenstein (figs. 26 and 27, 1902) published an almost identical set of pictures, but in this case, of an actual diplomatic audience in progress. It was almost as if the protocol in itself was insufficient. Much like the posting of imperial edicts in compliance with treaty provisions, visible proof was required to show that at long last the emperor of China had been made to conform to the "international" practices of "civilized" nation-states.

One curious dimension of this whole process, however, is the particular elements that Chinese plenipotentiaries insisted on as compromise solutions. As indicated with respect to the audience hall location, they suggested

---

12. Rockhill [1905] 1971: 49, 51. The official British military history included the audience protocol as well; see Norie [1903] 1995: 507–508.

that both general and specific audiences be held in a more inner hall. In the case of sedan chairs, while successfully resisting the request for a yellow chair like the emperor's, Court officials themselves brought to the attention of the powers the fact that being carried in close proximity to the Palace of Heavenly Purity in a small chair (*yijiao*) was a privilege accorded only the father and uncle of the emperor. They then pointed out that if the powers would accept this form, it would be "treating the foreign representatives with great courtesy" (FRUS 280). Such strategies on the part of imperial officials may well have been a last-ditch effort to enfold the powers into the Manchu house, positioned as it were as kin and allies against an increasingly resentful Chinese majority. Yet regardless of their intent, the effects of this courtesy opened the Qing Court to an unprecedented level of scrutiny.

Spectacles for Consumption

As the previous sections indicate, diplomats reworked the ground on which Euroamerican privilege was established in the Qing Empire. Through the new legal codes of the *Final Protocol*, foreign relations were elevated and buttressed by the promise of swift and remorseless force if violated. Public expressions of dissent by Chinese people were made illegal and could be punished. This unprecedented intrusion into daily life was paralleled by another phenomenon of historic importance: the turning of China itself into a spectacle for the visual consumption of foreigners inside and outside of the Qing Empire. Recall how the Triumphal March through the Forbidden City was understood to be a grand gesture striking at the heart of the Qing monarchy, performing a racial, cultural, military, and political humiliation of the Chinese emperor. It performed another operation as well.

Recent research on international exhibitions and tourism in the nineteenth century has argued that as a result of colonial expansion, Euroamerican culture itself underwent a series of transformations that affected numerous facets of everyday life. Although unevenly distributed across the societies of Europe and North America, among social classes, and between urban and rural populations, the effects of change are discernable in a number of domains of practice.[13] First, and perhaps most significant, there was a re-

13. Greenhalgh (1988), Mitchell (1988, 1989), and Rydell (1984) discuss the social transformations wrought in Europe and North American. Much of this work is indebted to the critical analysis of Walter Benjamin (1969). A more complete version of Benjamin's mus-

hierarchization of the human senses, with the ocular function taking precedence.[14] The eye became sovereign, and other senses, such as touch, became
physical extensions of visuality. This privileging of sight was encouraged by
new technologies of vision, such as photography, dioramas, displays in museums and expositions, and new print technologies, all of which suggested
that visual imagery was as important as the printed word. In fact, some could
even argue that images might be more important, particularly if they were
claiming to be mirrors of reality, because they presented the world even to
those who could not read.

The new visual technologies, like Latour's immutable mobiles on paper,
gathered together the physical objects or reproductions of them from distant
places and assembled and reassembled them in a new place and in different
relations to one another. The result, as Timothy Mitchell (1988, 1989) has argued, was not an exhibition of the world, but the presentation of the world as
if it were an exhibition. In this ocular regime, a viewer was constructed who
expected that the world and everything in it could be experienced as an exhibition for his or her viewing scrutiny and judgment and, in some instances,
tactile pleasure. It was this sensibility that appears to have been operating in
Beijing in 1900–1901. It was present in two significant formations, both of
which may be understood as not only having global significance, but as being
themselves mechanisms of reterritorialization: touring and photography.

DISENCHANTING THE FORBIDDEN CITY
Beginning in September 1900, the palaces were opened to a host of observers.
As most tourists wanted to enter on the route of the Triumphal March, the U.S.
army, which controlled the south gate, managed the arrangements (NARA,
RG395, 898). About 160 tour passes were issued between mid-October and
the following May. Groups numbering from six to thirty members were es-
corted by a U.S. officer. At first, only high-level diplomats and military officers
were allowed in, but beginning in October this changed. By the late fall, curious visitors from treaty ports with connections in the diplomatic corps began
to participate in the spectacle.

How did the tourists react to the palaces? When Colonel J. T. Dickman of

---

ings on the social and economic changes resulting from Euroamerican globalization can
be found in Benjamin 1999.

14. See, especially, D. Lowe 1982; Crary 1988; Jay 1988. These works provide the basis
for more recent studies collected in Jenks 1995 and Devereaux and Hillman 1995.

28. Exterior of the empress dowager's private rooms. Source: *Military Order of the Dragon*, 1912.

the U.S. army confided to the official staff diary that the Forbidden City was not a particularly good "exhibition," he hinted at how others would experience the site (NARA, RG395, 913, no. 33: 14; Lynch 1901: 157). "Good" or "bad," the Forbidden City, especially the empress dowager's quarters, was consumed as a visual and tactile exhibition (figs. 28 and 29). The few tour accounts that exist make this clear. Wilber Chamberlin, a reporter for the *New York Sun*, indicated that although the palaces were "a picture of degeneracy," there still were certain pleasures to be had. "I have sat upon every throne that the Emperor possesses and every throne ever occupied by the Dowager," he continued. "I have seated myself and lain upon the bed of the Emperor, and in fact I've had a regular picnic with things royal." Of interest here is the dynamic of his account, that is, the swing between utter contempt for "benighted Chinaland" and the obvious pleasure Chamberlin derived from sitting on "all" of the emperor's thrones and lying on the beds of the emperor and empress dowager (1903: 103–104, 117).

Chamberlin was not the only one to take advantage of this rare opportunity to make physical contact with imperial possessions and signs of Qing

29. Tourists explore the interior of the empress dowager's private rooms. Source: Military *Order of the Dragon*, 1912.

kingship.[15] Moreover, it was not a form of pleasure exclusively confined to men; there is at least one photograph of a woman sitting on the throne in the Qianqing Palace (fig. 30). But what sort of pleasures, shared presumably by men and women, were these? First, of course, there was the pleasure to be had from seeing and touching what was normally forbidden and, more important, to do so without fear of consequences. Second, one could put oneself, and be seen by others, in the place of the emperor of China. Similarly, there was pleasure to be had in cavorting through the private apartments of the empress dowager, the person held most responsible for failing to halt the Boxer depredations, allowing the siege of the legations, and, as Arthur Brown recalled, the person also referred to as "the only man in China" (1904: 193). Thus, seeing and touching her most intimate things brought both pleasure and a sense of triumph over the chief perpetrator of crimes against civilization. And, as she herself was nowhere to be seen, it may also have been understood as a form of punishment personally directed at her. Perhaps this was why, even in

15. G. E. Morrison indicated that he sat on the emperor's throne at the time of the Triumphal March; see Seagrave 1992: 367.

30. Woman tourist on imperial throne. Source: *Military Order of the Dragon*, 1912.

spite of strict rules to the contrary and concerted efforts at policing, visitors continued to pilfer items that fit into their pockets or could be hidden under coats. According to one report, such sleights of hand were justified on the grounds that one could not pass through the Forbidden City without taking a souvenir.[16]

Perhaps none of this is too surprising. In this era of international expositions, the exhibition of the exotic world of others at world's fairs involved a relationship of power marked most profoundly by a transgression of boundaries, of the movement across the barriers of everyday life into a realm of absolute otherness. For example, it was common from the Paris Exhibition of

16. Dillon 1901: 30. Mrs. A. Little (1901: 505) notes that one tourist complained that eunuchs lurked too close, making it impossible to take anything. All efforts to halt the activity proved futile and on 3 December, General Chaffee decided to close the palaces (NARA, RG395, 898, no. 428). For a report on thefts and altercations related to them, see NARA, RG395, 906, Box 2 (27 October 1900) and Box 3 (2 December 1900) and Yamaguchi to Chaffee, 30 November 1900, RG395, 906, Box 3. When the palaces were reopened, new regulations governing entrance to the city were issued (RG395, 906, Box 4). However, further incidents were reported in March (RG395, 906, Box 5, 5 and 20 March 1901).

1889 forward for full-size models of buildings or historical structures from various parts of the colonized world to appear, along with natives in their local dress, on display for the gaze of fairgoers. This move required, of course, a suspension of disbelief (how could Cairo be in Paris, after all?), which, if accomplished, offered a host of optical and tactile pleasures and opportunities for unusual forms of play—temporarily locating oneself in the place of the emperor of China, for instance.

At the same time, if the examples discussed above are indicative of a wider culture that saw the world as exhibition, then the act of viewing, entering, and possessing did something else as well. Tours of the Forbidden City were part of a more general process transforming Western societies, one that through the extension of scientific rationality into all areas of Euroamerican culture was disenchanting the everyday life of people throughout Europe and North America.

In the case of China, disenchantment operated on the imperial palaces, a world now colonized, like other parts of Asia and Africa, by Euroamericans who moved around freely, unencumbered by local strictures and certain of their own loftiness. The effect was profound: it turned the fantastic elements of Qing monarchy, of its belief in the superiority of the Chinese emperor as the Son of Heaven and his empire as celestial, into something quite ordinary and mundane.

Perhaps one of the best examples of the process of disenchantment can be found in the account of the Reverend Arthur Brown, who visited the Forbidden City, the Summer Palace, and the Temple of Heaven in mid-1901. In the Forbidden City, Brown noted that he and his companions "walked freely" through the vast grounds and buildings, even the throne rooms, where "the highest Chinese official can approach only upon his knees and with his face abjectly on the stone pavement." In addition to recalling the comment of Garnet Wolseley at the Summer Palace in 1860, Brown's brief encounter with the Qing Empire—his description of the palaces takes up less than one of the 370 pages of text—mimes the sovereign white male diplomat who refused to kowtow. Thus empowered, Brown completed the disenchantment of the palaces and their transformation into an exhibition. Upon leaving the throne rooms, he crossed the palace grounds and entered the apartments of the emperor and empress dowager: "I was impressed by the vastness of the Palace buildings and grounds, the carvings of stone and wood, and the number of articles of foreign manufacture. But thousands of Americans in moderate circumstances have more spacious and comfortable bedrooms than those of the

Emperor and Empress Dowager of China. All the living apartments looked cheerless . . . and of course everything was covered with dust" (1904: 197–198).[17]

Much like the assaults on what were understood to be symbols of importance to the Chinese mind, the process of disenchantment exemplified in Brown's comparison of Qing palaces to the homes of Americans of moderate circumstances undermined any local claims to the power of these buildings or to meanings independent of those imputed to the palaces or temples by visitors like Brown. The reduction of the Forbidden City to a mundane object of little or no value effectively colonized it, shifting it from a site for the performance of Qing imperial power to the residence of an impotent monarch of moderate means.

The physical presence of Euroamericans in throne rooms and private apartments and the theft of intimate imperial possessions was not the only way of disenchanting the Qing monarchy. As the previous discussion of sitting on thrones suggests, another means for accomplishing the same objective was through photography. Photographers were present from the time of the allied landings at Dagu, recording the devastation of Tianjin and the march on Beijing. Once in the capital, they set about, as the U.S. commander General Adna Chaffee put it, making "a record" of the occupation.[18] In the fall and winter of 1900–1901, Captain Cornelius Francis O'Keefe, the main army photographer, took well over five hundred photographs.[19] One taken of the Triumphal March itself became an exhibit, appearing in the Louisiana Purchase Exposition in St. Louis in 1904 (fig. 31). More important, O'Keefe's camera recorded, like others in Beijing at the time, iconic subjects, the physical sites that were understood to be intimately linked to the Qing monarchy. These included the Qianqing Palace and throne (fig. 32), which the *Final Protocol* stipulated as the site of future audiences, the empress dowager's private quarters, the forecourt and gates of the Taihe Palace, and the Temple of

17. Arthur Smith (1901b, 2: 529–530) performed a similar act of disenchantment by emphasizing the "scrimped pattern" in which the palaces were laid out.

18. See NARA, RG395, 906, box 2, 4 and 5 for requests from the French and German units.

19. O'Keefe had been a professional photographer working in Leadville, Colorado, when the Spanish-American War broke out. He enlisted in the army and was sent to the Philippines, where he covered the Filipino Insurrection during 1899–1900; see Sharf and Harrington 2000: 246–247. O'Keefe's photographs are available in the U.S. National Archives, College Park, Maryland.

31. Triumphal March by C. F. O'Keefe, shown at St. Louis Exposition, 1904. Courtesy National Archives and Records Administration.

Heaven prayer hall. Multiple photographs were taken of each of these structures and sent back to imperial centers for storage, reproduction, and combination with other media. In this easily manageable size, the Forbidden City had been transformed into an immutable mobile.

Another gesture of photographic disenchantment involved what was perhaps the most impressive documentary project launched at the Forbidden City, the results of which were published in an imposing two-volume work entitled *Shinoku Pekin kojo shashincho* (Photographs of the palace buildings of Peking, 1906), with text in Japanese, Chinese, and English. Carried out by a team of engineers from the University of Tokyo led by Itō Chuita and the photographer Ogawa Kazuma, the project documented virtually the entire palace complex in 170 photographs. The reason for this extensive coverage, according to the preface, was that it was designed to expose what had been "jealously kept from public sight" for the purpose of "architectural study," that is, for the analysis of "the arrangement, construction, and decoration" of the Forbidden City and other palace grounds in the area. It would seem, therefore, that the photographing of Qing palaces and temples produced exhibits for a Japan now imagined as the "museum of Asiatic civilization" (Okakura Teshin, cited in Tanaka 1993: 13). The Japanese team disenchanted the Forbidden City by treating it as if it were a specimen of a past that Japan had now transcended.

But if disenchantment was the dominant performance of power in the Forbidden City, there were at least a few responses that contrasted starkly with the dismissive attitudes or minimalist description to be found in accounts like those of Chamberlin and Brown. Sarah Pike Conger (1909) and Mrs. Archibald Little (1901), wife of a British missionary, both of whom had resided in the legation quarter for some time before the siege, wrote accounts of their visits to the Forbidden City that overflow with enthusiasm. In the 1890s, Conger developed an appreciation for Chinese aesthetics as embodied in the intricate symbology found on ceramics and in Court dress. Such encounters help to explain her unusual response to the palaces. Conger made no mention of dust, dragons, or decay. Instead of lamenting the failure of the city to evoke imperial grandeur, she saw "large, gorgeously decorated throne buildings," structures that were "elaborate, attractive, and rich in Oriental beauty, color and grandeur," which stood in stark contrast to the "dirty, cheer-

32. Principal throne in Qianqing palace by C. F. O'Keefe. Courtesy National Archives and Records Administration.

less, barren building" that housed the Qing foreign office (the Zongli yamen). Inside the buildings were rooms filled with "elegant" furnishings, "valuable treasures," and "exquisitely fine" objects of art.[20] While there are certainly world-as-exhibition elements at work here, there is nothing in Conger's account that in any way attempts to demean or dismiss what is before her. Indeed, her interest in finding meaning in Oriental splendor foreshadowed later reactions to the Forbidden City, ones that would reimagine the palaces and the city of Beijing itself as sophisticated works of art.[21] Little's account was similar, emphasizing the "imposing" majesty of the palaces, the art, and the absence of frivolous decoration like that found in many European buildings (1901: 504–505).

Perhaps their admitted desires to enter the "forbidden spot" — Little recalled fantasies of dressing up in Chinese clothing and sneaking in — accounts for their refusal to debase or disenchant the emperor's palaces.[22] Yet, longing generated by desire for the forbidden does not account for other positive responses to the palaces. This was especially the case with the reaction of Julian Viaud, a staff officer with the French forces, who was better known under the pen name Pierre Loti. In what was certainly the most idiosyncratic memoir to come out of the China relief expedition, Loti did more than simply avoid disenchanting the Forbidden City. In *Les Derniers Jours de Pékin* (*The Last Days of Pekin*, 1902), he exoticized and appropriated the palaces into an Orientalized realm of fantasy, infusing almost every page with seemingly unquenchable desires and fantasies triggered, he avers, by his encounter with the palaces. The contrast with Chamberlin and Brown is striking. Because the palaces were almost vacant, the two Americans reveled at being able to survey and judge the Qing monarchy. In Loti's case, the absence of the emperor produces a kind of lament.

Billeted in pavilions around the lakes to the west of the Forbidden City, Loti and a few French officers had free run of the palaces for several weeks in the winter of 1900. This daily contact with the Forbidden City plunged Loti, as Chris Bongie has observed, into a kind of funk. Yearning for contact with an actual imperial presence, he finds nothing but empty palaces and unin-

20. Conger discusses her growing awareness of the meaning of Chinese art in a number of her letters; see 1909: 70, 204, 260–261, 269, 311–312. The quotations are on 170–171, 189.

21. See, for example, Blofeld [1961] 1989; Bredon 1922; Johnston [1934] 1985.

22. See Conger 1909: 169; Mrs. A. Little 1901: 504. Issues of gender and Orientalism are also raised by these texts; see the discussions in L. Lowe 1991 and Lewis 1996, which focuses on women writing and painting the Islamic world.

habited residences. The absence of the sovereign at the center of the Orient transformed the palaces into a phantasmagoria of confusing and frightening ornamentation and hideous design. Confronted by this vacant "scene of exoticism" (Bongie 1991: 122), Loti wrote elegies on the demeaning fate of the emperor and his "poor Yellow City" (1902: 210). The sole respite from this melancholy came when, surrounded by imperial treasures, dressed up in imperial robes, and reclining on couches in one of the apartments of the Forbidden City, Loti and his friends smoked opium.

This play acting not only lifted Loti's dark mood, but inspired him to a new understanding of things Chinese; he claimed that for the first time he was able to experience and appreciate Chinese art and architecture. What had been "mere captivated admiration" was transformed into "respect and awe" (1902: 150–151). Opium, it would seem, had freed Loti's mind and allowed him to form a meaningful link between himself and the emperor's possessions, a process that he assumed would normally have been possible only in the presence of the Chinese emperor himself. But because the drug was a mere substitute for the more significant production of meaning that Loti imagined would occur when the emperor was in the palaces, it proved ephemeral. The result was a kind of longing for the meaning and order promised by the physical presence of the absolute sovereign in the Forbidden City.

From the absence of the emperor, Loti generated a trope that would recur in the writings of future observers of the Forbidden City, particularly among those who visited Beijing after the fall of the Qing Dynasty in 1911. Throughout *The Last Days*, Loti articulated a nostalgia for an imaginary past evoked by a "dream of being Chinese sovereigns," a fantasy standing in stark contrast to present time, an age of "weakness and mediocrity, when nothing is sacred and the future is full of fear" (1902: 190–201). Whatever we might think of Loti's assessment of the times he lived in, the desires he articulated are significant and important. They not only demonstrate that there were other ways of responding to the Forbidden City, they indicate an awareness of the processes of disenchantment going on in Beijing and the rest of the world at that moment. Moreover, as Loti constructed a counterdiscourse, or at least disrupted the regularities of colonial discourse, he also projected onto the "Orient" the function of producing, at least for some Westerners, a kind of antimodernism, a theme that would return in the writings of many visitors to Beijing after World War I. In 1900–1901, however, few had the patience of either Conger, Little, or Loti to attempt to find some common ground, even if wholly imaginary, between themselves and Qing rulership.

But if majority opinion strayed little beyond the assertions of domination over the (absent) emperor of China and the disenchantment of his rulership, perhaps what was most important was the nature of the transaction underway. The signs, sites, and symbols of Qing sovereignty had been forcefully brought low by means of "symbolic warfare" and Qing rulership had been repositioned within an "exhibitionary complex" (Bennett 1995: 59–88), in which aspects of its powers were neutralized and made nonthreatening. This was accomplished through the violation of the Forbidden City, textual violence, photographic reproduction, and the many articles of the *Final Protocol* that, like the imperial audience section, reterritorialized Qing rulership and incorporated it into a global order of Eurocentric international relations.

THE NEW AUDIENCE FORMAT AND
THE SPECTACLE OF THE QING COURT

The occupation of Beijing came to a close with the signing of the *Final Protocol* in September 1901, and with it ended the spectacle of the empty palaces. The following year, the Court returned and the new audience protocol went into effect. The implications of the new procedure soon became evident in the New Year's celebration of 1902. Held initially in the Palace of Heavenly Purity and later in the new Summer Palace, the number of Court audiences for Euroamerican diplomats escalated. From 1902 to the fall of the dynasty in 1911, there were thirty-two audiences with the diplomatic corps gathered en masse, twenty-one of which took place between 1902 and 1904. Participants ranged from a low of thirty-two to a high of 110 in 1904. In the process, the Qing monarchy was incorporated into a global formation of emperors and heads of state whose sovereignty was purported to be "perfectly equal."

The number of large-scale audiences pales in comparison, however, to individual audiences over the same time span, in which ministers might deliver their credentials or communications. Table 2 is based on sources in the Qing imperial archives and the *Veritable Records of the Qing Dynasty*.[23] When one recognizes that there were fewer than ten imperial audiences of any sort granted to the Euroamerican diplomatic corps between 1873 and 1902, the numbers recorded here are quite stunning. They tell only part of the story,

---

23. First Historical Archive, Beijing, Foreign Relations: Imperial Audience Participants List (Waijiaolei jinjian), boxes 2404 and 2405; *Zhupi zouzhe*, box 376, nos. 16–18, 22 and box 368, nos. 12–26; *Da Qing lichao shilu*, Guangxu, reign years 28–34 and Xuantong, reign years 1–3. I found no entries for 1905 in any of these sources.

TABLE 2. General and Individual Court Audiences for Foreign Ministers, 1902–1911

	1902	1903	1904	1906	1907	1908	1909	1910	1911	Total
Collective Audiences	10	6	5	1	2	4	2		2	32
Individual Audiences										
Japan		1	1	3	5	2	5	6	1	24
Germany	1	3	4	1	1		6	3	2	21
France	2	2	1	2	3	1	5	2		18
England		1	2	4		1	2	5	2	17
USA	5	4	1				2	4	1	17
Italy	1	1	3	1	1	1	2	2	4	16
Russia	2	1	1		1	1	2		2	10
Belgium			2	1	1		3	3		10
Austria		1				1	1	1	2	6
Holland		1	1			1	2			5
Mexico			1	1				1	1	4
Brazil							3			3
Sweden						1	1			2
Spain								1		1
Portugal							1			1
Misc.										6
Total individual annually	11	14	18	13	12	9	34	28	15	160
Total audiences	21	20	23	14	14	13	36	28	17	192

however. In the first few years of the new order, Sarah Conger (1909), who attended several of these functions, noted their imposing scale. From Conger's accounts, as well as one left by Alice Roosevelt Longworth, it would seem that the Qing Court had cleaned up its dusty palaces and shaken off some of its decay.[24] Qing efforts at restructuring the monarchy into a shape compatible with European state formations and constitutional monarchies (Ichiko 1980), particularly from 1905 forward, suggest that audience procedures were one vehicle for doing this. But there may have been other elements at work as

24. On audiences from 1902 forward, see Conger 1909: 216–233, 237–240, 242–246, 247–252, 271–273, 291–293, 299–305, 319, 352–353, 367–371. Also see Carl 1907: 165–170.

well. From the outset, the collective and individual audiences included more than the diplomatic corps. Indeed, the traffic became so heavy that Robert Hart, director of the Imperial Maritime Customs, was led to exclaim: "The Court is over-doing it in civility: not only will the Empress Dowager receive Minister's wives, but also Legation children!" (cited in Fairbank 1987: 139). Moreover, the Court seems to have been willing to receive a variety of visiting dignitaries and travelers who had connections at foreign embassies.

Whatever motives may be ascribed to the Court—and these surely involved a strategy of placating the powers and winning their support for the dynasty—the reason for Westerners flocking to the Qing Court is perhaps less clear-cut. Certainly, there was a wish among diplomats to make the Court like any other in the world—to standardize it, as it were. But there may also have been some connection involving the formal restructuring of relations between European imperial states and Oriental despotism as it was understood to exist in China. When Lord Macartney participated in an audience at the Qing Court in 1793, he noted the "calm dignity" and "sober pomp of Asian greatness, which European refinements had yet to achieve" (Cranmer-Byng 1963: 124). By the end of the nineteenth century, all that had changed. In the case of Great Britain, the imperial rulership that had been fashioned in the wake of the 1857 rebellion in India was an "Orientalized" hybrid formation that included grand imperial durbars, new imperial regalia, and public events designed to impress and awe the masses. This new formation shaped, for example, the jubilees of Queen Victoria, the weddings of her many children and grandchildren, and their funerals. And, because of the dominant position of the British, imperial spectacle, including the building of monuments and memorials to empire and the orchestration of spectacular events such as coronations and international expositions, played prominent parts in public culture throughout Europe, even in republics like France.

In this global reterritorialization of sovereignty, the Qing Court could serve the useful representational purpose of performing an authentic model of the "Orient," one with Chinese characteristics. Moreover, those so privileged could participate in this production through boat rides on the lake at the Summer Palace and reciprocal tiffins with Manchu nobility at the palaces or in the rebuilt legations. Visiting dignitaries might be treated to private performances of "real" Oriental despotism. Alice Roosevelt, daughter of the American president, appears to have been rather taken with a high court official "kowtowing at one's feet" and thought that at any moment in this Wonderland, the empress dowager might say "off with his head," and off it would go

(Longworth 1933: 100–101). It was almost as if the empress, the emperor, their palaces, and attendants had become a kind of living museum, an animated ethnographic display now defanged and declawed by an alien exhibitionary regime for the pleasure of well-connected globetrotters.

Lessons at Home: Recapitulating the Problem of China in Popular Media

Much as "just" punishment, spectacle, and the disenchantment of Qing kingship served to obscure or deflect criticism of the behavior of the allies in China, it did so in imperial metropoles as well. In Europe and North America, the wound in Euroamerican self-perceptions created by looting and atrocities was sutured by erasing ambiguities in the flood of publications that reported the various aspects of reterritorialization discussed in the previous sections. Critical to this process were presentations in the media that kept the distinctions between civilization and barbarism, violence and justice clear. Photographs and drawings, immutable mobiles produced by correspondents in China, were combined with textual accounts to accomplish this task.

In the United States, for example, *Leslie's Weekly* provided issue-by-issue coverage and devoted nine covers to events in China between June and November 1900. The overall emphasis of the paper was on the hard side of imperial pedagogy, the righteous conduct of the allied efforts, especially those of the Americans, and the barbarism of the benighted Chinese. Dealing with the entry into the Forbidden City, for example, the 1 September issue contained a series of panoramic photographs of the palaces over the caption a "much needed lesson." Emphasizing this point, the 3 November cover showed a group of startled mandarins in the palaces "watching with indignation and astonishment the desecration of the sacred city by the allied forces." This kind of lesson teaching culminated with a cover showing the decapitated body of a Qing official in a public execution that took place in March. An accompanying story detailed the hideous brutality of beheadings, firmly placing the onus for such executions solely on the Chinese (LW, 18 May 1901: cover, p. 484).

These kinds of image-text reports of punishment and humiliation were a major theme in the illustrated press in other countries as well, but perhaps nowhere more so than in Great Britain.[25] Uncritically presenting the atti-

25. The French illustrated weeklies *L'Illustration*, *La Vie Illustrée*, and *Le Monde Illustré* are also worth consideration. On the whole they maintained a similar narrative structure as the American and British papers discussed here. There were, as noted earlier, some disso-

tudes and pronouncements of British civil and military officials in China, the *Illustrated London News*, *The Graphic*, and *Black & White* placed heavy emphasis in drawings and photographs on acts of punishment, retribution, and symbolic violence directed against the Qing monarchy (e.g., pictures of private apartments in the Forbidden City) and the Chinese people (e.g., looting and burning villages).[26]

There are images of reputed Boxers shot by firing squad (fig. 33), rounded up and held under guard, tried by stern courts, and executed.[27] In other cases, suspected Boxers or thieves were shown being flogged or being humiliated as they were hauled around or tied together by their queues.[28] These depictions of assaults on Chinese male bodies was paralleled by attacks against objects Chinese people were supposed to value highly. Pictures showed the destruction of the walls of Tianjin (fig. 34), the new railway terminus at the Temple of Heaven, and "Getting to the Root of the Evil" by blowing up or burning temples where Boxers were believed to have conducted their rituals.[29] There were also numerous depictions of troops with Boxer banners, groups of officers posed in the Forbidden City, and objects from a Lama Temple that would go to Queen Victoria as trophies (fig. 35).[30]

But probably the best example of the smug superiority of British imperial masculinity appeared in the 20 April 1901 issue of the *Illustrated London News*. A drawing shows a British and an Indian soldier on the round altar at the Temple of Heaven, which, according to the accompanying text, provided a "humorous touch" to the occupation of Beijing. Called by the *News* Thomas Atkins — the name of Kipling's everyman British soldier — the Englishman stood on the round stone at "the center of the Chinese universe," above the "admiring gaze of an Indian orderly" (p. 566; fig. 36). This wholly colonial performance, reminiscent in numerous ways of British acts of subjugation in India, was

---

nant notes, such as the *Vie Illustrée* issue on plunder (1 February 1901) and *Le Monde Illustré*'s fantasies about China's revenge (25 August 1900).

26. ILN, 11 November 1900, 2 March 1901; *Black & White* (hereafter B&W), 3 and 17 November 1900.

27. ILN, 27 October 1900, 1 March 1901; *The Graphic*, 17 November, 8 December 1900, 5 January 1901, depicting the execution of officials at Baoding; B&W, 23 March 1901.

28. ILN, 23 April 1901; B&W, 2 March 1901. Also see LW, 30 March 1901 for a picture of a Chinese man being held by his queue.

29. ILN, 6 and 13 April 1901, 17 November 1900; *The Graphic*, 16 February 1901; B&W, 11 November 1900, 28 January 1901.

30. ILN, 29 December 1900; *The Graphic*, 1 and 8 December 1900.

33. Boxers executed by British firing squad. *The Graphic*, 17 November 1900.

34. Destruction of the Tianjin city wall. *Illustrated London News*, 6 April 1901.

35. "Presents for Queen Victoria." *Illustrated London News*, 29 December 1900.

36. British soldier at the center of the Chinese universe. *Illustrated London News*, 20 April 1901.

complemented soon afterward by the publication of photographs of the seals of the emperor and the empress dowager of China (ILN, 20 July 1901: 89–90).

These visual narratives of conquest, humiliation, punishment, and symbolic appropriation meshed with press coverage of "Queen Victoria's Little Wars," the outbreaks after 1861 of resistance to British imperialism that occurred more or less annually somewhere in the empire or on its frontiers. In the more than one hundred such incidents that have been recorded (Farwell 1972: 367–371), there were, as John Hobson, one of the foremost contemporary critics of British imperialism, observed, certain constants in the coverage of these wars: "hero-worship and sensational glory, adventure and the sporting spirit: current history falsified in coarse flaring colours, for the direct stimulation of the combative instinct." [31] The assault by Chinese "barbarism" against Christian civilization easily lent itself to the moral masculinity implicit in these representations of British imperial campaigns, enfolding China into a global narrative of righteous warfare and the just punishment of the guilty. In a sense, therefore, it was almost as if an actual photograph of "Tommy Atkins" at the center of the Chinese universe was unnecessary—a drawing, perhaps done at the home offices of the *Illustrated London News*, was sufficient.[32] Where else, after all, would Tommy Atkins be standing if he were in China?

If the illustrated press delivered a barbaric China now subjugated and offering few, if any, surprises, there was at least one other kind of image-text form disseminated in Great Britain at the time that was clearly designed to exploit the conditions in China and shock its audience. Earlier it was noted that sometime after the occupation of Beijing began, the allies altered the form of execution of alleged Boxers to mandate a procedure in which Chinese executioners publicly beheaded other Chinese. This was done in part because of growing concerns over barbarism within the civilized (i.e., occupation troops) and because beheading was understood to be an especially odious form of execution in the eyes of Chinese people. Although a substantial number of photographs were taken of executions by beheading, few seem to have

31. The quotation is from Hobson's *Imperialism: A Study*, cited in Springhall 1986: 49. See also Stearn 1992 for a discussion of war correspondents during the era of high imperialism.

32. Springhall (1986: 59–62) discusses the production process of pictures for the ILN, many of which were produced in London by local illustrators. One of the more famous of these was Richard Caton Woodville, who is credited with the drawing of a Bengali cavalryman escorting a Boxer prisoner that appeared on the 15 September 1900 cover of ILN.

appeared in print. Perhaps, as James Ricalton explained after seeing Japanese soldiers behead two supposed Boxers, such "heartless butchery" was too gruesome for presentation in a popular medium (cited in Lucas 1990: 184).

As we saw at the opening of chapter 1, however, such a sensibility did not deter the Visitors' Inquiry Association at Brighton from publishing *Unique Photographs of the Execution of Boxers in China* (ca. 1901). The photograph on which the title of this study is based was one of four that appeared in the booklet, which sold for a hefty 5 shillings (an illustrated tourist guide to Brighton was advertised in the same publication for 6 pence).[33] They were accompanied by a text that told a story about public executions in China within the framework of the unquestioned moral superiority of the British.

In the image-text genre, as we have seen, pictures do not necessarily speak for themselves; discourse often frames them as illustrations or evidentiary proof of the truth that the text narrates. The Brighton booklet provides a number of examples of this kind of image-text relationship. The first photograph, "Led to Execution," is followed with a full-page discussion by an author identified only as R. N. The opening sentences set the style of the commentary. It is a collection of clichés about China and the Qing realm, ones that the photograph purportedly confirm. China is a "remarkable" place made up of people with "some good traits of character" (i.e., they are industrious), but the bad predominates, making it difficult for Englishmen "to understand why such people are allowed to exist." It would, however, be a tedious job to wipe them out, R. N. explained, because there are so many of them.

This initial denigration of the population of China proceeds to the mandatory claim that they are a "treacherous" lot, devoid of religious feeling and belief, amoral, and wholly materialistic, characteristics that, taken together, place the Chinese "outside the pale of civilization." There follows a catalogue of other bad traits—callousness and indifference to death, daily forms of officially sanctioned torture and punishments done on open streets for all to see—and a detailed list and description of the forms of public execution in China, the cruelties of which are vividly detailed by the author. This catalogue of "barbarism" concludes with the observation that because the "Mongolian race is confessedly obtuse, nerved and insensible to suffering . . . Chinese

33. In 1994, the Forbidden City Publishing House published a large number of photographs from the Palace Museum's collection in a volume edited by Liu Beisi and Xu Qixian. It included two pictures shared by the Brighton publication labeled "Led to Execution" and "The Execution"; see B. Liu and Xu 1994: 243, 245.

criminals do not suffer nearly as much as members of more sensitive races would under similar conditions."

This is, of course, first-order imperial archive knowledge culled from sources on Chinese characteristics. In this case, the passage comes from the article on China written by Robert K. Douglas for the tenth edition of the *Encyclopaedia Britannica*—R. N. copied it verbatim without citation.[34] But that is not the most interesting point to be made about this instance of plagiarizing the imperial archive. R. N.'s mimicry of an unimpeachable source on the physical characteristics of the "Chinaman" does more than simply provide racial details to accompany the photographs. Here, the archive functions not only to create a precise interface between knowledge of a faraway place and the imperial metropole, but to ensure that the latter is not polluted by the former. There is no acknowledgment, indeed no hint that the activities of the British imperial state might in some way be connected to what is recorded in the photographs. Instead, we are told that although there is no apology for "the refined cruelties inflicted on Chinamen by Chinamen," the "presence of European officers at 'The Executions' prevented cruel and needless torture . . . torture of any description being very abhorrent to an Englishman."

From this position of superiority and distanced judgment, it was then possible to make a number of observations and pronouncements that reaffirmed for the reader the benign nature of British actions. First, we are told that "these vivid and unique illustrations, albeit gruesome, depict the punishment of the Boxers, for whom we can have little pity; even the most tender-hearted amongst us dare say nothing, but that 'they richly deserved all they got.' " This was because of their "blood-thirsty" depredations and "diabolical" crimes that the text briefly outlines. At the same time, however, all of this might have been prevented if Great Britain's hands were not "tied" by the considerations of "international tactics" (e.g., "diplomacy and red-tapism") embodied in the Eastern Question.

The results of these international complications were collusion between the Qing Court and the Boxers, with the accompanying disasters that followed. Once the rebellion was quelled, however, the Chinese government did

34. The tenth edition was first published in 1874. I have consulted the 1878 Scribner's edition. See "China" in vol. 5, pp. 626–672. The passage in question is on 669. Mackerras (1989: 60) cites a portion of the passage. The eleventh edition of the *Britannica*, while retaining much of the descriptive account of capital punishment from Douglas, dropped the elements cited here.

A STREET SCENE AFTER AN EXECUTION.

37. Street scene after execution. Source: *Unique Photographs of the Execution of Boxers in China*, ca. 1901.

an about-face and, in an effort to ingratiate itself with the allies, set about executing Boxers at a strenuous pace, until the streets of Beijing ran red with their blood. That is what these photographs show in gruesome detail. Yet, their display in these pages, R. N. assured readers, was not for purposes of exploitation: "These unique illustrations cannot be viewed without pain and repugnance. However, it is not with any view of gratifying a morbid curiosity that these are offered to the public, but for a three-fold purpose: To enlist our sympathy for an unfortunate people; to arouse in our hearts a strong abhorrence of cruel practices, and to cause us to feel thankfulness that we live in a land where Justice is tempered with Mercy."

Conflating the idealized social world of the viewer with the interests of the imperial state is unexceptional; it is repeated many times in the illustrated press coverage of this and other "little wars" of the era mentioned above. Moreover, given the content of the photographs, the last sentence is, to say the least, an extremely effective way to banish any doubts that might have been raised about the actions of British forces in China. Nor is it particularly surprising to see a denial of prurient interest in the pictures coupled with suggestions of humanitarianism and the responsibilities of the White Man's Burden to learn to abhor cruelty. What does stand out, however, is the incongruity between the purity of British civilization that the text insists on and the postures of the English officers standing at the center of "A Street Scene after an Execution" (fig. 37). The inability of R. N. or the Visitors' Inquiry Association to see the obscenity of those poses brings into sharp focus the power and force of racialized discourse. Such discourse not only performs the processes of reterritorializing the Qing Empire and erasing any ambiguities about the actions of the allies in China, it violently places China and the Chinese people firmly within a colonial world and its forms of power/knowledge.

· ·

CHAPTER 9

Mnemonic Devices: Memorializing

the West as Victim and Hero

IN HIS HISTORY OF THE SIEGE of the legations published in 1959, Peter Fleming noted that the Boxer Uprising was one of those events, like the Boston
Tea Party or the Black Hole of Calcutta, that formed "part of the iron rations
of general knowledge that everyone carries in his head" (1959: 9). These
"rations" can be understood as simplified or short-hand versions of complex
events, versions that distort, especially by their omissions, the truth of the
past. In the case of the Boxer Uprising, Fleming wished to restore some of the
integrity of history by telling a fuller story. He did not ask, however, about
the way the iron rations came into being, or how they acquired such a fixity
that he could characterize them in this way. It is the purpose of this chapter
to address those issues, to explore how the events of 1900 were edited and
then solidified into the form that Fleming later called attention to.

Some answers to these questions are, of course, related to the activities of
the Western powers in the wake of the uprising. The many forms of reterritorialization that have been discussed, including alterations of Qing Imperial
Court ceremony and the opening of China as a spectacle for the Western gaze,
helped to occlude the full scope of Western violence and vengeance visited
upon the Qing Dynasty and the Chinese people. Yet, in the activities discussed

in chapter 8, with the exception of photography and the illustrated press, the primary impact and the major arena on which the effects of reordering seemed to work were confined to China itself. The wound in Western self-perceptions created by looting and punitive expeditions in China also had to be sutured at home. This chapter considers ways in which the meaning of events in 1900 was stabilized through authoritative narratives and forms of memorialization that circulated well beyond China. I begin with narratives to be found in missionary writings about the Boxer Uprising and the creation of monuments to dead missionaries in both China and the United States. I then consider boys' adventure stories involving the Boxers and a China relief expedition veterans group. In each of these cases, the West is constructed as a victim, and the overcoming of Chinese savagery as a heroic act deserving of memorialization. Taken together, inspirational narratives about those who made sacrifices for the preservation of the Christian religion and international law and order served to operate as an effective way of reducing anxieties over the barbaric violence that had accompanied this civilizing mission.

Missionary Discourse

Ministers of the Western powers were able to establish legal responsibility for "crimes against humanity" in China in 1900, but they represented only the interests of nation-states, who were understood to be in jealous competition with one another for spheres of influence in China. As such, their version of events, particularly as it was shaped by the publication of official records such as the British parliamentary papers and the proceedings of the Congress of the United States, could not collectively constitute a unitary and authoritative narrative of events. Inserting themselves in the gap between the interests of states and the publics of the Western nations involved in the relief of the legations were Christian missionaries. Missionary authors were able to fashion narratives of events that simultaneously overlapped with and maintained a critical distance from the public documents of states. In so doing, they not only generated a plausible supplemental story about 1900, but lay the foundation of a popular version of the Boxer Uprising, elements of which continue to circulate into the present.

Through their various publications and their performance of mourning rituals, missionaries were able to substitute tales of suffering, martyrdom, and the triumph of Christian civilization over pagan barbarism for accounts of looting, revenge, and atrocities committed by the allied armies. In the process, missionary writers stabilized the imperial powers' explanation of the cause of the uprising as the sole version of events: the Boxer episode became nothing more than the outgrowth of Chinese antiforeignism. The event had been an assault on innocent people who had come to China to give selflessly to improve the conditions of the Chinese people. The story that resulted, with Chinese antiforeignism and heroic, self-sacrificing Western resistance to it the moral positions in the plot, appeared in opinion journals, periodicals, newspapers, and missionary publications almost as soon as the occupation of Beijing began.

Barely two months after the relief of the legations, Arthur Smith (1900), acting as special commissioner for *The Outlook* in China, detailed the "crimes of Peking," which included the Qing Court's support of the Boxers and the assault on anything with "a foreign aspect" or "in any way suggestive of foreigners." Chinese antiforeignism extended not only to the summer houses built by the legations in the Western Hills, he noted, but to the foreign race course (!) and the desecration of foreign cemeteries. Once the city was occupied, these evil actions were answered, in varying degrees of intensity, by the occupation forces. There followed a detailed list of the humiliations of Beijing. By the middle of 1901, these initial efforts by Smith (1901a, 1901c, 1901d) and others to control the meaning of the events of 1900 were followed by full-length books and were accompanied by dedication services of monuments to dead missionaries in many parts of China.

MISSIONARY HISTORIES, ATROCITY STORIES, AND THE REDEMPTION OF THE MISSIONARY CAUSE

By any standard, the volume of missionary publications is impressive. In 1901 alone, this corpus included Arthur Smith's two volumes of *China in Convulsion*, Reverend F. L. Hawks Pott's *The Outbreak in China*, Reverend Roland Allen's *The Siege of the Peking Legations*, Marshall Broomhall's *Martyred Missionaries of the China Inland Mission*, and Reverend Robert Coltman's *Beleaguered in Peking*. These works were followed in 1902 and 1903 with *The Tragedy of Paotingfu* [Baoding] by Isaac Ketler, *Chinese Heroes* by Isaac Headland, *Fire and Sword in Shansi* by E. H. Edwards, *Siege Days* by A. H. Mateer, and *China's Book of Martyrs* by Luella Miner. In 1904, Reverend Arthur Brown's *New Forces in Old China* and Robert Forsyth's *The China Martyrs of 1900* capped the initial outpouring.[1]

Among these works, one of the more impressive was that of Arthur Smith,

1. For a bibliography of missionary sources, see Forsythe 1971: 129–141.

who, as we have seen, was a widely recognized authority on China. His contribution to Boxer literature was markedly larger than any of the others; the two volumes came to 770 pages of text and included 96 photographs (some of which were discussed in the previous chapter) and 5 maps. The volumes were more than the work of an individual, however. Smith acknowledged, for example, the fact that he was privy to the communication between the U.S. minister E. H. Conger and the Chinese government, and also seems to have had good connections in the British legation. These relationships helped him to construct a narrative that, if not in full agreement with the actions of all the powers, was more informed, perhaps, than others about why certain things were done. In addition to his link to the official record, Smith was also closely aligned with missionary sources. He was able, for example, to draw on the work of Mrs. D. Z. Sheffield for firsthand accounts of the experiences of Chinese Christians and on other missionary sources to provide an overview of experiences in China's interior.

The vast resources at his disposal allowed Smith to ground his work in a tone of historical and practical realism that, unlike many of the martyrologies that will be addressed shortly, gave his work a flavor much like the hard-hitting reportage of the missionaries' critics. From that position, he was able to level criticism in equitable doses at the imperialist powers and the antiforeign elements within the Qing Court, at Chinese ignorance and superstition, at the excesses of the Euroamerican occupation forces, and at the unwillingness of some of the powers, including the United States, to punish China in a manner the Chinese both "expected" and "could understand." At the same time, Smith made it clear that he was still a missionary. His explanation for the survival of the besieged legation members and missionaries was unequivocal: it was divine intervention.

This curious mix of realpolitik and Christian faith points to the contradictions inherent in the missionary enterprise in China. On the one hand, missionaries were dependent on secular authority, Chinese and foreign, to enforce treaty rights, and yet they also sought to establish a moral ground aloof from this dependency. Insofar as Smith's opus drew attention to this contradiction, he was perhaps not the best writer for fixing unambiguously the meaning of 1900. Unlike Smith, and in contrast to the accounts of secular writers discussed above, missionary martyrologists kept matters relatively simple. Operating as a kind of united front, much like the British memoirists of the 1860 campaign, they created a concise and powerful party line about what had happened. Missionaries did not cause the Boxer outbreak, but were the innocent victims of it. Some missionaries were more than heroes—they were martyrs. These points were made within a narrative structure that presented the facts of incidents involving missionaries as stories of suffering and sacrifice. Critical to that framework was the atrocity story.

In her martyrology, for example, Luella Miner explained that in "the succeeding narratives, while it has not seemed best to crowd the pages with the heart-sickening details of butchery, neither is there any attempt to conceal the fact that cruelty was rampant. Thank God that lust was not rampant also, that women were spared what they would have suffered at the hands of Turks" (1903: 23). Although Miner went a bit further than most in alluding to the absence of rape, her decision to exclude details of atrocities was based on a concern not to offend contemporary sensibilities.[2] Others, however, rejected this strategy, deciding instead to present in graphic detail what the Reverend Gilbert Reid referred to as "a carnival of hell" (1901: 582).[3] Here is a typical account of the events in Baoding, where several missionaries were beheaded and their bodies buried in a mass grave, presented by the Reverend Arthur Brown concerning the ordeal of two American women:

> The fate of the young women, Miss Morrill and Miss Gould, thus deprived of their only protector, was not long deferred. After the fall of Mr. Pitkin, they were seized, stripped of all their clothing except one upper and one lower garment, and led by the howling crowd along a path leading diagonally from the entrance of the compound to the road just east of it. Miss Gould did not die of fright as she was taken from the chapel, as was first reported, but at the point where the path enters the road, a few hundred yards from the chapel, she fainted. Her ankles were tied together, and another cord lashed her wrists in front of her body. A pole was thrust between legs and arms, and she was carried the rest of the way, while Miss Morrill walked, characteristically giving to a beggar the little money at her waist, talking to people, and with extraordinary self-possession endeavoring to convince her persecutors of their folly. And so the procession of blood-thirsty men, exulting in the possession of defenseless women one of them unconscious, wended its way northward to the river bank, westward to the stone bridge, over it

2. Martin (1900: 140) concurred with Miner on how to approach the subject of atrocities.

3. More graphic accounts of atrocities are presented in A. Smith 1901b, 2: 619; Ketler 1902: 389–392; Conger 1909: 183.

and to a temple within the city, not far from the southeast corner of the wall. (1904: 206)

Throughout the telling of these atrocity stories certain common elements are repeated: (1) the particular sufferings of each individual; (2) the fact that chief among the victims were defenseless or "delicate" women and children (Reid 1902: 453); (3) the sequence of deaths; (4) the exact location of each death and how each person died (in almost every case, by beheading); (5) the words that each had spoken during the ordeal; (6) the extraordinary heroism displayed by most of the victims; and (7) the identification, if possible, of the responsible Chinese party.

At the same time, there is an irony in stitching together these elements. Where deaths occurred, there were seldom survivors. This meant that native informants had to be relied on to provide the necessary details, informants who themselves might have been involved in the killing of missionaries. Moreover, because most such interviews were done several months after the fact, informants gave contradictory and partial accounts of events and multiple versions of what happened in each case circulated. Brown indicates as much when he notes that "Miss Gould did not die of fright . . . as first reported." But there were other discrepancies as well. Accounts variously record that the two women were stripped of their clothing and paraded naked through the streets of Baoding; that they were only partially stripped, as Brown has it; or that they were not stripped at all, but that their clothing was torn by the hands of an enraged mob as they were taken through the streets. One report has Miss Gould suspended by her hair from the pole on which she was carried and another claims that Miss Morrill's breasts were cut off before she was beheaded. Each of these accounts was contradicted by other testimony.[4]

The point, however, is that although the facts remained elusive, none of the authors who wrote about the deaths of Morrill and Gould felt compelled to avoid telling these tales based, as they were, on sketchy evidence. What then, we might ask, are these atrocity stories about? What purpose do they have in the broader narratives of suffering, martyrdom, and resurrection? In most

4. For other descriptions of the treatment of Morrill and Gould, see R. Forsyth 1904: 24–5; Ketler 1902: 387; the report of U.S. Army Captain Grote Hutcheson in NARA, RG395, 913, no. 36; Lynch 1901: 204–205; Shanghai Mercury, 1967: 83; A. Smith 1901b, 2: 611; Conger 1909: 183.

cases, atrocity stories are either immediately followed by or closely linked to accounts of retribution. As such, they prepare the way for the return of light to Chinese darkness, and in so doing they give meaning to what might otherwise be construed as "blood and iron" triumphalism. They have, in other words, an ideological effect—they normalize revenge, transforming it into a reasonable reaction to "Chinese brutality" and, thus, help to banish critics like Mark Twain and Edward J. Dillon from the field. At the same time, the normalization of retribution was not inherent in the structure of the Christian metanarrative noted above, but was appended to it. In this respect, what happened in China, at least for some influential missionary writers, could just as well have happened elsewhere, for the appended tale, of which the narrating of atrocities made up a part, was an Old Testament story of the righteous struggle against heathenism and Satanic barbarism.

Yet, as powerful as the Baoding atrocity story was for placing the events in China within a Judeo-Christian moral universe, the story itself lacked the grandeur that the biblical framework relied on. There was no individual, either Qing official or Boxer, one could point to as the personification of satanic evil. The events in Taiyuan, where other missionaries had been executed, filled in the missing element by providing a profoundly demonized villain in the person of Yuxian, the governor of Shanxi province. Not only was he personally implicated in the death of several missionaries, but, as Arthur Brown explained, Yuxian was the epitome of the Qing official whose hands, rather than "restraining, actually guided and goaded the maddened rioters" (1904: 195).

Before coming to Shanxi, Yuxian had been governor of Shandong, where, according to most accounts, he "officially started the Boxer organization" (Reid 1902: 451).[5] After a number of incidents in which the governor was considered to be complicit, the Western powers demanded that he be removed from office. In March 1900 he was appointed governor of Shanxi; according to missionary accounts, Boxers began to appear soon afterward (Forsyth 1904: 32). Near the end of June riots occurred at missions in and around Taiyuan. Protestant and Catholic missionaries were gathered together and on 7 July taken to the governor's yamen, ostensibly for their protection. On 9 July Yuxian personally oversaw their executions, many of which were carried out by

5. For an evaluation of Yuxian's involvement in the Boxer movement, see Esherick 1987, especially 190–193, 255–270.

the governor's own troops. Almost all the victims were beheaded and the severed heads displayed outside the governor's yamen.[6]

Among the more spectacular accounts of these executions was one given by an "eyewitness" that appeared in the *North China Herald* on 17 October 1900. In it, Yuxian himself is condemned as a murderer:

> When the first batch of missionaries was brought to T'ai-yuan-fu . . . Yu Hsien [Yuxian] ordered them to be brought straight into his yamen and taken to an archery ground in the rear, and then placed standing at a distance of a few feet from each other. The sanguinary Governor then took off his outer official robe and necklace, mounted a horse ready saddled for him, and then taking a long sword from an orderly, cantered to the other end of the ground. As Yu Hsien turned his horse towards the victims, standing some 15 chang (about 200 feet) away, he started at a hard gallop towards them, swinging his long sword as he swept past them, carrying off four or five heads on the onrush. Then his horse balked and would go no further, so Yu Hsien had to get off his horse, and the rest of these unhappy missionaries were then massacred by the Boxers and soldiers who were present. This was Yu Hsien's way of "setting an example" to his myrmidons.[7]

In both this case and that of Baoding, the details of missionary suffering converged with the crimes of Chinese officials to generate a powerful rhetorical question. Were not retribution and justice synonymous? Moreover, with the truth of the crimes vividly depicted in the atrocity stories, the missionaries could now answer their critics. Recall that by the end of 1900, missionaries' seemingly blood-thirsty desire for revenge and their involvement in looting had engendered substantial criticism in newspapers and journals.[8] Even supporters of the missionary cause such as Leslie Grove and Sarah Conger (1909: 175) expressed concern over missionary attitudes in their letters, while Robert

6. For missionary accounts of the Taiyuan atrocities, see Edwards 1903: 64–82; R. Forsyth 1904: 32–41; A. Smith 1901b, 2: 613–615. Also see Stanley Smith 1901: 82–88.

7. Cited in Stanley Smith, 1901: 87. Following the executions, Yuxian was honored by the people of Shanxi. When he left Taiyuan, his "boots of honor" were hung on the city gate and a stone tablet was erected to glorify his achievements; see A. Smith 1901b, 2: 615; Edwards 1903: 139.

8. Dr. Hykes, for example, argued that missionaries wanted justice, not revenge; see the *Shanghai Mercury*, 1967: 83. Charges of revenge appeared in *Literary Digest* 21.2 (1900): 35.

Hart did so in print (1901a, 1901b). The retelling of atrocity stories could, at the very least, help explain why the passions of survivors ran so high once the fate of missionaries in Baoding and Taiyuan were known. Was it any wonder, therefore, that people like Arthur Smith, faced with Yuxian's atrocities and the complicity of the population of Taiyuan in these crimes, would write in clear and unambiguous terms that it was essential for an "indelible brand" to be affixed to Taiyuan and the governor's yamen destroyed (1901b, 2: 615–16)?

But that was the Old Testament side of the narrative. There was a New Testament aspect as well, one that proved, for missionary purposes, to be the more significant of the two. Common in the titles of books that appeared between 1901 and 1904 was the reference to deceased missionaries as martyrs. The books themselves might be understood, in turn, as martyrologies for the contemporary world, but martyrdom and martyrology are notions that require some explanation. The term martyr has a long history, dating back to the very beginning of Christianity. Martyr means to witness, to testify to the fact that Jesus is the Son of God, and involves the refusal to renounce one's faith in the face of persecution and death. A martyr's death has been characterized by some as a second baptism or a baptism in blood. In the early church, martyrs were venerated through ceremonies held at their gravesites, usually in extraurban cemeteries, on the date of their death, and miracles were associated with them. In the Roman Catholic Church, martyrdom was one road to sainthood, and cults of saints emerged in which the faithful prayed for martyrs to intercede with God on their behalf. Relics of martyrs, pieces of their body or their clothing, were used to sanctify altars in new churches and were thus a mechanism for incorporating ever more territory into Christendom. From the third century C.E. forward it was also held that "the blood of the martyrs is the seed of the Church," a notion repeated by Isaac Ketler in *The China Martyrs of 1900* (1902: 400).[9]

Here we are not dealing with Roman Catholic theology, however, but with Protestant sects and ideas. The historian of Christianity Robert Kolb has pointed out that from its inception Lutheranism rejected the notion of the intercession between man and God provided by saints and martyrs. At the same time, however, religious persecution during the Reformation led to

9. On martyrdom and sainthood, see Eliade 1987, 11: 251, 4: 172–174; Hastings 1916, 11: 53; Jackson 1910, 7: 216; Meagher et al., 1979, 2: 2276. Also see Weinrich's characterizations of martyrdom (1981: 78–79, 205–206). Aries (1974: 16–17) discusses martyr burials.

the emergence of new martyrologies and a recognition that martyrs could exist in the present. Foremost among the writings devoted to martyrdom, at least in the English-speaking world, was Foxe's *Book of Martyrs* (1856), a seventeenth-century Protestant text that enjoyed renewed interest as missionary enterprises expanded globally.[10] It was so well-known, in fact, that Reverend Frederick Brown could argue that it "must fall into the background in the presence of the history of the Christian Church in China during the year 1900" (1902: 122).

Rather than working miracles, Protestant martyrs called believers to confess or testify to their belief, provided models of exemplary actions in the face of persecution or, more humbly, of the virtue of piety, and supported the claim that the Christian God concerned himself with every aspect of his people's daily life (Kolb 1987: 148–156). Certainly, by these Protestant definitions, those who died at the hands of the Boxers could be considered martyrs. Atrocity stories maintained that they had suffered and borne witness to their belief, and that all had led pious and exemplary lives. And though one might argue that perhaps martyrdom does not necessarily call for retribution, there was little doubt that martyrs provided a powerful refutation of criticism of the missionary enterprise in China.

The construction of missionaries as martyrs had one other significance, for what these books also contained was evidence that the martyr's blood was indeed the "seed" of the church. They did this through the retelling of the memorial services that occurred in 1901 and after in Baoding, Taiyuan, and other places where missionaries had died. These services included reburials, the consecration of sacred ground, Christian services, and the dedication of memorial monuments. Moreover, they paralleled services held at the same time "by almost all Christian denominations, and in almost all lands" (Ketler 1902: 400), effectively incorporating China into Christendom and encouraging a major expansion of the missionary enterprise in China.[11]

10. Kolb 1987: 148. On the publishing history of Foxe's book, see Haller 1963: 251–253. An 1856 American edition contained an 1813 preface by John Malham, who argued for "disseminating" this text because popery and persecution were not dead.

11. I am indebted to Donald Lopez, who encouraged me to further explore Christian notions of martyrdom, and for his suggestion that having martyrs effectively turned China into a part of Christendom.

CONSTRUCTING CHRISTIAN SACRED
SITES IN BAODING AND TAIYUAN

Clouds lowered as we left Peking, July 6 [1901], on the Peking and Hankow Railway for
Paoting-fu, that city of sacred and painful interest to every American Christian.
—Arthur Brown 1904

Between the winter and fall of 1901, groups of missionaries returned to places
where their compatriots had been killed and performed rituals of sacred consecration. This process might be understood as the constructive phase of
retribution, a reterritorialization that was designed to inscribe on the land
and on the minds of the Chinese a perpetual memory of Christian martyrdom.
In February, missionaries arrived in Baoding and located the mass grave near
the southeast corner of the city wall. E. H. Edwards and others dug up the remains of the dead and placed them in coffins, after which a short service was
held (Forsyth 1904: 26). A month later, prominent members of the Presbyterian mission and the American Board in China, including Arthur Brown and
Arthur Smith, accompanied by German and French officers, came to Baoding
to carry out formal burial services for the missionaries and Chinese converts
at a new cemetery. On the "Crowning Day," [12] 23 March, services were performed in a tent pavilion that had been set up by Chinese officials where the
Presbyterian compound had stood. Those present appear to have included the
replacements for the Qing officials executed on the first Baoding expedition.[13]
According to the Reverend J. W. Lowrie:

> The service opened with some rich and plaintive strains from the band
> which were followed by a reading of Scripture by Rev. C. A. Killie,
> a singing in English of the beautiful hymn, "Asleep in Jesus, blessed
> sleep," which, especially the last verse, never seemed more appropri-
> ate, a memorial address by Rev. John Werry, D.D., who spoke of each
> individual whose death we had gathered to commemorate. The German
> musicians followed with two stanzas of "Ein fest Burg ist unser Gott."
> Rev. Dr. Sheffield of the American Board led in prayer, Mr. Lowrie fol-
> lowed in some remarks to the Chinese gathered there. The Chinese sang
> the native rendering of the hymn, "I'm but a stranger here, heaven is

12. The phrase is taken from J. W. Lowrie, cited in Ketler 1902: 394–395, which also
provides numerous photographs of the Baoding ceremony.
13. See the list of officials in Ketler 1902: 394.

my home." Rev. Dr. Arthur Smith of the American Board pronounced the benediction. The band followed with a soft and gentle air and the service ended.

On the following day, services were held at the site of the American Board where the remains of twenty-six persons were buried. Further services were held at Lowrie's residence that evening, during which the missionaries seemed to have discussed the possibility of constructing another burial ground on the site where the Baoding contingent had been executed (cited in Ketler 1902: 395).

In Taiyuan, the story was much the same. Although the city had avoided the sort of punitive expedition that had "branded" Baoding, it received a contingent for a memorial service held on 18 July 1901. Funeral services were held and wreathes presented by Chinese officials. At that point or perhaps later, the city's stone monument to Yuxian was replaced by one to the dead martyrs. In addition, the building where some of the missionaries had been imprisoned awaiting their fate was razed to the ground, a monument erected, and the site turned into a public garden. Finally, as a result of negotiations in July 1901 between missionaries and officials in Taiyuan, it was arranged that "the funeral ceremonies at T'ai Yuan Fu were to be repeated at every place in Shansi where foreigners had been massacred; cemeteries made and kept in order at public expense, and suitable commemorative tablets erected." Services were held at Xinshou on 29 July, Taigu xian on 9 August, and Shouyang on 29 November, 1902.[14]

At the same time, it is also clear from missionary accounts that this New Testament tale was not the only one operating in either Taiyuan or Baoding. There were, in other words, opportunities to make other kinds of reordering statements. For example, the services themselves reconfirmed the right of missionaries to proselytize in the Chinese hinterland. The common burial of Chinese converts and Western missionaries and the participation of Chinese converts in the memorial service in the presence of Chinese officials, gentry, and merchants all point to such a conclusion. Also, missionaries expected that the memorial services would be accompanied by Chinese admissions of remorse. This, according to all accounts, is what seems to have happened in Baoding. Robert Forsyth, in commenting on the memorial service held in Tai-

---

14. The quotation is from Edwards (1903: 132–154), who also provides the fullest account of services in Taiyuan and subsequent events. See also R. Forsyth 1904: 41, 499–502.

yuan, captured succinctly the attitude that missionaries hoped the Chinese population would display: "How different the scene then to the sight many bystanders saw about a year before! Then the martyrs stood pale and silent in the presence of their persecutors; now the officials stood silent and abashed in the presence of missionaries. The contrast was striking, and to the thoughtful must have afforded suitable food for reflection" (1904: 500).[15]

Such positive results led a number of missionaries to express a strong sense of optimism about the future. Often couched in millenarian terms, their statements turned what had been generally seen as a "cataclysm" into a confirmation of past success. As that old missionary hand W. A. P. Martin put it, "The fires kindled by Boxers throw light on the success of missions, and prove that Christianity *was* making no little headway." In this revivalist atmosphere, Martin believed that the uprising had opened the way for the total conversion of China to Christianity.[16] Others chimed in on the same note. The *Missionary Herald*, for example, argued that what remained in China was much more than had perished. "China's need of the Gospel," the editor continued, "is greater and more clearly revealed than ever before; the lessons of history lead us to expect that after these convulsions cease and peace has been secured, a wider door of opportunity than heretofore will greet us in this great Empire" (Forsythe 1971: 78).

Statements like these encouraged readers to view the disaster as something that would serve to regenerate Christian evangelism globally and breathe new life into the China missions. Marshall Broomhall went so far as to compare the crisis in China to the destruction of Jerusalem. Just as the old order of Judaism had become impossible as a result of that disaster, the old structure of the missionary enterprise in China had also become impossible. In its stead were "greater freedom and boundless opportunities" for which the Church must rouse itself (1901: 12). This call to revival was punctuated by citing the last words of the Reverend Pitkin, killed at Baoding, to his wife, words faithfully carried to the world by the Chinese convert Lao Man and transmitted to Mrs. Pitkin by J. W. Lowrie. According to these sources, Pitkin asked that his

15. Others found the Taiyuan population far from repentant and blamed it on the fact that no punitive expedition had been sent there; see Edwards 1903: 139.

16. Martin 1900: 170. Even those who might be less sanguine than Martin could still argue that the missionary's steadfast "work of love" in China could not be for "naught"; see Conger 1909: 167.

son Horace be told that "his father's last wish is that when he is twenty-five years of age, he may come to China as a missionary." [17]

Biblical images of sacrifice and renewal were not the only analogies missionaries employed. Some cited more recent examples of Christian suffering and indicated, in each case, that they had also begun a new and more successful age of missionary enterprises. Arthur Brown noted that "the faint-hearted said that the India mutiny of 1857 and the Syria massacre of 1860 ended all hope of regenerating those countries, but in both they ushered in the most successful era of missions" (1904: 28–29). W. A. P. Martin (1900: 175–185) and Marshall Broomhall (1901: 13) agreed.

Regeneration and revivalism were also connected to assertions that China and perhaps the world were on the verge of great change. According to Arthur Brown, the Boxer Uprising indicated that China was undergoing an "unwelcome" but "inevitable awakening," a situation that led him to ruminate on Asia's long history of "grandeur" and "horror":

> Has that mighty continent nothing more to contribute to the world than the memories of a mighty past? It is impossible to believe that this is all. The historic review gives a momentum which the mind cannot easily overcome. As we look towards the Far East, we can plainly see that the evolution is incomplete. Whatever purpose the Creator had in mind has certainly not yet been accomplished. More than two-thirds of those innumerable myriads have as yet never heard of those high ideals of life and destiny which God Himself revealed to men. It is incredible that a wise God should have made such a large part of the world only to arrest its development at its present unfinished stage, inconceivable that He should have made and preserved so large a part of the human race for no other and higher purpose than has yet been achieved. (1904: 16–17)

"Impossible," "incredible," "unfinished," and "inconceivable," when coupled with "innumerable myriads," are the key words here; they help to justify and focus the missionary enterprise in the aftermath of the Boxer movement. They also weld a Christian teleology to secular visions of evolution and progress in a universal pattern of natural historical development. [18] Like many

17. Cited in Ketler 1902: 385–386. A. Smith (1901b, 2: 618) also mentions Pitkin's message.

18. Brown, Arthur Smith, and others freely used the contemporary language of evolu-

other missionaries, Brown saw part of China's salvation lying in Westernization and industrialization, forces of change that could not be resisted. But he also saw these inevitable changes as incomplete without a corresponding Christianization of China.[19] It was Christianity, according to Arthur Smith, that would allow the Chinese to adapt to the impact of Western civilization. The combination of Christianity and Western science would, he asserted, "make the dry bones of Chinese scholarship live by unifying, and for the first time completing, their knowledge of 'Heaven, Earth, and Man' " (1901b, 2: 738). The Chinese would be doubly saved; thanks to the missionary enterprise they would have bestowed on them a Christianized modernity.

Indeed, such moral modernization, aided in no small measure by the application of New Testament principles, soon emerged. In a spirit of forgiveness that was favorably contrasted with the insistence by the Catholic Church on exorbitant indemnities, Protestant missionary writers noted a number of farsighted and commendable programs that were soon implemented under the leadership of the Reverend Timothy Richard. Richard negotiated a settlement with Qing authorities that, among other things, provided a fund for the education of the people of Shanxi, so that, as Robert Forsyth explained, "the ignorance and superstition which was the root cause of this terrible tragedy may be removed for ever" (1904: 42).[20] Provided the Chinese atoned for their sins, missionaries seemed willing to extend their charitable pedagogy to the masses who had so recently rebelled against their presence. They would forgive and help to reform and rehabilitate China.

There is one final observation to be made about the regenerative theme developed by these authors. As indicated earlier, the sites of massacres were consecrated by missionaries as sacred ground, ground that now entered a new order of symbolic construction in which it provided material signs of remembrance for Christian sacrifice and Chinese transgression. But such ground

tion, adaptation, and race. See Hofstadter 1955 and Bannister 1972 on the pervasiveness of these ideas in late nineteenth-century America.

19. A. Brown 1904: 116, 127–128. See also A. Smith, 1901b, 2: 736, who argued that only Christianity had proven capable of providing a moral foundation to civilizations experiencing rapid scientific and technological change.

20. See A. Smith's criticism of the Catholics in 1901b, 2: 729. Gilbert Reid (1902: 450) spoke of "erroneous suspicion" and "superstitious fear." Hastings (1916, 8: 741) claimed that the refusal of the Protestant missionary groups to accept money indemnities created a good impression in China and accounted for a doubling in the number of converts over the next decade.

could also serve to instill hope for the future by becoming sites for Christian pilgrimage. In a letter to one of her sisters written on 20 June 1904, Sarah P. Conger, the wife of the U.S. minister to China, implies as much: "We found the missions [in Baoding] rebuilt and all their many lines of work moving on with activity. The Chinese converts who survived the troubles of 1900 and bore their awful test are strong helpers to-day, and there is more interest manifested, far more sympathy offered, and more respect shown the Christian thought than ever before" (1909: 316).

The shifts evident in these developments — from a willful focus on retribution to an emphasis on the constructive possibilities the Boxer debacle offered to enterprising Christians — when combined with rituals of grief and remembrance and the erection of stone monuments memorializing the dead, were effective agents for recruiting and mobilizing allies for the missionary enterprise in the United States and Great Britain. These events not only provided models for secular powers to mimic, they helped to inaugurate what Harold Isaacs ([1958] 1980) has called the golden age of the missionary enterprise. According to one study, during the first decade of the twentieth century the number of missionaries in China increased from 2,785 to 4,175 (Hastings 1916, 8: 741). The missionary narrative of suffering, redemption, and revival appears, in other words, to have had a profound impact in the homelands of the missions. It effectively fixed the interpretation of the events of 1900 as one in which foreigners, not the Chinese people, were innocent victims. From that point forward, it would be difficult to contemplate Western imperialism in China without also conjuring up an image of Chinese irrationality and savage barbarism.

BUILDING AND DEDICATING THE OBERLIN ARCH

The flurry of memorialization that followed the suppression of the Boxer Uprising was not confined to China. In the United States and Great Britain, for example, monuments to the China relief expedition and to missionaries killed during the uprising appeared. One of the more prominent was built at the small Protestant college of Oberlin in Ohio. The Oberlin monument was specifically dedicated to eighteen American missionaries who were connected to the college. Moreover, rather than presenting the missionaries as mere victims, the arch constructs them more positively as massacred Christian martyrs.

The Oberlin Memorial Arch was dedicated on 14 May 1903, a year and a half after the idea for it was first conceived by the American Board of Com-

missioners for Foreign Missions.[21] It would appear that the notion took coherent form in the spring of 1901, at a time when memorial services and the
dedication of monuments to the missionary dead were underway in China. In
addition to mirroring those events, there are two other aspects of the Board's
decision worth noting. The first has to do with the resolution to build it at
Oberlin College. In a letter to James R. Severance, Oberlin College treasurer,
Judson Smith of the American Board explained that Oberlin had been determined to be the most appropriate site "because so many of the martyred
missionaries were educated at Oberlin or went directly from Oberlin to the
field" (Oberlin College Archives [OCA], Smith to Severance, 24 June 1901).
The second issue had to do with the meaning the Board wished to fix on the
memorial. It was not to be a monument to missionaries, even dead missionaries, but, as Smith put it, to Christian martyrs (OCA, Smith to Severance,
9 August 1902, box 37).

Smith's insistence on constructing the Oberlin monument in these terms
appears consistent with the notion of Protestant martyrdom discussed above.
As we have seen, missionaries who died at the hands of the Boxers could, by
various Protestant definitions, be considered martyrs. The arch itself further
affirms this relationship in its bold inscription of the legend "The blood of
the martyrs is the seed of the Church."

This phrase suggests that there was a mimetic relationship between the
Oberlin memorial and those in China, providing, as it were, a pilgrimage site
in the United States for evangelical Christianity. If this is in fact the case, then
the Oberlin memorial established a claim of importance that went well beyond the confines of this small Ohio town. And it is here, I think, that we
might find a point of entry for an exploration of the ideological import of
Boxer Uprising memorialization in general.

In recent years, there has been a marked increase in the study of memorial monuments, particularly those that are dedicated to groups of people
rather than to individuals. Prominent in this work is the war memorial, which
is usually dealt with as a site for collective remembrance. This focus easily
lends itself to functionalist interpretation—for instance, memorialization

21. Once the decision was made to build a memorial at Oberlin, the Board turned to
raising money and finding an architect to design the monument. D. Willis James contributed $20,000 and smaller contributions totaled $720. See OCA, *Publications and Special Projects*
(Memorial Arch), under subgroup II (RG 41), box 4.

as a means to reintegrate community following a disaster such as the mass slaughter of World War I—but recent studies have addressed memorialization in a variety of other ways: as sites where national and individual efforts to construct meaning converge and diverge; as willful efforts to remember as well as to mold and remold memory; as sites where the interests of state and the interests of groups or individuals might clash; and as spaces into which passersby are beckoned and the significance of the monument gradually revealed. These interpretations not only denaturalize the processes involved in the creation and initial reception of monuments, but equally important, they suggest that over time the meaning of "sites of memory" may alter and transform (Nora 1989). They also suggest that memory, like experience, is a complex construct that is collectively formed and sustained and is intimately linked to material objects (M. Evans and Lunn 1997; Gregory 1994; Moriarty 1997; Winter 1995).

These approaches are useful for exploring the history of the Oberlin memorial. There is no doubt, for example, that the creators of the monument intended to mold memory in a specific way—that is, to present the dead missionaries as martyrs. They also appear to have wanted the monument to serve as an inspiration for the future. As models of dedication to Christianity and self-sacrifice, the martyrs could serve to guide and motivate students at Oberlin and at other Christian colleges throughout the world. In addition, the monument was built in a way and on a site that invited passersby into the central arch, where the significance of the memorial was made clear. The site chosen was a park on the edge of the Oberlin campus (now called Tappan Square) where it would be accessible to the public at large. Inside the central arch, two bronze plaques, visible only when one actually enters the arch, are mounted on either side. Under the heading "MASSACRED," they carry the names of the martyred dead and the places and dates of their martyrdom.

From the moment of its inauguration, the arch not only worked to mold memory, but became a focal point for the fashioning of a series of interconnected and overlapping meanings that reinforced the inspirational aspects of the memorial. It was dedicated, for example, during the ceremonies for the inauguration of the college's new president, Henry Churchill King, on 14 May 1903. Prior to the dedication ceremony, faculty, students, and visitors marched through the arch to the First Congregational Church, where King was installed. The following day, during his dedicatory address, the Reverend Frank Fitch of Buffalo described the arch as "a permanently beautiful monument to the noble life sacrifice of the Shansi martyrs." Paul Leaton Corbin, another speaker, added that the arch was "a call to self-denial service of a very special sort."[22]

These gestures focused on the remembrance of missionary dedication and sacrifice, but there was also a generative element. The arch had inscribed on its other arm "Ye are Witnesses." This statement encouraged others to follow in the footsteps of the Oberlin martyrs, and, with the graduation of 1903, marching through the arch became a standard part of Oberlin commencement exercises. In addition, beginning in 1904 and continuing until 1951, memorial services for the Shanxi martyrs, initially sponsored by the college and later by the community of Oberlin, were held annually.

Such material embodiments of Christian witnessing linked the arch, the college, Oberlin's mission school at Taigu, and the Taigu martyrs cemetery into a tightly woven network capable of remembrance, regeneration, and the refashioning of meaning. The fit among the parts of the network was so tight, in fact, that it seems to have formed a powerful consensus on Oberlin's place in the missionary enterprise in China. While it operated, it not only served to recall the evangelical and secular missionary enterprise in China, but, by the 1930s, could symbolize an idealistic universalism of brotherhood and material progress. The network, in other words, was a superlative machine for reterritorialization.

. . . .

Missionary discourse and memorialization constructed dead missionaries as martyrs and the events surrounding their deaths as a sign of success in China. The narrative of victimhood and transcendence situated China within a global process of Christian evangelism promising redemption through conversion to the heathen races of Asia and Africa. Equally important, memorialization established a network that linked burial grounds in China to memorials outside of China, constituting a pilgrimage circuit that would be traveled and retraveled, both physically and in the imagination of those who might participate in a graduation at Oberlin College. This circuit was paralleled (and occasionally overlapped) by another, a masculine network of heroic confrontation with barbarism that, like the missionary network, produced its own forms of memory.

22. OCA, Hi-O-Hi, 1904: 117–122; OCA, Carl Jacobson, "The Memorial Arch: An Unfinished Story," unpublished manuscript; *Lorain Journal* (Ohio), 15 August 1964.

Boys' Adventure Stories, Manly Performances, and Masculine Memory

Missionary writings on the Boxer Uprising, like many other cases of resistance to Western imperialism, was fodder for narrative structures that thrived on the Manichaean confrontation between civilization and barbarism. In this form, tales of white suffering mimicked the narrative-monument fusion found, for example, in other colonial settings where there had been resistance to European domination (e.g., the Indian rebellion of 1857 and the monuments to the "innocent" English who had perished as a result). But it was not only martyrdom in China that fit into patterns of late nineteenth-century Euroamerican imperial expansion. There were also tales of heroic overcoming of barbarism. And like martyrologies, the events in China could be readily incorporated into these stories as well. One of the more formative genres for fusing Boxer events and Western heroic triumphalism was the adventure novel for boys.

TALES OF HEROISM

One of the more effective mechanisms for producing imperial subjects in the late nineteenth century was the factually based novel for adults and children set in exotic regions of Africa, the Middle East, and Asia. In the juvenile adventure genre, Great Game heroics and colonial warfare were a staple, and much ink was spilled describing the efforts by adolescents and young adults in fighting and overcoming barbarism in "uncivilized" parts of the world (MacKenzie 1992). Clearly, the events of 1900 offered ample material for incorporating China into the genre; they also corresponded nicely with the formulaic plot structures of these stories.

In his study of popular imperialism and juvenile literature, Jeffrey Richards notes that the protagonist of these stories is often a teenage boy who, at the outset of the book, has lost parents, a fortune, or his place in society and is thrown on his own resources in the wider world. In a sequence of "special missions, adventures, battles, sieges, chases, captures, escapes and rescues," the hero's character is tested and confirmed as flawless. Unlike other novel forms in which the protagonist might grow mentally and ethically as a result of life's challenges, the hero of juvenile literature came fully formed. The adventure merely put his qualities of courage, patriotism, resourcefulness, manliness, paternalism toward natives, service, and sacrifice on display, while demonstrating that such character traits were absent among those who opposed the civilizing mission (1992: 90–91). As such, the type of hero to be found in this literature provided a foundation for white supremacy and a basis of the claimed right to rule over others.

These heroic traits were given added force by drawing on popular name recognition for the setting of the story. George A. Henty, perhaps the most important author of the genre, whose formula was frequently copied by others, intercut these personal adventures with factual accounts of current events produced by war correspondents and campaign participants.[23] His boy heroes often encountered iconic figures of empire, telegraphed by such titles as *With Roberts to Pretoria* (1901), *With Clive in India* (1884), and *With Kitchener in the Soudan* (1902). In all, he authored six novels set in Africa, including one on Garnet Wolseley's campaign of 1873–1874 against the Ashanti (*By Sheer Pluck*, 1884), and another nine set in India, on the Afghan frontier, and in Burma.

Henty's contribution to the Boxer literature was *With the Allies to Pekin: A Story of the Relief of the Legations* (1904). Drawing on George Lynch, H. C. Thomson (*China and the Powers*, 1902), and the Reverend Roland Allen, Henty ingeniously managed to get Rex, his hero, into almost the entire Boxer affair. Like many of the protagonists of these tales, Rex is infinitely resourceful at disguising himself, and he can speak Chinese well enough to fool the natives. These skills make him the perfect messenger, and he manages to join the Seymour relief column, make his way in and out of the besieged legations more than once, fight in Tianjin and at the Tagu forts, and accompany the first relief group into Beijing.

Other authors, though perhaps less faithful to published details than Henty, still found the Boxer Uprising a useful setting for their boy heroes to cavort in. In the United States, for example, Elbridge S. Brooks and Edward Stratemeyer, both renowned authors of patriotic juvenile literature, produced *Under the Allied Flags: A Boxer Story* (1901) and *On to Pekin* (1900), respectively.[24] In Brooks's case, he added a third novel to a set that had placed his hero, Ned Pulver, in Cuba, South Africa, and the Philippines (*In Defense of the Flag* and *With Lawton and Roberts*). Stratemeyer located his China novel in his *Old Glory* series, which featured the exploits of a young American army lieutenant. As

23. Fleming (1959: 90) thought Henty's influence so profound on his times that he argued that novelists, not Clausewitz, inspired the strategy that doomed the Seymour expedition.

24. Stratemeyer is best known as the creator of the Rover Boys, Hardy Boys, Tom Swift, and Nancy Drew series of children's stories. See *The Legendary Edward Stratemeyer*, http://www.web-span.com/raven43/pers9.htm, accessed 30 June 2001. I am indebted to Eve Sawyer for bringing this site to my attention.

in the Henty book, both Brooks and Stratemeyer build their stories around the absolute distinction between civilization and barbarism and reproduce the racial typologies of the era. The only good Chinese people, it turns out, are servants who demonstrate loyalty and who gratefully accept the paternalistic gestures of their white masters. Indeed, here as in other settings, the only right-thinking natives are those who welcome and occasionally demand the particular kinds of order Euroamericans impose.[25]

Taken together, these works and others like them sutured the wounds of "civilization" much as missionary martyrologies had done—they fixed the meaning of the event in clear-cut terms of perpetrator and victim, while providing their young heroes the opportunity to perform the positive masculine virtues of empire builders. Moreover, in Henty's case, there was substantial value added. In one instance, for example, Rex was part of the Triumphal March in August 1900, and his reactions to the Forbidden City were much like those of others—he was "greatly disappointed." "It is a rotten place," he explained to female relatives who had survived the siege: "it looks as if it hadn't been inhabited for a hundred years. It is grimy, dusty, and dark" (Henty 1904: 370). But like many of those who expected so much more from the Forbidden City, Rex took a degree of solace in the ready access he now had to Chinese valuables. His uncle, Mr. Bateman, who ran a merchant enterprise in Tianjin, had returned to England just before Rex left for China. He had advised his nephew that there would be a great deal of looting by soldiers who seldom knew the value of what they had taken and would be ready to sell "for a song." Rex should keep an eye out for old vases and furs. Armed with his uncle's advice and a large amount of money furnished by his father, Rex entered the Beijing loot market, astutely buying an enormous amount of porcelain, jewelry, and furs well below their actual market value and hiring coolies to haul his purchases to the coast for him. On his way out of China with his plunder, Rex found time to save several Chinese women from being raped by Russian soldiers.

The lesson for juveniles in Great Britain and the rest of the English-speaking world was clear. Like all honest and chivalric Englishmen, Rex did what was right and served the cause of civilization when opportunity arose. He was, in other words, like all other heroes of the genre, performing imperial masculine virtues for others to understand and copy. At the same time, Henty

25. Jeffrey Richards (1992: 97) notes this theme in much of the British juvenile literature; though somewhat less bellicose, it is also present among American authors.

could not avoid dealing with looting and violence. The latter he handled by having Rex rescue the innocent; the former he explained in the following way: acknowledging that looting in China was a violation of international treaties, from the allied point of view, he argued, Chinese atrocities had negated the agreements (Henty 1904: 373–374, 376, 380). At the same time, his hero Rex did not loot; rather like the British army itself, he was sealed off from the stigma associated with plunder by British prize procedures, gaining his booty through the amoral marketplace of supply and demand.

In these and other ways, the boys' adventure stories of Henty, Stratemeyer, and Brooks helped either to occlude the many forms of violence perpetrated by the allied armies in China or lay the blame at the door of the Russians, French, or Germans and, of course, the Chinese. These sorts of displacements functioned in a manner similar to those operating in missionary martyrologies. Much as martyrs' blood effectively incorporated China into Christendom, juvenile literature, through its heroic accounts of the siege and relief of the legations, incorporated China and the Boxers into a global narrative of imperial policing actions, making them "morally legible" for the future rule of empire.[26]

In this form, the Boxer events lent themselves to ready appropriation by other media. Within a year of the relief, Buffalo Bill's Wild West Show staged "The Allied Powers at the Battle of Tien-tsin and the Capture of Pekin," and included actors wearing the uniforms of the U.S. 9th Regiment, U.S. Marines, Royal Welsh Fusiliers, India army units, and several of the European powers.[27] In Great Britain, meanwhile, the Belle Vue Gardens, an outdoor theater noted for its pyrotechnic extravaganzas representing Britain's many imperial wars, staged The Siege of Pekin (1901), a production that was nested neatly among other siege tales, including The Siege of Ladysmith, The Siege of Paadeburg, and The Defense of Mafeking, all Boer War events occurring in the same year as the Boxer Uprising.[28]

Even the new medium of motion pictures got into the act. In 1901, the British firm Walturdaw, playing on two of the most emotional elements in accounts of the Euroamerican reports on the Boxer Uprising, distributed At-tempted Capture of an English Nursery and Child by Boxers and Assassination of an En-

26. I take the term from Peter Brooks (1976), who is cited in Mayer 1992: 186.

27. Russell 1960: 419. I am grateful to Joy Kasson for bringing this source to my attention.

28. See Mayer 1992 on the Belle Vue Gardens, especially 192–194. Belle Vue had also staged the destruction of the Summer Palace in 1861; see 187.

glish Citizen by Boxers. That same year, James Williamson, a British filmmaker, produced *Attack on a Chinese Mission*. Shot at his Brighton villa with members of his family as the cast, Williamson had the women and children of the mission station rescued by British Marines at the moment the Boxers are about to put them to death. In France, the film pioneer George Méliès produced *La Chine contre les Allies*, which was shown in late 1900 (Leyda 1972: 4–5). Meanwhile, in the United States, Lubin Studios in Philadelphia made a 42-second film entitled *Beheading the Chinese Prisoner*, complete with a Chinese swordsman,[29] and Vitagraph Company produced *The Congress of Nations*. According to one description, the powers, represented in the person of characters such as John Bull and Germania, are about to dismember Boxer China when the Statue of Liberty appears to sort things out (5–6). The Open Door had, after all, to be maintained regardless of what went on in China.

In these various ways, the dominant narrative of missionary transcendence, military triumphalism, and, in the case of the United States, Western fair play in China was further disseminated and linked to sacrifices being made in other parts of empire, the effect of which was to solidify the victim-hero tale in popular print and nonprint culture. Indeed, it was through media such as the ones discussed in this section that powerful "memories" were shaped about fin de siècle China and the Boxer Uprising. A half century later, in oral interviews with Americans who grew up in the 1890s and the first two decades of the twentieth century, Harold Isaacs recovered images of China that can be dated to the Boxer era. In at least one case, Isaacs's interviewee pointed directly to literature for boys, in particular, harrowing tales of Boxer antiforeignism, as the vehicle through which his understanding of Chinese character and conditions was formed.[30] Such images, as we will see in the final chapter, continued to be a staple element in an Orient of the Western popular imaginary.

MILITARY MEMORIALIZATION

Of course, juvenile literature was not the only way that heroic sacrifices and the courage of soldiers could be memorialized and remembered. We have already seen that trophy acquisition was a commonly shared process by which

29. Gary Arbuckle, "An Exiting Novelty: The Exotic Orient in Early Film," http://www. interchg.ubc.ca/arbgary/excite.html, accessed 12 May 1998.

30. Isaacs [1958] 1980; see especially 106, where one respondent recalls having read one of the boy's adventure tales of the Boxer Uprising serialized in *Youth's Companion* as "The Cross and the Dragon."

regiments involved in action in China fixed institutional meaning about their participation. Boxer weapons, field guns, and imperial regalia could all take up a prominent position at a unit's regimental headquarters alongside items from other campaigns. Over time, they might also find a place in a regimental museum.[31] In other cases, appropriated items could be transformed to become a more suitable medium for remembrance. The Liscum bowl, dedicated to the commander of the U.S. 9th Infantry who had been killed at Tianjin, was made from a portion of silver found in a Qing government mint and placed in the care of the regiment.[32] The U.S. 14th Regiment followed suit, casting silver bars ostensibly awarded to them by the Qing government after the fall of Beijing into a regimental punch bowl. They named their bowl after Calvin P. Titus, who had been awarded the Congressional Medal of Honor for his heroism in the storming of the Qing capital.[33]

Regiments also designed recognition of the campaign into battle flags and, in some cases, altered their insignia and nicknames as a result of the action in China. As noted earlier, this was the case with two of the American units involved, the U.S. 9th and 14th Infantry Regiments. The 9th not only changed its nickname to "The Manchus," but added a five-toed Chinese dragon to the unit insignia and belt buckle. The 14th ("Golden Dragons") placed a dragon on its insignia as well. These incorporations of things Chinese into the living memory of U.S. military units was one way that effects of events in 1900 were carried through time, effects that remain visible today on the Internet Web sites of these army regiments.[34]

A third kind of memorialization also occurred after the China relief expedition. Perhaps the most common form of military memory retention, it involved the creation of a fraternal organization of campaign veterans. The U.S. army took the lead in establishing such an organization. On 13 February 1901, General Chaffee appointed three officers to a committee charged with organizing the Military Order of the Dragon (NARA, RG395, 906, box 4). When established, the Order included most of the officers in the U.S. army and Marine contingents, as well as officers from the other seven nations. In

31. This was the case with a number of items sent to the Royal Engineers' Barracks at Chatham and the Royal Welsh Fusiliers Museum in Caernarvon Castle.

32. See www.manchu.org/linage/liscum.htm, accessed 25 May 2001.

33. See www.25thida.com/14thinf.html, accessed 25 May 2001. The punch bowl can be seen at http://1-14th.com/titusbowl.htm, accessed 1 July 2001.

34. As of 1 July 2001, the Web sites of these regiments can be found by searching on their nicknames.

TABLE 3. Membership in the Military Order of the Dragon, ca. 1912

Country	Members
United States	346
Great Britain	416
Japan	302
Germany	75
Italy	35
Russia	28
France	19
Austria	1
Total	1,222

a publication it issued in 1912, the organization included over one hundred rare photographs and a membership list. The total number of members from each of the eight powers is summarized in table 3. These numbers reflected more than the interest in the Order of individual members; by 1912 the top three had formed alliances to "defend" themselves against Imperial Russia.

Based in Washington, D.C., the Order continued to be dominated by U.S. army officers until the beginning of World War I. When war broke out in Europe in 1914, the international composition of the Order was dissolved. Sometime around 1915, the organization changed its name to the Imperial Order of the Dragon and altered its constitution. Following the war, it seems to have developed affiliations with other U.S. veterans organizations, including the Veterans of Foreign Wars, and was invited to participate in the dedication of the Unknown Soldier Memorial in Washington.[35]

This change in itself is not of particular interest. Of note, however, is the language and terminology that emerged from the shift. Members of the Order used the fraternal greeting "Hello Chino," and when they died, they passed over "The Great Wall." The president of the Order became the "grand viceroy," his term of office a "dynasty," and his headquarters the "Great Yamen." Heads of local chapters were designated "provincial viceroys" and ordinary members became "mandarins." This use of terminology that mimics the Qing bureaucracy not only parallels various terminological and symbolic appropriations by the regiments discussed above, but suggests a certain degree

35. See http://www.army.mil/cmh-pg/faq/memday/90-1-ch1.htm, accessed 1 July 2001.

of knowledge, however limited, of the Qing state. Perhaps the Order had learned this language from its "grand custodian of archives," one Enoch R. L. Jones, who, in the 1930s, published in the group's newsletter accounts of late nineteenth-century Chinese history, drawn, it would seem, from "authoritative" sources such as *China Under the Empress Dowager* and *Annals and Memoirs of the Court of Peking* by Edmond Backhouse and J. O. P. Bland.[36] The Order's embrace of Oriental motifs might also stand as an example of the kinds of patchwork identities discussed by Robert Young in his comments on the imbrication of cultures in a colonial setting. In this case, the Great Yamen could be understood as the product of a joint history, an artifact holding fragments of that shared past that returns as an exaggerated form of mimicry.

Finally, there is one other kind of memorialization worth noting here, and it too involved American members of the Military Order of the Dragon. This was the quite literal inscription on China of material markers to commemorate the engagements of 1900. In April 1905, General Chaffee, now president of the Order, created a committee to determine where the markers should be placed. In December of the following year, seven bronze tablets were shipped to China for installation. Six of the tablets were placed at the entranceway of the U.S. legation in Beijing and bore the names of those Americans killed during the siege and relief of the legations.[37]

These tablets were not the only monuments erected in China to the American dead. In his report to the Order on the dedication ceremonies of the tablets, Lieutenant Colonel Webb Hayes noted that the British community in Tianjin had dedicated a tablet to the American dead and placed it in Gordon Hall, the structure in the British concession named after Charles "Chinese" Gordon, who, it will be recalled, had been part of the joint Anglo-French expedition of 1860. In addition, a monument to Colonel Emerson Liscum, commander of the 9th Infantry Regiment killed at Tianjin, was erected on the site where he fell. When Hayes arrived at Tianjin in 1908, the site had been made part of an enlarged Japanese concession and, he was delighted to report, Japanese officials had made the area around the Liscum monument into a public park.[38]

36. I take the terminology from the Order's newsletter, which appeared at least twice annually from the early 1930s forward. See USMHI, Lewis L. McKinney file 1898-W-619, Spanish-American War Survey Collection.

37. See *Military Order of the Dragon* ca. 1912 for photographs of the plaques.

38. See *Military Order of the Dragon* ca. 1912: 101–105. Also see NARA, RG92, file 214,

NEW KNOWLEDGE, MEMORIALIZATION, AND TOURISM

The consecration and preservation of monuments to the events of 1900 were, as argued in the case of missionaries, a significant way by which the barbarism within civilization could be suppressed and memory constituted around sacrifice and valor. These morally elevating sentiments encoded in the monuments themselves could, in turn, serve as objects for other kinds of activities. They could, for example, become part of a rebuilt Beijing, a post-Boxer environment in which not only diplomats, soldiers, missionaries, and businessmen came to visit, but a whole new species appeared: the international tourist seeking the most exotic of locales. Within a few years of the signing of the protocol of 1901, tourists began to arrive overland via the Trans-Siberian railway or by steamship from Shanghai or Yokohama. The sites of Boxer-era events and their memorialization in Beijing were key elements in creating another kind of circuit of remembrance. In turn, these events were located within a broader history, one that had produced uniquely new knowledge about Beijing and its inhabitants since the establishment of the first legations in 1861.

It is beyond the scope of this study to delve deeply into the development of global tourism and its extension to China at the beginning of the twentieth century. Still, it is clear from a perusal of a number of the guidebooks written before and in the decade following World War I that sites of Sino-Western conflict were a critical part of seeing Beijing. One of the earliest of these guidebooks was that of Mrs. Archibald Little, who drew extensively from the imperial archive of knowledge about Beijing, including the writings of Bushell and publications of the North China Branch of the Royal Asiatic Society, to provide authenticity and verisimilitude.

Little's guide was organized as a series of itineraries for tours of Beijing and its environs, depending on the amount of time visitors had to spend. Through this mechanism, it constructed a hierarchy of significant sites. Spatially, the hierarchy was anchored in the legation quarter and in its relationship to the Forbidden City. On their first day, for example, tourists were instructed to pass through the Ketteler Memorial Arch to see, in one day, the Lama Temple (Yonghe gong), Confucian Temple and Hall of Classics, the Yel-

no. 469 for correspondence and memoranda related to the monuments. The China memorial plaques were processed through the same correspondence that led to the erection of monuments in Cuba commemorating the U.S. soldiers who died in the Spanish-American War.

38. The "Lest We Forget" wall, British legation, Beijing. Source: *Military Order of the Dragon*, 1912.

low Temple outside the Anding Gate, the Great Bell Temple to the northwest of the city, the Peitang (Catholic cathedral), where "possibly the most miraculous siege recorded in history" had occurred, and observatory, "where the famed astronomical instruments used to stand" (Mrs. A. Little 1904: 5–6). On the second day, visitors were told to climb the city walls to see the relationship between the Forbidden City and the European enclave, now almost wholly rebuilt, and to scan the sights from one to the other. They were then directed to move through the legation quarter itself to see monuments to the siege. These included a second Ketteler memorial in the German legation, the chapel in the British legation with memorial plaques, one of which had been presented in gratitude by American siege survivors, and a remnant of the wall of the old British legation, on which Sir Claude MacDonald had painted the legend "Lest We Forget" (fig. 38), a line taken, no doubt, from Rudyard Kipling's "Recessional," which first appeared in 1897.

If tourists had additional time, Little guided them to sites outside of Beijing, including the Western Hills, where the British summer residence, destroyed by the Boxers, had stood, as well as a host of other famous temples, palaces, and pavilions. After providing a precis to the significance of these places for the local people (drawn, of course, from sinological sources with which she was familiar), she would often note their importance in the events of 1900–1901. It was possible, in other words, with Little's guidebook in hand, to follow out the movements of Boxers and Western military forces, and do so by repeatedly passing through the Ketteler Memorial Arch on Hatamen Street. Moreover—and this was unique to Little—it was also possible to see some of the sites of importance during the campaign of 1860, including the temple where Parkes and Loch had been held captive (1904: 40).

Although none of the guidebooks that followed in the wake of Little's was quite as openly Boxer-centered, the theme itself and Mrs. Little's itinerary are evident in them. For example, in the same year that her guide was published, Karl Baedeker added Beijing to his trans-Asian tour. The "Lest We Forget" wall, the Ketteler Arch, as well as a site near the Qing Western Tombs (Xiling) were prominent in Baedeker editions from 1904 forward (1904: 498, 501, 503, 1912: 533–534, 536, 1914: 557, 560, 562). Not to be outdone, Thomas Cook and Son had a similar guide in print by 1910, which was expanded in 1917 to include an entire section on the siege of the legations, as well as points of interest in Beijing and its environs (1910: 22, 1917: 13–15, 1924: 12–15). The pattern continued into the 1920s and 1930s, as more and more guides to the city appeared in print. In one of them, Emil Fischer noted that a small obelisk was in place near the entrance to the British legation, bearing the legend "20th June to 14th August 1900," a reminder of the dates of the siege. According to Fischer, the chancellery wall in the French legation was pockmarked with bullet holes, another reminder of 1900 (1924: 16–17). Even the *Peiping Chronicle* guidebooks of the 1930s, which tended to emphasize the modern hospitals, universities, libraries, hotels, and shopping areas around Beijing, noted the "Lest We Forget" wall and the Ketteler monument at the German legation (1933: 13–14).

By the 1920s, book-length studies of Beijing began to appear. More than guidebooks, they were written by long-time Western residents and sought to capture the history and flavor of the pre-Republican-era city. One of the more noted of these was by Juliet Bredon (1922, 1931), niece of Sir Robert Hart. In a chapter on the legation quarter, Bredon drew attention to the "Lest We Forget" wall in the British embassy and peppered her text with references to events of 1860 and 1900. In a similar vein, L. C. Arlington and William Lewisohn, in their guidebook *In Search of Old Peking* ([1935] 1987), also provided a chapter on the legations, reviewed the history of Westerners in Beijing from 1860 forward, discussed the Boxer Uprising at length, and reproduced the full text of the memorial tablet to the Europeans and Sikhs who had died in captivity in 1860. This was the monument, it will be recalled, that bore the legend "This stone replaces the original memorial destroyed by the Chinese in June 1900."

As a reinscription of history, this particular stone monument might stand as a fitting epitaph for all the works discussed in this section. In tourist guide-books and more detailed studies of Beijing, the Euroamerican presence was repeatedly reconfirmed and justified, and the notion that Westerners were the well-meaning victims of Chinese exclusionism or barbarism recycled. Chinese efforts to erase or rework that history were futile, as the destruction of the 1860 memorial stone in the Russian cemetery indicated. New generations of Westerners, whether they casually passed through north China or became longer-term residents, were acculturated to the special place of privilege, guaranteed by treaty rights, that citizens of the powers enjoyed in China.

"The Guy with the Flag"

This chapter has focused on many kinds of efforts to fix the meaning of events in 1900. In particular, it has addressed those that involved the construction of authoritative narratives and institutional forms of memory making. In each of the cases dealt with above, whether the building of monuments, the incorporation of the events of 1900 into various kinds of history, or the creation of a tourist network, China was reterritorialized yet again. Moreover, as the forms of meaning associated with this reordering process were disseminated and circulated through Europe and North America to treaty ports and back again, they became iconic talismans of heroism and sacrifice that were never to be forgotten. It was, in effect, these icons that formed the iron rations of general knowledge to which Fleming alluded over half a century later. In this form, they also served to drive a wedge between the Chinese and the Western community in China, epitomized by the high-walled exclusion of the legation quarter in Beijing, where Chinese were now forbidden to live. Yet, this divide was not absolute—there was seepage across the boundaries, a flow that produced its own peculiar and unique hybrid formations. One of the more interesting of these forms appeared in Tianjin, in the rebuilt concessions.

The Boxer protocol allowed the powers to station military contingents in Beijing and Tianjin. In 1912, the U.S. 15th Infantry Regiment, famous for members such as George C. Marshal and Joseph Stilwell, began a twenty-six-year stay at the U.S. barracks in Tianjin, a site at which, as in other foreign concessions in the city, memorial services were held regularly to remember the Boxer-era dead (Tuchman 1971: 99; Bickers 1999: 107). While attached to this unit in the late 1920s, Charles Finney noted that there were a large number of retired U.S. army noncommissioned officers still living in the American concession. According to Finney, many of them had taken up residence with young Chinese women. Although they used the Post Hospital and Exchange, they kept a distance from the active-duty soldiers at the barracks and had their own private club. By chance, Finney became friendly with one of them, Master Sergeant George Smith, who, after a time, introduced Finney to the club and invited him home. Smith was living with a woman he identified as a Manchu (Finney 1961: 245–258).

On one occasion, after Smith's Manchu companion had cooked them dinner, brought them hot towels and drinks, and massaged their necks, Smith told Finney that "she paints, too." He then proceeded to produce a long scroll from a cabinet, which when unrolled told a story. Finney's description of the scroll and Smith's commentary on it are worth citing in full: "The opening scene was of the mouth of a river: cannon mounted in forts were firing at warships out to sea. 'Taku,' said Smith. 'You know—at the mouth of the Hai Ho where those busted up gun emplacements are.' As he unrolled the scroll, the foreign armies fought their way up the Hai River and battled it out with the Boxers in Tien-tsin and raised the siege of Peking. 'I told her about it, and she painted it,' said Smith. 'She wasn't even born then. You see I fought in that particular scrap myself. That's supposed to be me there—the guy with the flag' " (1961: 257).

Here, then, was another sort of remembrance, a kind that was incised into the everyday life of a small group of veterans who had decided to spend their later years in the zone of privilege that warfare and treaty had created in China. Yet, if Sergeant Smith is any example, they were also there because they could practice their own form of transgression, living apart and in a way unimaginable for most foreigners. Their otherness, their nonconformity to the conventional boundaries of foreign and Chinese interaction presents another form of recollection and remembrance, another kind of intercultural contact in the wake of the China relief expedition.

Finney's account conjures a stunning image of the Manchurian woman, brush in hand, attentive to the verbal narrative of the soldier, perhaps his own stories, perhaps ones he heard at the club. For a moment, fixed in the imagination like a Benjaminian montage, we might catch a glimpse of that hand arrested over the scroll's visual trace of the route from Dagu to Beijing, the path of the deterritorialization and reterritorialization of China, but now as the imbrication and layering of cultures. It is this image, in its unmistakable density and complexity (one that I have not been able to shake off since first reading Finney's passage), more than any of the monuments erected in China in the wake of the Boxer Uprising—they are all gone now, erased by a revolution—that continues to haunt the present.

. . . .

CHAPTER 10

The Return of the Repressed, Recirculations,

and Chinese Patriotism

IMPERIAL WARFARE AND ITS forcible reordering of the Qing Empire profoundly shaped the history of twentieth-century China and China's relations
with North Atlantic nation-states. The twentieth century began with esca-
lating failures of Qing reform efforts, which resulted in the 1911 Revolution
and the end of two thousand years of monarchial government. Revolution
and warfare on a monumental scale marked the first half of the century; the
building of socialism and the turn toward a market economy the second half.
China's governments continued to deal with the machinations of the great
powers, though much external meddling came to an abrupt end in 1949 with
the establishment of the People's Republic of China. The Chinese communists formally negated all of the unequal treaties still in effect and reclaimed
most if not all of the territories and concessions that had been ceded away.
Although the era of Western imperialism in China was apparently at an end,
the often hostile relations between China and the great powers did not cease.
Nor did the Great Game. It was transformed into a cold war, one now designed to contain the spread of communism from the Union of Soviet Socialist Republics and the People's Republic to other parts of the greater Eurasian
land mass.

Clearly, the events of the nineteenth century powerfully shaped the actions and worldviews of leaders in China and Euroamerica. Moreover, they continue to influence how contemporary Chinese people understand China's relations with other parts of the world and, to a greater or lesser extent, how Westerners respond to China. This chapter seeks to look beyond the events of the late nineteenth century and explore their place within certain forms of cultural production that emerged in China, Europe, and North America from the early twentieth century forward. To put this another way, I want to consider the patterns of circulation and the sites at which the many kinds of English lessons that have been discussed came to rest in Euroamerica and China. My purpose is to demonstrate how consciously and unconsciously embedded that history is in our world, and how it continues to shape the world, a century after the occupation of Beijing ended.

Specters from the East

If . . . a taste for opium-smoking should once gain a footing in England, as it has already done in America, there may be reason to fear lest the *poison which Britain has so assiduously cultivated for China,* may eventually find its market amongst our own children—*a retribution too terrible to contemplate,* though one against the possibility of which it were well to guard. —C. F. Gordon Cumming 1886

The author of this warning wrote these lines following a trip to China in 1885. They reference a history that, for educated English people like her, was common knowledge: Britain's "opening" of China to the West and the lever that was employed, the evil drug opium. In the Christian moral universe in which she lived and circulated, Gordon Cumming knew that there was often a balancing of the books, that evil was often repaid with retributive justice. At the time, China was weak and did not appear to have the capacity for effective action, but the fear of Chinese retribution could not disappear. It merely lay dormant, beneath or perhaps adjacent to the periodic obsessions with cross-channel invasions that occasionally mesmerized various strata of the British public before World War I (Pick 1993: 115–135). All this changed after the war, when, as a result of a peculiar convergence of elements, Great Britain found itself in the midst of an unprecedented drug panic.

Although, as Gordon Cumming suggests, concern with the infiltration of exotic drugs into Britain dated back at least to the 1880s (Berridge and

Edwards 1981; Milligan 1995; Parssinen 1983), the particular hysteria that took shape in the early 1920s seems to have had its source in the unusual cultural mixture that connected jaded aristocrats, the lower orders in the theater and dance hall districts of London, and men of color. The immediate cause was the drug-related deaths of several chorus girls and actresses. According to reports in the tabloid press, all of the women had died as a result of combining forbidden sex with dangerous drugs, and had been enticed into doing so by yellow and black men. Moreover, such concerns over the mixture of white women with opium and men of color was not confined to the tabloids. D. W. Griffith's film Broken Blossoms (1919) took up the same theme, including scenes of white women in languid poses at opium dens in the Limehouse section of London (Marchetti 1993: 32–39). What made this conjunction unusual, at least according to the tabloids, was that the deaths of London women appeared to be part of a vast conspiracy, one designed to degrade white women and to undermine the moral and physical strength of the British imperial center. The point of origin of the conspiracy lay on the frontiers of the empire, in those zones of contact that were not quite inside, yet not quite outside the imperial purview—zones often labeled "spheres of influence"—where Great Games were played.

In this case, the frontier in question was China and those areas adjacent to it where opium was grown for the vast China market and for global distribution. From these sources, opium was being smuggled into England by an organization at the head of which stood a criminal mastermind, a crafty "Chinaman." Dubbed by the press "Brilliant" Chang, partly because of his purported intelligence and partly because of his un-Oriental style of dress, he was arrested in 1924 and deported after being convicted of cocaine possession. Yet, like archvillains of popular fiction such as Professor Moriarty and Fu-Manchu, both of whom also threatened the stability and health of the imperial center, Chang did not disappear. It was said that he jumped ship before reaching China and resumed operations out of Zurich, Antwerp, Brussels, or even Paris. Characterized as the "Emperor of Dope" at the head of a "dope octopus," Chang was blamed for drug-related deaths throughout Europe well into the next decade.[1]

These references to race, degradation, gender, and conspiracy are not un-

---

1. Moreover, his reputation extended into the 1950s. This description of the drug panic in Great Britain is taken from Kohn 1992. On Chang, also see Parssinen 1983: 169–172.

usual features of tabloid journalism or the social world of the spectacular that emerged in the imperial centers of Western Europe and North America in the second half of the nineteenth century. Nor is it unusual to see the specter of a threat posed to white women by men of color; it is a kind of mimicry in the imperial metropole of the alarmism often found among colonial officials concerning the secret or hidden activities of the colonized. What is peculiar about this case, however, is that it does not invoke the usual colonial sites, but implicates the new Republic of China. Perhaps the history Gordon Cumming made reference to a third of a century earlier was, in fact, far more alive than one might at first suspect.

There was, for example, the emergence of an imaginative literature that, like the tabloids, luridly dealt with sex, drugs, and Oriental retribution, the flip side, as it were, of the juvenile hero tales. One prominent author of the genre was Arthur Ward, better known as Sax Rohmer, the creator of Fu-Manchu. In two non–Fu-Manchu novels, The Yellow Claw,[2] first published in 1915, and Dope, which appeared in 1919, Rohmer wrote about mastermind Chinese criminals like Brilliant Chang who spun drug conspiracies in England and sought to entrap upper-class women, actresses, and effeminate men in the nefarious world of drug use, thereby undermining the high moral order of the British Empire. The Fu-Manchu series extended these anxieties well into the 1950s and 1960s, recycling fantasies of the many threats to white masculinity and femininity posed by an awakened Asia.[3]

Rohmer's foreshadowing of the 1920s drug panic appears, therefore, to have been firmly rooted in the same fears articulated by Gordon Cumming (i.e., the problems of empire coming home to roost in England), which themselves were grounded in widely diffused understandings of the history of the Anglo-Chinese contact in the nineteenth century. As we have seen, a vast archive of knowledge about China had been produced that, by the early twentieth century, had taken on the status of common sense about China and the characteristics of the Chinese people. Rohmer's fiction drew from this archive to create plausible fantasies about Chinese ambitions toward the West. As such, Fu-Manchu novels provide a useful site for locating China in the

2. The Boston Sunday Globe serialized the novel from 2 April to 28 May 1916 and began a Fu-Manchu serialization in September of the same year.

3. Invariably stalwart white men thwart the conspiracy. But it is also clear from Rohmer's novels that in the era of global empire and imperial capitalism, the threat from many forms of social pollution were never completely eliminated.

broader discourses on global conflict and competition between powerful imperial formations in the past century and a half.

For much of the twentieth century, this "specter out of the east"[4] was the emblem par excellence of deep-seated Western anxieties about global cross-cultural relations and, for many, the sign of a world fundamentally, and perhaps irreconcilably, divided between East and West.[5] As Nayland Smith, Rohmer's heroic British protagonist, put it, Fu-Manchu was not only "the yellow peril incarnate in one man" (Rohmer [1913] 1975: 17), he threatened to inundate the West with even greater numbers of yellow, black, and brown aliens than had already made their way there.[6] Yet, as powerful as this racial imagery might appear, it is in itself insufficient to explain how Fu-Manchu could become such a dominant and long-lived iconic figure in the Euroamerican imaginary about Asia (Isaacs [1958] 1980: 86, 116–122; Moy 1993). To explore both the magnitude of Fu-Manchu's threat and his ongoing emblematic significance, it is worth cataloging some of the structural elements around which Rohmer organized the first four Fu-Manchu novels ([1913] 1975, [1916] 1975, [1917] 1976, [1930] 1976).

Like other members of his "race," Fu-Manchu demonstrated standard Chinese characteristics; he was clever, cunning, insensitive to his own pain and that of others, cruel, industrious, and pragmatic. He was also well-educated, sophisticated, aloof, arrogant, and convinced, in spite of the many military defeats suffered at the hands of Western powers, of his own and China's superiority. Rohmer's invention was, in other words, an almost perfect copy of the imperial upper-class "mandarin," the antagonist of upright Englishmen that had been generated in the reports of diplomats, consuls, Imperial Maritime Customs agents, and in the flood of accounts and reminiscences that poured out of China after 1860. Moreover, like other members of

4. The phrase is used on the back cover of the 1975 Pyramid reprint of the first novel, *The Insidious Dr. Fu-Manchu*.

5. Rohmer wrote thirteen Fu-Manchu novels between 1913 and 1959. Perhaps the only thing more astonishing than this long period of production has been the extent of the dissemination of the novels and their transference into other media. The Fu-Manchu Web site at http://www.njin.net/~knapp/FuFrames.htm (accessed 17 June 2002) indicates that the novels have been translated into over twenty languages worldwide, made into films, television and radio serials, comic books, and board games.

6. See Rohmer [1916] 1975: 62 for a particularly distasteful description of a multiethnic London. A telling comparison between rats from merchant vessels docked in London and humans from Africa and Asia is drawn in Rohmer [1917] 1976: 99–103.

imperial China's ruling elite, he was decadent, addicted to opium, capable of disarming charm, with a confusing mix of feminine and masculine features, at times an honorable man of his word, and yet susceptible to the "childish trifles which sway the life of intellectual China" (Rohmer [1916] 1975: 79). He was, in other words, the embodiment of the Chinese official toward whom Parkes, Wade, and others had directed their English lessons.

At the same time, however, Fu-Manchu (not unlike Brilliant Chang) possessed some characteristics that distinguished him from the old ruling class and from ordinary Chinamen. These included his command of esoteric Eastern knowledge (e.g., "Indo-Chinese jugglery," sorcery) alongside modern Western scientific knowledge, the combination of which gave him unique powers over nature, making him "seemingly . . . immune from natural laws."[7] As a result of this combination of elements, the danger Fu-Manchu posed was more unsettling than the relatively straightforward European fantasy of barbarian invasions from the East, and more profound than the alarmism about an inundation of "coolie" labor into Europe and North America. His fusion of Eastern and Western knowledge, because it threatened the imperial archive itself, had the potential to undermine the whole structure of empire and of global white supremacy, and could conceivably topple the British and other Western empires like a row of dominos.

This universalist and totalizing dimension of the Fu-Manchu challenge is extremely important. It not only mimics the British imperial archive project and generates fears for its safety, but points directly to a common "misreading" of China produced by the information-gathering network in China. This is the notion that because historically the Chinese Empire saw itself as the "Middle Kingdom," the center of the universe, the Chinese emperor must also claim to rule the entire world.[8] Such pretensions could be contrasted with those of the Westernizing republican nation-state that had been established in Nanjing in 1912. Fu-Manchu was not, however, part of this reform movement. Rather, he was a throwback, a mandarin of imperial China, and as such he sought retribution against those who had humiliated and degraded the Chinese Empire. His project, in other words, was to restore the old order and expand its dominion; he wanted to create "a universal Yellow empire"

7. These seem to include Daoist alchemy and "Lamaist" sorcery. On the latter, see Rohmer [1917] 1976: 130–138. Also see Rohmer [1913] 1975: 16–17, [1917] 1976: 49.

8. Emperors certainly might claim to be above other monarchs in the world, but this was a cosmological claim, not an instance of personal arrogance; see Hevia 1995b; Zito 1997.

(Rohmer [1916] 1975: 162), first by absorbing Russia and then the Asian and African empire of Great Britain, thereby reversing the direction of the flow of power in the epistemological empire and ending the Great Game once and for all.

At his disposal for reconstituting a Chinese empire were two primary instruments. The first of these was a secret organization called the Si-Fan. Headquartered high above India and China in the vastness of Tibet (Rohmer [1913] 1975: 155), the Si-Fan was a "huge secret machine" and "the greatest mystery of the mysterious East." According to Nayland Smith, "hidden behind a veil of Lamaism," the organization was "a sort of Eleusinian Mystery holding some kind of dominion over the Eastern mind, and boasting initiates throughout the Orient" (Rohmer [1917] 1976: 8, 19, 67). It was also a kind of central intelligence agency over which Fu-Manchu operated as a spymaster. In this capacity, he organized his conspiracy through a number of fronts, all of which drew on the rich imagery of Asian and African malcontents within or bordering the British Empire; they included fanatical Muslim fundamentalist sects, drug-smuggling criminal organizations, more conventional Chinese secret societies, and a host of anti-British fanatics, such as Kali-worshiping Indian Thuggees and acrobatic Burmese robber-assassins called Dacoits.[9]

Through these agencies, Fu-Manchu delivered a threat that was local and immediate: he invaded London, the imperial center par excellence. Yet, although the terrain was familiar, Rohmer's protagonists seldom felt comfortably at home. Literally working beneath and on the margins of the imperial center, Fu-Manchu was able to transform London into a fantastical and horrific alien space. Mobilizing dark and mysterious powers, he induced in others "horrible phantasmagoria," waking dreams, and "subjective hallucinations." As reality became more and more distorted, paragons of empire like Nayland Smith and Dr. Petrie found it increasingly difficult to separate illusion from fact, thus creating in them a profound sense of epistemological crisis.[10]

The ability to cause this confusion, to destabilize white male rationality, was in turn a function of Fu-Manchu's unusual mental capacities, the second instrument at his disposal for building a new empire. Fu-Manchu's prodi-

9. By 1930, the Si-Fan is said to control the global underworld; see Rohmer [1930] 1976: 88–89.

10. All the novels considered here are rich in description of such states, but the general pattern is nicely laid out in the first one; see Rohmer [1913] 1975: 82–92.

gious brain made him more than a master of ancient Oriental science, more than a clever Chinaman, and more than a manipulator of various sorts of drugs. He also possessed encyclopedic knowledge of Western science, which he had learned at European universities—and he sought even more! To do so, he first secretly infiltrated the colonial periphery of the British Empire and then the imperial center itself. In London, he set about assassinating those who had suspicions about what he was up to and (this, I think, is perhaps the most wonderful part of Sax Rohmer's mania) kidnaping the greatest scientists of the age and transporting them back to the "head center," where their knowledge was to be forcibly extracted from them ([1913] 1975: 140, 154, 168).[11]

These monstrous schemes were the product of a mental genius who was anything but normal. Through the fusion of ancient and modern knowledge, Fu-Manchu had been able to physically transform himself, to induce a kind of mutation. His unusually large head and emerald-green eyes, central signs of his mutation, testified to the fact that he had not only learned how to manipulate opium and other mind-altering drugs, but had been able to do so to enhance his already formidable mental capacities. He then used his mutant brain to unlock other secrets of nature and to create additional frightening monstrosities like himself.[12]

Such fictional presentations of Fu-Manchu's conspiracies serve to establish a powerful link between Rohmer's narrative and the machinations of the Great Game, British interests in Tibet, and the threat an alien archive posed to Britain's actual epistemological empire. Whereas such concerns were usually associated with the secret activities of Britain's rivals in Europe, the Fu-Manchu narrative centers on the possibility of a thoroughly alien archive that has suddenly awakened after a prolonged Oriental slumber and is attempting to alter the direction of the Great Game. As embodied in the figure of Fu-Manchu, the alien archive is not content to remain simply Oriental; it also works to transform itself by absorbing other archives, encompassing their networks, and thereby reversing the flow of information toward an alien center far from London. It would then add modern technological knowledge to its own ancient and secret store of knowledge (much of which had yet to be

11. In the second novel, Fu-Manchu nearly succeeds in spiriting off Dr. Petrie, Nayland Smith's Watson; see Rohmer [1916] 1975: 106–110.

12. See the exchange with Petrie about opium in Rohmer [1913] 1975: 87–88; also see [1936] 1976: 113.

decoded by British agents) and thereby create an almost invincible adversary for the imperial state.

Plots like these involving nefarious conspiracies by people of color, matched by puzzle solving on the part of white males, were not unique to Sax Rohmer. This particular imaginary, however, is peculiar precisely because it is not reducible simply to Yellow Peril anxieties. A suddenly awakened China becomes in Rohmer's hands a supreme threat to British mastery in Asia. This construction was made credible by widely diffused anxieties over the possibility that the Chinese would exact revenge for the opium trade and Western aggression in China. Indeed, in at least one early film version of a Rohmer story, Fu-Manchu was motivated by the murder of his wife and family by allied soldiers during the suppression of the Boxer Uprising.[13] The Fu-Manchu threat also gained validity from the fact that the networks of empire allowed bidirectional flows, from fears over the dissemination of technologies and technological knowledge to the nonwhite races, and from the permanent mixture of hot and cold war that empire seemed to entail. In such an atmosphere, it was perhaps not too difficult to imagine or believe in Chinese conspiracies or in the possibility that some clever Oriental might fuse ancient and modern scientific knowledge. From there it was a short step to conjuring a China that could lead the Orient against Western empires, first pushing out Great Gamesmen, then entire colonial administrations from Asia, and rolling Europe's power back to the tiny peninsula it historically occupied on the isolated western edge of the enormous Eurasian landmass.

From the Alien Archive to Cold War Containment

If Fu-Manchu is understood as a product of early twentieth-century British fears projected onto China, he is also something more. By working the symbolically rich representations of China knowledge and Great Gamesmanship into the structure of the Fu-Manchu stories, Rohmer literally fixed a set of narrative elements that became staples in the succession of paranoid fantasies that have sustained the archive state in this century.[14] Threats would always

13. Entitled *The Mysterious Fu-Manchu*, the film was produced by Paramount Pictures in 1929 and starred Warner Oland, who would later go on to fame as Charlie Chan. See http://www.njedge.net/~knapp/FuFrames.htm and follow link to movies; accessed 13 September 2002.

14. Rohmer's novels remain in publication to the present. In the 1920s and 1930s, new

be total, the prize would always be the world, victories would never be absolute, the danger could never be completely eliminated. Fu-Manchu could be shot through his prodigious brain at the end of one novel and return restored to malignant life in the next.

The state of apprehension that such horrific possibilities engender is related to the postwar drug panic that gripped England in the early 1920s. Such anxieties have become a part of our collective culture, infusing the descendants of the British imperial archive—the United States and its North Atlantic allies—with a permanent sense of unease, a sense of a world perpetually on the brink of chaos, with an endless series of global crises, external terrors and terrorists who threaten to destroy the Western way of life. Who among us can recall when there was not a cold war? Or when the state was not declaring an emergency? Or when Asia didn't pose a global threat (Red China, Japan as Number 1, the Asian economic crisis of 1998, and, more recently, an "axis of evil," including Iraq, Iran, and North Korea)? When wasn't the sense of secret conspiracy a normal part of the rhetoric of the archive state or deeply embedded in popular culture? From the plots of Ming the Merciless in Alex Raymond's *Flash Gordon*[15] to the Japanese conspiracy for world domination uncovered by Jimmy Cagney in the film *Blood on the Sun* to Ian Fleming's *Dr. No*, the dangerous fusion of the archive project with a modernizing Oriental menace has been a staple in popular consciousness.[16] And the plot seldom has changed—mind manipulation, deadly mutant technologies, underground invasions, and horrific weapons of mass destruction return again and again.[17]

With the creation of the People's Republic of China in 1949 and the explosion of a Chinese atomic bomb a little over a decade later, fears of a modernizing China were reinvigorated. In the process, the Fu-Manchu narrative returned to animate the culture of the most recent cold war and its global anticommunist crusade. In this climate, the insidious doctor replicated himself;

---

ones were serialized in *Collier's* magazine. For a complete publication list see http://www.njedge.net/~knapp/FuFrames.htm under *Collier's Magazine*; accessed 13 September 2002.

15. This particular variation was so powerful that it was honored on a U.S. commemorative postage stamp in 1995. Quite appropriately, Ming the Merciless occupies the entire foreground of the design.

16. John F. Kennedy, it will be recalled, loved James Bond; see Nadel 1995: 157.

17. British fears of underground invasions went back at least as far as discussions of a Channel tunnel in the 1880s; see Pick 1993.

his avatars continued the assault against the sanity and ingenuity of white men. In the novel and movie *The Manchurian Candidate*, American POWs in Korea have their brains "washed" and "dry-cleaned" by a Chinese communist Pavlovian psychologist who, "smiling like Fu-Manchu," makes them "commit acts too unspeakable to cite."[18] In the film *Battle Beneath the Earth* (1967), the Red Army, led by a mandarin-like figure, creates an atomic- powered drilling device used to tunnel under the Pacific Ocean and all the major cities and military installations in the United States. During the Vietnam War, Wo Fat, a Chinese communist agent, spun one global conspiracy after another, only to be foiled by Nayland Smith's reincarnation, *Hawaii Five-o's* Steve McGarrett.[19]

At the same time, in a literal reversal of the history of Sino-Western contact, Milt Caniff's daily comic strip *Steve Canyon*, witnesses before the Senate Judiciary Committee, and a host of "authoritative" publications, including ones by the head of the Federal Bureau of Narcotics and a representative of the American Federation of Labor in Asia, charged that Red China had become the center of the international opium and heroin trade. The goal, they argued, was to poison the West with drugs as a means to global supremacy.[20] In an atmosphere rich in symbolic demonology, fears of pollution, and mania over Red Chinese science, Fu-Manchu himself returned in five British-made films between 1965 and 1968.[21]

More recently, following the collapse of the Soviet Union and renewed

18. In the film, Yen Lo, the psychologist, brags about his power over the American mind, and Major Marco makes the link to Fu-Manchu and unspeakable acts. Richard Condon's 1959 novel also has certain similarities to Rohmer [1936] 1976.

19. Parenthetically, Khigh Dhiegh, who played the parts of the Oriental mastermind in *The Manchurian Candidate* and *Hawaii Five-O*, seems to have gotten little work following diplomatic recognition between the United States and the People's Republic of China in 1978. However, he reemerged briefly after the 4 June 1989 Beijing massacre as the heartless party secretary in the made-for-TV version of the Liang Heng–Judith Shapiro romance, *China Nights*.

20. See Caniff 1987: 118, 127; *Hearings before the Subcommittee on the Improvements in the Federal Criminal Code of the Committee in the Judiciary, U.S. Senate, 84th Congress, 1955*, especially vol. 3: 739, vol. 8: 3894–3899; Anslinger and Tompkins 1953: 10–11; Deverall 1954. In his masterful study of the heroin trade, McCoy (1973, especially 145–147) demolishes the allegations made in these works. They were not simply anticommunist propaganda, but more than likely part of CIA disinformation campaigns designed to protect its network of agents, some of whom were engaged in the drug trade.

21. They were *The Face of Fu-Manchu* (1965), *The Brides of Fu-Manchu* (1966), *The Vengeance of Fu-Manchu* (1968), *The Blood of Fu-Manchu* (1968), and *The Castle of Fu-Manchu* (1968).

interest in the history of the Great Game (Hopkirk 1992, 1995), familiar tropes from the Fu-Manchu corpus have provided helpful ways to represent the threat post-Mao China poses to the West. High atop his John M. Olin Foundation chair at Harvard University, Samuel P. Huntington has a waking nightmare of the "Clash of Civilizations," of a "Confucian-Islamic" alliance that, armed with homemade conventional and nuclear weapons and outside the rule of law, threatens Western civilization.[22] Meanwhile, in his novel *Pax Pacifica*, Tom Clancy's collaborator Steve Pieczenik worries about the consequences of China's "Middle Kingdom Complex" becoming fused with advanced technology and a dynamic economy. As Sax Rohmer might have put it, "China versus America is really a contest between which moral, ethical, and religious philosophy will dominate the world—Oriental or Occidental."[23] Others, such as Richard Bernstein and Ross Munro (1997), raise the specter of a "coming conflict" between the United States and an expansive China with sophisticated military technology (1997).[24] All of these writers suggest that the cold war has hardly ended, that containment of an Oriental peril is still necessary, and that more and better knowledge is needed to defend against the new Chinese threat. Thus, just as the Chinese mind constructed by diligent British agents in the nineteenth century remains relatively stable, so does the project of the archive state. Monotonously linked together, they produce a seemingly interminable repetition of Rohmer's fundamental scenario: the danger of an alien archive and the necessity for determined efforts to contain it. Even those who may balk at Fu-Manchu revivalism and are aware of the history of Western imperialism in Asia can only conclude that the Chinese must be taught that there is "no profit in expansion."[25]

22. In the original piece that eventually resulted in a book, Huntington placed a question mark in his title (1993). By 1996, whatever doubts he may have had seem to have disappeared, along with the question mark.

23. Pieczenik 1995: 153. Actually, Rohmer more or less did put it this way; see [1913] 1975: 86. Fu-Manchu fails because in spite of his superior brain power and ability to mimic certain virtues of the British homosocial world (he is brave and keeps his word), he underestimates British masculinity and the loyalties and ethics of that world.

24. Bernstein was *Time* magazine correspondent in Beijing in 1989; Munro is a member of the Foreign Policy Institute in Philadelphia and the human rights organization Asiawatch.

25. The quotation is from James R. Lilley, former CIA chief in Beijing and U.S. ambassador to China from 1989 to 1991, in an a piece entitled "The 'Fu-Manchu' Problem"; see *Newsweek*, 24 February 1997: 36. At the same time, Lilley endorsed *Pax Pacifica*, arguing that

Recirculations

If Euroamerican violence returned to haunt later generations in the malignant form of Fu-Manchu, other forms of return and circulation were consistent with the patterns of political economy laid down in China in the nineteenth century. Here I want to provide two brief examples of the way the history of the repeated waves of deterritorialization and reterritorialization of China continues to be layered into and imbricated with contemporary Euroamerican culture. I begin with a discussion of 55 Days at Peking, a movie released in 1963 about the siege of the legations and one that appears regularly on the American Movie Classics cable station. I then consider the ongoing circulation of Summer Palace loot through auction markets in Europe and Asia.

Made on the eve of the U.S. buildup in Vietnam and in the era of big-budget Hollywood historical epics, 55 Days at Peking stars Charlton Heston as Major Matt Lewis, commander of the Marine detachment at the U.S. legation, David Niven as Sir Arthur Robertson, the British ambassador, Flora Robson as the empress dowager Cixi, and Ava Gardner as Baroness Natalie Ivanoff, who (this being a Hollywood movie) provides the love interest for Major Lewis.[26] Though much could be said about the handling of race and gender in this film,[27] here my concern is with how the film concisely restates the Euroamerican pedagogical project in China and Asia for yet another generation. Perhaps the key moment of instruction occurs in an exchange between Sir Arthur and the empress dowager just prior to the beginning of the siege.

The sequence takes place in a palace within the Forbidden City. Although no such event occurred, the scene is otherwise faithful to British perceptions of China in the nineteenth century. Sir Arthur enters the imperial presence and, like Garnet Wolseley, walks directly in front of the throne. Before speak-

---

few have "dramatized the protracted struggle between East and West" as well as Pieczenik (1995) has.

26. Directed by Nicholas Ray and released by Allied Artists, the film was shot in Spain on a set built with some accuracy to show the legation quarter and the walls around the Forbidden City. For a discussion of the cold war and Hollywood movies, see Nadel 1995.

27. The baroness has a Chinese lover, a high official in the Qing government, which in the end gets her killed. A female child of a Chinese mother and an American officer is orphaned during the siege. The movie ends with Major Lewis, in spite of the reservations he has previously expressed, taking the child with him when the Marines withdraw from Beijing after the relief.

ing, he delicately moves aside a pillow with the toe of his boot—the British minister does not kowtow before an Oriental monarch—and coolly proceeds to exchange pleasantries with the empress. Sir Arthur has come to protest the murder of the German minister by the Boxers, but before he can begin, the empress points out that although the Boxers will be dealt with, the anger of the Chinese people will not disappear—the Western powers have gone too far. Foreign ships dominate China's harbors, foreign armies occupy her forts, foreign merchants control her banks, and foreign gods disturb the spirits of the ancestors. "Is it surprising," she wonders, "if the people are aroused?" China, she adds, is like a prostrate cow; the foreigners are no longer content to simply milk her, they want to carve her up for her meat. Sir Arthur listens politely and then delivers the lesson: The violence of the Boxers is no solution, especially since China has been learning the "arts of peace from the West"; if she will be patient, all will be well. "And if China is not patient?" the empress asks. "If not, if the counsels of violence and impatience prevail," Sir Arthur warns, "then the blood of millions will be shed and the agony prolonged."

The empress does not listen or learn; instead, she suggests that the legations leave Beijing for their own safety. Sir Arthur retires and returns to the legations to present matters to the other ministers. With the Americans abstaining—the United States has no territorial concession in China and does not want one, states the U.S. minister—the ministers vote to leave. Sir Arthur thereupon begins the second lesson. He convinces the others that if they stay and stand united, peace will be preserved in China and perhaps the whole world. In the end, he is proven right. But more important, Major Lewis, who spends most of the film doubting the feasibility of the British position, not only acknowledges that Sir Arthur is right, but suggests that maybe others will remember this lesson someday.

This was, of course, nineteenth-century pedagogy, but given the global cold war tensions of the nuclear age and U.S. efforts to contain Chinese communism, the message seems clear enough. China remains impatient, and its long-standing antiforeignism has been refueled by the Chinese communists. It was important, therefore, for white men to learn from Sir Arthur and Major Lewis. If the nuclear-age generation does not remember how to stand firm, millions might actually die and the agony might be prolonged.

At the same time, there was at least an acknowledgment that China's grievances were not based on fantasies; that the powers had, in fact, milked and were about to cut up the cow. No such admissions are evident in museum displays in Great Britain or in the international auction market, where plunder from China has been displayed and sold without apologies. In other words, deterritorialized Qing imperial objects and the art of aristocratic or wealthy Beijing residents continue to be reterritorialized in the West via market mechanisms and the routines and rituals of museums. In the course of researching this book—a fifteen-year period dating from 1986—I have seen, read about, or been told about numerous objects looted from China in 1860 and 1900 and have found some of them for sale or on display in museums. Let me catalogue some of these instances.

As noted earlier, 1900 loot is difficult to locate. However, in the form of military trophy, it can be seen in the Royal Welsh Fusiliers Museum at Caernarvon Castle and the United States Military Academy at West Point. No doubt there are other military museums in Europe and North America with similar collections. In other cases, trophies are on display at military bases. The Garden Island Dockyard in Sydney has a cannon sent by Phillip II of Spain to the emperor of China, and the Australian War Memorial in Canberra has a bronze temple bell (Nicholls 1986: 127–129). In the United States, the Norfolk Naval Shipyard has a Qing army field gun on display.[28]

The "shortage" of identifiable objects taken from Beijing in 1900 is more than made up for, however, by the seeming omnipresence of 1860 loot. In the Royal Engineers Museum at Chatham sits "the throne" of the emperor of China, sent back by the magic Christian, Charles George "Chinese" Gordon. In 1987, when I first saw it, it was displayed in the central alcove of the officers' mess and required permission to be seen by outsiders. Now the throne is in the museum proper, which is open to the public.[29] In the dusty records of museums such as the Victoria and Albert can be found bequests of objects "from the Summer Palace of the Emperor of China." Still other records tell the story of Royal Engineers bringing a throne cushion to the Victoria and Albert in 1912 for comparison with one in the possession of the museum.[30] In addition, the museum has several thrones, including a red lacquer one, said

28. See http://www.nnsy1.navy.mil/History/SEMIAUTO.HTM, accessed 11 July 2001. One can also purchase memorabilia of the era from Web sites. See, for example, http://www.collect.at/boxer_rebellion.htm, accessed 13 September 2001. In 1997, I found for sale what was reported to be a Boxer Rebellion–period executioner's sword; www.auctions-on-line/wallis/auction/b970429/page69.html; accessed 28 October 1997.

29. Personal correspondence from Simon Jones, 12 June 1992.

30. See Victoria and Albert Acquisition Records, "Miss Gordon file." The Victoria and Albert throne cushion was on display when I visited the museum 24 June 2001; it was part of an exhibit commemorating the hundredth anniversary of Queen Victoria's death.

to be that of the Qianlong emperor. Apparently taken from the South Park palaces outside Beijing in 1900, the museum bought it in 1922. A companion lacquer screen is in the Museum of Ethnography in Vienna.[31] The Victoria and Albert and the British Museum also have books taken from Beijing collections and a number of pages from the *Huangchao Liqi tushi*, a volume of diagrams of ritual implements and imperial robes taken from the Summer Palace in 1860. And although the tell-tale legend "from the Summer Palace of the Emperor of China" was less visible in the display rooms of these museums by 1998,[32] acquisition records make it possible to identify other Summer Palace items.[33]

Institutions in Great Britain are not alone in putting China loot on display. As noted earlier, just outside Paris, Le Musée Chinois de l'Impératrice Eugénie at the Château de Fontainebleau was restored and opened to art connoisseurs and tourists. Originals of the objects that appeared in the *Illustrated London News* drawing of 1861 (see chapter 5) are quite visible in this collection, and one item has been published on a postcard. Even the tale of "Looty," the Pekinese dog presented to Queen Victoria, continues to circulate. Not only did Rumer Godden (1977) make the story a centerpiece of her history of the Pekinese dog, but reference to Looty turned up not so long ago in an article written by Ivor Smullen (1991) for the inflight magazine of Singapore Airlines, *Silver Kris*. But perhaps this latest site of repetition is not so curious, especially if one considers that the purpose of the magazine is to stimulate the desires of tourists for the fine objects (not unlike those from the Summer Palace) that can be bought in Asia's markets.[34]

It is the market, in fact, where Summer Palace loot continues to appear and to make the news. The pattern of circulation from private collections to the marketplace evident in the nineteenth century has continued into the present.

31. See Clunas 1991: 44–50, 1994: 336–338; *Nominal File: J. P. Swift*, Victoria and Albert Museum Registry.

32. An exception was the Victoria and Albert's centenary of Queen Victoria's death. The throne cushion mentioned above and a cloisonné ice chest were identified as from the Summer Palace.

33. For example, in 1987 the British Museum had a jade sutra on loan from the Queen (OR. 54) and several books, including the *Shiquan ji* (Ten great campaigns of the Qianlong era, OR. 1234), which was registered in 1872. The Victoria and Albert has imperial seals dating from the Qianlong era (T. 80474/04).

34. I am indebted to Tani Barlow for bringing Smullen's article to my attention. The links between neocolonialism and the sort of tourism that seems to be promoted in the pages of magazines like the *Silver Kris* has been admirably explored by Enloe 1989 and Truong 1990.

In 1988, Sotheby's London auctioned off what it termed "original paintings from the Summer Palace Peking," and included reference to the first sale of these paintings in London in 1863 as part of their provenance. They were, in fact, pages from the *Huangchao Liqi tushi*, with a suggested opening bid of £80,000–100,000.[35] In 1993, Christie's offered a white jade bowl said to have come via an American private collection from the estate of Sir John Michel, commander of the 1st Division of the British expeditionary force in 1860; the asking price was between $150,000 and $250,000.[36] A year later, Christie's put up for auction the "Gordon" incense burner; it fetched £20,000.[37] Even more recently, items identified as from the Summer Palace turned up in "The Imperial Sale" held by Christie's in Hong Kong in 1996. Some of these pieces, according to Michael Gillingham in the *Daily Telegraph*, appeared in a Burlington Fine Arts fair in London in 1915. That same exhibition, Gillingham added, contained a jade horse and buffalo that had been taken from Beijing in 1900 and that now resided in the Fitzwilliam Museum, Cambridge University.[38]

Finally, in 2001, Sotheby's and Christie's Hong Kong included four items from the Summer Palace in a second "Imperial Sale." Two bronze animal heads (a monkey and an ox) were identified as among the zodiac of twelve animals that made up part of the water clock the Qianlong emperor had commissioned his Jesuit missionaries to build in the European section of the Yuanming Garden. This sale proved to be the last straw. Outraged, the PRC government formally protested, requesting that Christie's and Sotheby's withdraw the items. When they refused, an unprecedented event occurred: mainland Chinese companies intervened and bought the objects, paying in excess of $6 million for the four pieces, three times the asking price. Carleton Rochell, Sotheby's managing director in Hong Kong, characterized the exchange and his company's windfall as an example of the repatriation of

35. See Sotheby's 1988: 34–39. According to the provenance provided in the catalogue, the first sale was by Puttick and Simpson on 4 February 1863; they were bought by Sir Thomas Phillips. I am grateful to Craig Clunas for bringing the sale to my attention.

36. Susan Naquin was kind enough to tell me about the Christie's sale; it took place on 2 December 1993 in New York.

37. *Daily Telegraph*, 12 November 1994. This may have been the same item sold in the disposition of the Wilfred Peek Museum collection in London in 1929. Notice of the sale actually appeared in the *China Express and Telegraph* of 2 July. Robert Bickers kindly passed this information to me, also noting that objects that were supposed to be from the Summer Palace turned up in the *Times* personals during the interwar years.

38. See the Christie's catalogue *The Imperial Sale*, Hong Kong, 28 April 1996 (1996); *Daily Telegraph*, 19 April 1996, 18.

looted objects to China (*New York Times*, 29 April, 1 and 3 May 2001)! No doubt market fundamentalists would applaud Rochell's assessment.

I would prefer to think of it, however, as only the most recent English lesson: if China is willing to pay the exorbitant price, imperial treasures can be "repatriated." This may not be a particularly welcome tutorial, but the truth is that with the exception of Li Hongzhang's souvenir spoon from Niagara Falls and the objects that the French government refused to accept in 1900 (see chapter 7), little has been returned to China outside of the extortionate realm of the marketplace. To the best of my knowledge (and I would be happy to be proven wrong), there has been only one instance of true repatriation since 1901. It came from the now defunct German Democratic Republic. In 1955, in a ceremony held in Beijing, Otto Grotewohl returned to Zhou Enlai a Boxer banner and other artifacts taken by the German army in 1900.[39] This sole exception to the dismal record of repatriation does little to alleviate the sense of national humiliation for recent generations of Chinese people.

National Humiliation (Guochi), Liberation (Jiefang), and the Construction of the Patriotic Chinese Subject

Perhaps contemporary Euroamericans can forget or flaunt the past, but Chinese people have not had such a luxury. The occupation of Beijing in 1900 was the culmination of a Western assault on Qing sovereignty led by Great Britain that began with the first Opium War. It proved to be a major turning point in modern Chinese history. Lessons, it would seem, were learned and remembered. It was no longer possible to rationalize the weaknesses of the Qing political and economic system. Imperial sovereignty, gutted by the Western powers of its material and symbolic force, could no longer remain a viable political entity. In the first decades of the twentieth century, China's intelligentsia, like those in other colonial settings, constructed a nationalism that, though antagonistic toward Western imperialism, accepted the "framework of knowledge created by post-Enlightenment rationalist thought" because it had equipped Europeans with attributes for "power and progress" (Chatterjee 1986: 50–51). It is here, indeed, that we can see the effectiveness of English lessons; they explain the resounding success of the Western penetration of China, as well as other parts of Asia and Africa. It followed from this

---

39. Felber and Rostek 1987: 43; personal correspondence from Klaus Mühlahn, Freie Universität Berlin.

logic that Chinese people did not possess similar attributes—the objective evidence was there in the ruins of the Dagu forts—and that China's "traditional" culture was, as demonstrated by the Boxers, incapable of generating such attributes. If China was to throw off the shackles of foreign exploitation and recover "sovereign rights," a new China with new Chinese people would have to be created (Wright 1968: 1–4). This colonization of Chinese consciousness resulted not in rebellion, but in revolution, a whole new way of thinking about the world derived from English lessons.

At the heart of the historical transformation the nationalists sought were two linked concepts, two lessons that had been well learned. First, Western imperial powers had had their way in China because they possessed superior military technologies. The result had been not only a succession of military defeats for the Qing Dynasty, but the humiliation of all of the Chinese people. The second proposition followed from this. If dignity was to be regained, many young and progressive Chinese thinkers felt, China would not only have to eliminate its archaic form of government and society, it would also have to acquire modern military hardware to defend itself and thereby instill national pride in the people. These two elements—the acquisition of military technologies and the elimination of a sense of national humiliation—run like a thread through the entire history of twentieth-century China. More important, perhaps, they indicate that the people of China understood, both at the turn of the century and later, that the actions of the Western powers in China were deliberate and explicit attempts to humiliate the Qing emperor and the Chinese people. In other words, the symbolic warfare of the powers outlined in the previous chapters was neither experienced nor interpreted as random, unconnected acts of violence, but as calculated procedures meant to humble China's rulers and people and to teach them not to trifle with these particular foreigners. This was certainly the understanding shared by Qiu Jin, an early revolutionary heroine, and others who went through the shame of the occupation of Beijing in 1900–1901 (Spence 1982: 84).

The lessons taught by the imperial powers were learned, though perhaps not in the way they had imagined. In the immediate aftermath of the Boxer Uprising, as Paul Cohen has indicated, the term "national humiliation" (*guochi*) was used by Chinese nationalists to rally support in anti-imperialist campaigns (1997: 242–243). Turn-of-the-century reformers such as Liang Qichao and Kang Youwei also played on the image of a humiliated Chinese population in their writings. More significant, in these two cases, their sense of humiliation was enhanced by having seen Summer Palace loot on public display in American and French Museums—Liang in New York in 1893, Kang while in Paris a few years after the Boxer Uprising. Liang wrote of a sense of shame (hanyen); Kang spoke of a wound that broke his heart (shangxin) and caused him great grief (Yuanming yuan [YMY] 2: 17, 158–159). Such experiences led him to form the "Know Our Humiliation Society" (Spence 1982: 47).

This sense of collective shame and personal grief could be dealt with in various forms of direct action such as protest demonstrations or as positive acts of eradicating signs of humiliation. For example, following Germany's defeat in World War I, the Ketteler Memorial Arch was moved into Zhongshan Park, southwest of the Meridian Gate (Wumen), and rededicated to Sun Yat-sen (Arlington and Lewisohn [1935] 1987: 150). By the 1920s, however, national humiliation was more commonly institutionalized as a collective malaise represented through a succession of memorial days throughout the year (Steve Smith 2002: 78, 197). Public institutions such as schools and government offices recognized up to twenty-four such days. Occurring two and occasionally three a month from January through November, National Humiliation Days included the dates of the signing of the "unequal treaties" and the Boxer protocol imposed by the Western powers, the dates Chinese territory was leased to foreigners (e.g., Weihaiwei to Great Britain), the dates of protest rallies in which demonstrators were killed (e.g., the May 30 Incident in Shanghai), and the dates on which the armies of foreign powers entered Beijing in 1860 and 1900 (NARA, RG127-38, box 3). As a form of public remembrance, these commemorations seem to have provided a foundation on which to build a modern Chinese national consciousness. The new historical subject, the national subject, whether an individual or a collectivity, would be a muscular, pure, self-sacrificing anti-imperialist who would rise above historical shame and reclaim China's sovereign rights. This larger than life figure would become the model of the new man and woman who would build socialism in China.

The constitutive role of national humiliation and its resulting anti-imperialism were, therefore, a central element in the construction of a new China by Chinese communists. Indeed, one might argue that the very foundation of the People's Republic was established on a unity forged through liberation (jiefang) from the humiliations of Western imperialism. When addressing the First Plenary Session of the Chinese People's Political Consultative Conference on 21 September 1949—just a few weeks before the formal inauguration of the PRC—Mao Zedong entitled his remarks "The Chinese People Have Stood Up!" and added that China would "no longer be a nation subject to insult and humiliation" (1977, 5: 17). With the advent of the Korean War and the implementation of the cold war "containment policy" of the United States, such imagery became a staple of verbal and visual propaganda. The human figures visible in the socialist realist genre of artistic representation that dominated Chinese public space for over two decades stood proudly defiant in the face of imperialist provocations (fig. 39).

I do not know whether the monthly national humiliation days continued into the PRC era. Nevertheless, a strong anti-imperialist strain of communist thought, built on remembrance and transcendence of what came to be called the century of humiliation, was clearly commonplace in public art, school books, radio, film, and later television. Furthermore, Chinese history in the nineteenth century was periodized into two segments, from the Opium War of 1840 to the May 4 Movement of 1919 as modern history and after 1919 as contemporary history. The latter date marked the birth of a new national consciousness and culminated in the founding of the Chinese Communist Party.

Within this periodization, Chinese historians built on a number of Mao's observations concerning the nature of Western imperialism to transform tales of Qing failures into the narrative of the heroic resistance of Chinese peasants and patriotic officials against the Western onslaught. In the process, other kinds of martyrs were created, ones who gave their lives in the anti-imperialist revolutionary struggle. The history that resulted was a counternarrative to British imperial historiography and scholars influenced by it. In general, historians in Europe and North America have generally been critical of this counternarrative, arguing that historical facts have been shoe-horned into ideological or mythical structures in the service of the party-state.[40] Yet it is also the case that elements of the critical position generated by Chinese historians remain difficult to ignore and in some respects find common ground, in the United States at least, in a thread of anti-imperialist historiography running from Mark Twain through the anti–Vietnam War movement of the 1960s and beyond.[41]

Among Chinese historians, this strong and vocal anti-imperialist strain can be found in the writings of Hu Sheng, whose *Imperialism and Chinese Politics* (1955; *Diguozhuyi yu Zhongguo zhengzhi*, 1952) is probably the best known

40. The latter assessment is well represented in Feuerwerker 1968. More recently, Cohen (1997) has discussed the mythologization of the past.

41. With respect to East Asia, I think in particular of the Committee of Concerned Asia Scholars, who were both sympathetic with the Chinese Revolution and critical of U.S. policy in the Pacific.

決定战争胜负的不是物，是人！

39. Socialist soldier-hero atop U.S. and Republic of China tanks, ca. 1955. Collection of the author.

of the genre outside of China. It is a scathing and sarcastic critique of the powers, the Qing Dynasty, and Chinese bourgeois "collaborators." This kind of verbose anti-imperialism remained evident to the end of the Maoist era and continued to be disseminated internationally in English and other European languages. For example, *The Yi Ho Tuan Movement of 1900*, a publication of the Compilation Group of the "History of Modern China" Series of the Foreign Language Press (1976) in Beijing, is much like the early work of Hu and identical to other PRC histories of the era. It is filled with quotations from Chairman Mao and stinging attacks on imperialists, reactionaries, and their lackeys. Yet, as clichéd as these works may appear, they can be read as performances of very real defiance, the kind that Frantz Fanon ([1963] 1966) saw as part of a process of unlocking the mental shackles of colonialism and realizing liberation. Humiliation, a general outcome of Western imperialism and colonialism for the colonized, is here turned into something positive and productive, the impetus for leading the Chinese people and other oppressed peoples of the world to stand up. The feisty language of international class struggle evident in both the Chinese and English versions of these works may have performed only a symbolic violence, but it was neither less real nor less effective than the symbolic warfare of the powers in 1900. And it had an effect in Europe and North America as well, generating a host of anxieties over communist-sponsored revolutions in the "third world."

These works are also of interest for reasons other than their polemical thrust. In many respects, they build their case by drawing directly from the Euroamerican imperial archive. There is extensive quotation and citation of British parliamentary papers (Blue Books), personal memoirs, and, in the case of the Boxer Uprising, the writings of Henry Savage Landor, Bertram Simpson, and Pierre Loti. The Foreign Language Press Compilation Group, for example, cited Field Marshal Waldersee's account of pervasive looting by soldiers and civilians of all of the eight nations to make a point about the occupation of Beijing that would be important, regardless of the ideological formation in which it is lodged (Compilation Group 1976: 67, 79, 81, 90–96). I want to return to this use of Western source material shortly. For now, it is sufficient to note that whatever criticism might be leveled at Chinese historians for the ideological structure of their works, they knew how to make use of the Euroamerican imperial archive to support their anti-imperialist arguments.

There is one other point worth noting in Maoist-era historiography. It is not only anti-imperialist but finds certain resonances with the more recent phenomenon dubbed postcolonial studies. One example of this can be found in a collection of essays, almost all of them penned by Western historians, published in 1968 under the title *History in Communist China* (Feuerwerker 1968).[42] In what was otherwise a critical review of the shortcomings and unhistorical quality of communist Chinese historiography, there was at least one voice from China's present. It was that of Liu Danian, deputy director of the Modern History Institute at the Chinese Academy of Social Sciences and an editor of *Historical Studies* (*Lishi yanjiu*). Liu's essay makes two points worth emphasizing. The first is that Western historians continue to place Europe at the center of world history, while treating other areas of the world and other civilizations as backward. Second, he notes that Euro-centered global history is grounded on notions of superior and inferior races. Liu reminded readers that both these habits — Eurocentrism and racialized worldviews — are a product of European colonialism in Asia and Africa (1968: 364–365). And they had hardly disappeared, even though much of Africa and Asia by 1968 had been liberated from European colonial rule.

The strident anti-imperialism in the writing of Hu, Liu, and the Compilation Group is also evident in what proved to be another major turning point in modern Chinese history, the Great Proletarian Culture Revolution (GPCR). As Paul Cohen has shown, historical events such as the Boxer movement could be used as a potent weapon in the internecine warfare that consumed the decade 1966–1976. Charges of spying, of being a capitalist-roader, or of being an agent or lackey of Western capitalism and imperialism were brought to bear in the context of purported attitudes toward the Boxers or other popular movements, including the campaigns against Liu Shaoqi, Confucius, and Soviet revisionism (Cohen 1997: 261–288). Although there is no question that the Boxer past was distorted to fight contemporary political battles, the image of the Boxers as peasant-proletarian heroes that circulated in these campaigns was especially potent. The Boxers had stood up at a time when China was otherwise humbled and humiliated. In the context of a global cold war and with U.S. forces fighting on China's borders, the patriotic message of Boxer resistance to imperialism must certainly have been clear to all.

With the death of Mao Zedong in 1976 and the arrest of the key leaders of the Maoist faction (the Gang of Four) that closed the GPCR, the strident tones

---

42. Although there was much criticism in these essays of Chinese communist historiography, there was no discussion about the historical methods, theoretical frameworks, or narrative structures that Western historians of China use and prefer.

of the anti-imperialists were muted and reshaped. In the world of scholarship, this meant a new and much deeper analysis of the events of the nineteenth century, particularly regarding anti-imperialist popular movements such as the Boxers. In the various publications that resulted, the nature and meaning of the Boxer movement and, by extension, the Chinese people's struggle against Western imperialism were explored, debated, and reworked.[43]

The result has been a broad spectrum of views that have diffused the unitary ideological structure of early PRC historiography. For example, while not completely abandoning the category of superstition in his consideration of Boxer invulnerability rituals, Lu Yao (1987, 2000) has avoided neat bifurcations of Boxer minds into progressive and feudal elements. Instead, he has sought to broaden understanding of Boxer beliefs by locating them in the context of Chinese popular religion, a move that has an effect not unlike Esherick's and Cohen's efforts to humanize the Boxers. In other cases, younger scholars have sought to credit the missionary enterprise with having made a positive contribution to China's modernization in the fields of higher education, medicine, and the natural sciences (e.g., L. Wang 1997; Tao and Wu 1998). Yet, even with these reappraisals of the past, patriotic anti-imperialism has not been lost. *Baguo lianjun qinhua shi* (A history of the eight-power invasion), the single most comprehensive work in any language on the multinational occupation of north China in 1900–1901, was produced in this same period by scholars in the Shandong University Department of History, the primary site of Boxer studies in China. Coauthors Li Dezheng, Su Weizhi, and Liu Tianlu (1990) toned down the angry rhetoric of Hu Sheng, but delivered a no less scathing indictment of Western violence, one that was built on a massive amount of source material in Chinese, English, French, and Russian.

The shifts in historical interpretation discussed above, as well as the kind

---

43. At Shandong University, for example, a group of researchers have been exploring the Boxer base areas in Shandong through oral and documentary history projects, part of which were published in Modern Chinese History Section, Shandong University History Department, 1980. The unit also directed the Chinese Boxer Studies Association and sponsored international conference volumes on the Boxer movement in 1980, 1990, and 2000. For conference volumes see *Yihetuan yundongshi taolun wenji* (Collected articles on the history of the Boxer movement) 1982; Chinese Association for Boxer Studies 1992; W. Su and Liu 2000, which includes a five-hundred-page bibliography of Boxer-era source materials in Chinese, Japanese, Korean, English, French, Russian, and German. Also see the exemplary translations of the 1980 conference at Shandong University in Buck 1987. There are also discussions of the proceedings of the 1980 and 1990 conferences in Xu 1981 and Buck 1991.

of empiricist-based methodology capable of retaining the key threads of modern Chinese history evident in the work of Li, Su, and Liu, was paralleled by developments in other domains of practice, ones that were stimulated and encouraged by the reform policies of the new leadership that came to power after the death of Mao Zedong. Within this dynamic process of change, the party-state itself, much like nation-states in Europe and North America, "appropriated the life of the nation into the life of the state" (Chatterjee 1986: 161)[44] and became a major actor in producing, preserving, and restoring national history. The state not only protected sites such as the Forbidden City, the Temple of Heaven, and the New Summer Palace, but worked to internationalize them by, among other things, petitioning to have them placed on the World Heritage List, a global preservation project run by the United Nations Educational, Scientific and Cultural Organization (UNESCO).[45] Such state-sponsored historical preservation is clearly part of a developmental strategy designed to promote external and internal tourism and perhaps to safely ensconce the feudal *and* revolutionary pasts under an apolitical and sanitized sign of heritage,[46] yet such activities also have the effect of contributing to a broader discourse on patriotism (*aiguo*, love of country) and national pride.

Such patterns of cultural production are especially discernible at some of the most highly charged sites of national humiliation. The Yuanming yuan, the Summer Palace destroyed by the British in 1860, is a case in point. For much of the PRC period, the ruins of the gardens were officially neglected. At various times, the parkland had been used for a people's commune and as a place where professors and teachers from nearby universities could perform the manual labor necessary to alter their class consciousness. Although the latter practice ended with the close of the Cultural Revolution, farmers continued to live and grow crops within the grounds of the park. In the 1980s, however, things began to change. A historical research unit was set up and launched a journal in 1981, and a small museum was organized. Among other

44. One could argue that a similar process was underway during the Maoist era, but I believe that the purpose was somewhat different. The primary goal was to recover the history not of the nation, but of worldwide social classes in various periods of historical development, with particular emphasis on the Chinese peasantry.

45. There are now twenty-eight World Heritage sites in China; for a complete list see http://whc.unesco.org/nwhc/pages/doc/mainf3.htm, accessed 17 June 2002.

46. I have discussed this issue in greater detail in Hevia 2000, where the focus is on the Bishu shanzhuang, the Qing summer palace at Chengde, and its link to the UNESCO World Heritage Project.

40. Diorama of British
soldiers looting the
Yuanming yuan.
Photograph by the
author.

things, this museum held an extraordinary diorama of British soldiers looting
the palaces in 1860 (fig. 40).

By the 1990s, an even greater change was evident. At the same time the
garden was being turned into a somewhat tacky leisure center, historical restoration and museumification were also in evidence: the Yuanming yuan was
reconstituted as a signifier of high cultural art from the past and as a different
sort of historical memory text.[47] If, as I have argued above, one of the hall-
marks of the reform era has been the marked decline of ideological orthodoxy
in publications on modern Chinese history, coupled with the reconfiguring of
the past as a heritage of both humiliation and resistance, the Yuanming yuan,
at one and the same time, is in and out of step with these trends. There are,
for example, publications that dwell on the beauties of the gardens, projects
to digitally reconstruct portions of the garden,[48] and large signs scattered

47. Parts of the garden was transformed into an amusement park with power boats and
mechanical rides, a paintball arena and shooting gallery, and an odd display of "primitive
totems" on an island in one of the garden lakes; see Barmé 1996: 142–154.

48. The Beijing-based Zhuda Cumputer Company is responsible for the effort; see
Barmé 1996.

41. "Never Forget National Humiliation Wall," Yuanming yuan. Photograph by the author.

around the garden referencing the art history of the site. In all these cases, an effort is made to position the meaning of the Yuanming yuan as a place for the aesthetic appreciation of China's cultural heritage.[49] At the same time, attention is even more stridently drawn to the British destruction of the palaces than was the case in the early decades of the PRC.

In the European garden area of the Summer Palace, new commemorative structures were erected in 1997 as part of the official celebration of the return of Hong Kong to the Chinese nation-state. One of these is a wall bearing fifty-one plaques tightly packed with text that provides a synopsis of the history of imperialism in China from 1840 through the war with Japan that ended in 1945. Large golden ideograms next to the first plaque proclaim "Never Forget National Humiliation" (*wuwang guochi*; fig. 41). Nearby is a museum that displays a history of the destruction of the palaces, including the old diorama of

49. See, for example, D. Wang 1999; Barmé 1996: 153. There is also a project on the Internet, where a virtual Yuanming yuan is being built; see http://www.cs.ubc.ca/spider/wang/, accessed 10 July 2001.

looting, and the records of the occupation of Beijing in 1900 in photographs and text. Of particular interest is the inclusion of photographs taken by Felice Beato in 1860 and Western photographers in 1900.

Like the citation of Western sources in the 1976 Foreign Language Press history of the Boxers, these references operate as a powerful condemnation of imperialism by the imperialists themselves. There is also at least one critical Western voice to be heard, that of Victor Hugo, whose comments, presented in French and Chinese, eloquently condemn the looting and destruction of the Summer Palace. As if to emphasize this point, the display also contains an important public recognition of where Summer Palace loot exists today. On one wall, there are photographs of imperial objects that General Montauban had sent to the Empress Eugénie in 1860 for her Oriental collection. The pictures are taken from Colombe Samoyault-Verlet's *Le Musée Chinois de l'impératrice Eugénie*, published in 1994 when the restored museum was reopened at the Château de Fontainebleau.[50] The message seems clear: As reform China reconstructs itself as a modernized nation-state and global power, can it tolerate the presence of objects marking national humiliation outside of China? The question is partly answered by the uproar over the sale of Summer Palace loot in Hong Kong in 2001.

The Yuanming yuan museum, as I have indicated, is a new project, but it is not the sole such undertaking in which the state apparatus is engaged. The Dagu forts is another. Even as the barren salt flats around Dagu are being transformed by an enormously ambitious land reclamation project for a new port, and as summer resort condominiums begin to appear along the coast to the north and south of where the forts once stood, there is nested within and juxtaposed to this new "Chinese modern" a museum of modest proportions that also recalls the century of national humiliation.

On a cold March day in 2001, I visited Dagu for the first time. The forts, it will be recalled, were destroyed as a condition of the *Final Protocol* of 1901. What stands there today is a walled mound with an ancient gun atop it. Below are a large stone monument, a modest rectangular structure containing a museum, and a Korea War–vintage Mig fighter jet. (These icons of modern military might are occasionally found in public parks and historic sites all around north China.) The monument notes a brief history of the military actions at

50. The original photographs are in Samoyault-Verlet 1994: 21, 24–25, 52, 59, 67. I am grateful to Craig Clunas for being kind enough to send me a copy of this publication, and to Regine Thiriez for arranging a special visit to the museum in 1997.

Dagu and indicates that it was dedicated by the Tianjin municipality in 1997 as part of the celebration of Hong Kong's return. Inside the museum, the historical humiliations from 1840 to 1900 are laid out chronologically. Detailed maps trace the global opium trade of the nineteenth century; diagrams show the military actions at Dagu in 1858, 1859, 1860, and 1900; and heroic paintings of Chinese soldiers depict them hurling themselves at the superior guns of foreign soldiers. There are also reproductions of original documents, including the Treaty of Tianjin, with the most galling passages highlighted in red; a painting of the sack of nearby Tanggu; and Beato's photographs of Lord Elgin and Hope Grant, as well as one of Harry Parkes, over which angry graffiti has been scrawled. In addition, there is a picture, which also appears at the Yuanming yuan, of a column of Western soldiers marching toward the Meridian Gate (Wumen) in the welcoming ceremonies for Field Marshal Waldersee.

Here, as in Beijing, visual evidence keeps the memory of national humiliation alive, but one may well wonder if the same sense of shame and its transcendence that marked Liu Danian's charges against Western historiography are still relevant. Liu's comments pointed, after all, to the fundamental bifurcation of history that was built into the processes of deterritorialization and reterritorialization in both East and West over the past century and a half. On the side of the colonized, the era of Western imperialism remained an open wound. Moreover, when Liu was speaking, formal empire was barely in the past—parts of Africa had only recently been "decolonized," others remained under white rule, and colonial-style warfare was still much in evidence in Southeast Asia. On the other side, the populations of Euroamerican nation-states and their scholars had seemingly lost sight of that violence, living, as Liu suggested, in blissful or perhaps willful ignorance of its savagery. Had the global confrontation between capitalism and socialism not been in full swing, had China not been in the grips of the Great Proletarian Cultural Revolution, perhaps Liu's statement could have been understood as a cry of anguish, as a plea that some form of acknowledgment was required in the present of the dubious grounds on which violence had been justified against the Qing Dynasty and the Chinese people.

But what are we to make today of the "Never Forget National Humiliation" wall or of the Dagu fort memorial museum? What relation can they possibly have to the era of socialist construction and self-reliance in which Liu's observations were embedded? How are we—or contemporary Chinese citizens, for that matter—to evaluate the new state-sponsored productions of history outlined here in relation to the globalizing forces that are reterritorializing China at the same moment that state socialism is deterritorialized? As the Chinese party-state rushes toward integration into a global economy that a generation ago was the archenemy of everything it stood for, the authors of official Chinese history are sponsoring more than heritage; they may also be caught in a nostalgia for the clarity and purity of a time when moral certitude was much more easily defined.

Yet, are they any worse off than we are? Perhaps contemporary Americans and Europeans need to remain ignorant of the events of the nineteenth century if they are to retain the moral high ground in relations with the current government of China. Blindness to Western imperialism and colonialism in China makes it difficult to understand expressions of patriotism and pride not only by party officials, but by ordinary Chinese. Such was the case with the announcement that China would host the 2008 Olympic games. Western newspaper reports that followed the announcement acknowledged the groundswell of emotion that burst forth in Beijing on 13 July 2001. But they only occasionally referred to events of the previous century, preferring instead to focus on the unacceptable character of China's political order.[51] Few seem to have noticed that part of the Chinese government's response to the announcement included references to past humiliations and to the respect that appeared to have been newly won from at least part of the world.

For much of the past century, Westerners have consistently interpreted Chinese patriotic expressions and protests against imperialism as at best tainted by state propaganda, at worst as a residual, unresolved hostility to all foreigners. In the wake of the events of 1900, Arthur von Rosthorn, Austria's minister in Beijing and a survivor of the siege of the legations, cautioned against such views. His assessment is worth recalling. Rejecting the conventional view of his peers on Chinese antiforeignism, von Rosthorn argued that "Europeans do not credit to Asians the feelings of patriotism which move us ourselves." Such myopia, he concluded, was a "great mistake" (cited in Mackerras 1989: 69). It remains no less a mistake today.

51. *Washington Post*, 14 July 2001 and *Chicago Tribune* 13 July 2001 did make reference to the past. The *Post* noted that it was a common view in that many Chinese feel that foreign governments continue to persecute China decades after the "humiliation" by foreign powers had formally ended.

THIS BOOK BEGAN with a horrific image of public executions in Beijing. The elements to be found in that image signaled the two sides of imperial pedagogy: the punitive and the constructive, the deterritorialization and reterritorialization of China. Although China-centered historians have addressed various aspects of this history, they have seldom identified the processes here referred to as English lessons or their global implications, preferring instead to interpret imperialism as an unfortunate effect of a quasi-natural Euroamerican expansion and to declare colonialism irrelevant to the China case. With only a few exceptions (Cohen 1997; Bickers 1999; Scully 2001), they have tended to treat the West as a known quantity requiring little if any further interrogation. Here I have attempted to build on and reach beyond the geographical and theoretical characteristics of China-centered approaches and address the following questions: What was colonial about Euroamerican activities in nineteenth-century China? What forms of political and material development in Europe and North America affected other parts of the world? How can these transnational processes be clarified by a study of their effects in China?

There is certainly no question that by the usual standards through which nineteenth-century colonialism has been understood, China was not a European colony. I have argued, however, that those standards, most of which involve degrees of political control, provide only a partial view of the many manifestations of nineteenth-century Euroamerican empire building. When colonialism is understood in broader, cultural terms or as a series of hegemonic projects, European and American diplomats, merchants, missionaries, and soldiers acted much like their counterparts in Africa and other parts of Asia. Certainly, this was the case with the forms of violence deployed by Western nation-states in China. Either as the rhetoric of physical force or the coercion of language, violence was used to modify the behavior and consciousness of recalcitrant others. Scenes like those evident in figure 1 were far more common than we care to remember. Added to them were the mundane daily humiliations that accompanied British, French, German, and American assumptions of their own racial, intellectual, and religious supremacy.

A second link to other colonial settings was the universalization of psuedo-scientific racial categories. Their conceptual apparatuses, when mobilized and disseminated, organized individuals into prison houses of purportedly uniform types with consistent physical and mental characteristics. Thus, any effort of colonizer or colonized to escape the cul-de-sac of imperial pedagogy was severely handicapped because it was first necessary to overcome the "common sense" of stratified categories of essentialized racial differences. For Chinese this meant remaining a patient of paternalistic Western action; for Euroamericans it meant that "civilization" was always at issue, particularly if one of their own number acted like tainted others.

Anxiety over civilization and barbarism is a third important link between China and other colonial settings. Such anxieties were made evident in a number of ways. Increasingly, by the end of the century, the violence of slaughter and plunder signified to some commentators atavistic remnants in the Western psyche and reminded observers of the thin veneer that was civilization. Discourse on civilization had other consequences as well. As in other colonial settings, Euroamericans agreed that the achievements of Chinese civilization lay in the past. Yet unlike the uniform dismissal of the present-as-degenerate to be found in characterizations of peoples in other parts of Asia, many Westerners preferred to think of China as somnambulant. At the very least, this meant that if the Chinese were to awaken and accept Western technology and revealed religion, they might be salvageable. Hence the frequent emphasis on the softer side of imperial pedagogy, the lessons of the classroom.

A fourth area in which China can be connected to other colonial settings is through the practices of military plunder, the public exhibition, and the art market. There is no question that British military practices worked out during the conquest of India were transposed onto China. Moreover, although the British army certainly had the most elaborate procedures for dealing with loot, other powers mimicked the form, if not all of the content of these practices. Meanwhile, in the imperial metropoles, China was organized into a representational order at international exhibitions and in museums that celebrated and helped to construct new forms of Euroamerican imperial sovereignty. At the same time, like the artifacts of aboriginal groups from Pacific islands, things Chinese were located as singular curiosities from which their market value was derived.

However, they did not remain so fixed. Over the course of the last four decades of the nineteenth century, the representational order in which these objects were located, as well as the general Euroamerican perception of China, shifted. That change can be accounted for by another similarity between colonialism in China and that to be found in other parts of Asia and Africa: the production of positive knowledge about China and the constitution of an imperial archive through which that knowledge was circulated and stored. Although this study has only scratched the surface of this topic, it should be clear from its findings that China knowledge was produced in ways identical to those found in other colonial settings, and it functioned in some cases through similar institutional structures. The knowledge produced by the China branch of the imperial archive not only transformed the daily life of objects taken from China by altering their status in collections and the marketplace; it also generated, as in India and parts of Southeast Asia, organizational and classificatory schemes that reterritorialized China and hence the lived relations between Chinese people at numerous levels of their social world. One outcome of these impositions was a "colonial modernity" in China, one that was shaped by and through continual dialogue with transnational forces and formations. Those processes continue into the present as contemporary Chinese people seek to craft a usable past out of the struggle with English lessons.

Last, as in other colonial settings, resistance of the colonized produced a powerful discourse on the colonizer as victim. Whether missionaries or settlers died as a result of indigenous rebellion, all the dead were understood to be innocent victims of savage barbarism. In the case of China, missionary writers took on the critical role of not only fixing this meaning to the events of 1900, but propelling that interpretation into the future. As a result, China shares with other former colonies the stigma of having rejected the opportunity to be tutored into Christian modernity.

If, as I argued in chapter 10, generations of Chinese and Euroamericans have been haunted by the English lessons of the past, it should also be clear that, as in other colonial contexts, neither Westerners nor Chinese have arrived at a mutual reconciliation. Instead, the traumatic events of the past century live on, refracted and distorted through nightmarish dreamscapes about Oriental menaces and obsessions with national humiliation. Perhaps little more could be expected from the violent oscillations between deterritorialization and reterritorialization that shaped global history in the past two centuries. But because no reconciliation was ever arrived at, because the past continues to be selectively plundered by the present, the scars, both physical and mental, remain, shaping the consciousness of the current generation. Where a more detailed account of humiliation exists, as is the case in China, contemporary Chinese are sometimes puzzled by, sometimes resentful of what men from the West did there. In North America, and to a degree in Europe as well, there is also questioning, but it tends even now to base itself on Fleming's iron rations of (misleading) general knowledge. Chinese still are thought to have attacked foreigners for no rational reason and, foreigners to have heroically resisted at the siege of the legations in unquestionably noble ways.

Occasionally, however, the dreamscape is disrupted, the surreal cycle of repetition traced in the painted scroll from Dagu to Beijing is halted. In 1958, at Oberlin College, site of the memorial arch to martyred missionaries of 1900, a group of faculty and students, including Asians and Asian Americans, constructed a wooden arch to the memory of the Chinese people killed in 1900. Put up on the night before an alumni reunion, the counter arch was placed on Tappan Square across from the martyrs' memorial. Although college administrators had it torn down, the idea of a memorial to the Chinese dead did not disappear. Eventually, in 1995, a plaque was dedicated for such remembrance.[1] At the same time, the original arch has undergone reinterpretation, serving repeatedly as a site of protest against social injustice and against U.S. military adventurism, including the Vietnam War.

The revision of the meaning of the Oberlin arch is instructive. It suggests that however powerful the memory machine of 1901 has been, the meaning that it fixed is mutable. One way of inscribing new meanings of the past in the present, as the Oberlin example also suggests, is to compose visible alterna-

1. OCA, letter from Tom Firor, 10 July 1991; *Oberlin Alumni Magazine* (summer 1991): 6.

tive versions of the events of the nineteenth century, ones that highlight suppressed or marginalized elements of dominant historical narratives. Much of this book has undertaken that project, and it has tried to do so in the same spirit as recent postcolonial studies of other parts of Asia and Africa. It has also attempted to locate within China other visions of the past that do not focus exclusively on humiliation. Perhaps it is time for all of us, Euroamericans and Chinese alike, to unroll in our imaginations the scroll painted by the nameless Manchurian artist, Sergeant Smith's companion, and think anew about ways to construct our shared history, ways that will accord a measure of dignity to all of us. Then, perhaps, we can put English lessons aside and move together beyond Fu-Manchu phobias in the West and fixations on national humiliations in the People's Republic.

BIBLIOGRAPHY

Archival Sources and Public Documents

British Library and India Office Records, London (IOR)
British Museum, Acquisition Records, London
First Historical Archive of China, Beijing
    Foreign Relations: Imperial audience participants lists
    Zhupi zouzhe: Imperially rescripted palace memorials
Library of Congress, Washington
National Army Museum, London (NAM)
Oberlin College Archives, Oberlin, Ohio (OCA)
Public Record Office, Kew Gardens, London
    Foreign Office Archives (FO)
    War Office Archives (WO)
    Wolseley Papers
Royal Engineers Museum, Brompton Barracks, Chatham
    Acquisition Records and Collections
United States Army Military History Institute, Carlisle, Pennsylvania (USMHI)
    Spanish-American War Era Veterans Survey, China Relief Expedition
United States National Archives and Records Administration, Washington (NARA)
    War Office Records

Victoria and Albert Museum. MSS. Acquisition Records. *Liqi tushi* plates; Arthur Wells Bequest; Miss Gordon File; and National Art Library, Auction Sales Catalogues, 1861–1902

Newspapers and Periodicals

Blackwood's Magazine
Celestial Empire (CE), Shanghai, 1900–1901
Chinese Repository, Canton, 1832–1851
Daily Telegraph, London, 1994, 1996
The Graphic, London, 1900–1901
Illustrated London News (ILN), London, 1860–1861, 1900–1901
Journal of the North China Branch of the Royal Asiatic Society (JNCBRAS), Shanghai, 1859–1948
La Vie illustrée, Paris, 1900–1901
Le Monde Illustré, Paris, 1900–1901
Leslie's Weekly (LW), New York, 1900–1901
L'Illustration, Paris, 1900–1901
Literary Digest, 1900–1901
New York Times, New York, 2001
North China Herald (NCH), Shanghai, 1900–1901
Peking and Tientsin Times, 1900–1901
Review of Reviews, London, 1900–1901

Published Sources

Adams, Charles F., ed. 1853. *The Works of John Adams*. 10 vols. Boston: Little, Brown.
Adams, John Q. 1909–10. "J. Q. Adams on the Opium War." *Proceedings of the Massachusetts Historical Society* 43: 295–324.
Adas, Michael. 1989. *Machines as the Measure of Men*. Ithaca: Cornell University Press.
Ahmed, Aijaz. 1992. *In Theory*. London: Verso.
Allen, Rev. Roland. 1901. *The Siege of the Peking Legations*. London: Smith, Elder.
Allgood, George. 1901. *China War 1860: Letters and Journal*. London: Longmans, Green.
Altick, Robert. 1978. *The Shows of London*. Cambridge, Mass.: Belknap Press.
Ament, William. 1901a. "A Bishop's Loot." *Independent* 53: 2217–18.
———. 1901b. "The Charges against Missionaries." *Independent* 53: 1051–52.
Anderson, Benedict. 1983. *Imagined Communities: Reflections on the Origin and Spread of Nationalism*. London: Verso.
Anglesey, George C. 1975. *A History of the British Cavalry, 1816 to 1919*. 4 vols. London: Leo Cooper.
Anslinger, H. J., and W. F. Tompkins. 1953. *The Traffic in Narcotics*. New York: Funk and Wagnalls.

Aries, Philippe. 1974. *Western Attitudes toward Death*. Baltimore: Johns Hopkins University Press.

Arlington, L. C., and W. Lewisohn. [1935] 1987. *In Search of Old Peking*. Reprint, Hong Kong: Oxford University Press.

Atkins, Martyn. 1995. *Informal Empire in Crisis*. Ithaca: Cornell University Press.

Ayers, J. 1985. "The Early China Trade," 259–266. In O. Impey and A. MacGregor, eds., *The Origins of Museums: The Cabinets of Curiosities in Sixteenth- and Seventeenth-Century Europe*. Oxford: Clarendon.

Backhouse, Edmond, and John O. P. Bland. 1911. *China under the Empress Dowager*. London: W. Heinemann.

———. 1914. *Annals and Memoirs of the Court of Peking*. London: W. Heinemann.

Baedecker, Karl. 1904, *Russland nebst Teheran*. Leipzig: Karl Baedecker.

———. 1912. *Port Arthur*. Leipzig: Karl Baedecker.

———. 1914. *Peking*. Leipzig: Karl Baedecker.

Ball, J. Dyer. 1893. *Things Chinese*. London: Sampson, Low and Marston.

Bannister, Robert. 1972. *Social Darwinism*. Philadelphia: Temple University Press.

Banno, Masataka. 1964. *China and the West, 1858–1861*. Cambridge, Mass.: Harvard University Press.

Barfield, Thomas. 1989. *The Perilous Frontier*. Cambridge, Mass.: Blackwell.

Barlow, Tani. 1993. "Colonialism's Career in Postwar China Studies." *positions* 1.1: 224–267.

———, ed. 1997. *Formations of Colonial Modernity*. Durham, N.C.: Duke University Press.

Barmé, Geremie. 1996. "The Garden of Perfect Brightness: A Life in Ruins." *East Asian History* 11: 111–158.

Barrow, George de S. 1942. *The Fire of Life*. London: Hutcheson.

Barrow, John. [1806] 1972. *Travels in China*. Reprint, Taipei: Ch'eng Wen.

Basu, Dilip. 1993. "Barbarians: Construction of Chinese Xenology and the Opium War." Paper presented at the conference *Beyond Orientalism?*, University of California, Santa Cruz, 12–13 November.

Bayly, C. A. 1996. *Empire and Information*. Cambridge, England: Cambridge University Press.

Bazancourt, César Lecat. 1861. *Les expéditions de Chine et de Cochinchine; d'après les documents officiels par le baron de Bazancourt*. Paris: Amyot.

Beeching, Jack. 1975. *The Chinese Opium Wars*. New York: Harcourt, Brace, Jovanovich.

Benjamin, Walter. 1969. "The Work of Art in the Age of Mechanical Reproduction," 217–251. In *Illuminations*. New York: Schocken.

———. 1999. *The Arcades Project*. Trans. Howard Eiland and Kevin McLaughlin. Cambridge, Mass.: Belknap Press.

Bennett, Tony. 1995. *The Birth of the Museum*. New York: Routledge.

Bernstein, Richard, and Ross Munro. 1997. *The Coming Conflict with China*. New York: Alfred A. Knopf.

Berridge, Virginia, and Griffith Edwards. 1981. *Opium and the People*. New York: St. Martin's.

Bevans, Charles I. 1918–30. *Treaties and Other International Agreements of the United States of America, 1776–1949*. Washington: U.S. Government Printing Office.

Bhabha, Homi. 1983. "Difference, Discrimination, and the Discourse of Colonialism," 194–211. In Francis Barker et al., eds., *The Politics of Theory*. Colchester, England: University of Essex Press.

Bickers, Robert. 1993a. "History, Legend and Treaty Port Ideology, 1925–1931," 81–92. In R. Bickers, ed., *Ritual and Diplomacy*. London: British Association for Chinese Studies and Wellsweep Press.

———. 1993b. "Treaty Port History and the Macartney Mission." Paper presented at the *Symposium Marking the Bicentenary of the First British Mission to China*, Chengde, PRC, 14–18 September.

———. 1999. *Britain in China*. Manchester, England: Manchester University Press.

Biggerstaff, Knight. 1934–35. "The T'ung Wen Kuan." *Chinese Social and Political Science Review* 18: 307–340.

———. 1961. *The Earliest Modern Government Schools in China*. Ithaca: Cornell University Press.

Bishop, Heber. 1900. *The Heber Bishop Collection of Jade and Other Hard Stones*. New York: Metropolitan Museum of Art.

Blofeld, John. [1961] 1989. *City of Lingering Splendor*. Boston: Shambala.

Bongie, Chris. 1991. *Exotic Memories*. Stanford: Stanford University Press.

Bottomore, Tom, et al., eds. 1983. *A Dictionary of Marxist Thought*. London: Blackwell.

Boulger, D. C. 1879. *England and Russia in Central Asia*. London: W.H. Allen.

———. 1885. *Central Asian Questions: Essays on Afghanistan, China, and Central Asia*. London: T.F. Unwin.

———. 1897. *The Life of Gordon*. London: T.F. Unwin.

———. 1900. "The Scramble for China." *Contemporary Review* 78: 1–10.

Brantlinger, Patrick. 1988. *Rule of Darkness*. Ithaca: Cornell University Press.

Breckenridge, Carol. 1989. "The Aesthetics and Politics of Colonial Collecting: India at the World Fairs." *Comparative Studies in Society and History* 31.2: 195–216.

Bredon, Juliet. 1922. *Peking*. Shanghai: Kelly and Walsh.

———. 1931. *Peking*. 3d ed. Shanghai: Kelly and Walsh.

Brooks, Elbridge S. 1901. *Under the Allied Flags*. Boston: Lothrop.

Brooks, Peter. 1976. *The Melodramatic Imagination*. New Haven: Yale University Press.

Broomhall, Marshall. 1901. *Martyred Missionaries of the China Inland Mission: with a Record of the Perils and Sufferings of Some who Escaped*. New York: Fleming H. Revell.

Brown, Arthur J. 1904. *New Forces in Old China*. New York: Fleming H. Revell.

Brown, Frederick. [1902] 1970. *From Tientsin to Peking with the Allied Forces*. Reprint, New York: Arno Press.

———. 1913. *China's Dayspring after Thirty Years*. London: Murray and Everden.

Buck, David, ed. 1987. *Recent Chinese Studies of the Boxer Movement*. Armonk, N.Y.: M.E. Sharpe.

———. 1991. "The 1990 International Symposium on the Boxer Movement and Modern Chinese Society." *Republican China* 16.2: 113–120.

Burlington Fine Arts Club. 1878. *Exhibition of Japanese and Chinese Works of Art.* London: John C. Wilkes.

———. 1895. *Catalogue of Blue and White Oriental Porcelain exhibited in 1895.* London: Printed for the Burlington Fine Arts Club.

———. 1896. *Catalogue of Coloured Chinese Porcelain exhibited in 1896.* London: Printed for the Burlington Fine Arts Club.

Bushell, Stephen W. 1899. *Oriental Ceramic Art: Collection of W. T. Walters.* New York: D. Appleton.

———. [1904] 1924. *Chinese Art.* London: Victoria and Albert Museum.

———. 1908. *Chinese Porcelain.* Oxford: Clarendon Press.

———. 1977. *A Description of Chinese Pottery and Porcelain.* Oxford: Oxford University Press.

Bushell, Stephen, and W. M. Laffan. [1904] 1907. *Catalogue of the Morgan Collection of Chinese Porcelains.* New York: Metropolitan Museum of Art.

Butler, Smedley D. 1933. *Old Gimlet Eye.* New York: Farrar and Rinehart.

Cameron, Nigel. 1970. *Barbarians and Mandarins.* Chicago: University of Chicago Press.

Caniff, Milt. 1987. *Steve Canyon: May 15, 1953–April 30, 1954.* Princeton, WI: Kitchen Sink Press.

Cannadine, David. 1983. "The Context, Performance and Meaning of Ritual: The British Monarchy and the 'Invention of Tradition,' c. 1820–1977," 101–164. In E. Hobsbawm and T. Ranger, eds., *The Invention of Tradition.* Cambridge, England: Cambridge University Press.

Carl, Katherine. 1907. *With the Empress Dowager of China.* New York: Century.

Carnegie Endowment for International Peace. 1914. *Signatures, Ratifications, Adhesions and Reservations of the Conventions and Declarations of the First and Second Hague Peace Conferences.* Washington: Carnegie Endowment.

Carter, W. H. 1917. *The Life of Lieutenant General Chaffee.* Chicago: University of Chicago Press.

Chakrabarty, Dipesh. 2000. *Provincializing Europe.* Princeton: Princeton University Press.

Chamberlin, Wilber. 1903. *Ordered to China.* New York: Frederick A. Stokes.

Chatterjee, Partha. 1986. *Nationalist Thought and the Colonial World: A Derivative Discourse.* London: Zed Books.

Cheng, Tien-fong. 1957. *A History of Sino-Russian Relations.* Washington: Public Affairs Press.

Chia Ning. 1992. "The Li-san Yuan in the Early Ch'ing Dynasty." Ph.D. diss., Johns Hopkins University.

Chien, Helen Hsieh, trans. 1993. *The European Diary of Hsieh Fucheng.* New York: St. Martin's.

China No. 2. [1869] 1975. *Correspondence respecting the Attack on British Protestant Missionaries at Yang-Chow-Fu, August 1868.* Reprint, San Francisco: Chinese Materials Center.

China No. 1. 1876. United Kingdom. House of Commons. Sessional Papers. London: Harrison and Sons.

China No. 3. 1877. United Kingdom. House of Commons. Sessional Papers. London: Harrison and Sons.

China No. 3. [1891] 1975 (CC91). *Correspondence respecting Anti-foreign Riots in China.* Reprint, San Francisco: Chinese Materials Center.

China No. 1. [1892] 1975 (CC92). *Further Correspondence respecting Anti-foreign Riots in China.* Reprint, San Francisco: Chinese Materials Center.

China White Paper: August 1949. 1967. Stanford: Stanford University Press.

Chinese Association for Boxer Studies, eds. 1992. *Yihetuan yundong yu jindai Zhongguo shehui guoji xueshu taolunhui lunwenji* (The collected papers of the International Symposium on the Boxer Movement and Modern Chinese Society). Jinan: Qilu.

Chirol, Valentine. 1896. *The Far Eastern Question.* London: Macmillan.

Chouban yiwu shimo, Xianfeng chao (YWSM, XF; The complete account of the management of foreign affairs, the Xianfeng Court). 1979. 8 vols. Beijing: China Press.

Chrisman, Laura. 1990. "The Imperial Unconscious? Representations of Imperial Discourse." *Critical Quarterly* 32.3: 38–58.

Christie's. 1996. *The Imperial Sale, Hong Kong, 28 April 1996.*

Clubb, O. Edmund. 1971. *China and Russia.* New York: Columbia University Press.

Clunas, Craig. 1991. "Whose Throne Is It Anyway?" *Orientations* 22.7 (July): 44–50.

Cochran, Sherman. 2001. *Encountering Chinese Networks.* Berkeley: University of California Press.

———, ed. 1999. *Inventing Nanjing Road.* Ithaca: East Asia Program, Cornell University.

Cocks, A. S. 1980. *The Victoria and Albert Museum: The Making of the Collection.* London: Windward.

Cohen, Paul. 1978. "Christian Missions and Their Impact to 1900," 543–590. In J. K. Fairbank, ed., *The Cambridge History of China*, vol. 10, part 1. London: Cambridge University Press.

———. 1984. *Discovering History in China: American Historical Writing on the Recent Chinese Past.* New York: Columbia University Press.

———. 1997. *History in Three Keys.* New York: Columbia University Press.

Cohn, Bernard. 1987. "The Census, Social Structure and Objectification in South Asia," 224–254. In *An Anthropologist among the Historians.* Delhi: Oxford University Press.

———. 1996. *Colonialism and Its Forms of Knowledge.* Princeton: Princeton University Press.

Colombos, C. J. 1940. *A Treatise on the Law of Prize.* London: Grotius Society.

Colquhoun, Archibald. 1898. *China in Transformation.* New York: Harper.

———. 1900. *Overland to China.* New York: Harper.

Coltman, Rev. R. 1901. *Beleaguered in Peking: The Boxer's War against the Foreigner; The Yellow Crime.* Philadelphia: F.A. Davis.

Compilation Group for the "History of Modern China" Series. 1976. *The Yi He Tuan Movement of 1900.* Peking: Foreign Language Press.

Conger, Sarah P. 1909. *Letters from China.* Chicago: A.C. McClurg.

Cook, Thomas. 1910. *Cook's Tourist Handbook to Peking, etc.* London: Thomas Cook and Son.

———. 1917. *Peking and the Overland Route.* London: Thomas Cook and Son.

———. 1924. *Peking, North China, South Manchuria and Korea.* London: Thomas Cook and Son.

Cooley, James. 1981. *T. F. Wade in China.* Leiden: E.J. Brill.

Cooper, Frederick. 1997. "The Dialectics of Decolonization: Nationalism and Labor Movements in Postwar French Africa," 406–435. In F. Cooper and A. Stoler, eds., *Tensions of Empire.* Berkeley: University of California Press.

Cooper, Frederick, and Ann Stoler, eds. 1997. *Tensions of Empire.* Berkeley: University of California Press.

Cordier, Henri. 1876. "A Classified Index to the Articles Printed in the Journal of the North-China Branch of the Royal Asiatic Society, from the Foundation of the Society to the 31st of December, 1874." JNCBRAS 9: 201–215.

Correspondence relative to the Earl of Elgin's Special Missions to China and Japan, 1857–1859 (CESM). 1859. Parliamentary Papers. London: Harrison and Sons.

Correspondence Respecting Affairs in China, 1859–1860 (CRAC). 1861. Parliamentary Papers. London: Harrison and Sons.

Costin, William C. 1937. *Great Britain and China, 1833–1860.* London: Oxford University Press.

Covell, Ralph. 1978. *W. A. P. Martin: Pioneer of Progress in China.* Washington: Christian University Press.

Cranmer-Byng, J. L., ed. 1963. *An Embassy to China.* Hamden, Conn.: Archon Books.

Crary, Jonathan. 1988. "Modernizing Vision," 29–44. In Hal Foster, ed., *Vision and Visuality.* Seattle: Bay Press.

Crosby, Christina. 1991. *The Ends of History.* London: Routledge.

Crossley, Pamela. 1999. *The Translucent Mirror.* Berkeley: University of California Press.

Crow, Carl. [1913] 1973. *The Travelers Handbook for China.* Reprint, Taipei: Ch'eng Wen.

Curzon, George. 1967. *Russia in Central Asia in 1889 and the Anglo-Russian Question.* London: Cass.

Da Qing lichao shilu (Veritable records of the Qing Dynasty). 1964. 13 vols. Taiwan: Huawen shudian.

Daggett, A. S. 1903. *America in the China Relief Expedition.* Kansas City: Hudson-Kimberly.

Davidson-Houston, J. V. 1960. *Russia and China.* London: Robert Hale.

Davis, John. 1887–1906. *The History of the Second, Queen's Royal Regiment (Royal West Surrey).* 6 vols. London: Eyre and Spottiswoode.

Deleuze, Gilles, and Félix Guattari. 1983. *Anti-Oedipus: Capitalism and Schizophrenia.* Minneapolis: University of Minnesota Press.

Denby, Charles. 1900. "The Duty of Securing Protection for Foreigners in China." *Independent* 52: 2485–86.

Deverall, Richard. 1954. *Mao Tze-Tung: Stop This Dirty Opium Business! How Red China Is Selling Opium and Heroin to Produce Revenue for China's War Machine.* Tokyo: Toyoh.

Devereaux, Leslie, and Roger Hillman, eds. 1995. *Fields of Vision.* Berkeley: University of California Press.

d'Hérrison, Maurice. 1901. "The Loot of the Imperial Summer Palace at Pekin," 601–635.

In *Annual Report of the Smithsonian Institution*. Washington: U.S. Government Printing Office.

Dillon, Edward J. 1901. "The Chinese Wolf and the European Lamb." *Contemporary Review* 79: 1–31.

Douglas, Robert K. 1894. *Society in China*. London: A.D. Innes.

Duden, Alexis. 1999. "Japan's Engagement with International Terms," 165–191. In Lydia Liu, ed., *Tokens of Exchange*. Durham, N.C.: Duke University Press.

Duyvendak, J. J. L. 1939. "The Last Dutch Embassy to the Chinese Court (1794–1795)." *T'oung Pao* 34.1–2: 1–116.

Eagleton, Terry. 1990. *The Ideology of the Aesthetic*. Oxford: Blackwell.

Eames, James. [1909] 1974. *The English in China*. London: Curzon Press.

Eastman, Lloyd. 1967. *Throne and Mandarins*. Cambridge, Mass.: Harvard University Press.

Edwardes, Michael. 1975. *Playing the Great Game*. London: Hamilton.

Edwards, E. H. [1903] 1970. *Fire and Sword in Shansi: The Story of the Martyrdom of Foreigners and Chinese Christians*. Reprint, New York: Arno Press and New York Times.

Eliade, Mircea, ed. 1987. *The Encyclopedia of Religion*. 16 vols. New York: Macmillan.

Elliott, Mark. 2001. *The Manchu Way*. Stanford: Stanford University Press.

Ellis, Henry. 1817. *Journal of the Proceedings of the Late Embassy to China*. London: John Murray.

Elvin, Mark, and G. William Skinner, eds. 1974. *The Chinese City between Two Worlds*. Stanford: Stanford University Press.

Enloe, Cynthia. 1989. *Bananas, Beaches and Bases: Making Feminine Sense of International Politics*. Berkeley: University of California Press.

Esherick, Joseph. 1987. *The Origins of the Boxer Uprising*. Berkeley: University of California Press.

Evans, John. 1987. *The Russo-Chinese Crisis*. Newtonville, Mass.: Oriental Research Partners.

Evans, Martin, and Ken Lunn, eds. 1997. *War Memory in the Twentieth Century*. New York: Berg.

Fabian, Johannes. 1983. *Time and the Other*. New York: Columbia University Press.

Fairbank, John K. 1942. "Tributary Trade and China's Relations with the West." *Far Eastern Quarterly* 1: 129–149.

———. 1953. *Trade and Diplomacy on the China Coast*. Stanford: Stanford University Press.

———. 1957. "Synarchy under the Treaties," 204–231. In J. K. Fairbank, ed., *Chinese Thought and Institutions*. Chicago: University of Chicago Press.

———. 1958. *The United States and China*. Cambridge, Mass.: Harvard University Press.

———. 1968. "The Early Treaty System in the Chinese World Order," 257–275. In J. K. Fairbank, ed., *The Chinese World Order*. Cambridge, Mass.: Harvard University Press.

———. 1987. *The Great Chinese Revolution 1800–1985*. New York: Harper and Row.

———, ed. 1978. *The Cambridge History of China: Late Ch'ing 1800–1911*. Vol. 10, part 1. London: Cambridge University Press.

Fairbank, John K., Katherine F. Bruner, and Elizabeth M. Matheson, eds. 1975. *The I.G. in Peking*. Cambridge, Mass.: Harvard University Press.

Fairbank, John K., Martha H. Coolidge, and Richard J. Smith. 1995. *H. B. Morse*. Lexington: University of Kentucky Press.

Fairbank, John K., and K. C. Liu, eds. 1980. *The Cambridge History of China: Late Ch'ing 1800–1911*. Vol. 11, part 2. London: Cambridge University Press.

Fanon, Frantz. [1963] 1966. *The Wretched of the Earth*. New York: Grove Press.

Farquhar, Judith, and James Hevia. 1993. "Culture and Post-war American Historiography of China." *positions* 1.2: 486–525.

Farwell, Byron. 1972. *Queen Victoria's Little Wars*. New York: Norton.

———. 1981. *Mr. Kipling's Army*. New York: Norton.

———. 1989. *Armies of the Raj*. New York: Norton.

Favier, Adolph. 1901. "An Answer to Charges of Looting." *Catholic World* 74: 387–390.

Felber, Roland, and Horst Rostek. 1987. *Der "Hunnenkrieg" Kaiser Wilhelms II: Imperialistische Intervention in China 1900/01*. Berlin: VEB Deutscher Verlag der Wissenschaften.

Feuerwerker, Albert, ed. 1968. *History in Communist China*. Cambridge, Mass.: MIT Press.

Finney, Charles G. 1961. *The Old China Hands*. New York: Doubleday.

Fischer, Emil. 1924. *Guide to Peking and Its Environs Near and Far*. Tientsin: Tientsin Press.

Fisher, Arthur. 1863. *Personal Narrative of Three Years' Service in China*. London: Richard Bentley.

Fleming, Peter. 1959. *The Siege of Peking*. New York: Harper.

Fletcher, Joseph. 1978a. "Ch'ing Inner Asia c. 1800," 35–106. In J. K. Fairbank, ed., *The Cambridge History of China, Late Ch'ing, 1800–1911*, vol. 10, part 1. Cambridge, England: Cambridge University Press.

———. 1978b. "The Heyday of the Ch'ing Order in Mongolia, Sinkiang and Tibet," 351–408. In J. K. Fairbank, ed., *The Cambridge History of China, Late Ch'ing, 1800–1911*, vol. 10, part 1. Cambridge, England: Cambridge University Press.

———. 1978c. "Sino-Russian Relations, 1860–62," 318–350. In J. K. Fairbank, ed. *The Cambridge History of China, Late Ch'ing, 1800–1911*, vol. 10, part 1. Cambridge, England: Cambridge University Press.

Foreign Relations of the United States (FRUS). 1902. *Affairs in China*. Washington: U.S. Government Printing Office.

Forsyth, Robert C. 1904. *The China Martyrs of 1900*. London: Religious Tract Society.

Forsyth, Thomas D. 1875. *Report of a Mission to Yarkand*. Calcutta: Foreign Department Press.

Forsythe, S. A. 1971. *An American Missionary Community in China, 1895–1905*. Cambridge, Mass.: Harvard East Asian Monographs 43.

Fortune, Robert. 1857. *A Residence among the Chinese*. London: John Murray.

Foucault, Michel. 1991. "Governmentality," 87–104. In Graham Burchell, C. Gordon, and P. Miller, eds., *The Foucault Effect*. Chicago: University of Chicago Press.

Fox, Grace Estelle. 1940. *British Admirals and Chinese Pirates, 1832–1869*. London: K. Paul, Trench, Trubner.

Foxe, John. 1856. *Foxe's Book of Martyrs*. Philadelphia: James B. Smith.

Frodsham, J. D. 1974. *The First Chinese Embassy to the West: The Journals of Kuo Sung-t'ao, Liu Hsi-hung, and Chang Te-yi*. Oxford: Clarendon Press.

Gatrell, T. J. N. 1901. "The Expedition to Paotingfu." *Independent* 53: 148–150.

Gibson, Tom. 1969. *The Wiltshire Regiment*. London: Leo Cooper.

Giles, Herbert. 1898. *A Catalogue of the Wade Collection of the Chinese and Manchu Books in the Library of the University of Cambridge*. Cambridge, England: Cambridge University Press.

———. 1915. *Supplementary Catalogue of the Wade Collection of Chinese and Manchu Books in the Library of the University of Cambridge*. Cambridge, England: Cambridge University Press.

Giles, Lancelot. 1970. *The Siege of the Peking Legations: A Diary*. Nedlands: University of Western Australia Press.

Gillard, David. 1977. *The Struggle for Asia 1828–1914*. London: Methuen.

Gilman, Sander. 1985. *Difference and Pathology*. Ithaca: Cornell University Press.

Godden, Rumer. 1977. *The Butterfly Lions: The Story of the Pekingese in History, Legend and Art*. New York: Viking.

Goldman, Charles, ed. 1905. *The Empire and the Century*. London: John Murray.

Gordon Cumming, C. F. 1886. *Wanderings in China*. 2 vols. Edinburgh: Blackwood.

Gould, Stephen J. 1981. *The Mismeasure of Man*. New York: Norton.

Graham, Gerald. 1901. *Life, Letters, and Diaries of Lieut.-General Sir Gerald Graham*. Ed. R. H. Vetch. London: Blackwood.

Greenhalgh, Paul. 1988. *Ephemeral Vistas*. Manchester, England: Manchester University Press.

Gregory, Adrian. 1994. *The Silence of Memory*. New York: Berg.

Guha, Ranajit. [1981] 1996. *A Rule of Property for Bengal*. Durham, N.C.: Duke University Press.

Hall, Ronald. [1931] 1966. *Eminent Authorities on China*. Reprint, Taipei: Ch'eng-wen Publishing.

Haller, William. 1963. *Foxe's Book of Martyrs and the Elect Nation*. London: Jonathan Cape.

Hansard's Parliamentary Debates. 1830–91. Ser. 3: vols. 1–356. London: T. C. Hansard.

Hao, Yen-ping. 1970. *The Comprador in Nineteenth Century China*. Cambridge, Mass.: Harvard University Press.

———. 1986. *The Commercial Revolution in Nineteenth-Century China*. Berkeley: University of California Press.

Hao, Yen-ping, and Erh-Min Wang. 1980. "Changing Chinese Views of Western Relations, 1840–95," 142–201. In J. K. Fairbank and K. C. Liu, eds., *The Cambridge History of China*, vol. 11, part 2. London: Cambridge University Press.

Harris, David. 1999. *Of Battle and Beauty: Felice Beato's Photographs of China*. Santa Barbara, CA: Santa Barbara Museum of Art.

Harris, James. 1912. *China Jim*. London: William Heinemann.

Hart, Robert. 1901a. "China and Non-China." *Fortnightly Review* 75: 278–293.

———. 1901b. *These from the Land of Sinim*. London: Chapman and Hall.

Hastings, James, ed. 1916. *Encyclopedia of Religion and Ethics*. 13 vols. New York: Scribner's.

Haswell, Jock. 1967. *The Queen's Royal Regiment*. London: Hamish Hamilton.

Hayford, Charles. 1985. "Chinese and American Characteristics: Arthur H. Smith and His China Book," 153–174. In Susan Barnett and J. K. Fairbank, eds., *Christianity in China*. Cambridge, Mass.: Harvard University Press.

Headland, Isaac. 1902. *Chinese Heroes*. New York: Eaton and Mains.

Headrick, Daniel. 1981. *Tools of Empire*. New York: Oxford University Press.

———. 2000. *When Information Came of Age*. New York: Oxford University Press.

Heathcote, T. A. 1974. *The Indian Army*. New York: Hippocrene.

Henty, George A. 1884. *By Sheer Pluck*. London: Blackie.

———. 1884. *With Clive in India*. London: Blackie.

———. 1901. *With Roberts to Pretoria*. New York: Scribner's.

———. 1902. *With Kitchener in the Soudan*. New York: Scribner's.

———. 1904. *With the Allies to Pekin*. London: Blackie and Son.

Hevia, James. 1993. "Lamas, Emperors, and Rituals: The Political Implications of Qing Imperial Ceremonies." *Journal of the International Association of Buddhist Studies* 16.2: 243–278.

———. 1995a. "An Imperial Nomad and the Great Game: Thomas Francis Wade in China." *Late Imperial China* 16.2: 1–22.

———. 1995b. *Cherishing Men from Afar: Qing Guest Ritual and the Macartney Embassy of 1793*. Durham, N.C.: Duke University Press.

———. 1996. "Imperial Guest Ritual," 471–487. In Donald Lopez, ed., *Religions of China*. Princeton: Princeton University Press.

———. 1998. "Postpolemical Historiography: A Response to Joseph W. Esherick." *Modern China* 24.3: 319–327.

———. 2000. "World Heritage, National Culture and the Restoration of Chengde." *positions* 9.1: 219–244.

Hibbert, Christopher. 1970. *The Dragon Wakes*. New York: Harper and Row.

Hinsley, F. H. 1969. "The Concept of Sovereignty and the Relations between States," 275–288. In W. J. Stankiewicz, ed., *In Defense of Sovereignty*. New York: Oxford University Press.

———. 1986. *Sovereignty*. Cambridge, England: Cambridge University Press.

Hirth, Friedrich. 1885–88. *Text Book of Documentary Chinese, with a vocabulary for the special use of the Chinese customs service*. Shanghai: Kelly and Walsh.

Hobsbawm, Eric. 1989. *The Age of Empire, 1876–1914*. New York: Vintage.

Hochschild, Adam. 1998. *King Leopold's Ghost*. Boston: Houghton Mifflin.

Hoe, Susanna. 2000. *Women at the Siege, Peking 1900*. Oxford: Holo.

Hofstadter, Richard. 1955. *Social Darwinism in American Thought*. Boston: Beacon.

Holmes, R. 1896. *Naval and Military Trophies and Personal Relics of British Heroes*. London: John C. Nimmo.

Hooker, Mary. [1910] 1987. *Behind the Scenes in Peking*. Reprint, Hong Kong: Oxford University Press.

Hope, E. 1885. *General Gordon, The Christian Hero*. London: Walter Scott.

Hopkirk, Peter. 1992. *The Great Game*. New York: Kodansha International.

————. 1995. *On Secret Service East of Constantinople*. Oxford: Oxford University Press.

Hostetler, Laura. 2001. *Qing Colonial Enterprise*. Chicago: University of Chicago Press.

Hsü, Immanuel C. Y. 1960. *China's Entry into the Family of Nations*. Cambridge, Mass.: Harvard University Press.

————. 1965a. *The Ili Crisis: A Study of Sino-Russian Diplomacy, 1871–1881*. Oxford: Clarendon Press.

————. 1965b. "The Great Policy Debate in China, 1874: Maritime Defense vs. Frontier Defense." *Harvard Journal of Asiatic Studies* 25: 212–228.

————. 1990. *The Rise of Modern China*. 4th ed. New York: Oxford University Press.

Hu Sheng. 1952. *Diguozhuyi yu Zhongguo zhengzhi*. Beijing: People's Press.

————. 1955. *Imperialism and Chinese Politics*. Beijing: Foreign Languages Press.

Hummel, Arthur. 1943. *Eminent Chinese of the Ch'ing Period*. Washington: U.S. Government Printing Office.

Hunt, Michael. 1979. "The Forgotten Occupation: Peking, 1900–1901." *Pacific Historical Review* 48: 501–529.

————. 1983. *The Making of a Special Relationship*. New York: Columbia University Press.

Huntington, Samuel. 1993. "The Clash of Civilizations." *Foreign Affairs* 72.3: 22–49.

————. 1996. *The Clash of Civilizations and the Remaking of the World Order*. New York: Simon and Schuster.

Hurd, Douglas. 1967. *The Arrow War*. London: Collins.

Ichiko, Chuzo. 1980. "Political and Institutional Reform, 1901–1911," 375–415. In J. K. Fairbank and K. C. Liu, eds., *The Cambridge History of China*, volume 11, part 2. Cambridge, England: Cambridge University Press.

Impey, O. 1977. *Chinoiserie*. London: Oxford University Press.

————. 1985. "Japan: Trade and Collecting in Seventeenth-Century Europe," 267–273. In O. Impey and A. MacGregor, eds., *The Origins of Museums: The Cabinets of Curiosities in Sixteenth- and Seventeenth-Century Europe*. Oxford: Clarendon.

Impey, O., and A. MacGregor, eds. 1985. *The Origins of Museums: The Cabinets of Curiosities in Sixteenth- and Seventeenth-Century Europe*. Oxford: Clarendon.

Isaacs, Harold. [1958] 1980. *Scratches on Our Minds: American Images of China and India*. New York: John Day.

Jackson, S. M., ed. 1910. *The Schaff-Hersog Encyclopedia of Religious Knowledge*. 12 vols. New York: Funk and Wagnalls.

Jay, Martin. 1988. "Scopic Regimes of Modernity," 3–23. In Hal Foster, ed., *Vision and Visuality*. Seattle: Bay Press.

Jenks, Chris, ed. 1995. *Visual Culture*. New York: Routledge.

Jensen, Lionel. 1997. *Manufacturing Confucianism: Chinese Traditions and Universal Civilizations*. Durham, N.C.: Duke University Press.

Johnston, Reginald. [1934] 1985. *Twilight in the Forbidden City*. Reprint, Hong Kong: Oxford University Press.

Jones, D. V. 1984. *Splendid Encounters*. Chicago: University of Chicago Libraries.

Kaestlin, J. P. 1963. *Catalogue of the Museum of Artillery in the Rotunda at Woolwich, Part I: Ordnance*. London: Her Majesty's Stationery Office.

Kelly, John S. 1963. *A Forgotten Conference: The Negotiations at Peking, 1900–1901*. Geneva: Librairie E. Droz.

Kennedy, Paul. 1987. *The Rise and Fall of Great Powers*. New York: Vintage.

Ketler, Isaac C. 1902. *The Tragedy of Paotingfu*. New York: Fleming H. Revell.

Kiernan, V. G. 1986. *The Lords of Human Kind*. New York: Columbia University Press.

Kipling, Rudyard. [1901] 1981. *Kim*. Mahwah, N.J.: Watermill.

Kipnis, Andrew. 1995. " 'Face': An Adaptable Discourse of Social Surfaces." *positions* 3.1: 119–148.

Kirshenblatt-Gimblett, B. 1991. "Objects of Ethnography," 386–443. In Ivan Karp and S. Lavine, eds., *Exhibiting Cultures*. Washington: Smithsonian Institution Press.

Knight, Charles R. B. 1935. *Historical Records of the Buffs*. 3 vols. London: Medici Society.

Knollys, Henry. 1875. *Incidents in the China War of 1860 compiled from the private journals of General Sir Hope Grant*. Edinburgh: William Blackwood and Sons.

———. 1894. *Life of General Sir Hope Grant*. 2 vols. London: Blackwood.

Kohn, Marek. 1992. *Dope Girls: The Birth of the British Drug Underground*. London: Lawrence and Wishart.

Kolb, Robert. 1987. *For All the Saints*. Macon, Ga.: Mercer University Press.

Krausse, Alexis. [1899] 1973. *Russia in Asia*. Reprint, New York: Barnes and Noble Books.

———. [1900a] 1973. *China in Decay*. 3d ed. Reprint, Taipei: Ch'eng Wen.

———. 1900b. *The Story of the China Crisis*. New York: Cassell.

Kuhn, Phillip. 1978. "The Taiping Rebellion," 264–317. In J. K. Fairbank, ed., *The Cambridge History of China, Late Ch'ing, 1800–1911*, vol. 10, part 1. Cambridge, England: Cambridge University Press.

Kuo, Ting-yee. 1978. "Self-strengthening: The Pursuit of Western Technology," 491–542. In J. K. Fairbank, ed., *The Cambridge History of China*, vol. 10, part 1. Cambridge, England: Cambridge University Press.

Lamb, Alastair. 1960. *Britain and Chinese Central Asia*. London: Routledge.

Landes, David. 1998. *The Wealth and Poverty of Nations*. New York: Norton.

Landor, Henry Savage. 1901. *China and the Allies*. 2 vols. New York: Scribner's.

Lane Poole, Stanley. [1901] 1968. *Sir Harry Parkes in China*. Reprint, Taipei: Ch'eng-wen.

Langer, Walter. [1935] 1965. *The Diplomacy of Imperialism, 1890–1902*. 2d ed. New York: Knopf.

Latour, Bruno. 1990. "Drawing Things Together," 19–68. In Michael Lynch and Steve Woolgar, eds., *Representations in Scientific Practice*. Cambridge, Mass.: MIT Press.

———. 1993. *We Have Never Been Modern*. Cambridge, Mass.: Harvard University Press.

Lattimore, Owen. 1940. *Inner Asian Frontiers of China*. New York: American Geographical Society.

Lee, Leo. 1999. *Shanghai Modern*. Cambridge, Mass.: Harvard University Press.

Leonard, Lawrence. 1944. *Catalogue of the United States Military Academy Museum*. West Point: United States Military Academy.

Leslie, N. B. 1970. *Battle Honours of the British and Indian Armies, 1865–1914*. London: Leo Cooper.

Lewis, Reina. 1996. *Gendering Orientalism*. New York: Routledge.

Leyda, Jay. 1972. *Dianying: Electric Shadows*. Cambridge, Mass.: MIT Press.

Li Dezheng, Su Weizhi, and Liu Tianlu. 1990. *Baguo lianjun qinhua shi* (A history of the eight-power invasion). Jinan: Shandong University Press.

Li Wen-hai et al., eds. 1986. *Yihetuan yundong shishi yaolu* (YHTYDSSYL; Essential historical records of the Boxer movement). Jinan: Ji-lu shu-she.

Little, Mrs. Archibald. 1901. "Peking Revisited." *Eclectic Magazine* 137: 501–511.

———. 1904. *Guide to Peking*. Tientsin: Tientsin Press.

Little, L. K. 1975. Introduction, 3–34. In J. K. Faribank, K. F. Bruner, and E. M. Matheson, eds., *The I.G. in Peking*. Cambridge, Mass.: Belknap.

Liu Beisi and Xu Qixian. 1994. *Exquisite Figure-Pictures from the Palace Museum*. Beijing: Forbidden City Publishing House.

Liu, Danian. 1968. "How to Appraise the History of Asia," 356–368. In A. Feuerwerker, ed., *History in Communist China*. Cambridge, Mass.: MIT Press.

Liu, Kwang-Ching. 1978. "The Ch'ing Restoration," 409–490. In J. K. Fairbank, ed., *The Cambridge History of China*, vol. 10, part 1. Cambridge, England: Cambridge University Press.

Liu, Kwang-Ching, and Richard J. Smith. 1980. "The Military Challenge: The Northwest and the Coast," 202–273. In J. K. Fairbank and K. C. Liu, eds., *The Cambridge History of China*, vol. 11, part 2. Cambridge, England: Cambridge University Press.

Liu, Lydia. 1995. *Translingual Practice*. Stanford: Stanford University Press.

———. 1999. "Legislating the Universal," 127–164. In Lydia Liu, ed., *Tokens of Exchange*. Durham, NC: Duke University Press.

Lo, Hui-min, ed. 1976. *The Correspondence of G. E. Morrison*. 3 vols. London: Cambridge University Press.

Loch, Henry B. [1869] 1900. *Personal Narrative of Occurrences during Lord Elgin's Second Embassy to China in 1860*. London: John Murray.

Longworth, Alice R. 1933. *Crowded Hours*. New York: Scribner's.

Loomba, Ania. 1998. *Colonialism/Postcolonialism*. London: Routledge.

Loti, Pierre. 1902. *The Last Days of Pekin*. Boston: Little, Brown.

Lowe, Donald. 1966. *The Function of "China" in Marx, Lenin, and Mao*. Berkeley: University of California Press.

———. 1982. *History of Bourgeois Perception*. Chicago: University of Chicago Press.

Lowe, Lisa. 1991. *Critical Terrains*. Ithaca: Cornell University Press.

Lu Hanchao. 1999. *Beyond the Neon Lights*. Berkeley: University of California Press.

Lu Yao. 1987. "The Origins of the Boxers," 42–86. In David Buck, ed., *Recent Studies of the Boxer Movement*. Armonk, N.Y.: M.E. Sharpe.

———. 2000. *Shandong minjian mimijiaomen* (Shandong popular secret sects). Beijing: Contemporary China Press.

Lucas, Christopher, ed. 1990. *James Ricalton's Photographs of China during the Boxer Rebellion.* Lewiston, N.Y.: E. Mellen.

Lynch, George. 1901. *The War of Civilizations.* London: Longmans, Green.

MacDonnell, John. 1901. "Looting in China." *Contemporary Review* 79 (March): 444–452.

MacDonnell, Ranald, and Marcus Macauley. 1940. *A History of the 4th Prince of Wales's Own Gurkha Rifles, 1857–1837.* 2 vols. Edinburgh: William Blackwood and Sons.

MacGregor, John. 1850. *Commercial Statistics.* 5 vols. London: Wittaker.

MacKenzie, John M. 1992. "Heroic Myths of Empire," 109–138. In John MacKenzie, ed., *Popular Imperialism and the Military.* Manchester, England: Manchester University Press.

Mackerras, Colin. 1989. *Western Images of China.* Hong Kong: Oxford University Press.

MacMurray, John. 1921. *Treaties and Agreements with and concerning China 1894–1919.* 2 vols. New York: Oxford University Press.

Mahan, Alfred Thayer. 1899–1900 "The Problem of Asia." *Harper's New Monthly Magazine* 100: 536–547, 747–759, 929–994.

———. 1900. *The Problem of Asia and Its Effect upon International Policies.* Boston: Little, Brown.

Malone, Carroll B. 1934. *History of the Peking Summer Palaces under the Ch'ing Dynasty.* Urbana: University of Illinois Press.

Mancall, Mark. 1971. *Russia and China: Their Diplomatic Relations to 1728.* Cambridge, Mass.: Harvard University Press.

Mani, Lata. 1985. "The Production of an Official Discourse on Sati in Early Nineteenth-Century Bengal," 1: 107–127. In Francis Barker et al., eds., *Europe and Its Others.* Colchester, England: Essex University Press.

Mao Zedong. 1977. *Selected Works of Mao Tsetung.* Beijing: Foreign Language Press, vol. 5.

Marchetti, Gina. 1993. *Romance and the "Yellow Peril."* Berkeley: University of California Press.

Marshall, Peter, and G. Williams. 1982. *The Great Map of Mankind.* London: J.M. Dent.

Martin, W. A. P. 1900. *The Siege of Peking.* New York: Fleming H. Revell.

Marx, Karl. 1973. *Grundrisse.* Harmondsworth, England: Penguin.

Mason, P. 1974. *A Matter of Honour.* London: Jonathan Cape.

Mateer, A. H. 1903. *Siege Days.* New York: Fleming H. Revell.

Matheson, James. 1836. *The Present Position and Prospects of Trade with China.* London. Smith, Elder.

Mayer, David. 1992. "The World on Fire . . . Pyrodramas at Belle Vue Gardens, Manchester, c. 1850–1950," 179–197. In John MacKenzie, ed., *Popular Imperialism and the Military.* Manchester, England: Manchester University Press.

Mayers, William F. [1877] 1966. *Treaties between the Empire of China and Foreign Powers.* Reprint, Taipei: Ch'eng-wen.

———. [1897] 1970. *The Chinese Government.* 3d ed. Revised by G. M. H. Playfair. Reprint, Taipei: Ch'eng-Wen.

Mayers, William F., N. B. Dennys, and Charles King. [1867] 1977. *The Treaty Ports of China and Japan*. Reprint, San Francisco: Chinese Materials Center.

McClintock, Anne. 1995. *Imperial Leather*. New York: Routledge.

McCoy, Alfred W. 1973. *The Politics of Heroin in Southeast Asia*. New York: Harper and Row.

McCulloch, John R. 1842. *A Dictionary, Practical, Theoretical, and Historical of Commerce, and Commercial Navigation*. London: Longman, Brown, Green, and Longmans.

McFarland, Earl. 1929. *Catalogue of the Ordnance Museum United States Military Academy*. New York: U.S. Military Academy Printing Office.

McNeill, William. 1982. *The Pursuit of Power*. Chicago: University of Chicago Press.

Meagher, Paul, et al. 1979. *Encyclopedic Dictionary of Religion*. 3 vols. Washington: Corpus Publications.

M'Ghee, R. J. L. 1862. *How We Got to Peking*. London: Richard Bentley.

Michie, Alexander. 1864. *The Siberian Overland Route from Peking to Petersburg*. London: John Murray.

———. 1893a. "Balance of Power in Eastern Asia." *Blackwood's Edinburgh Magazine* 154 (September): 397–308.

———. 1893b. "The Russian Acquisition of Manchuria." *Blackwood's Edinburgh Magazine* 153 (May): 631–646.

Middleton, Ben. 2001. "Spectres of Imperialism, Scandals of Empire: The Boxer War and the Japanese Public Sphere." Paper presented at the international conference 1900: *The Boxers, China and the World*, London, 24 June.

Miles, Robert. 1989. *Racism*. London: Routledge.

Military Order of the Dragon, 1900–1911. ca 1912. Washington: Press of B.S. Adams.

Millard, Thomas F. 1901. "Punishment and Revenge in China." *Scribner's Magazine* 29: 187–194.

Miller, S. C. 1974. "Ends and Means: Missionary Justification of Force in Nineteenth Century China," 249–282. In J. K. Fairbank, ed., *The Missionary Enterprise in China and America*. Cambridge, Mass.: Harvard University Press.

Milligan, Barry. 1995. *Pleasures and Pains*. Charlottesville: University Press of Virginia.

Millward, James. 1998. *Beyond the Pass*. Stanford: Stanford University Press.

Miner, Luella. 1903. *China's Book of Martyrs*. Cincinnati: Jennings and Pye.

Mitchell, Timothy. 1988. *Colonizing Egypt*. Cambridge, England: Cambridge University Press.

———. 1989. "The World as Exhibition." *Comparative Studies in Society and History* 31.2: 217–236.

Morgan, Gerald. 1981. *Anglo-Russian Rivalry in Central Asia: 1810–1895*. London: Frank Cass.

Moriarty, Catherine. 1997. "Private Grief and Public Remembrance: British First World War Memorials," 125–142. In M. Evans and K. Lunn, eds., *War and Memory in the Twentieth Century*. New York: Berg.

Morrill, Samuel. 1926. *Lanterns, Junks and Jade*. New York: Frederick A. Stokes.

Morse, Hosea B. [1905] 1907. *Currency, Weights, and Measures*. Reprint, Shanghai: Kelly and Walsh.

———. 1908. *The Trade and Administration of the Chinese Empire*. London: Longmans, Green.

———. 1909. *The Gilds of China*. London: Longmans, Green.

———. 1910–18. *The International Relations of the Chinese Empire*. 3 vols. London: Longmans, Green.

———. 1926–29. *Chronicles of the East India Company Trading to China, 1635–1843*. 5 vols. Oxford: Oxford University Press.

Moy, James S. 1993. *Marginal Sights*. Iowa City: University of Iowa Press.

Mumm, Alfons Freiherr von Schwarzenstein. 1902. *Ein Tagebuch in Bildern*. Berlin: Graphische Gesellschaft.

Murphy, Rhoads. 1974. "The Treaty Ports and China's Modernization," 17–71. In Mark Elvin and G. William Skinner, eds., *The Chinese City between Two Worlds*. Stanford: Stanford University Press.

Murray, Hugh, et al. 1836–43. *An Historical and Descriptive Account of China*. 3 vols. London: Simplin, Marshall.

Mutrécy, Charles de. 1862. *Journal de la campagne de Chine 1859–1860–1861; par Charles de Mutrécy; précédé d'une préface de Jules Noriac*. 2 vols. Paris: A. Bourdilliat.

Nadel, Alan. 1995. *Containment Culture*. Durham, N.C.: Duke University Press.

Nicholls, Bob. 1986. *Bluejackets and Boxers*. Sydney: Allen and Unwin.

Nora, Pierre. 1989. "Between History and Memory: Les Lieux de Memoire." *Representations* 26: 7–24.

Norie, E. W. M. [1903] 1995. *Official Account of Military Operations in China 1900–1901*. Reprint, Nashville: Battery Press.

Oliphant, Laurence. [1859] 1970. *Narrative of the Earl of Elgin's Mission to China and Japan in the Years 1857, '58, '59*. Reprint, New York: Oxford University Press.

Oudendyk, William. 1939. *Ways and By-ways of Diplomacy*. London: Peter Davies.

Paine, S. C. M. 1996. *Imperial Rivals*. Armonk, N.Y.: M.E. Sharpe.

Pakenham, Thomas. 1979. *The Boer War*. New York: Avon.

Palgrave, F. T. 1862. *Handbook to the Fine Arts Collection in the International Exhibition*. London: Macmillan.

Parker, E. H. 1886. "From the Emperor of China to King George the Third." *Nineteenth Century* (July): 45–54.

———. 1901. *China*. New York: E.P. Dutton.

Parry, Benita. 1987. "Problems in Current Theories of Colonial Discourse." *Oxford Literary Review* 9.1–2: 27–58.

Parssinen, Terry. 1983. *Secret Passions, Secret Remedies*. Philadelphia: Institute for the Study of Human Issues.

Pauthier, J.-P. G. 1861. "Des Curiosités Chinoises." *Gazette des Beaux-Arts* 9: 363–369.

Pearce, Nick. 1998. "From the Summer Palace of the Emperor of China." Paper presented at the International Convention of Asian Scholars, 25–28 June, Leiden.

Pearl, Cyril. 1967. *Morrison of Peking*. Sydney: Angus and Robertson.

Peiping Chronicle. 1933. *Guide to "Peking."*

Pelcovits, Nathan. [1948] 1969. *Old China Hands and the Foreign Office*. Reprint, New York: Octagon.

Perdue, Peter. 1996. "Military Mobilization in Seventeenth Century China, Russia, and Mongolia." *Modern Asian Studies* 30.4: 757–793.

Pick, Daniel. 1993. *The War Machine*. New Haven: Yale University Press.

Pieczenik, Steve. 1995. *Pax Pacifica*. New York: Warner.

Playfair, G. M. H. [1910] 1978. *The Cities and Towns of China*. Reprint, Taipei: Ch'eng Wen.

Pomian, K. 1990. *Collectors and Curiosities: Paris and Venice 1500–1800*. Cambridge, England: Polity Press.

Pong, David. 1975. *A Critical Guide to the Kwangtung Provincial Archives Deposited at the Public Records Office of London*. Cambridge, Mass.: Harvard University Press.

Porter, D. 1983. "Orientalism and Its Problems," 179–193. In Francis Barker et al., eds., *The Politics of Theory*. Colchester, England: University of Essex Press.

Porter, Whitworth. 1889. *History of the Corps of Royal Engineers*. 7 vols. London: Longmans, Green.

Pratt, Mary Louise. 1992. *Imperial Eyes*. London: Routledge.

"Progress in China." 1863. *Blackwood's Magazine* 93: 44–61.

The Queen. 1862. Exhibition Supplement 20, 18 January.

Rabinow, Paul. 1986. "Representations Are Social Facts: Modernity and Post-Modernity in Anthropology," 234–261. In J. Clifford and G. Marcus, eds., *Writing Culture*. Berkeley: University of California Press.

Ralston, David B. 1990. *Importing the European Army*. Chicago: University of Chicago Press.

Rawlinson, Henry. 1875. *England and Russia in the East*. London: J. Murray.

Rawlinson, John L. 1967. *China's Struggle for Naval Development, 1839–1895*. Cambridge, Mass.: Harvard University Press.

Rawski, Evelyn. 1998. *The Last Emperors*. Berkeley: University of California Press.

Rawski, Thomas. 1970. "Chinese Dominance of Treaty Port Commerce and Its Implications, 1860–1875." *Explorations in Economic History* 7: 451–473.

Read, S. P. 1900. "Similarities in the Peking Expeditions of 1860 and 1900." *Independent* 52: 2627–2629.

Reid, Gilbert. 1901. "The Ethics of Loot." *Forum* 31: 581–586.

———. 1902. "The Ethics of the Last War." *Forum* 32: 446–455.

Rennie, David F. 1864. *The British Arms in North China and Japan: Peking 1860; Kagoshima 1862*. London: John Murray.

———. 1865. *Peking and the Pekingese*. 2 vols. London: John Murray.

Report of the Commissioners appointed to inquire into the realisation and distribution of Army Prize; with minutes of Evidence, and Appendix. 1864. London: Her Majesty's Stationery Office.

Ricalton, James. 1901. *China through the Stereoscope*. New York: Underwood and Underwood.

Richards, Jeffrey. 1992. "Popular Imperialism and the Image of the Army in Juvenile Literature," pp. 80–108. In John MacKenzie, ed., *Popular Imperialism and the Military*. Manchester, England: Manchester University Press.

Richards, John. 2002. "The Opium Industry in British India." *Indian Economic and Social History Review* 39: 149–180.

Richards, Thomas. 1990. *The Commodity Culture of Victorian England.* Stanford: Stanford University Press.

———. 1992. *The Imperial Archive.* London: Routledge.

Richthofen, Ferdinand von. 1877–1912. *China: Ergebnisse eigner reisen und darauf gegründeter studien, von Ferdinand freiherrn von Richthofen.* 7 vols. Berlin: D. Reimer.

Ridpath, John. 1893. *Great Races of Mankind.* 8 vols. Cincinnati: Jones Brothers.

Rockhill, William W. [1905] 1971. *Diplomatic Audiences at the Court of China.* Reprint, Taipei: Ch'eng Wen.

Rohmer, Sax [Arthur Ward]. [1913] 1975. *The Insidious Dr. Fu-Manchu.* New York: Pyramid.

———. [1915] 1966. *The Yellow Claw.* New York: Pyramid.

———. [1916] 1975. *The Return of Dr. Fu-Manchu.* New York: Pyramid.

———. [1917] 1976. *The Hand of Fu-Manchu.* New York: Pyramid.

———. 1919. *Dope.* New York: A.L. Burt.

———. [1930] 1976. *The Daughter of Fu-Manchu.* New York: Pyramid.

———. [1936] 1976. *President Fu-Manchu.* New York: Pyramid.

Rowe, William. 2001. *Saving the World.* Stanford: Stanford University Press.

Russell, Don. 1960. *The Lives and Legends of Buffalo Bill.* Norman: University of Oklahoma Press.

Rydell, Robert W. 1984. *All the World's a Fair.* Chicago: University of Chicago Press.

Samoyault-Verlet, Colombe. 1994. *Le Musée chinois de l'impétrice Eugénie.* Paris: Editions de la Réunion des musées nationaux.

Sand, Jordan. 2000. "Was Meiji Taste in Interiors 'Orientalist'?" *positions* 8.3: 637–673.

Scully, Eileen. 2001. *Bargaining with the State from Afar.* New York: Columbia University Press.

Seagrave, Sterling. 1992. *Dragon Lady.* New York: Vintage.

Shanghai Mercury. 1967. *The Boxer Rising.* Reprint, New York: Paragon Book Reprint Corp.

Sharf, Frederic, and Peter Harrington. 2000. *China, 1900.* London: Greenhill.

Simpson, Bertram L. [1907] 1970. *Indiscreet Letters from Peking.* Reprint, New York: Arno Press and New York Times.

Singh, Sarbans. 1993. *Battle Honors of the Indian Army, 1757–1971.* New Delhi: Vision Books.

Skidmore, Eliza. 1900. *China the Long-lived Empire.* New York: Century.

Smith, Arthur. 1894. *Chinese Characteristics.* Port Washington, N.Y.: Kennikat Press.

———. 1900. "The Punishment of Peking." *Outlook* 66: 493–501.

———. 1901a. "China a Year after the Siege in Peking." *Outlook* 68: 969–975.

———. 1901b. *China in Convulsion.* 2 vols. New York: Fleming H. Revell.

———. 1901c. "China Six Months after the Occupation of Peking." *Outlook* 67: 865–871.

———. 1901d. "The Transformation of Peking." *Outlook* 68: 157–162.

Smith, D. Warren. 1900. *European Settlements in the Far East.* New York: Scribner's.

Smith, Judson. 1901. "The Missionaries and Their Critics." *North American Review* 172: 724–733.

Smith, Richard, John Fairbank, and Katherine Bruner, eds. 1991. *Robert Hart and China's Early Modernization: His Journals, 1863–1866*. Cambridge, Mass.: Harvard University Council on East Asian Studies.

Smith, Stanley. 1901. *China from Within: or the Story of the Chinese Crisis*. London: Marshall Brothers.

Smith, Steve A. 2002. *Like Cattle and Horses*. Durham, N.C.: Duke University Press.

Smullen, Ivor. 1991. "Pekes of Perfection." *Silver Kris* (January): 116–120.

Sotheby's. 1988. *The Library of Philip Robinson: Part 2, The Chinese Collection*. Auction catalogue. London.

Spence, Jonathan. 1969. *To Change China*. New York: Penguin.

———. 1982. *The Gate of Heavenly Peace*. New York: Penguin.

Spivak, Gayatri. 1985. "The Rani of Surmur," 128–151. In Francis Barker et al., eds., *Europe and Its Others*, vol. 1. Colchester, England: University of Essex.

Springhall, John O. 1986. " 'Up Guards and at Them!' British Imperialism and Popular Art," 49–72. In J. MacKenzie, ed., *Imperialism and Popular Culture*. Manchester, England: Manchester University Press.

Stallybrass, Peter, and Allon White. 1986. *The Politics and Poetics of Transgression*. Ithaca: Cornell University Press.

Statutes of the United Kingdom of Great Britain and Ireland. Vols. 54 (1814), 61 (1821), 72 (1832). London: Her Majesty's Stationery Office.

Stearn, Roger. 1992. "War Correspondents and Colonial War, c. 1870–1900," 139–161. In J. MacKenzie, ed., *Popular Imperialism and the Military*. Manchester, England: Manchester University Press.

Steel, Richard A. 1985. *Through Peking's Sewer Gate: Relief of the Boxer Siege, 1900–1901*. Ed. George W. Carrington. New York: Vantage.

Stephenson, Frederick. 1915. *At Home and on the Battlefield*. London: John Murray.

Stewart, Norman. 1908. *My Service Days*. London: John Ouseley

Stocking, George W., Jr. 1968. *Race, Culture, and Evolution: Essays in the History of Anthropology*. New York: Free Press.

Stoler, Ann. 1991. "Carnal Knowledge and Imperial Power," 51–101. In Micaela di Leonardo, ed., *Gender at the Crossroads of Knowledge*. Berkeley: University of California Press.

Stratemeyer, Edward. 1900. *On to Pekin*. Boston: Lothrop, Lee and Shepard.

Student interpreter. 1885. *"Where the Chinese Drive": English Student Life at Peking*. London: W. H. Allen.

Su Ching. 1985. *Ch'ing-chi t'ung-wen-kuan chi ch'i-shih* (The late Qing translation bureau and its instructors and students). Taipei: Shanghai Publishing House.

Su, Weizhi, and Tianlu Liu, eds. 2000. *Boxer Studies–100 years*. Jinan: Qilu.

Swinhoe, Robert. 1861. *Narrative of the North China Campaign of 1860*. London: Smith, Elder.

Swisher, Earl. 1953. *China's Management of the American Barbarians: A Study of Sino-American Relations, 1841–1861, with Documents*. New Haven: Yale University Press.

Tanaka, Stefan. 1993. *Japan's Orient*. Berkeley: University of California Press.

Tao Feiya and Wu Ziming. 1998. *Jidujiao daxue yu guoxue yanjiu* (Christian universities and national education). Fuzhou: Fujian Educational.

Taussig, Michael. 1987. *Shamanism, Colonialism and the Wild Man*. Chicago: University of Chicago Press.

Teng, Ssu-yu, and John K. Fairbank. 1963. *China's Response to the West*. New York: Atheneum.

Thackeray, William M. 1991. *The History of Henry Esmond, Esq*. Ed. Donald Hawes. Oxford: Oxford University Press.

Thomas, Nicholas. 1991. *Entangled Objects*. Cambridge, Mass.: Harvard University Press.

———. 1994. "Licensed Curiosity: Cook's Pacific Voyages," 116–136. In Roger Cardinal and John Elsner, eds., *The Cultures of Collecting*. Cambridge, Mass.: Harvard University Press.

Thomson, H. C. [1902] 1981. *China and the Powers*. Reprint, Westport, Conn.: Hyperion Press.

Torr, Dona, ed. 1968. *Marx on China, 1853–1860*. London: Lawrence and Wishart.

Truong, Than-dam. 1990. *Sex, Money and Morality*. London: Zed.

Tsiang, T. F. 1929. "China after the Victory of Taku, June 25, 1859." *American Historical Review* 35.1: 79–84.

Tsin, Michael. 1999. *Nation, Governance and Modernity in China*. Standford: Stanford University Press.

Tuchman, Barbara. 1971. *Sand against the Wind*. New York: Macmillan.

Tulloch, Alexander B. 1903. *Recollections of Forty Years' Service*. Edinburgh: William Blackwood and Sons.

Twain, Mark. 1901a. "To My Missionary Critics." *North American Review* 172: 520–534.

———. 1901b. "To the Person Sitting in Darkness." *North American Review* 172: 161–176.

Unique Photographs of Executions of Boxers in China. Ca. 1901. Brighton: Visitors' Inquiry Association.

United Kingdom. House of Commons. 1971. *British Parliamentary Papers (BPP). Sessional Papers*. Irish University Press Area Studies Series, *China*. 22 vols. Reprint, Shannon: Irish University Press.

United Kingdom. War Office. 1884, 1887, 1893, 1899, 1907, 1914. *Manual of Military Law*. London: Her Majesty's Stationery Office.

U.S. Navy. Hydrographic Office. 1919. *General Catalogue of Mariner's Charts and Books*. Washington: U.S. Government Printing Office.

U.S. War Department. 1901. *Reports on Military Operations in South Africa and China*. Washington: U.S. Government Printing Office.

U.S. War Department, Adjutant General's Office. 1900. *Notes on China*. Washington: U.S. Government Printing Office.

Varin, Paul. 1862. *Expédition de Chine, par Paul Varin*. Paris: Michel Lévy frères.

Vattel, Emmerich de. 1916. *The Law of Nations*. 3 vols. Washington: Carnegie Institute.

Vaughan, H. B. 1902. *St. George and the Chinese Dragon*. London: Arthur Pearson.

Volontaire au 102e. 1861. *Lettres d'un volontaire au 102me/recueillies et mises en ordre par Émile Maison*. Paris: B. Duprat.

Wade, Thomas F. [1867] 1886. *Yü Yen Tzu Erh Chi* (A progressive course designed to assist the student of colloquial Chinese as spoken in the Metropolitan Department). 3 vols. Shanghai: Kelly and Walsh.

————. [1867] 1905. *Wen-chien tzu-er chi* (A series of papers selected as specimens of documentary Chinese designed to assist students of the language as written by the officials of China). Shanghai: Kelly and Walsh.

Wakeman, Frederic. 1966. *Strangers at the Gate: Social Disorder in South China, 1839–1861.* Berkeley: University of California Press.

————. 1975. *The Fall of Imperial China.* New York: Free Press.

Wakeman, Frederic, and Carolyn Grant, eds. 1975. *Conflict and Control in Late Imperial China.* Berkeley: University of California Press.

Wakeman, Frederic, and Yeh Wen-hsin, eds. 1992. *Shanghai Sojourners.* Berkeley: Institute of East Asian Studies, University of California.

Waldersee, Alfred von. 1924. *A Field Marshal's Memoirs.* Trans. Frederic White. London: Hutcheson.

Waley-Cohen, Joanna. 1991. *Exile in Mid-Qing China.* New Haven: Yale University Press.

Walker, C. P. Beauchamp. 1894. *Days of a Soldier's Life.* London: Chapman and Hall.

Walrond, Theodore, ed. 1872. *Letters and Journals of James, Eighth Earl of Elgin.* London: John Murray.

Wang, Daocheng, ed. 1999. *Yuanming yuan* (Yuanming gardens). 2 vols. Beijing: Beijing Publishing House.

Wang, Lixin. 1997. *Meiguo chuanjiaoshi yu wan Qing Zhongguo xiandaihua* (American missionaries and China's modernization in the Late Qing). Tianjin: Tianjin People's Publishing House.

Wang, Tseng-tsai. 1971. "The Audience Question: Foreign Representatives and the Emperor of China, 1858–1873." *Historical Journal* 14.3: 617–633.

Ward, A. W., and G. P. Gooch. 1923. *The Cambridge History of British Foreign Policy 1783–1919.* 3 vols. New York: Macmillan.

Waring, J. B. 1863. *Masterpieces of Industrial Art and Sculpture at the International Exhibition, 1862.* 3 vols. London: Day and Son.

Weaver, Lawrence. 1915. *The Story of the Royal Scots.* New York: Scribner's.

Weinrich, William. 1981. *Spirit and Martyrdom.* Washington: University Press of America.

Williams, Frederick W. [1889] 1972. *The Life and Letters of Samuel Wells Williams, LL.D.: Missionary, Diplomatist, Sinologue.* Reprint, Wilmington, Del.: Scholarly Resources.

Williams, S. Wells. [1848] 1883. *The Middle Kingdom.* 2 vols. New York: Scribner's.

Wilson, Angus. 1977. *The Strange Ride of Rudyard Kipling.* London: Secker and Warburg.

Wilson, James H. 1901. *China.* 3d ed. New York: D. Appleton.

————. 1912. *Under the Old Flag.* 2 vols. New York: D. Appleton.

Winter, Jay. 1995. *Sites of Memory, Sites of Mourning.* Cambridge, England: Cambridge University Press.

Wolseley, Garnet J. [1862] 1972. *Narrative of the War with China in 1860.* Reprint, Willmington, Del.: Scholarly Resources.

———. 1904. *The Story of a Soldiers Life.* 2 vols. New York: Scribner's.

Wong, J. Y. 1976. *Yeh Ming-ch'en, Viceroy of Liang Kuang, 1852–8.* Cambridge, England: Cambridge University Press.

———. 1983. *Anglo-Chinese Relations 1839–1860.* London: Oxford University Press.

———. 1998. *Deadly Dreams: Opium, Imperialism, and the Arrow War (1856–1860) in China.* Cambridge, England: Cambridge University Press.

Wright, Mary C. 1968. "Introduction: The Rising Tide of Change," 1–66. In M. C. Wright, ed., *China in Revolution: The First Phase, 1900–1913.* New Haven: Yale University Press.

Wykes, Alan. 1968. *The Royal Hampshire Regiment.* London: Hamish Hamilton.

Xu Xudian. 1981. "The 1980 Conference on the History of the Boxer Movement." *Modern China* 7.3: 379–384.

Yihetuan yundongshi taolun wenji (Collected articles on the history of the Boxer movement). 1982. Jinan: Qilu.

Young, L. K. 1970. *British Policy in China, 1895–1902.* Oxford: Clarendon.

Young, Marilyn. 1968. *The Rhetoric of Empire: American China Policy, 1895–1901.* Cambridge, Mass.: Harvard University Press.

Young, Robert. 1990. *White Mythologies: Writing History and the West.* London: Routledge.

———. 1995. *Colonial Desire.* New York: Routledge.

Younghusband, Francis. [1910] 1985. *India and Tibet.* Reprint, Hong Kong: Oxford University Press.

Yuanming yuan 2. 1983. Peking: Yuanming yuan Museum.

Yule, Henry, and A. C. Burnell. [1886] 1994. *Hobson-Jobson.* Ed. William Cooke. Reprint, New Delhi: Munishiram Manoharlal.

Zhongguo shehui kexueyuan jindaishi yanjiu suo "Jindaishi ziliao" bianjizu, eds. 1982. *Yihetuan shiliao* (YHTLS; Historical materials on the Boxers). 2 vols. Beijing: Chinese Academy of Social Sciences.

Zito, Angela. 1997. *Of Body and Brush.* Chicago: University of Chicago Press.

Yi, translated as "barbarian," 57

Yi, Prince of (Caiyuan): arrest of Parkes and Loch and, 45, 103; flees with emperor to Chengde, 46; residence as British legation, 112

Young, Robert: critique of Deleuze, 22–23; imbrication of cultures and, 23, 308, 313

Yuanming yuan [Garden of Perfect Brightness] (Summer Palace): British and French accounts of, 100; complex of gardens, 108; destroyed, 48, 103–111; looted, 47, 76–80; museum, 340–343; "Never forget national humiliation" (wuwang guochi) wall and, 342; objects from in Western museums, 329–330, 335; "solemn act of retribution" and, 76, 105

Yuxian: atrocities and, 288–289

Zeng Jice: negotiates Treaty of St. Petersburg, 173

Zongli [geguo shiwu] yamen (Office for managing affairs with various countries): abolished in Final Protocol (1901), 249; established, 48

Zuo Zongtang: maritime vs. frontier policy debate and, 172; opposition to treaty with Russia (1878), 173; reconquest of Central Asia and, 171, 172–173

James L. Hevia is Associate Professor of History
and International Studies at the University of
North Carolina at Chapel Hill. His previous book
is *Cherishing Men from Afar: Qing Guest Ritual and the
Macartney Embassy of 1793* (Duke University Press,
1995), which won the 1997 Joseph Levenson Prize
from the Association for Asian Studies.

. . . .

Library of Congress Cataloging-in-Publication Data
Hevia, James Louis.
English lessons : the pedagogy of imperialism
in nineteenth-century China / James L. Hevia.
p. cm.
Includes bibliographical references and index.
ISBN 0-8223-3151-9 (cloth : alk. paper)
ISBN 0-8223-3188-8 (pbk. : alk. paper)
1. China—Foreign relations—Great Britain.
2. Great Britain—Foreign relations—China.
3. China—Foreign relations—1644–1912.
4. Great Britain—Foreign relations—1837–1901.
5. Imperialism—History—19th century.
I. Title: Pedagogy of imperialism in nineteenth-
century China.   II. Title.
DS740.5.G5H484   2003
951'.033—dc21   2003009460